# LONGSTREET HIGHROAD GUIDE
## TO THE

# FLORIDA
# KEYS & EVERGLADES

### BY RICK FARREN

D1456022

**LONGSTREET**
ATLANTA, GEORGIA

Published by
**LONGSTREET PRESS, INC.**
a subsidiary of Cox Newspapers,
a subsidiary of Cox Enterprises, Inc.
2140 Newmarket Parkway
Suite 122
Marietta, Georgia 30067

Great efforts have been made to make the information in this book as accurate as possible. However, over time, trails are rerouted, beaches erode, towns are developed, and signs and landmarks may change. If you find a change has occurred to a beach, island, or trail in the book, please let us know so we can correct future editions. *A word of caution:* Outdoor recreation by its nature is potentially hazardous. All participants in such activities must assume all responsibility for their own actions and safety. The scope of this book does not cover all potential hazards and risks involved in outdoor recreation activities.

Printed by RR Donnelley & Sons, Harrisonburg, VA

1st printing 1999

Library of Congress Catalog Number 98-89180

ISBN: 1-56352-543-7

Book editing, design, and cartography
by Lenz Design & Communications, Inc., Decatur, Georgia

Cover illustration by Harry Fenn, *Picturesque America*, 1872

Cover design by Richard J. Lenz, Decatur, Georgia

Illustrations by Danny Woodard, Loganville, Georgia

Photographs courtesy of Visit Florida and Rick Farren

Second excerpt on page iii is from the book, *The Everglades: River of Grass*, 50th Anniversary Edition copyright © 1997 by Marjory Stoneman Douglas. Original edition copyright © 1947 by Marjory Stoneman Douglas. Used by permission of Pineapple Press, Inc.

But the one vast, continuing marvel is the sea itself. Never for one hour of
the day is the magic of its coloring alike; always each new phase is
more wonderful than the last. Within its heart of mystery are continually
born new dreams that pulse in nascent beauty to the rhythm of its tides,
quivering to the mind of him who looks upon them with all fond longings
and the bliss of noble desires. He who is privileged to see it must be base
indeed if it does not call some answering glow from within him.

—Winthrop Packard, *Florida Trails*, 1910


There are no other Everglades in the world.
They are, they have always been, one of the unique regions on the earth,
remote, never wholly known. Nothing anywhere else is like them:
their vast glittering openness, wider than the enormous visible round of
the horizon, the racing free saltness and sweetness of their massive winds,
under the dazzling blue heights of space; They are unique also
in the simplicity, the diversity, the related harmony of the forms of life
they enclose. The miracle of the light pours over the green and brown
expanse of saw grass and of water, shining and slow-moving below,
the grass and water that is the meaning and central fact of the Everglades.
It is a river of grass.

—Marjory Stoneman Douglas, *The Everglades: River of Grass*

# Contents

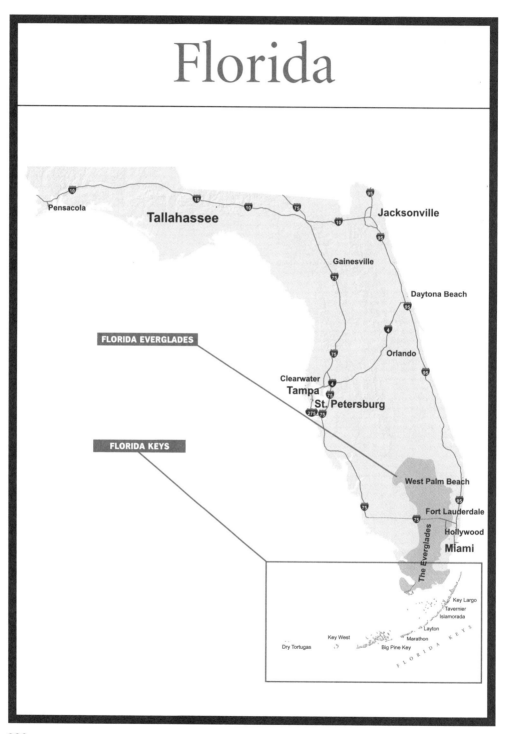

Florida

**Legend**

| | | |
|---|---|---|
| Amphitheater | Camping | Ranger Station |
| Parking | Bathroom | Misc. Special Areas |
| Telephone | Wheelchair Accessible | Town or City |
| Information | First Aid Station | |
| Picnicking | Picnic Shelter | Physiographic Region/ Misc. Boundary |
| Dumping Station | Shower | Regular Trail |
| Swimming | Biking | State Boundary |
| Fishing | Comfort/Rest Station | 70 Interstate |
| Interpretive Trail | Park Boundary | 522 U.S. Route |
| Good Diving | Good Snorkeling | 643 State Highway |

# How Your Highroad Guide is Organized

*The Florida Keys are split into three sections: upper, middle, and lower; the Everglades are divided into the eastern and western entrances. Naples and its nearby sites are the final section.*

Tampa

ATLANTIC OCEAN

LAKE OKEECHOBEE

Naples
Pages 261-290

Sanibel Island

Immokalee

Delray Beach

Boca Raton

Pompano Beach

Naples

Alligator Alley

Fort Lauderdale

GULF OF MEXICO

Hollywood

Hialeah

Miami Beach

**Area Enlarged**

Miami

Tamiami Trail

Florida Everglades:
Everglades National
Park to Shark Valley
153-222

Kendall

Homestead

Western Everglades:
Big Cypress to Ten
Thousand Islands
223-260

Upper Keys
Pages 27-74

Key Largo

Flamingo

Tavernier

Plantation

Islamorada

Middle Keys
Pages 75-92

Layton

Lower Keys
Pages 93-152

Marathon

Big Pine Key

Key West

THE EVERGLADES

FLORIDA KEYS

Dry Tortugas

Stock Island

N

# How to Use Your Longstreet Highroad Guide

The *Longstreet Highroad Guide to the Florida Keys & Everglades* offers detailed information about some of the best places in Florida to pursue your favorite outdoor activities, including hiking, camping, freshwater and saltwater fishing, boating, snorkeling, diving, canoeing, wildlife watching, and touring of historic sites. The book also includes distinctive restaurant, lodging, and night life information. These attractions are known to change over time, altering their operating hours, quality of food and service, and ownership, so it is wise to call ahead before making a long drive to visit an establishment profiled here. Also, there is detailed information on the natural and human history of most areas, which can add dimension and depth to any outdoor pursuit.

This book is divided into three sections on the Florida Keys, two on the Florida Everglades, and one on the Naples area. An additional chapter covers the natural history of the Keys and the Everglades. At the beginning of the Upper Keys chapter there is a more detailed introduction to the natural history of the Keys, and at the front of the Everglades: Everglades National Park to Shark Valley chapter is a detailed discussion of the natural features of the Everglades.

The Florida Keys and Everglades are sensitive and valuable areas. Many of the natural communities profiled here are fragile and should be treated with great respect. Refrain from collecting live plants and feeding wild animals.

*A word of caution*: For the most enjoyment, visitors to wilderness areas should prepare themselves for heat and insects. Bring water for drinking, use insect repellant, and wear a hat, long sleeves, and pants. The waters of the Keys and Everglades can be dangerous for swimming, fishing, and boating. Be very aware of your surroundings and make safe decisions. If boating, use common sense and a personal floatation device.

# Preface

"I'm hoping to see an otter," said the English tourist standing next to me on the Anhinga Trail boardwalk in Everglades National Park. We were watching the wildlife in Taylor Slough. Actually she was watching, I was busy taking notes and pictures to help with the writing of this book.

Around us the slough teemed with wildlife—anhingas, cormorants, alligators, kingfishers, great blue herons, and snapping turtles were either searching for one last unsuspecting meal or settling in somewhere to await the night. But her trip would only be complete she said, if she got to see an otter.

Many visitors come to the Everglades on a sort of quest, a determined desire to see a certain animal—maybe a crocodile, a panther, or a manatee. I've been on those quests, and the only problem with being on one is that you risk overlooking some of the other incredible sights and sounds.

After her party moved on, I put down my pen, stored my camera, and just watched the slough as the light slowly dimmed. As often happens in those moments, old memories had a chance to resurface.

I was 12 years old the first time I stood at this very spot on this trail. My family had moved from Iowa to South Florida that year, 1964, and our initial trip into the Everglades might as well have been a trip to another planet.

To a young man accustomed to corn fields and farm ponds, here was a vast wilderness of sawgrass and tree islands. A place with unimaginably strange wildlife— a bird, with a neck like a snake, swimming beneath the surface and spearing fish with its sharp beak; an alligator lying next to the trail oblivious to the people passing by only a few feet away; a water moccasin coiled on a mat of reeds totally uninterested in a purple gallinule walking daintily by on its big yellow feet.

A couple months later we loaded up the old '59 Ford and took the long drive over the bridges to Key West. Again, here was another world—a chain of emerald green islands connected by a series of narrow, and somewhat scary bridges. The Keys are neighbors to the Everglades, yet completely different in every way.

We stopped at an attraction where dolphins leaped out of the water on command, and where boats with glass bottoms revealed an incredible undersea world that before I had only known in black-and-white television shows like Sea Hunt. In Key West we visited the "southernmost" point in the United States and ate lobster fresh off the docks.

I was hooked, and for the next 35 years, from the time I was old enough to drive, explored every part of both of these strange new worlds, sometimes with friends, sometimes with my wife, and sometimes alone. There were diving trips to the coral reefs, wild weekends in Key West, and week-long wilderness adventures into the Everglades backcountry.

Throughout this book I've tried to call upon those experiences, to provide not only an accurate guide to the various destinations in the Keys and the Everglades but also to provide a personally detailed guide that should help you look behind the scenes a little, where only longtime residents and repeat visitors know to look.

I've also tried to recommend the best restaurants and lodging facilities, but that's difficult in places like Key West or Naples that have so many from which to choose. And I've included dive shops and marinas and guide services that I have personal knowledge of, or have interviewed specifically for this book.

The best advice I could give for enjoying your visit, however, might be to recognize that the Florida Keys and the Everglades are two vastly different landscapes that should be approached with somewhat different attitudes.

Visit the Keys with an open, bright spirit, looking for fun in the sun. Snorkeling, swimming, diving, fishing, dining, and shopping are all part of the

## ROSEATE SPOONBILL
### (Ajaia ajaja)
This pink and white bird preys on small fish, shrimp, and shellfish. When its catch is a fish, it may beat the fish on the water before swallowing it. In the past, this species was shot for its wings, which were made into fans.

Keys experience—so are crowds in the winter, some traffic problems and sometimes endless commercial strips of development. But the islands, and the blue pastel seas that surround them, have a way of grabbing hold and taking over.

A trip into the vast Everglades should be approached with a little more composure, with an expectation of coming closer to nature if only to observe, to learn, or to understand a little more about life itself. It's a land where wildlife is a constant part of the landscape, where binoculars and a good pair of hiking boots are more important than a restaurant guide, and where a little planning can make a big difference in the experience you come away with.

You'll also discover a great deal of history on these pages. How else would it be possible to know the whole story of South Florida? In the Keys and Everglades it's a history that lies very close to the surface where evidence of the area's earliest inhabitants is still obvious in huge shell mounds that they left behind. The Everglades are so young that man had been living in Florida more than 5,000 years before they even formed.

The Keys and Everglades have changed during all the years I've been coming here. Bulging population centers on the southeast and southwest coasts continue to push against these lands. The Keys have grown ever more commercial, both thriving and suffering from a still-growing tourist trade. The Everglades have been dealt one severe blow after another from political battles over land use and water supply; either there's too much or too little.

Nevertheless, despite these pressures and problems the Keys and Everglades still hold the same fascination and opportunities for recreation and adventure they always have. And as Floridians we are far more proud of the arching Florida Keys and magnificent coral reefs than we are of the condominiums or the Interstates, and we are far more proud of the Everglades and its still bountiful wildlife than we are of the politicians and developers that place profit ahead of protection.

It is the Everglades and the Keys that make this special state even more special. For the people of South Florida and the world, they represent nature that is not yet lost, not yet paved over. So when you visit, step lightly, but enjoy thoroughly these unique destinations. Every decision not to pluck a flower blossom from the sawgrass prairie, or not to touch a piece of fragile coral will ensure it's there for the next person to enjoy.

One thing is certain, you won't go away unaffected by the stunning beauty of the Keys or the deep emotional context of the Everglades. My career as an outdoor writer and conservationist all started with my first trip in 1964. What the Keys or the Everglades mean to everybody who visits, however, is up to them. It can be a life-changing experience, or just a chance to see an otter; both are important.

—Rick Farren

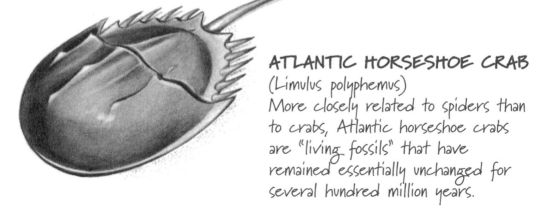

**ATLANTIC HORSESHOE CRAB**
(Limulus polyphemus)
More closely related to spiders than to crabs, Atlantic horseshoe crabs are "living fossils" that have remained essentially unchanged for several hundred million years.

# Acknowledgments

I wish first of all to recognize freelance writer William Schemmel of Atlanta, Georgia for his valuable contributions to this book. His experienced and insightful critiques of restaurants, lodging, and attractions in the Florida Keys and Naples will benefit every person who uses this guide. Mr. Schemmel also provided important historical and natural history information that has been included in those two sections as well as the introduction.

Any mention of individuals who helped with this book must also include at the top of the list Claudia Farren, my proofreader, researcher, business partner, and loving wife of 25 years. Just as valuable as Claudia's help with the writing of this book, however, were the long hours she spent walking trails, toting camera equipment and wildlife identification books, and paddling canoes these past years while we explored, enjoyed, and wrote about the Everglades, the Keys, and the rest of natural lands of South Florida.

Similar appreciation goes to lifetime friends Jim Schroeder and Tim Schroeder for often filling the other seat in the canoe and pounding in the other tent stake on many early trips into the Everglades. And thanks also to my parents Retta Farren and Bill Farren, who gave me the Everglades and Keys, and the wonders of Florida with a brave move to South Florida more than 35 years ago.

My deepest gratitude to Marge McDonald, Director of Development for Longstreet Press, and Richard Lenz and Pam Holliday of Lenz Design & Communications, who entrusted me to complete this book without overly stretching the deadlines. Thanks too for providing invaluable direction and editing support. Everything good about this book is due to Pam and Richard's skilled oversight of the project.

I am indebted to the staff of Everglades National Park for many years of always providing every assistance possible when asked. Although the names have changed from time to time, the information specialists, park rangers, and scientists have always been ready to help with any project or provide any information requested about the park's varied ecosystems and wildlife.

In particular I would like to credit Park Naturalist Stephen Robinson, who for 20 years has provided expert advice on everything from camping to the intricacies of the Everglades ecosystem with an unmatched dedication to the land. My appreciation also to Richard Dawson, a former research scientist with the park who was always willing to patiently explain complicated scientific information to a confused layman. Thanks also to Pat Toole, former head of public relations, who always had an open office door, and a quick response to any requests. I would like to thank Linda Roehrig for reviewing the sections of the book on Everglades National Park and Dry Tortugas National Park.

Jennifer Huber, Sales Manager with AmFac Parks and Resorts in Flamingo was also very helpful to this book in providing both hospitality and assistance with information regarding visitor opportunities in the Flamingo area and Florida Bay.

Appreciation also goes to the staff of the Florida Wildlife Federation and President Manley K. Fuller for information regarding Florida's wildlife, the Everglades, the Everglades Restudy, and Florida Keys environmental issues.

Thanks also to Kris W. Thoempe, Ph.D., Everglades Project Director for the National Wildlife Federation at the joint Florida and National Wildlife Federation Southeast Florida Office for his knowledge of the Western Everglades and the Everglades Restudy plan. Similar appreciation goes to the staff of the Big Cypress National Preserve for its guidance regarding visitor opportunities in the Big Cypress Swamp. Thanks to Sandy Snell-Dobert at Big Cypress for reviewing a portion of the manuscript.

The staff of the Coastal Conservation Association Florida and Executive Director Ted Forsgren have my gratitude for providing valuable assistance and information on fishing guides and marine conservation issues.

*Florida Sportsman Magazine* and its publisher Karl Wickstrom have also been invaluable to the writing of this book due in part to their sharp coverage of South Florida conservation issues and for assistance with charts, tide tables, and other information regarding fishing and other outdoor opportunities in the Everglades, Florida Bay, and the Florida Keys.

My appreciation also goes to the staff of John Pennekamp State Park, and to Andy Newman of Captain Slate's Atlantis Dive Center for information on Key Largo diving opportunities and the coral reef system.

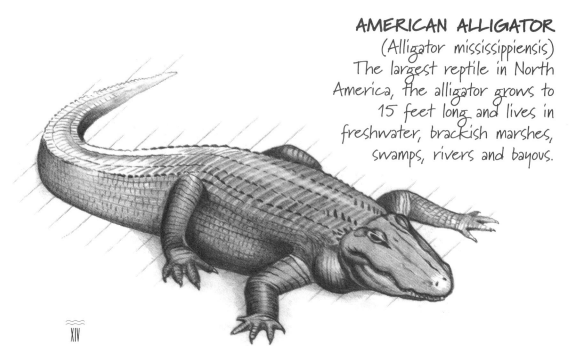

**AMERICAN ALLIGATOR**
(Alligator mississippiensis)
The largest reptile in North America, the alligator grows to 15 feet long and lives in freshwater, brackish marshes, swamps, rivers and bayous.

**WATERLILY**
(Nymphaea)
The waterlily is rooted
to the bottom of the
lake, river or pond
and has a bright
blossom and notched pad
floating on the surface of
the water.

And my thanks go to the Monroe County Tourist Development Council for providing invaluable assistance and guidance on visiting the Florida Keys along with essential information on the most current eco-tourism opportunities.

Thanks also go to Kenny Brown of Outdoor Resorts on Chokoloskee Island for always being ready and willing to share his special knowledge of southwest Florida's unique history as well as the best spots to catch a redfish or snook in the Everglades backcountry.

The U.S. Fish and Wildlife Service, especially Jim Bell at the Florida Keys National Wildlife Refuges Office on Big Pine Key, and the staff of the Ten Thousand Island National Wildlife Refuge, were very helpful in providing natural history information and background on the six national wildlife refuges covered in this book.

Thanks also to Lucy Evanicki of the Seminole Tribe of Florida for information on Florida's Indian tribes, their history, and visitor opportunities on the Seminole Indian Reservation.

Sincere thanks also go to Eric Hathaway with Banana Bay Resorts on Marathon and Key West, for his hospitality and knowledge of the Florida Keys; and to Julie Perrin-Olsen and the Cheeca Lodge resort, for their hospitality and help with Islamorada fishing information.

I would like to thank Beth Preddy Public Relations, particularly Beth Preddy and Howard Goodman, for coordinating review of the Naples chapter for factual accuracy. And thanks to Pat Wells at Lignumvitae Key State Botanical Site and Michelle Sheldone, Stuart Newman Associates, Miami, for their help and input.

Last, I wish to extend special recognition to my father-in-law Dean Losey, who passed away during the writing of this book. Dean and his wife Betty Losey took the time to track down valuable information for this book concerning the Everglades Restudy, South Florida water and population issues, and the Sawgrass Recreation Area.

—Rick Farren

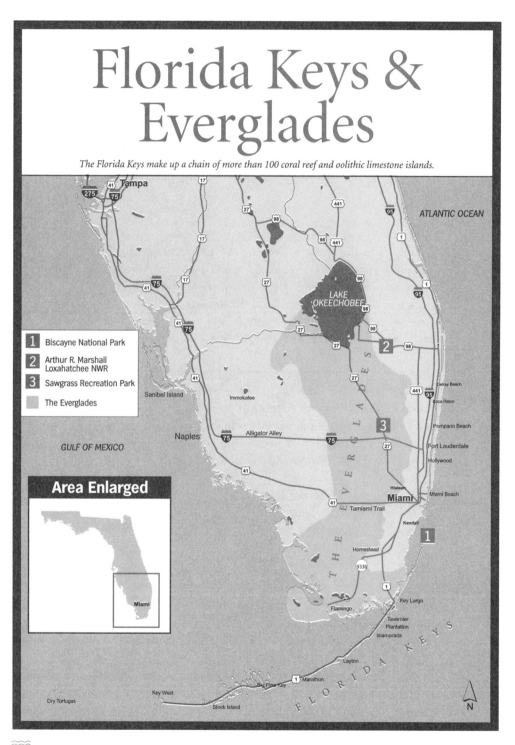

# Florida Keys & Everglades

*The Florida Keys make up a chain of more than 100 coral reef and oolithic limestone islands.*

**Legend:**

1. Biscayne National Park
2. Arthur R. Marshall Loxahatchee NWR
3. Sawgrass Recreation Park

The Everglades

**Area Enlarged**

# The Natural History of the Florida Keys & Everglades

Jutting into the sea between the Atlantic Ocean and the Gulf of Mexico for more than 400 miles, the Florida Peninsula looks like a land caught in a tug of war between the United States and the Caribbean—a sort of half-sister to both, not fully a part of either. Nowhere is this dual nature more evident than in the Everglades and the Florida Keys, where plants and animals, and even cultures from both worlds, live side-by-side in a unique and remarkable land.

The two distinct yet connected coastal regions covered in this book are the Florida Keys and the Everglades. The Florida Keys encompass a loose string of 822 islands scattered from Biscayne Bay just south of Miami to the Dry Tortugas, about 200 miles to the southwest. Thirty-two of the islands are inhabited and a few, like Key Largo, Islamorada, Marathon, and Key West, are heavily developed for tourism.

The Everglades is a low, flat plain shaped by the action of water and weather—a

[ *Above:* An endangered Key Deer peers out of the foliage on Big Pine Key ]

# Geologic Time Scale

| Era | System & Period | Series & Epoch | Some Distinctive Features | Years Before Present |
|---|---|---|---|---|
| CENOZOIC | Quaternary | Recent | Modern man. | 11,000 |
| | | Pleistocene | Early man; northern glaciation. | 1/2 to 2 million |
| | Tertiary | Pliocene | Large carnivores. | 13 ± 1 million |
| | | Miocene | First abundant grazing mammals. | 25 ± 1 million |
| | | Oligocene | Large running mammals. | 36 ± 2 million |
| | | Eocene | Many modern types of mammals. | 58 ± 2 million |
| | | Paleocene | First placental mammals. | 63 ± 2 million |
| MESOZOIC | Cretaceous | | First flowering plants; climax of dinosaurs and ammonites, followed by Cretaceous-Tertiary extinction. | 135 ± 5 million |
| | Jurassic | | First birds, first mammals; dinosaurs and ammonites abundant. | 181 ± 5 million |
| | Triassic | | First dinosaurs. Abundant cycads and conifers. | 230 ± 10 million |
| PALEOZOIC | Permian | | Extinction of most kinds of marine animals, including trilobites. Southern glaciation. | 280 ± 10 million |
| | Carboniferous | Pennsylvanian | Great coal forests, conifers. First reptiles. | 310 ± 10 million |
| | | Mississippian | Sharks and amphibians abundant. Large and numerous scale trees and seed ferns. | 345 ± 10 million |
| | Devonian | | First amphibians; ammonites; Fishes abundant. | 405 ± 10 million |
| | Silurian | | First terrestrial plants and animals. | 425 ± 10 million |
| | Ordovician | | First fishes; invertebrates dominant. | 500 ± 10 million |
| | Cambrian | | First abundant record of marine life; trilobites dominant. | 600 ± 50 million |
| | Precambrian | | Fossils extremely rare, consisting of primitive aquatic plants. Evidence of glaciation. Oldest dated algae, over 2,600 million years; oldest dated meteorites 4,500 million years. | |

unique geologic feature that contains habitats found nowhere else in the world. A watery marsh of some 4,000 square miles, the Everglades covers much of the tip of the Florida Peninsula from Lake Okeechobee south to Florida Bay and the Ten Thousand Islands. It includes the famous river of grass, the Big Cypress Swamp, the Ten Thousand Islands, the vast Everglades mangrove backcountry, and Everglades National Park. For more specific information on geology and history of the Keys and the Everglades, see Florida Keys, page 27, and the Florida Everglades, page 153.

Unlike many coastlines where one road winds along the shoreline leading from one scenic or historical site to the next, the roads leading to the coast along the tip of Florida travel straight to the sea. One of these roads, the incredibly scenic Overseas Highway (US 1) skips for 100 miles across the Florida Keys to Key West following the route of the original Flagler railroad. Everything that happens in the Keys starts somewhere along this road.

A few miles to the west there's a road of discovery that crosses through Everglades National Park on the way to Flamingo, a small National Park Service community on the very tip of the Florida Peninsula. The park road literally crosses sawgrass prairies and travels past pineland forests, dwarf cypress forests, and tropical hammocks. It ends on the shore of Florida Bay, a body of water made famous by television anglers and a struggle to protect this important estuary.

On the southwestern coast there's State Road 29, which passes through the Big Cypress Swamp on its way into the middle of the Ten Thousand Islands. It ends on the rustic and historic Chokoloskee Island and on the edge of the Everglades National Park's mangrove backcountry. It's a road that has brought outlaws, drifters, and millionaires to the edge of the wilderness.

Connecting the southwestern and southeastern coasts, and cutting across the tip of the peninsula, is the famous Tamiami Trail (US 41), a scenic highway that is its own attraction. Crossing through the heart of the Everglades, it cuts across the Shark River Slough and right through the middle of the Big Cypress Swamp. Along the road you'll discover numerous opportunities to explore these extraordinary lands.

# Climate

The Everglades and the Florida Keys basically have two seasons. A warm, humid season runs from May to November, during which about three-quarters of the 57 to 60 inches of annual rainfall falls. (The Keys average only about 40 inches of rain per year). A much more pleasant, cool, dry season lasts from December to April.

Summer temperatures can reach the mid-90s for many days in a row. Winter temperatures average around 70 degrees Fahrenheit, but can rise into the mid-80s during any month, or drop into the low 50s when occasional cold fronts push far enough south. Frost in South Florida is extremely rare.

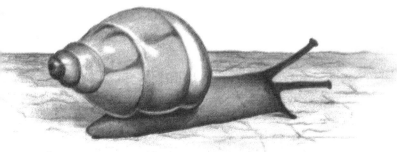

## FLORIDA TREE SNAIL

(*Liguus fasciatus*)

Liguus tree snails feed on fungi growing on the sides of tropical trees. They use their mouths to scrape fungi so completely off trees that they leave clearly marked trails on the trunks.

Located at the northernmost extreme of the tropical belt and the southernmost point in the temperate belt, the Florida Peninsula's climate evolves from temperate in the northern panhandle to tropical in the south. Although technically even Key West is 1 degree above the Tropic of Cancer, the warmth provided by the Gulf Stream creates a true tropical climate in extreme South Florida and the Keys.

Literally a river within the sea, the 45-mile-wide Gulf Stream carries warm tropical waters from west to east between Cuba and Key West, and then up along the southeastern coast of Florida. In the lower Keys, the deep blue waters of the Gulf Stream can be seen just outside of the barrier reef.

Trade winds blowing predominately from the southeast steadily carry the warmth of the Gulf Stream and Caribbean waters across South Florida, creating a true tropical weather pattern. As a result, Key West is the hottest city in America with a year-round average temperature of 77.7 degrees Fahrenheit. Miami falls second in that category at 75.6 degrees Fahrenheit.

Overall, Florida has the highest average temperatures nationwide. Yet the moderating trade winds also protect South Florida from the triple-digit summer temperatures that occur in more northern climes.

South Florida's unique climate, geology, and balance between temperate and tropic climates have created a vast interconnected mosaic of unique natural features and unusual habitats populated by a great diversity of plants and animals.

# Tropical Hardwood Hammocks

Tropical hardwood hammocks flourish on coastal ridges, islands, and on ground that is slightly elevated above the level of neighboring marshes and other wetland habitats. They are found both in the Florida Keys and the southern portions of the Everglades. Some of the finest examples can be seen on the northern end of Key Largo and in Everglades National Park.

Dozens of native West Indian plant species can often be found in a single hammock. Most began as seeds brought here by winds, tropical storms, tides, or migratory birds. More than 200 varieties of West Indian species of trees, vines, ferns, mosses, and lichens have been identified in the region.

A typical hammock is made up of four major structural parts: the canopy or overstory, the midstory, the understory, and the ground cover. The canopy contains the tops of the largest trees such as gumbo-limbo *(Bursera simaruba)*, Jamaica dogwood (*Piscidia piscipula*), and poisonwood (*Metopium toxiferum*). The mix of smaller trees in the midstory often includes black ironwood (*Krugiodendron ferreum*), pigeon plum *(Coccoloba diversifolia)*, and Spanish stopper (*Eugenia foetida*). Young canopy tree species are also found in the midstory mix. Tropical shrubs in the understory and ground cover include wild coffee (*Psychotria nervosa*) and cockspur (*Crataegus crus-galli*).

The hammocks also support a variety of birds, small mammals, and butterflies, including the endangered Schaus' swallowtail (*Heraclides aristodemus*).

One interesting hammock-dweller, the Florida tree snail (*Liguus fasciatus*) is a very colorful, hard-shelled mollusk that feeds on the bark of trees growing in tropical hardwood hammocks. During summer, tree snails can be seen crawling slowly along, scraping off and ingesting fungi, lichen, and algae. In the winter dry season, they seal their shell to a tree with a gluey mucus and wait for the next wet season.

A state species of special concern, the Florida tree snail, like many other Florida creatures, has been undone by its beauty. The snails' 1.5- to 3-inch whorled shells, which range in color from white to buff to yellow and are often brilliantly striped in pink, yellow, green, and white, make them a natural collector's item.

Due to long isolation the snails in some individual hammocks have actually developed distinct color variations. To date, there are 58 separately named color forms. Tragically, some collectors took advantage of this evolutionary situation by gathering as many snails as possible from a specific hammock, then burning the hammock to insure the uniqueness of the snails they intended to sell.

# Pine Rocklands

Pine rockland forests grow out of thin layers of porus caprock (limestone) and oolite substrate. In the United States they are found only in South Florida with examples in Everglades National Park and the middle region of the Florida Keys.

The pinelands have an upper canopy, an understory or subcanopy, and a thin layer of ground cover plants. Although there is little underbrush, frogs, snakes, insects, orchids, and ferns live in soil accumulated in deep crevasses and holes in the porus, rocky surface.

Slash pine (*Pinus elliottii*) is this woodland community's predominant tree. Maturing at 120 to 130 feet, it has a crown rounded to a flattened top, long yellow-green needles, and cones up to 6 inches in diameter. Along with a variety of birds and small mammals, animals found here include white-tailed deer (*Odocoileus virginia*) on the mainland and endangered Key deer (*Odocoileus virginianus clavium*) on Big Pine Key and No Name Key.

Periodic fires are one of nature's ways of safeguarding the health of the pinelands. A thick bark almost impervious to fire protects adult pines. In addition, needles are found only near the crown of the trees and lower limbs drop off as the tree grows taller. At full maturity, the lowest limbs may be 30 or 40 feet above the ground, well away from any fast-moving brush fire.

Fires forestall an accumulation of dead wood and dried organic matter, which could result in catastrophic fires that might reach into the upper canopy and destroy the mature trees. They also keep in check the hardwood understory that would shade out pine seedlings and eventually replace the pines.

A number of venomous and nonvenomous snakes make their home in the pinelands and along nearby wet areas. The Eastern coral snake (*Micurus fulvius fulvius*) grows up to about 2 feet long and is distinguished by alternating black, yellow, and red bands. Normally not aggressive, the coral snake's bite paralyzes the nervous and respiratory systems and can be fatal if antivenom isn't injected within a short time.

The Eastern diamondback rattlesnake *(Crotalus adamanteus)*, a member of the Pit Viper family, is one of the more feared reptiles. It coils and shakes its tail rattles as a warning before striking, although it can also strike without coiling. Normally not aggressive, it will on occasion stand its ground.

The dusky pigmy rattlesnake (*Sisturus milarius barbouri*) is also a member of the pit viper family. It matures at about 2 feet in length and is gray with three rows of black spots. The pigmy rattlesnake's warning rattle can sound like a cricket or a grasshopper. It is found both in marshes and pine woodlands.

The Florida cottonmouth moccasin (*Agkistrodon piscivorus conanti*) can sometimes be spotted swimming in fresh water with its head patrolling above the surface like a submarine periscope. Dark brown, with wide yellowish brown bands, it usually avoids human contact but its bite can be deadly.

The nonvenomous yellow rat snake (*Elaphe obsoleta quadrivittata*) is also very common in the Everglades and can often be spotted slithering up a tree. As its name suggests, the snake feeds on rodents, which it bites and squeezes to death. When disturbed the snake releases a strong smelling musk, which acts like catnip to wild cats.

The Eastern indigo snake (*Drymarchon corais couperi*), also known as Florida's blue indigo snake, is the largest snake in America. Reaching lengths of 8 feet or more, the nonvenomous species suffers from overcollection and habitat destruction. It's protected as a threatened species in Florida.

# Mangrove Forest

Mangrove forests are one of South Florida's most important natural features. The mangrove tree has adapted so well to living in a saltwater environment that it is the prevalent plant found in gently sloping shoreline areas regularly washed by low tidal wave intensity. Trapping detritus with their roots, the trees also provide food and habitat for a variety of crabs, fish, mollusks, and insects.

Brown pelicans (*Pelecanus occidentalis*), great white herons (*Ardea herodias*), magnificent frigatebirds, white-crowned pigeons (*Columba leucocephala*), double-crested cormorants *(Phalacrocorax auritus)*, and anhingas *(Anhinga anhinga)* roost and nest in mangrove trees. Water snakes and raccoons forage among the mangrove roots, and American crocodiles *(Crocodylus acutus)* rely on the forest as a sanctuary from man.

Three mangrove species are prevalent in the Everglades and Keys. The red mangrove (*Rhizophora mangle)* is the most dominant member and the species found nearest to the water. It has elliptical dark green leaves and long green seed pods that drop into the water and can float for miles before taking root. The tallest member of the mangrove family, usually growing to an average of 20 feet, it anchors itself against the tide with hundreds of reddish-brown prop roots that arch from the trunk and take hold of the muck below the water. The black mangrove *(Avicennia germinans)* is the second tallest species. Its oblong leaves have a salt-encrusted underside, and tasting the leaf is one way to tell the black from other mangroves. Its twisted aerial roots, called pneumatophores, that jut up like cigars or skeletal fingers all around the base of the tree, are the plant's respiratory organs. Indians and early white settlers burned black mangrove wood as a mosquito repellent.

The shrublike white mangrove (*Laguncularia racemosa*) is the smallest of the three species. It favors higher ground and grows away from the shorelines, often forming hammocks along with tropical species like West Indian mahogany (*Swietenia mahagoni*) and gumbo-limbo trees. It can be identified by wide, flat leaves with rounded ends and seeds that look like small peas. Its fruit is red when mature.

Buttonwood *(Conocarpus erectus)* is a member of the white mangrove family and is found most often in swamps and hammocks at least 2 feet above sea level where tidal flooding is unlikely. It has 4-inch elliptical leaves, gray to dark brown bark, and small greenish flowers in egg-shaped clusters.

## RED MANGROVE
(Rhizophora mangle)
The sturdy, arching prop roots of this tree bind the nutrient-rich silt in tidal marshes and build new land.

7

# Coral Reefs    .

Stretching along the Atlantic side of the Florida Keys is the only living coral reef system in North America and the third largest barrier reef in the world. Each year millions of snorkelers and divers come to discover this alien yet startlingly beautiful world.

Composed of coral structures that grow one upon the other, coral reefs are one of the most complex of all ecosystems. Florida's coral reefs, which extend from Biscayne Bay to the Dry Tortugas, are estimated to have taken from 5,000 to 7,000 years to develop.

Every coral structure is actually a colony made up of thousands of microscopic, soft-bodied animals, called polyps. Each tiny polyp extracts building material—calcium—from the sea and uses it to make a protective tube-type skeleton. Hundreds of these skeletons make a coral. Untold numbers of corals growing side by side and on top of each other form a reef.

The reefs then become host to a diverse community that includes sponges, shrimp, crabs, turtles, lobsters, and fish. Any unoccupied hole, crack, or ledge quickly becomes a home, and every bare spot a likely anchor site.

Many of the Keys' vast array of marine invertebrates can be found on or near the reefs, including sponges, sea anemones, jellyfish, and of course several species of living coral. Beautiful to look at, some invertebrates are dangerous to humans who come into contact with them. Fire sponge (*Tedania ignis*) can be recognized by its brilliant red or orange coloration and wide, irregular lobes. Anchored to coral, rocks, and mangrove roots, it causes serious rashes and blisters. Crenelated fire coral (*Milepora alcicornis*), which is actually a hydrozoan disguised as a creamy-yellow, tree branch-looking coral, is covered with small, white, hairlike tentacles that cause a serious rash.

Made obvious by their 9- to 10-inch-long, gas-filled, balloon-shaped bodies, with blue and pink highlights, Portuguese man-of-wars (*Physlia physalia*) are often seen floating on the ocean surface in large schools or washed up on the beaches. Their stinging 50- to 60-foot tentacles can cause severe burns and blisters, which should be treated immediately. Meat tenderizer or warm water applied to the welts will help to break down the poison proteins until medical help can be obtained.

Tropical reef fish like sergeant majors (*Abudefduf saxatilis*), butterflyfish, and parrotfish rely on multicolored displays of bars and stripes to help them hide from predators against the colorful reef. Reef fish popular as sport-fishing targets include a wide array of snappers and groupers, which take up residence in available holes and beneath ledges in the reef.

Barracudas (*Sphyraena barracuda*), which average from 2 feet to 3 feet long but can grow much larger, cruise through the water column above the reef and are regularly caught by anglers. The barracuda's massive lower jaw, with pointed, protruding teeth, makes it a terrifying sight and potential danger to swimmers and divers. However, it rarely intentionally attacks humans.

Beyond the reefs, the waters of the Gulf Stream beckon to charter boats stationed in the Keys that carry clients into the warm waters to troll for wahoo, dolphin, king mackerel, bonita, yellowfin tuna, and blackfin tuna. Perhaps the greatest prize is a chance to tangle with a trophy sailfish or marlin. Atlantic sailfish (*Istiophorus platypterus*), which are members of the Billfish family, are dark blue and silver and they mature at between 6 and 8 feet in length. They are distinguished by two spectacular dorsal fins that can be folded into a groove on the back for increased speed when pursuing prey on or near the surface. Underwater, groups of sailfish unfold their sails to herd schools of smaller fish.

Blue marlin (*Makaira nigricans*), also a member of the Billfish family, are one of the Keys' most prized trophy fish. Today, very few fish are killed to make trophy mounts; instead a replica is made of the catch, which is released alive. Marlin are found in deep open seas, where their speed helps them capture tuna, squid, and other prey. They mature at 6 to 12 feet, and fishermen rarely capture one of these silvery-blue fighters without an exhausting battle.

# Cypress Forests

Cypress domes and broad cypress strands dominate inland coastal areas where the water is slightly deeper than in the grasslands. Domes are dense clusters of cypress trees growing in water-filled depressions in the landscape. The depressions are widening solution holes in the porous limestone rock caused by rainfall that becomes slightly acidic after percolating through the surface layer of organic material.

Although they require occasional droughts to germinate, cypress trees can survive in year-round standing water their entire life. The dome shape results from trees in the deeper soil at the center of a depression growing taller than those on the outside. Stunted cypress trees, called dwarf cypresses, are a result of poor soil and dry land. While only a few feet tall, they can be as old as their stately brothers.

Huge cypress strands are found in the Big Cypress Swamp (*see* page 225). The word strand refers to linear swamp forests that develop along large sloughs in the Big Cypress Swamp. These densely vegetated forests may contain thousands of acres of cypress trees and stretch for up to 20 miles. The sloughs are created by water flowing over and beneath the landscape, slowly dissolving the limestone base.

The Fakahatchee Strand is a 20-mile-long and 3- to 5-mile-wide major drainage slough of Big Cypress Swamp. It contains the largest stand of native royal palms and largest concentration and variety of tree orchids in North America, as well as a number of other plants that are extremely rare. It's believed that the unique forest of cypress trees and royal palms may be the only one in existence in the world.

# Coastal Prairies

Coastal prairies can be found in Everglades National Park behind the beaches of Cape Sable and behind the mangroves that line the northern edge of Florida Bay. The open prairies are low, flat lands that have been formed and are maintained by passing hurricanes and tropical storms that carry salt water and marl (a limey mud) miles inland from Florida Bay.

Only low-growing desertlike succulents and cacti are capable of survival in these dry, salty conditions. Common plants are the multichambered glasswort *(Salicornia birginica)*, sea oxeye daisy *(Borrichia frutescens)*, saltwort *(Batis maritima)*, also known as pickle weed; and prickly pear cactus *(Opuntia stricta).*

Marsh hawks (also known as northern harriers) *(Circus cyaneus)* and red-shouldered hawks commonly hunt over the coastal prairies. Marsh hawks are easy to spot because of their kite-like ability to glide on wind currents low to the ground. The rare Cape Sable seaside sparrow *(Ammodramus maritimus mirabilis)* also inhabits these prairies. This 6-inch-long, greenish-colored endangered species is a member of the American Sparrow subfamily. Rarely seen, it is hard for even trained bird watchers to spot.

# River of Grass

The most distinguishing feature of the Everglades, and that for which it was named, is a wide, shallow marshy river that was brought to the world's attention in Marjory Stoneman Douglas's groundbreaking book, *The Everglades: River of Grass.* Forty to 50 miles wide, and only inches deep, the historic river of grass originated as water flowing out of the southern end of Lake Okeechobee and across the nearly flat prairies at an almost imperceptible rate of no more than 100 feet per day. Sawgrass *(Cladium jamaicense)* is the dominate species growing profusely across this vast wilderness, which is also interspersed with torpedo-shaped tree islands and the rounded domes of cypress heads. The land is so flat, dropping only 2 or 3 inches per mile, that changes in elevation of only inches result in entirely different and distinct habitats and landscapes each with their own community of plants and animals.

Freshwater sloughs are the deeper and faster-flowing centers of a broad, marshy river. Everglades National Park contains two distinct sloughs (pronounced "slew"), the Shark Valley Slough, which is the true "river of grass," and Taylor Slough, a narrow eastern branch of the "river."

Common mammals found in the sloughs include river otters *(Lutra canadensis)*, which are very active and well adapted to aquatic life. They can often be seen playing or hunting for food in the open freshwater areas. Their permanent dens are often dug into mud banks and have both an underwater and an exposed entrance.

Another unusual aquatic creature is the marsh rabbit (*Sylvilagus palustris*), which uses its large feet to cross wet, muddy marshes and to swim in deep water. The rabbit can be seen along roadsides near freshwater lakes and marshy areas. When threatened the marsh rabbit takes to the water where it can float with only its eyes and nose exposed.

Several species of freshwater fish are found in sluggish streams and swamps. Common species include largemouth bass *(Micropterus salmoides)*, bluegill *(Lepomis macrochirus)*, black crappie (*Pomoxis nigomaculatus*), Mozambique tilapia (*Tilapia mossambica*), chain pickerel (*Esox niger*), and redbreast sunfish *(Lepomis auritus)*.

The Eastern mosquitofish (*Gambusia affinis*), a member of the Live-bearer family, is a small but important player in the ecology of the Everglades. About 1.5 inches long, the olive brown fish lives in ponds, lakes, drainage ditches, and brackish waters, where it feeds greedily on hordes of mosquito larvae that begin life underwater. In accordance with nature's plan, mosquitofish, which reproduce by the thousands during rainy seasons, are a mainstay in the diets of numerous birds, mammals, and reptiles throughout the region.

# Estuaries

In estuaries such as Florida Bay, all the right ingredients, salt water and fresh water, nutrients from soil and decaying plants, and sunlight, come together to give rise to some of the most productive habitats in the world.

Wedged between the Florida Keys and the Everglades, and situated entirely within Everglades National Park, Florida Bay is a triangular-shaped body of water covering an area of 400,000 to 550,000 acres, depending on where the western boundary with the Gulf of Mexico is measured. Its waters are dotted with 237 mangrove islands. Sea turtles, dolphins, game fish, and a unique mix of bird life rely on the bay for food and in some cases nesting sites.

The bay's productivity depends upon a bountiful underwater "forest" of turtle grass (*Thalassia testudinum*). The most common seagrass in the bay, turtle grass continues to survive despite problems with the bay's salinity. Other less-tolerant types of seagrass have died back due to changes in the natural plumbing system of the Everglades.

Under natural conditions, the bay received enough fresh water from the Everglades to maintain a brackish water estuary. In more recent times, the bay has suffered from a periodic lack of freshwater inflow, which has caused the massive die-off of hundreds of acres of valuable seagrass habitat.

On the southwestern coast, the Ten Thousand Islands mangrove-dominated estuary is the final destination for the vast amounts of water flowing through the Big Cypress Swamp. Often described as the Florida equivalent of a tropical rain forest, the whole life-propelling estuary system actually begins with the mangrove trees, which act as solar panels for the estuary.

Powered by the sun, they capture and store energy. As the trees grow, older leaves turn yellow and drop into the water, sending energy into the system. The leaves are colonized by algae and fungi and then either decay or are eaten by small crabs, snails, and fish—initiating the tropical food chain. More than 3 tons of leaves can fall from a single acre of mangroves every year.

Many of Florida's estuaries are popular with sport-fishermen. Among the more sought after species are redfish (*Sciaenops ocellatus*), which are also know as red drum. Bronze colored with white undersides, redfish always have one or more prominent ringed spots on their sides. Known as tough competitors with a good food value, redfish are highly prized by anglers. Although reaching weights of more than 90 pounds, redfish in the 10 pound range are commonly caught in the estuary waters around South Florida.

Another popular species is spotted seatrout (*Cynoscion nebulosus*), one of Florida's most common game fish. It is caught throughout the coastal waters of the Gulf and Atlantic, but rarely in the Lower Keys. It has a silver body with black spots, but the fish becomes darker when it lives in back bays or inland creeks. The species can reach weights of 10 to 15 pounds, but most spotted seatrout that are caught weigh 2 to 3 pounds.

Tarpon (*Megalops atlanticus*) is another popular and protected game fish. Olive-gray and silvery colored, tarpon can reach lengths of 4 to 6 feet and weights up to 200 pounds. Its favorite habitats are open seas, shallow coastal waters, and estuaries. Snook (*Centropomus undecimalis*) is also one of South Florida's premier game fish. Silver colored, with a distinctive black line running down its side, snook are caught in mangrove estuaries and inland brackish-water rivers and creeks. Also called "linesides," they can reach weights of 50 pounds but average much smaller.

# Beaches

The South Florida region also sports some of the most attractive beaches in the world. The beach at Bahia Honda State Park, with its long strands of soft, white sand bordered by swaying palm trees, is without question the best beach in the Keys, and is often rated as one of the best in the nation. On the southwestern coast, the Naples area has more than 40 miles of beaches accessible at various points. Most are heavily visited and have varying levels of facilities (*see* Naples Area Beaches, page 264). Some of the Naples beaches also rank among the best in the nation.

The 10 miles of bright white, isolated beaches on Cape Sable in Everglades National Park are among the few wild beaches left in Florida. They can only be reached by a 15-mile boat trip. The whiteness of a beach is determined by how much of the sand is composed of crushed seashells and how much of crushed rock. On Cape Sable, the pure white beaches are made almost entirely of shell.

Sea purslane *(Sesuvium portulacastrum)* and sea oats (*Uniola paniculata*) are two of the plants that are able to brave the harsh conditions at the top of the beach and anchor the soft ground. The long roots of the sea oat help to secure dunes against wind and storm. The seeds and the plants are protected from harvest by state law. Sea oats have narrow, pale green leaves and a prominent 3-foot stem displaying a thick seed head that waves in the wind like a small flag. The individual seeds look like oats.

Florida's beaches are also very important as nesting sites for many of the world's sea turtles. Sea turtles mate in shallow waters close to nesting beaches. From early spring to mid-September, females come on shore after dark and lay eggs in holes they dig above the high tide line. They deposit anywhere from 40 to 180 eggs, which are covered with sand. The eggs are warmed by the sand and sun, and several weeks later the young break out of their shells at the same time and dig their way to the surface. From there they follow their instincts across the sand toward the slighter brighter horizon over the sea. Many perish on the way, eaten by birds, raccoons, crabs, and other predators lying in wait for the slowly moving feast. Street lights and other artificial lights attract some baby turtles inland, away from the water.

Those that reach the comparative safety of the water are often eaten by fish and diving birds. The few that miraculously reach maturity will some day follow an inner compass back to their birthing beach, where they will continue the turtles' uphill battle against extinction.

Loggerhead sea turtles (*Caretta caretta*), which are classified as a threatened species, are some of the most commonly encountered sea turtles in South Florida waters. Maturing at up to 3 to 4 feet in length, they're dark reddish brown and have a large head and pointed beak. They make their home in bays, estuaries, and the open ocean. The endangered green sea turtle (*Chelonia mydas*) has a large head and olive-green scales. It nests mainly on the Atlantic coast of Florida between Palm Beach and Cape Canaveral. Although once common in South Florida waters, it suffered from

## LOGGERHEAD SEA TURTLE
(Caretta caretta)

After mating in shallow water, a female loggerhead comes ashore, digs a deep hole in the beach, lays more than 100 eggs, covers them with sand, and heads back to the sea. The eggs will hatch in about eight weeks, and the baby turtles will make their way to the water.

overharvest for use as food and to make cosmetic oils, and it is now rarely seen as far south as the Keys. The endangered Atlantic hawksbill sea turtle (*Eretmochelys imbricata*) and the endangered Atlantic ridley sea turtle (*Lepidochelys kempi*) are occasionally seen in the clear waters in Florida Bay (*see* page 189), Dry Tortugas National Park (*see* page 143), and Biscayne National Park (*see* page 32).

# Endangered and Threatened Wildlife of the Everglades and Florida Keys

The numerous and distinctive habitats found in the Everglades and Florida Keys support a variety of endangered and threatened wildlife. Some species, like the Florida panther (*Felis concolor coryi*) or the wood stork (*Mycteria americana*), move freely between various habitats. While others, like the Florida tree snail or the Cape Sable seaside sparrow (*Ammodramus maritimus mirabilis*), are restricted to small niches in the ecosystem.

In fact, many of the 74 federally endangered plants and animals found in Florida, the most in any state except California and Hawaii, are found within South Florida coastal habitats. This unfortunate list includes the American crocodile, the Atlantic green sea turtle, Atlantic ridley sea turtle, leatherback sea turtle (*Dermochelys coriacea*), red-cockaded woodpecker (*Picoides borealis*), Cape Sable seaside sparrow, Key deer, snail kite (*Rostrhamus sociabilis*), Key Largo wood rat (*Neotoma floridana smalli*), Queen conch (*Strombus gigas*), Schaus' swallowtail butterfly, West Indian manatee (*Tricechus manatus*), and Florida panther. Threatened species include the American alligator (*Alligator mississippiensis*), loggerhead sea turtle, southern bald eagle (*Haliaeetus leucocoephalus leucocephalus*), peregrine falcon (*Falcon peregrinus*), and roseate tern (*Sterna dougallii*).

Florida's standing among states with high numbers of endangered species is due in part to the unique habitats that are found nowhere else in the continental United States, and to the overall distribution of many of the listed species. Like many states, Florida contains remnant populations of species that have been eliminated elsewhere. The Florida panther, for example, was once found throughout the Southeast, but now only exists in South Florida.

A number of other endangered species, however, such as the West Indian manatee, American crocodile, and snail kite, exist in Florida at the very edge of their natural range and are still found in the West Indies and South America. Yet another group of endangered species, which includes the Schaus' swallowtail butterfly, the Florida tree snail, and the Cape Sable seaside sparrow, are endemic to specific habitats (in this case tropical hardwood hammocks and coastal prairies) and have always only existed in small and fragile populations.

Following is a detailed description of five threatened and endangered species. For more information on endangered species in Florida, contact the U.S. Fish and Wildlife Service and the Florida Fish and Wildlife Conservation Commission (*see* Appendix C). Contact information is provided in the glossary of this book.

## FLORIDA PANTHER

Florida panthers are very rarely seen by anyone other than the scientists who keep track of them with radio collars. Before European settlement, the big cats roamed all of Florida. Primarily out of fear for themselves and their livestock, early settlers actively tried to rid the state of these elusive creatures. Bounty laws in the nineteenth century granted a cash payment for panther hides even though there are no documented reports of Florida panther attacks on humans.

In the 1950s and 1960s, destruction of the panthers' habitat for urban and agricultural development severely reduced their living space, and the panther population dwindled dangerously low. The Florida panther was placed on the federal endangered species list in 1967. In 1979, the State of Florida made it a felony, with a five-year prison sentence, to kill a panther. Somewhere between 40 and 70 of the majestic cats remain in the wild.

Even with the best efforts of state and federal biologists, dwindling habitat and road kills continue to take their toll on the species. Underpasses have been installed beneath some highways to provide safe passage for the cats, which can roam up to hundreds of square miles.

Despite its name, the Florida panther is not a close relative of panthers that live in Africa and Asia. It's actually a subspecies of the western cougar or mountain lion. Adult males mature at up to 8 feet from tail to nose and weigh 110 to 125 pounds. Females average about 6 to 7 feet and weight 75 to 85 pounds. The Florida panther has a short, tawny-brown or golden coat, a long tail, long legs, and wide paws with retractable claws. The panther doesn't roar; instead it purrs, screams, and hisses, similar to a house cat only with a chillingly high increase in volume.

In pursuit of prey, a Florida panther can run for short distances at 30 to 35 miles an hour. Acute senses of smell and hearing also aid in the hunt. White-tailed deer and wild hogs are the mainstays of its diet, which it supplements with birds, rabbits, armadillos, rodents, and even small alligators.

Mainly nocturnal, panthers spend the daylight hours resting in hardwood hammocks, swamps, and pine forests. They are typically solitary creatures, and adult males hardly ever share the same territory. Litters are usually born in the spring with the female giving birth to between two and four cubs. She nurses them for about eight weeks, until they are ready for their first fresh meat.

The female stays with her cubs for about two years, teaching them hunting skills and survival techniques. When she is ready to find another mate, the cubs are pushed out on their own. Only a small number survive to adulthood.

## WEST INDIAN MANATEE

Manatees aren't particularly graceful or photogenic or adept at performing and interacting with humans. They just go on about their grazing oblivious to most interruptions. Manatees have a bulbous, grayish-black, seal-like body that tapers to a flat, paddle-shaped tail. A pair of small front flippers propels them slowly through fresh, brackish, and shallow ocean waters. Vegetarians, they feed exclusively on seagrasses, water hyacinths, and other water plants. Every few minutes they rise to the surface for air.

Commonly known as sea cows, full-grown West Indian manatees average 8 to 10 feet and weigh 1,800 to 2,500 pounds. Among the most beloved of Florida's wildlife, manatees are protected by state and federal law as an endangered species. A specialty license tag is sold by the State of Florida to raise money for their protection. The U.S. Fish and Wildlife Service estimates that about 2,300 now live in Florida.

Docile, with no defense mechanisms, the species is distantly related to elephants. Both sides of manatees' split upper lip grasp vegetation and roll it into their mouth, similar to the way an elephant uses its trunk to gather food.

Manatees' gentle nature has also contributed to their endangerment. Many are killed every year in boat locks, and through collisions with power boats and even barges, which sometimes trap the animals beneath their wide hulls. During the 1990s hundreds of manatees also fell victim to a massive outbreak of red tide (a toxic algal bloom) that appeared on the southwestern coast of Florida.

Manatees communicate with high-pitched squeaks and chirps, similar to dolphins. Females give birth to a single calf about every two to three years, and nurse for about two years. They closely protect their young and remain with them for at least two years.

In summer, manatees travel in small groups as far north as the coasts of Georgia, the Carolinas, and Virginia. They have a low tolerance for water colder than about 65 degrees Fahrenheit, and in winter they migrate to warm springs in coastal Florida and more southerly habitats in the Keys.

## AMERICAN ALLIGATOR

American alligators were once nearly wiped out for their hides and meat but have since made an exceptional comeback across Florida. Only a few thousand remained 25 years ago, but the Florida Fish and Wildlife Conservation Commission estimates the state's alligator population is now more than 1 million. Although alligators are no longer on the endangered species list, they remain under federal protection on the threatened species list.

During the late spring breeding season, female alligators construct 4-foot-tall pyramid-shaped mounds of mud, reeds, twigs, grass, and other vegetation as nests for laying their eggs. Several dozen hard-shelled, leathery eggs are laid in the center of the mound. During the nine-week incubation period, the decaying vegetation and hot sun keep the interior of the nest warm, while the mother remains on constant vigil against birds, raccoons, and other potential predators.

The eggs begin to hatch in late summer and the young claw their way out of the shells. Alerted by the chirping of her hatchlings, the mother digs them out of the nest and carries them to the water in her mouth. At birth, alligators are about 8 inches long and weigh about 2 ounces. They grow about 1 foot per year for the first five years. Those that survive for a year reach 18 inches and 10 ounces. At 30 years, a male can attain 12 to 13 feet and weigh as much as 850 pounds.

Adult alligators have huge, incredibly strong jaws, 80 strong teeth, and a brain about the size of a walnut. When the jaws are closed, only teeth of the upper jaw are visible. Eyes, ears, and nostrils are on the top of the head, enabling alligators to see, hear, and smell when swimming just beneath the surface with the tops of their heads exposed.

When an alligator submerges, a series of natural mechanisms are triggered. The throat closes so the alligator can grab prey without taking water into the lungs. Flaps of skin close the outside ear openings and protect the eardrums. Nostrils close, and a thin, soft, third eyelid protects the eyes from water and allows the alligator to see as well underwater as it does on the surface.

Alligators are usually docile but can be dangerous to humans who surprise them or come too close to their nests. They are unpredictable and never should be approached. On land they can run incredibly fast for short distances. By nature, alligators fear adult humans and prefer to hunt smaller prey, such as birds, raccoons, fish, and crabs. Nevertheless, wading into murky water or swimming at night where alligators are known to reside carries obvious risks. Special care should be taken with small children and pets, which are more the size of an alligator's natural prey. Dogs swimming in canals and ponds, or straying too close to shorelines often become alligator victims.

Nine people have been killed in gator attacks in Florida, about half of them children, since 1972. The state averages about 4 to 5 serious bites every year, and about the same number of minor bites. With more than 1 million alligators and a human population of more than 15 million, Florida officials say that makes the odds of being bitten less than being struck by lightning.

## AMERICAN CROCODILE

A small, endangered population of American crocodiles exists in the Upper Keys and Florida Bay area. The American saltwater crocodile is one of the least aggressive members of the world's Crocodile family. Shy and reclusive, it avoids all contact with humans.

The American crocodile is broadly distributed along the coastal and estuarine shores of the Caribbean, including the coasts of Venezuela, Colombia, Central America, and Mexico. In Florida, American crocodiles were once found from Lake

Worth (near West Palm Beach) down the southeastern coast to Key Largo and across the northern shore of Florida Bay to Cape Sable.

Scientists estimate that the number of American crocodiles in Florida is 600 or less. Only about 50 of those are mating pairs. The population is centered around northeastern Florida Bay and Key Largo.

Crocodiles are distinguished from broad-snouted, darker-colored alligators by their grayish-olive green color and their long, tapered snouts. They also have a long, pointed tooth near the front on each side of the lower jaw that remains exposed even when the mouth is closed. Their large mouths and huge, tearing teeth enable them to capture snakes, turtles, fish, birds, raccoons, and rabbits. They can go for long periods without eating. They store up heat by lying in the sun. Adult crocodiles can measure up to 12 feet in length. The largest ever recorded in Florida was nearly 16 feet.

Mating takes place in March and April, and in early summer, female crocodiles lay their eggs in a mud or sand nest in brackish or salt water along canal and creek banks and away from the vegetation line of Florida Bay. They lay an average of 30 to 50 eggs, and incubation takes 80 to 90 days. Females remain near the nest but don't protect the nest as zealously as female alligators.

When the young are born, they measure about 10 inches long. The mother crocodile digs them out of the nest and carries them to the water in her mouth, then abandons them. The young stay together for about a month for mutual protection. Some find their way to muddy water holes, where they feed on small snakes, fish, and insects.

### QUEEN CONCH

Also known as pink conch, the queen conch is a marine snail that is a victim of its own beauty. The large, spindle-shaped shell, with the lustrous, flaring pink lip, is a prized souvenir that thousands of tourists take home as a reminder of the Florida Keys' stunning beauty. Lovely to look at, conchs are also delightful to eat. Their tasty meat has been a mainstay of Keys and Caribbean residents for hundreds of years. Conch fritters, conch chowder, and conch salads are popular restaurant fare. They were once so plentiful, they could be gathered up by the bucketful in beaches and shallow waters.

Overaggressive harvesting has severely decimated their numbers. In 1985, the State of Florida put them on the protected species list. The conch meat and shells sold in restaurants and stores throughout the Keys is imported legally from other countries.

Queen conch mating takes place between February and October. Females lay their eggs on sandy sea bottoms in depths ranging from a few feet near shore to more than 400 feet.

Females lay their eggs three weeks after mating and can produce five to eight egg masses a season. Each egg mass, looking like a mound of soggy cooked noodles, contains up to 500,000 eggs, which hatch in three to five days into microscopic larvae. The young conchs then drift through the sea currents, feeding on single-cell plants. In another month those few that survive settle to the sea bottom and metamorphose into bottom-feeding snails about the size of a grain of sand. Those that survive for three years reach their full size of 9 to 10 inches. Their many predators include sharks, octopuses, sea turtles, and humans.

# Birds

*"We observed great flocks of wading birds flying overhead towards their evening roost...they appeared in such numbers to actually block out the light for some time."*
— John James Audubon, *Remembrances of a Trip to South Florida*, circa 1832.

Birds of the Everglades and Florida Keys deserve a special mention. From backyard feeders to tropical hardwood hammocks in the Everglades wilderness, from roadside canals to isolated keys far from land, bird life in the Keys and Everglades is both startling and commonplace.

What Audubon witnessed in 1832 was one of the greatest wildlife spectacles ever known—millions of wading birds nesting and feeding in Florida's wetlands. By 1900 these flocks had been hunted down to near extinction for their beautiful feathers. Legal protection passed in 1905 partially restored the birds' numbers, but ongoing draining of the Everglades combined with extensive habitat loss has resulted in a 90 percent decline in their historic, overall numbers.

Nevertheless, birds and bird watchers are still a constant part of the landscape of coastal South Florida. Following are a few of the more interesting species you're likely to encounter, but there are literally hundreds or others waiting to be discovered by the veteran birder or the casual observer. Don't forget your binoculars!

**Brown pelican** (*Pelecanus occidentalis*). This marine bird dives head first into the water using its huge throat pouch as a dip net to catch fish. Brown pelicans have special air sacs beneath their chests to cushion the impact as they hit the water. During the summer brown pelicans nest in mangrove areas.

**Great white heron** (*Ardea herodias*). The largest of all herons, the great white has brilliant white plumage and light colored legs, which differentiate it from the similar-looking, black-legged great egret (*Casmerodius albus*). A color variation of the great blue heron (*Ardea herodias*), it is frequently seen in and around Florida Bay where it stalks a variety of large prey including rodents and other birds.

**Osprey** (*Pandion haliaetus*). This hawk is well adapted to catch the fish that make up its diet. The soles of the osprey's feet have sharp projections that help it grip its slippery prey. It hovers until spotting a fish near the surface, then it suddenly plunges feet first into the water, grasping the fish in its talons. Osprey are a frequent sight throughout the Keys and the Everglades. Their nests can often be see on the top of electrical poles and in tall trees.

**Peregrine falcon** (*Falcon peregrinus*). Like the bald eagle, the population of this small, powerful, threatened raptor is increasing since the use of the pesticide DDT has been discontinued. With a raucous "kak kak" cry, the peregrine falcon patrols the skies for sick and slow-flying birds and dives to the ground for mice and other small animals. It is a frequent sight in Florida's marshes and coastal areas during fall migrations.

**Pileated woodpecker** (*Dryocopus pileatus*). Despite its large size, this elegant black and white woodpecker with a bright red crest is adept at keeping out of sight. In the Everglades it often builds its nest in the trunk of a palm tree. You can hear its strong and loud drumming on trees from a great distance and sometimes spot its fast, undulating wing beat as it flies from tree trunk to tree trunk.

**Piping plover** (*Charadrius melodus*). This diminutive, gray and white, 7-inch to 8-inch bird is a member of the Plover family and is on the threatened species list. With a short black bill and "peep-lo" call, it can be sighted in sandy flats and coastal areas.

**Purple gallinule** (*Porphyrula martinica*). This striking green and purple bird can be seen in freshwater sloughs and ponds in the Everglades walking gingerly on spatterdock leaves using its very long toes to lift the leaves in search of insects. The gallinule's long toes also enable it to climb low bushes. When walking or swimming it constantly jerks its head and tail.

**Roseate spoonbill** (*Ajaia ajaja*). This is a species of special concern in Florida, and the number of roseate spoonbill breeding pairs is estimated at only about 500. The striking pink and white wading birds feed in shallow water by moving their beaks from side to side, catching small fish, crustaceans, and insects. Their primary nesting areas are mangrove islands in Florida Bay, which they share with other wading bird species.

**Snail kite** (also known as Everglades kite) (*Rostrhamus sociabilis*). An endangered member of the same family as hawks and eagles, snail kites feed almost entirely on Florida apple snails, which they extract from the shell with their sharply hooked beaks. Destruction of freshwater marsh habitats has reduced this once abundant species to only a few hundred, placing it in grave peril of total extinction.

**Southern bald eagle** (*Haliaeetus leucocoephalus leucocephalus*). While it remains on the threatened species list, this magnificent national symbol has been making a comeback since being placed under federal protection. Hundreds of nesting pairs now exist throughout Florida. It is often seen perching near coastal and inland waterways.

**Tricolored heron** (*Egretta tricolor*). This small, blue and gray heron walks quietly through still water to stir up prey, or stands motionless waiting for prey to swim within reach of its long neck and quick beak. Sometimes it extends its wings to cast a shadow across the water to make the prey below the surface more visible.

**White-crowned pigeon** (*Columba leucocephala*). A threatened species, the white-crowned pigeon is found only in the southern portion of Everglades National Park, the Keys, and neighboring Caribbean islands. It breeds in summer on islands in Florida Bay, where it feeds on the fruit of tropical hammock trees.

**White pelicans** (*Pelecanus erythrorhynchos*). Flocks of these majestic white migrants with distinctive black wing tips fill the sky each winter, forming long lines and flapping their enormous wings in unison. They fish in formation as well, swimming on the surface and using their wings to drive their prey into shallow water where they seize the fish in their large pouched bills.

**Wood stork** (also known as wood ibis) (*Mycteria americana*). The wood stork is the only member of the Stork family that can be found in the United States. On the endangered species list, the tall bird is clumsy looking on land but graceful in flight. With white feathers and long, skinny black legs, wood storks stand about 3.5 feet high, with a wingspread of 5.5 feet. They nest together in large colonies and feed by stalking patiently through muddy water with their beaks submerged, ready to grab and immediately swallow anything that comes within range.

# History and Human Habitation

South Florida's first human inhabitants may have arrived as early as 10,000 years ago. They lived in an arid climate on a flat land that held little surface water, and they hunted Paleolithic megafauna like bison and mammoths. Around 5,000 years ago, as a result of a changing climate, melting glaciers, and a rising sea level, a subtropical terrain began to form composed of islands, cypress swamps, hardwood forests, and sawgrass prairies. The large animals disappeared, and the inhabitants responded by establishing other patterns of subsistence.

The descendants of these early arrivals, the Tequesta Indians on the southeastern coast and Calusa Indians on the southwest, built their villages at the mouths of rivers, on offshore islands, and on elevated pockets of tropical forest. They turned their hunting skills to smaller reptiles and mammals and they took to the sea to catch fish and harvest shellfish.

There are accounts of Tequesta Indians who, when they spotted a pod of whales offshore in the Atlantic, would paddle after them in canoes. When a whale surfaced within range, an Indian would leap aboard its back and plug the animal's breathing hole with a stake. After the whale suffocated, it was hauled to shore. The North Atlantic right whale may have been the most common species taken this way.

The Calusa on the southwestern coast used huge dugout canoes that held as many as 40 paddlers. As the Indians expanded their realm of influence, the big canoes were used for carrying trade goods through the Gulf and Caribbean. The Calusa also built huge shell mounds, as large as 40 acres, throughout the Ten Thousand Islands.

The Calusa Indians are known to have had a highly evolved political structure and are believed to have dominated the Tequesta and other tribes, including the Jeaga and Ais who lived on the Florida east coast north of the Tequesta, and the Mayaimi, who lived in the interior near Lake Okeechobee.

In 1896, Smithsonian archeologist Frank Hamilton Cushing excavated a Calusa Indian shell mound on Marco Island and discovered tools, weapons, utensils, wooden ceremonial masks, and wood carvings including heads of animals such as a wolf, sea turtle, pelican, and alligator. The most famous artifact uncovered is known today as the Marco Cat—a breathtaking, fully preserved wooden statuette of a panther 6 inches in height that was carved from a "gnarled block of fine, dark brown wood." Cushing speculated it had either been "saturated with some kind of varnish, or more probably had been frequently anointed with the fat of slain animals or victims. To this, doubtless, its remarkable preservation was due."

The article that most fascinated Cushing, however, was a wooden deer head. He wrote: "This represents the finest and most perfectly preserved example of combined carving and painting that we found…it portrayed with startling fidelity and delicacy, the head of a young deer or doe…The muzzle, nostrils, and especially the exquisitely modeled and painted lower jaw, were so delicately idealized that it was evident the primitive artist who fashioned this masterpiece loved, with both ardor and reverence, the animal he was portraying…"

Spanish explorers are believed to be the first Europeans to see the Florida Peninsula. Estimates place the number of Indians occupying South Florida when the Spanish arrived to be 20,000 with perhaps 100,000 living throughout the state.

On April 2, 1513, Don Juan Ponce de Leon made landfall near present-day St. Augustine. He christened the land *La Florida*, in deference to the Easter season, which Spaniards called the Feast of Flowers. The 53-year-old was not really seeking a fountain of youth. The hardened soldier and explorer, in fact, was seeking new lands for his king and country, and gold and glory for himself.

As the Spanish sought to establish forts and religious missions in *La Florida*, and slave traders raided Indian villages, the Tequestas and Calusas grew increasingly unfriendly. In 1521, Ponce de Leon and 200 Spanish soldiers were ambushed by a large force of Calusas at Charlotte Harbor, near present-day Fort Myers. Ponce de Leon was struck in the chest by an arrow believed to have been dipped in the poisonous sap of the manchineel tree. He was taken to Cuba, where he died and was buried.

Undeterred, the Spaniards fortified their hold on the New World. On August 28, 1565, the feast day of Saint Augustine, ground was blessed in northeastern Florida for what is still the oldest continuous settlement in the United States, St. Augustine.

Less than 200 years later, decimated by their wars with the Spanish and English, by constant slave trader raids, and by European diseases such as typhus, measles, yellow fever, and smallpox, the Calusas and Tequestas had become virtually wiped out. By 1763, when Spain ceded Florida to the British as part of the treaty ending the

Seven Years War, the few remaining native peoples were reported to have migrated to Cuba with the Spanish.

In their place came bands of Creek Indians, who migrated south from the Carolinas, Georgia, and Alabama ahead of European expansion. Collectively known as Seminoles, they lived and hunted throughout the state and provided refuge for runaway slaves. When Congress ordered all Native Americans east of the Mississippi River to move to present-day Oklahoma in 1830, many of these Indians resisted and fought three wars with the U.S. Army.

Although harassed and hounded for decades, a small group of Indians, sometimes estimated at about 300, simply refused to surrender, eventually taking refuge in the Big Cypress Swamp and the Everglades. From these strong and proud people have come the Seminole and Miccosukee people that live in South Florida today.

The Miccosukee, who were originally known as Mikasuki and who spoke the Hitichi language, were given tribal status in 1962 following an international campaign that was supported by Fidel Castro, who among other international leaders at that time recognized the Indians' nationhood.

Today the Miccosukee occupy a reservation straddling Interstate 75, with a small tribal headquarters area along the Tamiami Trail (Highway 41), next to Everglades National Park. The Seminoles, who spoke the Muskogee language, occupy four reservations, with the largest (69,900 acres) located in the Big Cypress Swamp.

Following statehood in 1845, and the end of the Indian conflicts in 1856, South Florida became the target of northern tycoons and would-be land barons who sought to gain wealth from the lands' natural resources. Since large areas of the state were periodically under water, great schemes were developed to drain the swamps and the Everglades—schemes that continued until the latter half of the twentieth century.

Hamilton Disston, a wealthy young man from Philadelphia who inherited his role as the country's largest manufacturer of saws and files, initiated the first broad plans to drain the Everglades in 1877. Rivers were straightened where possible, natural limestone barriers were blown away, and canals were dredged to carry the unwanted water to the sea (see The Florida Everglades, page 153).

An era of steamboat traffic that had begun early in the nineteenth century reached its peak during the later part of that century as more waterways were opened. By 1880 railroads were being pushed down both the east and west coasts and settlement quickly followed.

On the east coast, in the late 1880s, Henry Morrison Flagler, a wealthy Standard Oil executive, purchased a small North Florida railroad. In St. Augustine and other Florida cities, he began building resort hotels that he hoped would entice affluent northerners to visit and subsequently invest in the state.

In 1896, Flagler completed his Florida East Coast Railroad to Miami. The extension was part of an agreement with Mrs. Julia Tuttle, who offered him half her property in the small, unincorporated community of Miami, if he would complete the railroad, map out a town, and build a hotel worthy of upper class guests. Flagler carried out the plan, and Miami was incorporated in July 1896.

Flagler continued to pursue a dream of extending his railroad all the way to Key West, a feat he achieved in 1912 just prior to his death the following year (*see* Florida Keys, page 27).

On the west coast, Barron G. Collier, a wealthy advertising executive, had purchased more than 1 million acres in what would become Collier County. He brought the railroad south to Everglades City and initiated the completion of the Tamiami Trail (*see* Western Everglades, page 223).

Florida's population growth, although beginning slowly following statehood in 1845, would eventually come to threaten every major habitat and body of water in South Florida. A federal census taken during the territorial period (1821–1845) showed a mere 34,000 residents within the state. Most of the population was centered in St. Augustine on the northeast coast, Pensacola on the western end of the Panhandle, and Tallahassee right in the middle of the state. Cotton farming, commercial fishing, and timber harvesting were the dominant industries.

By the beginning of the twentieth century, Florida had acquired more than half a million inhabitants. Jacksonville, a port city on the northeast coast near the Florida/Georgia border, was the largest city with 23,000 inhabitants. But on the heels of newly drained land and rapid railroad expansion down both coasts, growth patterns were quickly changing in favor of South Florida.

By 1930 the state's population had reached 1.5 million residents, and the beginnings of large metropolitan areas were developing around Miami on the southeastern coast and around Tampa and St. Petersburg on the central west coast. Following World War II, a developing tourism industry combined with rapidly expanding retirement communities initiated an explosion in population that changed the face of the state.

Huge expanses of wetlands were rapidly transformed into farming, ranching, and residential communities. The majority of urban development took place at first along the Atlantic coastal ridge in southeastern Florida where Dade, Broward, and Palm Beach counties, with a combined estimated population of 4.5 million, still make up one of the fastest growing areas in the country.

As development continued in southeastern Florida, it pushed west into the Everglades, draining the land and pushing the wilderness farther and farther away. On the southwestern coast, urban sprawl in the Naples area created a more recent struggle over protecting that area's unique habitats that continues today (*see* Naples, page 261).

Averaging 9,000 new residents arriving per week during the latter part of the twentieth century, Florida's population continues to grow. By the beginning of 1999, the state was home to an estimated 15 million residents, four-fifths of whom reside along the coasts. That number swells annually with the arrival of more than 40 million tourists.

# A Land Preserved

Fortunately, millions of acres of South Florida's native habitats survived and are protected within a vast network of public lands including Everglades National Park, Biscayne National Park, Big Cypress National Preserve, Dry Tortugas National Park, and dozens of other state and federal refuges, parks, recreation areas, marine sanctuaries, and wildlife management areas described in this book.

So when you visit the Keys and the Everglades, and you should, please remember that despite the unbridled growth and mounting pressure on the natural resources, most Floridians are proud of their state and their relationship to the land and its wildlife. With public support, the State of Florida has already purchased more than 1 million acres of fragile lands for preservation. In 1998, Florida voters passed a constitutional amendment by a 72 percent majority that provided a permanent funding source to continue purchasing and protecting important wildlife habitat.

Floridians have also learned that with wildlife so close, it has to be respected. Alligators in swimming pools are common, as are deer in backyards, wading birds in roadside ditches, spiraling flocks of white pelicans over coastal condominiums, and beaches used by people in the daytime and nesting turtles at night.

South Florida is also a place accustomed to visitors, so there are many attractions, both natural and man-made, that will vie for your attention. But while you're here take at least one long walk along a beach, exploring for tiny treasures in the line of shells thrown up by the waves. Go swimming at least once in the salt water, and eat in a restaurant that serves real Key lime pie. Sample a platter of seafood, and maybe try something a little different like gator tail, Florida lobster, frog legs, cracked conch, or Indian fry bread. Try not to miss a sunset, and catch at least one sunrise over the water or the grassy plain of the Everglades; you'll never forget it.

Please be careful with the fragile land and fragile wildlife. Note the signs protecting turtle nests and bird rookeries. Follow the boating rules to protect manatees, fragile seagrass, and coral reefs, and watch for wildlife on the roads when traveling anywhere in the Keys or Everglades.

All that's left is to bring your camera and your sunscreen, wear your hat and sunglasses, and have fun. You'll discover a land that is as unique and enchanting as any on earth.

# Upper Keys

The Upper Keys are the most heavily visited of the Florida Keys.

THE EVERGLADES

PALO ALTO KEY
CARD SOUND
LITTLE CARD SOUND
997
Grayvik
Angelfish Key
905 A
905
MANATEE BAY
LONG SOUND
JOE BAY
LITTLE BLACKWATER SOUND
BARNES SOUND
Key Largo
DAVIS COVE
TROUT COVE
ALLIGATOR COVE BAY
LITTLE MADEIRA BAY
905
Eagle Key
BLACKWATER SOUND
Key Largo
Key Largo
FLORIDA BAY
BUTTONWOOD SOUND
John Pennekamp Coral Reef State Park Apx. Boundary
Black Betsey Keys
Rock Harbor
Newport
1
Rodriguez Key
Thompson
N
1
Tavernier
Plantation
Plantation Key
HAWK CHANNEL
Islamorada
2
3
4
Windley Key
TEATABLE KEY
LIGNUMVITAE KEY
5
Upper Matecumbe Key
Overseas Hwy
MATECUMBE BIGHT
Indian Key
Teatable Key
7
8
6
ATLANTIC OCEAN
Fiesta Key
Overseas Hwy
Lower Matecumbe Key
Layton
9
LONG KEY BIGHT
10
Long Key Point
Long Key

Ref: Delorme Florida Atlas and Gazetteer

| 1 | Florida Keys Wild Bird Rehabilitation Center |
| 2 | World Wide Sportsman |
| 3 | Theater of the Sea |
| 4 | Windley Key Fossil Reef State Geologic Site |
| 5 | Lignumvitae Key State Botanical Site |
| 6 | Indian Key State Historical Site |
| 7 | Robbie's Marina |
| 8 | San Pedro Underwater Archaeological Preserve |
| 9 | Layton Nature Trail |
| 10 | Long Key State Recreation Area |

# The Upper Florida Keys

The Florida Keys—a chain of more than 100 coral reef and oolitic limestone islands—began evolving more than 100,000 years ago when shallow seas covered most of the present-day Florida peninsula. They are still being shaped by hurricanes, tides, and slow-marching mangroves.

Although they extend out from the southernmost point in the continental United States, the Keys don't follow a north-to-south path. They instead lie mainly in a northeast to southwest line for 106 miles from Key Largo, south of Miami, to Key West, 90 miles north of Cuba. Seventy miles west of Key West, the Dry Tortugas are a cluster of tiny remote islands populated by a remarkable array of birds and marine life.

The Everglades, Florida Bay, and Gulf of Mexico lie to the north of the island chain, the Atlantic Ocean and the Straits of Florida to the south. Fantastic and fragile

[ *Above:* Scuba diving in the Florida Keys is a popular activity ]

## Visitor Assistance

The Florida Keys have a visitor assistance program for travelers who have questions or encounter difficulties once they arrive in the Keys.

Travelers can call (800) 771-KEYS to talk with a multilingual operator, 24 hours a day, seven days a week.

Operators are able to help with directions, medical facility locations, automobile repair service locations, or other difficulties a traveler might encounter.

living coral reefs lie below the waters all along the Atlantic shoreline. These reefs support over 650 species of fish and 40 species of coral, as well as a large array of sponges, marine worms, and other invertebrates.

Reefs that now are the foundation of the Key's islands probably formed about 200,000 years ago during the Sangamon interglacial period. Sea level was about 25 feet higher than it is today, and warm ocean water washed over all of southern Florida.

Living coral flourished on a platform reef covering a shallow, submerged plateau at the edge of the continental shelf. This mammoth reef tract extended from what is now Miami all the way to the Dry Tortugas. Key Largo Limestone forms the surface bedrock of the upper keys from North Key Largo to Big Pine and the Newfound Harbor Keys. From Big Pine to Key West, the reef drops down and lies beneath a 20- to 30-foot-thick layer of finely grained calcium carbonate known as Miami Oolite.

During the warm interglacial periods, which lasted thousands of years, large animals such as horses, camels, mastodons, mammoths, sabertooth tigers, jaguars, and panthers, and a huge array of birds, reptiles, alligators, and crocodiles, roamed the area. Isolated from the Florida peninsula, many species were extirpated and in their place the islands fostered indigenous species of birds, animals, and reptiles, including the tiny Florida Key deer, an indigenous subspecies of the common white-tailed deer. The nearly sea-level topography—the average elevation is 10 feet and the highest point is only about 16 feet—and the warm, humid climate provided the wildlife with a lush landscape of mangrove thickets, tropical hardwood hammocks, and pine forests.

The people that would eventually form the Tequesta and Calusa Indian tribes migrated to South Florida and the Florida Keys as early as 10,000 years ago. They built villages on offshore islands and on hammocks. They hunted small mammals, turtles, and deer, ate wild plants, and took to the sea in dugout cypress canoes to catch fish and harvest shellfish. Tools, household implements, knives, and fishhooks were made from shells and sharks teeth.

Spanish adventurers are believed to be the first Europeans to see the Florida Keys. Don Juan Ponce de Leon, during his explorations in the early 1500s, called the chain of small islands at the tip of the peninsula, "*cayos,*" (small islands), a name later anglicized to "keys." He also called them "*Los Martires*" because to him they resembled a group of martyrs hunkering down on the low horizon. A smaller group of islands to the west was called *Tortugas*, the Spanish word for sea turtles.

In the 1760s after the conclusion of the Seven Years War, Spain ceded Florida to the British in exchange for Havana, and pulled out of Florida. By that time, decimated by their battles with the Spanish and English, by constant slave trader raids, and by European diseases, the Calusas and Tequestas were almost extinct. In their place came bands of Creeks, who migrated south from the Carolinas, Georgia, and Alabama ahead of European settlement. Collectively known as Seminoles at the time, they lived and hunted throughout the state and provided a refuge for runaway black slaves.

In 1830, Congress ordered all Native Americans east of the Mississippi River to move to present day Oklahoma. Seminoles who resisted fought three wars with the U.S. Army in the 1800s. Some bands of Indians never surrendered and took refuge in the Everglades and Big Cypress Swamp.

Isolated and accessible only by boat, and plagued by hurricanes and tropical fevers, the Keys' human population remained small through most of the nineteenth century. Except for Key West, which had a small merchant and professional class, most of the islands were inhabited by a scattering of fishermen, farmers, smugglers, and salvagers.

In the late nineteenth century, the Keys were invaded by plume hunters seeking the long, flowing plumage of snowy egrets, great egrets, herons, ibis, roseate spoonbills, and other wading birds. The feathers had become worth their weight in gold to apparel manufacturers, who used them as decorations on women's hats and dresses.

Birds were slaughtered by the thousands and several species came close to extinction. In 1905 National Audubon Society investigator Guy Bradley was shot to death by poachers in a Keys bird rookery. Public outrage over his death moved state and federal governments to enact protective legislation.

The Keys' modern history began in 1904, when Henry Morrison Flagler implemented his improbable dream of constructing a railroad 127 miles from Homestead, south of Miami, across vast stretches of water, down the chain of islands to Key West. From there he envisioned barges carrying freight and passengers across open seas to Cuba. Key West's deep port would also be a gateway to the Caribbean and the Panama Canal.

During the first year of construction, a hurricane drowned 130 laborers and washed away much of their efforts. More men, tracks, and embankments were destroyed in a 1909 hurricane. Undaunted, the nearly blind, 82-year-old Flagler pressed on. Then on January 22, 1912, "The Extension Special," carrying Flagler and a host of dignitaries and reporters, arrived to a wildly joyous celebration in Key West. "Now I can die a happy man, my dream is fulfilled," he said. He died in May 1913 and was buried at St. Augustine.

"The Railroad That Went to Sea," the once-upon-a-time, "Eighth Wonder of the World," was destroyed in a catastrophic hurricane on Labor Day 1935. The most powerful storm in the recorded history of the Keys, with winds of more than 200 miles an hour, killed hundreds of railroad laborers and residents, and in the height of the Great Depression left the railroad beyond all hope of resurrection.

The massive bridges and trestles that Flagler's crews constructed so sturdily defied the storm, however, and three years later, "The Highway That Went to Sea," superimposed on their framework, was opened to automobile traffic. Almost immediately, the Overseas Highway (US 1) began to attract intrepid tourists and ambitious land speculators and developers. Since the 1970s, newcomers have flocked to the Keys in ever-increasing numbers, turning once-pristine wilderness into housing tracts, shopping centers, and other developments that imperil the tropical paradise most new residents hope to find.

Today, 80,000 Keys residents live on 32 of the islands. Their numbers are dwarfed, however, by the estimated 4,000,000 visitors that journey to the Keys every year on vacation. Businesses catering to tourists—dive shops, marinas, hotels, and restaurants—line the Overseas Highway in long, often crowded, commercial strips on some of the larger islands, and in scattered clumps on the smaller keys.

The estimated $1.2 billion that visitors channel through these various businesses helps bring prosperity to an area where the main industry, tourism, is tightly tied to its fragile ecology. Tourism spending is also responsible for an estimated 50 percent of all the jobs in the Keys. Another result of the tourism-based economy is that Monroe County, which includes the Keys and Everglades National Park, has the highest cost of living of any of Florida's 68 counties.

All those visitors unwittingly bring other problems. Degradation of the Keys' marine ecology has ceased to be a debatable issue. Scientists contend that human waste from more than 12,000 septic tanks is irreversibly polluting waters close to shore and is endangering the only living coral reef in the United States.

Underwater visibility, conservationists and scientists say, is only about half what it was a decade or so ago. Healthy coral is disappearing. Algal blooms are suffocating seagrass meadows and reefs. Reduced freshwater input in Florida Bay has hurt fish and bird populations. What to do with the tons of garbage created every day is another problem. Dumping it in the ocean is out of the question, and the Florida mainland has its own waste disposal problems. Except for a couple bridges that are elevated over shipping channels, the Key Largo landfill is the highest point in the Keys.

The State of Florida has designated Monroe County an "area of critical concern." That means the state must review any plans for major construction that might affect the ecology. But "big government" supervision rubs against the grain of independent-thinking Keys residents, many of whom view themselves as political and social exiles from oppressive bureaucracy.

As a case in point, in 1990 when the U.S. Congress was considering legislation that would establish the Florida Keys National Marine Sanctuary, and place the bulk of the world's third largest living coral reef system under federal protection, there was tremendous opposition from Keys residents. Most agreed that the reef needed safeguarding, but they wanted to do it themselves. Although the sanctuary was eventu-

# National Marine Sanctuary Program

Established by Congress in 1972, the National Marine Sanctuary Program is designed to protect nationally significant marine areas for their ecological and historical value. Thirteen such sanctuaries have been established around the nation. Three of these, along with Biscayne Bay National Park and John Pennekamp State Park, protect the vast tropical coral reef ecosystem off Florida's coast.

**Key Largo Marine Sanctuary**

The Key Largo Marine Sanctuary was designated in 1975 to protect more than 100 square nautical miles of submerged coral reefs off the northernmost Florida Keys. The boundaries enclose five major fore reefs and seven major patch reef communities. For more information: Upper Keys Regional Office, PO Box 1083, Key Largo, FL 33037. Phone (305) 852-7717.

**Looe Key National Marine Sanctuary**

The Looe Key National Marine Sanctuary was designated in 1981 to protect 5.32 square nautical miles located off the coast of Big Pine Key. It protects one of the best examples of a spur-and-groove reef system. For more information: Lower Keys Regional Office, 216 Ann Street, Key West, FL 33040. Phone (305) 292-0311.

**Florida Keys National Marine Sanctuary**

Designated in 1990, the Florida Keys National Marine Sanctuary is charged with providing comprehensive management for 2,800 square nautical miles of the marine environment surrounding the Florida Keys. It encompasses the third largest barrier reef in the world and is the second largest marine sanctuary in the United States. For more information: Florida Keys National Marine Sanctuary Administrative Office, PO Box 500368, Marathon, FL 33050. Phone (305) 743-2437.

ally established, it was only after years of heated negotiations, contentious meetings, and battles in the press.

Meanwhile, most visitors are blissfully unaware of the ecological perils and bureaucratic battles facing the Keys. They come to spend time in one of the nation's great outdoor playgrounds. They come to dive and snorkel, to swim and fish, and hike, and sail, and visit for awhile with nature. They come to sample the beauty and to savor the Keys' still-incomparable natural grandeur.

As visitors our responsibility is to leave as light a footprint as possible. It's our job to learn the rules for boating and diving and to properly dispose of litter. We should know not to feed the wildlife, or touch the coral, or collect live sea life. We should practice catch-and-release fishing, and in all ways respect this special place.

# Biscayne National Park

[Fig. 3(1)] Less than an hour's drive from Miami, and overlooked by many visitors intent on getting started on their Overseas Highway adventure in the Keys, Biscayne Bay National Park preserves a sampling of marine ecosystems including a thick mangrove shoreline, a shallow brackish-water bay, isolated keys, and a living coral reef.

The park is not overlooked, especially on weekends, by a portion of the 2.5 million Miami residents, or the 8 million annual Miami tourists looking for a recreational outlet. They come to cruise over the emerald green, crystal-clear waters and vast seagrass beds; they come to dive and snorkel the shallow coral reefs and explore the miracle of life here; or they come to visit, explore, and maybe camp on one of the small keys equipped with boat slips and nature trails.

Although Key Largo is often referred to as the northernmost island in the Florida Keys chain, 44 additional keys extend the line of islands north into the boundaries of Biscayne Bay National Park and almost to the city of Miami. Like their counterparts in the rest of the Keys, many of the islands support a tangled, tropical hardwood forest where exotically named trees like the gumbo-limbo, mahogany, poisonwood, strangler fig, and torchwood fight for space. A fringe of red mangroves and button-wood trees encircles most of the islands.

Also like the rest of the Keys, the Atlantic side of the islands is home to a share of North America's only living coral reef. Made up of brain coral, staghorn coral (which resembles deer antlers), branching elkhorn coral, tube coral, and star coral the reefs extend south and join those in John Pennekamp Coral Reef State Park and Key Largo National Marine Sanctuary.

Because the living reefs are so shallow, snorkelers and even glass bottom boat riders are treated to a close-up kaleidoscopic array of tropical fish. Among them are the flamboyantly hued queen angelfish, yellow-headed wrasse, queen and spotlight parrotfish, blue tang, blue triggerfish, Spanish hogfish, damselfish, and neon gobies (*Gobiosoma oceanops*).

Although most fish seem to live quiet lives, it's not uncommon for snorkelers and divers to hear the sharp-beaked parrotfish munching on coral polyps. Other reef inhabitants include spotted moray eels (*Gymnothorax moringa*), lobsters, sponges, sea fans, anemones, and Christmas tree worms (*Spirobranchus giganteus*).

Biscayne Bay, lying between the mainland and the string of barrier islands, adds another ecological dimension to the park. Sunlight easily penetrates the crystal-clear 5- to 10-foot depths, supporting a vast forest of waving, wide-bladed turtle grass. Sponges of many species and shapes are common in the bay's waters, as are immature lobster hiding among the grasses until they grow large enough to venture onto the reef.

Manatees commonly graze lazily on the seagrasses. Sea turtles weighing hundreds of pounds glide through the clear water as if weightless. Southern stingrays float across the bottom, while seatrout, redfish, and barracuda roam through the tall grass looking for an unsuspecting meal.

Bonefish and permit are among the most sought after prey by local anglers, especially the fly-fishing crowd. Both species feed over the sand and grass flats and are known for their blistering run after feeling the hook. Snook, bluefish, barracuda, and Spanish mackerel are also caught in the bay. Since the park's boundary extends out to a depth of 60 feet offshore, anglers go in search of grouper, snapper, king mackerel, and dolphin as well.

The park also encompasses a narrow strip of almost unbroken mangrove coastline. Red mangroves with their thick prop roots dominate the vegetation immediately next to the salt water. Buttonwoods take over when the land is drier and a little higher. The mangroves are important both as filters for rainwater runoff, and to insure a low-level flood of nutrients from the mainland.

By renting a canoe and exploring the coastline you'll have a chance to see many of the species associated with the mangroves. Wading birds like snowy egrets, great blue herons, white ibis, brown pelicans, and roseate spoonbills feed in shallow mangrove-lined pools. Many of these same species also nest in the low trees. Wood storks and yellow-crowned night herons (*Nyctanassa violacea*) can often be seen along the base of the mangroves, searching for food among the prop roots. Osprey perch on the highest branches.

In the 1960s, developers proposed construction of resort hotels and other facilities on some of Biscayne Bay's small keys. Marjory Stoneman Douglas, Ernest F. Coe, and other conservationists successfully campaigned to protect the pristine islands, and in 1968, Congress designated Biscayne Bay National Monument, in recognition of its "rare combination of terrestrial, marine, and amphibious life in a tropical setting of great natural beauty." In 1980, its status was changed to a national park, and with the acquisition of additional keys and offshore reefs it was expanded to its current size of 181,500 acres. About 95 percent of the park is under water.

The park's concessionaire, Biscayne National Underwater Park Inc., conducts three-hour glass bottom boat tours from the Convoy Point Visitor Center. Across the bay there are 66 boat slips at Elliott Key Harbor, and other docks at Boca Chita Key, where boaters can tie up and spend the day free of charge or overnight for a fee. Docking is on a first-come, first-served basis. Rental canoes are also available.

The Elliott Key Campground has 40 primitive campsites with cold showers, restrooms, and drinking water available. Permits are required. Picnic tables and grills are available on a first-come, first-served basis. Campers are required to take away all trash. The island also has a self-guided nature trail, which begins at the harbor and winds through a tropical hardwood forest with rare flowers, trees, and vines. A longer hike follows the old road that runs the length of the 7-mile island.

To the north of Elliott Key, Boca Chita Key's landmark is a 65-foot decommissioned lighthouse and a beautiful harbor. Amenities include primitive tent camping (no permit required), a boat dock (overnight fee), a picnic area, restrooms, and a short nature trail.

To the south of Elliott Key, Adams Key is open only for daylight use. There is a free boat dock, a picnic shelter, restrooms, and a nature trail. There is no fresh water.

There is a public boat ramp at the Convoy Point Visitor Center and navigation charts are for sale. Florida state saltwater fishing and license rules and regulations apply. Licenses may be acquired at marinas and bait shops. (*See* Appendix E, page 298 for more information on Florida fishing licenses.) There is no camping allowed in the mainland areas of the park, but several privately owned campgrounds and RV parks are nearby in Homestead, Florida City, and south Miami.

**Directions:** The park's Convoy Point Visitor Center is 7 miles east of Florida Turnpike's Exit 2 (Campbell Drive) or 9 miles east of US 1 on SW 328 Street (North Canal Drive).

**Activities:** Snorkeling, diving, swimming, boating, camping, picnicking, fishing, hiking.

**Facilities:** Convoy Point Visitor Center with exhibits on the park's natural and cultural history, vending machines, picnic tables, and restrooms. Offshore campgrounds on Elliott Key, nature trails, picnic areas, and boat docks.

**Dates:** Open daily.

**Fees:** There is a fee for glass bottom boat trips, and guided snorkeling and diving trips. There is also a charge for overnight docking on Elliott Key and Boca Chita Key.

**Closest town:** Homestead and Miami.

**For more information:** Biscayne National Park, PO Box 1369, Homestead, FL 33090. Phone (305) 230-7275.

# The Upper Keys

[Fig. 4] Although there are 44 keys located within Biscayne National Park, the area described as the Florida Keys generally refers to the islands between Key Largo and Key West that are connected by the Overseas Highway. They are loosely divided into three geographical sections: upper, middle, and lower. The Upper Keys includes the communities and islands of Key Largo, Tavernier, Plantation Key, Lignumvitae Key, Indian Key, Upper and Lower Matecumbe Keys, Islamorada, and Long Key. This is the most heavily visited part of the Florida Keys, receiving both out-of-state tourists and regular barrages of weekend warriors from densely populated South Florida.

Driving south from Miami, the Homestead Extension of the Florida Turnpike merges with US 1 just south of Homestead. The Homestead Extension is also called the West Dade Expressway on some maps. From here, US 1 continues south to Key Largo 20 miles away. Use caution on this stretch of road. The two-lane highway is heavily traveled by impatient drivers. Passing lanes are periodically provided for their benefit.

The road passes a grassland prairie and travels along a small canal in which you can see a variety of wading birds, including great blue herons, white ibis, great white egrets

(*Casmerodius albus*), American coots (*Fulica americana*), and pied-billed grebes (*Podilymbus podiceps*). Swamp lilies (*Crinum americanum*) are the white flowers that are often in bloom mixed in among the sawgrass.

Watch the tops of the power poles along the road for osprey nests. Anhingas and a variety of hawks also roost on the poles.

Soon you'll have your first (but hardly your last) sight of mangrove trees standing with their out-stretched prop roots looking as if they are stopped in mid-wade. Mangroves are the predominant species of vegetation in the Keys. The road then passes over Jewfish Creek and soon swings onto Key Largo.

An alternative, and perhaps a little more scenic route forks left onto Card Sound Road (CR 905A) just below Florida City, about 0.7 mile from the end of the Florida Turnpike. The road is very narrow and uneven with few places to pull off. It passes by a small marina and a couple rustic looking fishing shanties and fish houses. Live blue crabs are always for sale.

Tall, skinny Australian pines, a non-native tree that has taken a firm foothold in South Florida, line much of the north side of the road while red and black mangroves dominate the opposite side.

The road leads over the Card Sound toll bridge, which provides a wonderful view of Biscayne Bay to the north and Key Largo stretching out to the south. Readers of Carl Hiaasen will recognize it as the bridge in the novel *Stormy Weather* that Skink had himself tied to in order to await the hurricane.

Beyond the bridge the road passes a fenced portion of Crocodile Lake National Wildlife Refuge. The shallow body of water beyond the fence is named Crocodile Lake for the refuge's most famous resident. Although saltwater crocodiles regularly use these lakes, they are very reclusive, and nearly impossible to see from a passing automobile. They are also seldom seen in the daytime.

The road ends on the island of Key Largo. Take a right on CR 905 through scenic hammocks of West Indian mahogany, Jamaica dogwood, and wild coffee. The hammocks in this area have been a U.S. Fish and Wildlife Service study site for the Key Largo wood rat, an endangered species that uses leaves, sticks, and debris to build 5-foot-high dens with multiple entrances. The rats also establish highways through the thick foliage that they can travel along at night while foraging.

CR 905 rejoins the Overseas Highway, 11 miles to the south at the north end of the town of Key Largo.

**QUEEN CONCH**
(Strombus gigas)
Also called the pink conch, this conch occurs off southern Florida. Conchs move rapidly with the aid of their claw-shaped operaculums.

# Key Largo

*The largest of the Florida Keys, Key Largo is 30 miles long.*

EVERGLADES
NATIONAL
PARK

Old Rhodes Key

Palo Alto Key
Pumpkin Key

CARD SOUND

Angelfish Key

Landing Flat

1

5

997

LITTLE CARD SOUND

905

905 A

Middle Key

4

Short Key

905

MANATEE BAY

Main Key

BARNES SOUND

LONG SOUND

LITTLE BLACKWATER SOUND

Shell Key

COVE POINT LAKE SURPRISE

TROUT COVE
Stump Pass

Cross Key

Deer Key

1  GARDEN COVE

BLACKWATER SOUND

Rattlesnake Key

Near Keys

Boggy Key

LITTLE BUTTONWOOD SOUND

Key Largo

TARPON BASIN

LARGO SOUND

El Radabob Key

Whaleback Keys

3

John Pennekamp Coral Reef State Park Apx Boundary

HAWK CHANNEL

ATLANTIC OCEAN

BUTTONWOOD SOUND

2

Swash

Newport

Pam Keys

Butternut Key

Rock Harbor

Point Charles

Pigeon Key

1

ROCK HARBOR

Rodriguez Key

5  Thompson

Tavernier

Plantation Key

N

| | Key Largo Hammocks State Botanical Site |
| 1 | |
| 2 | Dolphins Plus |
| 3 | John Pennekamp Coral Reef State Park |
| 4 | Crocodile Lake NWR |
| | Mangrove |
| | Marsh |

Ref: Florida Atlas and Gazetteer

# Key Largo

[Fig. 4, Fig. 5] Key Largo is the first island motorists come to as they drive south from Miami on the Overseas Highway (US 1). The largest of the Florida Keys, it's about 30 miles long. With nearly 14,000 year-round residents, the town of Key Largo is the second most populous town in the Keys after Key West and a major destination for many of the millions of visitors who descend on the Keys every year. The facilities are here, however, to handle the crowds: diving operations, fishing charters, boat tours, shell shops, motels, campgrounds, restaurants, and resorts line the highway.

Key Largo will ring a bell with movie buffs. The town was called Rock Harbor until Humphrey Bogart, John Huston, and company produced *Key Largo* in 1948. The film's director, John Huston, made a few atmospheric shots inside the old Caribbean Club, but Bogie and Bacall remained on the Hollywood sound stage where the Keys were re-created. That didn't deter resolute citizens from pressing to take advantage of the movie's popularity. With the blessings of the U.S. Post Office, Rock Harbor became Key Largo in 1952.

To further enhance the Bogart aura, the river boat used in the 1952 Bogie-Katherine Hepburn classic, *The African Queen*, was purchased by the owners of the Holiday Inn and takes guests on trips from the hotel dock. You can also see, but not ride in, *The Thayer IV*, the Chris-Craft boat Henry Fonda piloted in *On Golden Pond*.

The island's main attraction and international claim to fame is the magnificent coral reef system that parallels the keys on the Atlantic side. Scuba divers and snor-kelers come from all over the world to explore the incredibly diverse and scenic formations. The minute you drive into Key Largo you'll see dive shops, dive flags (red with a white stripe), and signs advertising dive trips to the coral reefs of John Pennekamp Coral Reef State Park and the Key Largo National Marine Sanctuary.

Key Largo is also a magnet for fishing enthusiasts, ranging from the lifetime fanatic to the rank amateur who barely knows which end of the rod to hold. Whether your skills equal that of Zane Grey or Homer Simpson, you can go fishing in the Florida Keys and have fun. And probably catch some fish. More than 10 percent of the International Game Fish Association's saltwater line class fly-fishing records were recorded out of Key Largo.

The first of the more than 1,000 fishing guides and charter boat captains working out of the Florida Keys are based out of Key Largo. A walk past the various charter booths at the Fishing Village at the Holiday Inn Marina (MM 100) will give you a full sample of what's available. Talk to the captains and mates about what's in season and look at the photos they have on display.

Fishing out of Key Largo is basically divided into two categories: offshore reef fishing and backcountry fishing. Offshore trips take place aboard charter boats that carry a limited number of people and usually troll for large game fish like king mackerel (*Scomberomorus cavalla*), Atlantic sailfish, wahoo (*Acanthocybium solandri*), cobia (*Rachycentron canadum*), and dolphin (*Coryphaena hippurus*). Party boats carry more people and generally bottom fish on the reefs for grouper and yellowtail snapper (*Ocyurus chrysurus*). Trips are usually half days or full days. Incidentally, most restaurants in the Keys will cook your catch in the manner of your choice.

Backcountry fishing takes place among the mangrove islands and grass flats of Florida Bay. A typical trip aboard a flats boat includes casting for snook, redfish, tarpon, permit (*Trachinotus falcatus*), or bonefish. Some guides out of Key Largo like to fish at different spots all the way to Flamingo 35 miles away, stop in there for lunch and gas, then fish all the way back to the island. Most backcountry guides cater to fly-fishing and conventional tackle use.

A number of dive boats, eco-tour boats, and glass bottom boats are also based at the Holiday Inn Marina and other sites along Key Largo. Most businesses offer package trips or will provide any type of trip you desire, including bird-watching endeavors. Eco-tours explore the mangrove-lined creeks and channels along the Atlantic coast and the mangrove islands and shallow grass flats of Florida Bay.

You don't need to be a scuba diver to enjoy the reefs off Key Largo. Most operations offer easy snorkel trips and will provide instruction and equipment. Wet suits are also provided during cool weather. It takes about 45 minutes to reach the reefs and trips usually last two- to two-and-a-half hours, depending on the winds and the tides.

A kayak rental concession at the Howard Johnson Key Largo (MM 102 Bayside) offers guided or self-guided tours of the mangrove coastline. This is a good way to see many of the wading birds that frequent the Florida Bay shoreline. It's also a reliable way to see West Indian manatees during the colder months.

**For more information:** You can get the full list of businesses in the area by contacting or stopping at the Key Largo Chamber of Commerce, MM 106, 105950 Overseas Highway, Key Largo, FL 33037. Phone (800) 822-1088. Local phone (305) 451-1414.

### JOHN PENNEKAMP CORAL REEF STATE PARK

[Fig. 5(3)] John Pennekamp Coral Reef State Park and the adjacent Key Largo National Marine Sanctuary include about 178 nautical square miles of coral reefs, seagrass beds, and mangrove swamps. Named for a late Miami newspaper publisher who championed the establishment of Everglades National Park and the Florida state park system, it was the country's first underwater state park.

Tropical vegetation, a huge variety of shorebirds, and marine life can be seen on land portions of the park and on reefs a few miles offshore. The mangrove swamp provides visitors with an opportunity to explore fascinating water channels. Unusual tropical-looking trees can be seen in the hardwood hammock in the park's upland limestone areas. During the winter this is one of the busiest parks in Florida. It's a good idea to arrive early. If you'd like to stay overnight, reserve well in advance one of the 47 full-service camping sites for tents and RVs.

Fishing is allowed in Pennekamp within guidelines of Florida state law. Saltwater licenses are required, and spearfishing, possession of spearfishing gear, and collection of tropical fish by any means is illegal inside the park's boundaries. Ask for a copy of fishing regulations when you buy a fishing license.

The park's Mangrove Trail uses a boardwalk to explore a portion of the mangrove estuary. It passes over clear, grassy channels in which you'll see gray snapper milling around the roots of the mangrove trees. Sometimes a redfish will even swim by, easily identified by the one or two large spots on its silver body.

Watch for black-crowned night herons (*Nycticorax nycticorax*), great blue herons, and tricolored herons feeding around the bases of the mangrove tree prop roots. A short lookout tower is still

## Mile Markers

Since the Keys have only one main road running their entire length, a convenient system of Mile Markers has been developed. The green and white markers (MM) stand about 4 feet tall on the shoulder of the road. They guide travelers from just south of Florida City (MM 126) down the chain of islands to MM 0 at the corner of Whitehead and Fleming streets in downtown Key West.

The markers are frequently used as addresses and directions. They are also a convenient way to differentiate between locations on the "bayside" (also "gulfside") and the "oceanside" of the road. A typical address will be "MM 90 Oceanside," or "MM 90 Bayside." Traveling southwest toward Key West, the Atlantic Ocean is on the left, and the Gulf of Mexico and Florida Bay on the right.

tall enough to allow you to see over the top of the mangrove forest. Canoes and kayaks can be rented in the park for exploring the mangroves in more detail.

The parking lot at the trail entrance also serves one of the small beaches. A pay-as-you-view telescope that looks out over a mud flat is mounted on the porch of a bathhouse next to the beach. At low tide look for a variety of feeding birds—willets (*Catoptrophorus semipalmatus*), piping plovers, sanderlings (*Calidris alba*), herons, and terns gathered on the exposed flats. During high tide sea gulls, brown pelicans, and double-crested cormorants sit on the rocks that encircle the swimming area.

The park's visitor center's outstanding natural history exhibits interpret the park's unique marine environment. There's also an entrancing, circular, 30,000-gallon saltwater aquarium in which you see sharks, yellowtail snapper, gray snapper, lane snapper (*Lutjanus synagris*), Spanish hogfish (*Bodianus rufus*), rock beauty (*Holacanthus tricolor*), southern lobster (*Panulirus argus*), and a variety of grunts, groupers and angelfish swim in, out of, and around a coral reef. For a special treat be there at feeding time.

People come to John Pennekamp to experience the coral reefs, and the park is geared to provide that experience. Snorkeling, scuba diving, and glass bottom boat tours operate right out of the park. Or you can rent a boat and plan your own reef trip. You can rent snorkeling equipment and wet suits for use on the reefs or swimming off the beaches. Scuba instruction is also available. The Dive Shop inside the park, a PADI five-star facility, offers two-tank, two-location tours to certified divers. A full range of instructional courses is also available.

Swimming and snorkeling are excellent at John Pennekamp's three small beaches. Although it hardly compares with a reef dive, there's a variety of sea life to be discovered around the rocks and seagrasses in shallow water. A reconstruction of a sixteenth-century Spanish shipwreck, complete with cannons, lies 130 feet offshore from Cannon Beach. It allows you to get a little of the feel of a wreck dive without boarding a boat. The cannons off the beach and many of the other cannons on display in the park are from the 1715 and 1733 Spanish gold fleets that were scattered and driven onto reefs throughout South Florida by hurricanes.

If you aren't into snorkeling and diving, you can get a limited idea of the reefs' grandeur on the glass bottom boat *San Jose*. Daily it makes three, two-and-a-half-hour trips from John Pennekamp to Molasses Reef, where it stays for about a half hour. On days when visibility is good, the majesty and color of the reef, and animals that live there, are plainly visible through the boat's underwater viewing windows.

The magnifying effect of the water makes it seem as if the bottom is only inches away. As the boat drifts along, a constantly changing panorama of reef life passes by. A shimmering school of bright yellow and blue yellowtail snapper comes into view, then disappears. Multicolored parrotfish nuzzle around on the bottom chewing on the coral. The log-shaped silhouette of a barracuda passes over them. Domes of hard coral round out some of the reef's rough edges. Soft corals and seafans stand like bushes without branches unwavering in the current.

Considered the most complex of all ecosystems, coral reefs are also the most beautiful underwater gardens man has the privilege to observe. Reefs are found only in shallow oceans, such as those in South Florida, with clear, perpetually warm waters.

Scientists estimate that Florida's coral reefs have taken from 5,000 to 7,000 years to develop. Biologists once believed corals were plants. But in more recent times, they've come to realize that every coral is actually a colony made up of thousands of microscopic, soft-bodied animals, called polyps, that have a hard, stony skeleton, much like a sea anemone.

Rarely visible during the day, polyps emerge at night and feed on plankton that drifts within reach of their tentacles. The yellowish-brown or green color visible to the human eye is the coral's living tissue—less than 0.0625 of an inch thick. The animal is wounded each time its surface is touched by a boat anchor, a swim fin, or a human foot or hand.

These primitive microorganisms are the architects of the reefs, and the creation of one small reef requires the joint effort of billions of individuals. Each extracts building material—calcium—from the sea and uses it to make a protective tube-type skeleton. Hundreds of these skeletons make a coral. Untold numbers of corals grow side by side and on top of each other to form a reef.

The huge and incredibly diverse coral reef community includes sponges, shrimp, crabs, turtles, lobsters, and about 600 species of fish. Living space is unbelievably hard to come by. Every hole, every crack, and every cranny is some creature's

## Nature's Underwater Rainbows

Why do tropical fish come in so many iridescent colors? The answer is different for each species. Spanish hogfish and other members of the Wrasse family use their stripes and brilliant hues to signal larger fish to come to be cleaned of parasites and dead tissue. In return the "cleaners" get a free meal. Multicolored bars, stripes, and splotches blur the outline of sergeant majors (*Abudefduf saxatilis*), foureye butterflyfish (*Chaetodon capistratus*), spotfin butterflyfish (*Chaetodon capistratus*), rock beauty, and spotlight parrotfish (*Sparisoma viride*) making them difficult for predators to see against the coral reef's complex background.

Some fish can change colors at night, to conceal themselves from nocturnal predators. The moray eel blends imperceptibly with the reefs, catching unwary fish with its vise-like jaws and needle-sharp teeth.

habitat. The old and unfit are evicted by younger, stronger tenants. Some, like the Christmas tree worm (*Spirobranchus giganteus*), live their whole life anchored to the coral, which they feed on. Flamingo tongue (*Cyphoma gibbosum*), a snail-like mollusk, eats the coral and, in turn, is eaten by small fish, which are eaten by larger fish that often end up on our dinner tables.

Although the reefs are hard enough to bring down ships that run aground on them, they are also extremely fragile in that they can take centuries to rebuild. Severe penalties are imposed for deliberately and accidentally harming any part of the reef. Boat damage carries especially severe penalties. Destruction of coral formation through grounding or anchoring can result in fines up to $50,000 for small boats. Larger ship owners have been assessed millions of dollars.

**Directions:** Overseas Highway, MM 102.5.

**Activities:** Snorkeling, scuba diving, swimming, hiking, camping, boating, and picnicking.

**Facilities:** Snorkeling and diving trips; sailboat, canoe, and reef boat rentals; scuba instruction and certification; boat ramp; glass bottom boat tours; snack bar; restrooms; changing rooms; visitor center; gift shop; orientation film; and camping sites.

**Dates:** Open year-round.

**Fees:** There is a charge for admission and activities.

**Closest town:** Key Largo.

**For more information:** John Pennekamp Coral Reef State Park, PO Box 487, Key

Largo, FL 33037. Phone (305) 451-1202. For information on rentals and reservations: Coral Reef Park Company, PO Box 1560, Key Largo, FL 33037. Phone (305) 451-1621.

## DIVE SITES

Many of the park's diving sites have their own fascinating features. Park Service boats usually go to Molasses Reef, French Reef, White Bank Dry Rocks and the *Benwood* wreck.

The *Christ of the Deep* statue at Key Largo Dry Rocks is one of the park's best-known landmarks. The 9-foot replica of a bronze statue in the Mediterranean near Genoa, Italy, was presented to the Underwater Society of America by Italian industrialist and sportsman Edigi Cressi in 1961.

The statue's base sits on the sandy sea bottom, 20 feet under, surrounded by enormous formations of various types of brain coral and elkhorn coral (*Acropora palmata*). Stingrays, barracuda, and other marine life regularly mill around the site. The top of the statue is easily spotted only 10 feet below the surface. Its outstretched arms seem to beckon all to enjoy the wonders of nature all around it.

The shallow reefs and mild currents at Grecian Rocks, near the statue, are popular with snorkelers. Also nearby, the Cannon Patch Reef, with an average depth of 4 feet, has a scattering of coral-encrusted cannons waiting to be discovered. Even though you know they are there, it's still exciting to find one of the ancient cannons and wonder about the action it might have seen, or the men who built it and fired it hundreds of years ago.

Molasses Reef is the park's largest and most popular scuba diving site. Located 6 miles offshore, it got its name from two shiploads of Caribbean molasses that went aground here. It is noteworthy for overhanging ledges, high-profile coral ridges, towering coral wells, swim-through tunnels, hard bottoms, and large sponges. Divers often are shadowed by barracuda, manta rays, silver tarpon, permit, Spanish hogfish, snapper, and squirrelfish (*Holocentrus adscensionis*). An 8-foot-long Spanish anchor is a landmark and a popular rendezvous point for divers.

French Reef is noted for its undercut ledges and swim-through tunnels. Several large caves and ledges are covered with lavender-colored sea fans, tube sponges (*Callyspongia plicifera*), anemones, and soft corals. They are home to schools of mangrove snapper, barracuda, grouper, sea turtles, and lobsters.

The *Benwood*, a 285-foot steel-hulled freighter, located 1.5 miles northeast of French Reef, was torpedoed by a German submarine during World War II. As she tried to make her way home, the ill-fated vessel accidentally collided with another vessel. Years later the hull was used as a bombing practice target and finally dynamited and sunk. Although the superstructure was salvaged, a large section of the hull remains underwater and attracts large numbers of colorful fish. A spar buoy and four mooring buoys mark the location.

White Banks Dry Rocks is the largest snorkeling reef. Its 5- to 15-foot depths are excellent for novices, who are rewarded by a large sea garden of rounded domes of

# Reef Types

John Pennekamp and the Key Largo Marine Sanctuary contain three unique types of coral reefs: outer bank reefs, inner bank reefs, and patch reefs. Outer bank reefs include popular Pennekamp diving sites such as Elbow, Molasses, French, and Carysfort reefs. They are characterized by a series of long limestone ridges that alternate with sandy channels. The ridges support live coral formations, called spur-and-groove, along their length. The spur-and-groove formations can be found in depths from 5 to 30 feet.

A flat sand and seagrass area can also be found on the back side of the reefs. These shallow areas contain many important invertebrates and young corals. A part of the outer reef bank known as the intermediate reef extends from 30 to 70 feet and is characterized by low-profile corals, large fish, and sponges.

Key Largo Dry Rocks, where the *Christ of the Deep* statue is located, is a prime example of an inner bank reef. Unique to Florida, these reefs have smaller spur-and-groove formations on the seaward side, but also the flat, shallow top and well-formed circumference of the larger patch reefs.

Found in the park's shallow waters, patch reefs are distinguished by a sandy perimeter, or "halo." Inhabited by many varieties of tropical fish, they are ideal for snorkeling and shallow scuba diving. The sides of these reefs are usually quite steep beginning near the surface and going as deep as 20 feet. Many flexible corals, such as sea fans and sea whips, grow on the patch reefs.

brain coral and the intricate branches of staghorn (*Acropora cervicornis*) and elkhorn coral, along with waves and waves of small, colorful fish.

The 112-foot-tall Carysfort Reef Lighthouse, built in 1853, marks the site of Carysfort Reef, at the far northern boundary of the park. Named for the HMS *Carysfort*, a 20-gun British frigate that went aground here in 1770, the reef offers protected snorkeling and scuba diving to 75-foot depths. The lighthouse is about 7 miles from shore, where the reef is one of the closest to the Gulf Stream. In earlier times, ships headed south usually sailed inside the Gulf Stream to avoid its currents, and frequently found grief on the reef.

In addition to the *Carysfort,* more than 200 ships were either damaged or sunk on the reef before the lighthouse was built to guide them through. In 1852, the U.S. Army Corps of Engineers sent Lt. George Gordon Meade to oversee construction of the lighthouse. Of iron-pile design with a skeleton tower, its 18 lamps with 21-inch reflectors were first lighted in March 1853. The lamps were subsequently upgraded to solar-powered optics. The lighthouse was taken out of active service after World War II.

Public and privately funded efforts are now under way to turn the lighthouse into a "beacon" that could help save the reef itself. The National Oceanic and Atmospheric Administration (NOAA) and the nonprofit Pennekamp Coral Reef Institute are

## Artificial Reefs

Artificial reefs, when placed on non-living bottom, can be a boon to divers and a boost to marine life. The Florida Keys Artificial Reef Association, founded in the early 1980s, has created a number of new reefs throughout the Keys from tons of concrete left over from the removal of some of the Keys' original bridges.

Decommissioned naval vessels have also been intentionally sunk at other sites. Off Plantation Key, south of Key Largo, the *Duane*, a 327-foot Coast Guard cutter, was sunk in 120 feet of water. Today, it's a popular diving destination. The *Bibb*, another former Coast Guard vessel, sits nearby.

cooperating on plans to convert the lighthouse keeper's quarters into a marine science center.

Scientists who have visited the area have expressed interest in studying coral bleaching, salinity levels, and other factors that are contributing to the decline of this and other coral reefs in the Keys. A laboratory would enable scientists to continuously monitor water quality and marine life populations. When the project is completed, NOAA will manage the project under an agreement with the Coast Guard.

**Directions:** Overseas Highway, MM 102.5.

**Activities:** Snorkeling, scuba diving.

**Facilities:** Snorkeling and diving trips; reef boat rentals; scuba instruction and certification; boat ramp; glass bottom boat tours.

**Dates:** Open year-round.

**Fees:** There is a charge for activities.

**Closest town:** Key Largo.

**For more information:** For information on rentals and reservations contact the Coral Reef Park Company, PO Box 1560, Key Largo, FL 33037. Phone (305) 451-1621.

### KEY LARGO HAMMOCKS STATE BOTANICAL SITE

[Fig. 5(1)] John Pennekamp park also manages the 2,000-acre Key Largo Hammocks State Botanical Site. Along with the adjacent Crocodile Lake National Wildlife Refuge, the sites contain the largest continuous tract of hardwood forest remaining in the Keys. The hardwood forest, or hammock, supports a wide diversity of plant species. About 80 percent of them originated in the West Indies. Nearly 100 species of native trees and shrubs also flourish here.

A short nature trail (less than 1 mile) takes you past gumbo-limbo, paradise tree (*Simarouba glauca*), blue morning glory vines (*Ipomoea indica*), wild bamboo (*Lasiacis divaricata*), West Indian mahogany, and willow bustic (*Dipholis salicifolia*). The forests are also habitats for endangered species such as the Key Largo wood rat, Key Largo cotton mouse (*Peromyscus gossypinus allapaticola*), Schaus' swallowtail butterfly, Eastern indigo snake, and Stock Island tree snail (*Orthalicus reses*). The hammock also provides important seasonal food sources for migratory neotropical songbirds, and permanent homes for other colorful butterflies and tree snails.

The trail starts at the gate of the former entrance to Port Bouganville 0.5 mile north of the intersection of US 1 and CR 905. Look for the pink walls of the defunct subdivision. There are no state personnel on duty. A pamphlet explaining the trail is available in the old guard house.

A number of structures were built as part of the Port Bouganville project, including a deep water canal with boat slips, a hotel, private villas with boat access, tennis courts and sauna. After the development failed, the state was able to purchase the land and now the hammock is beginning to reclaim its former glory.

The state plans to eventually remove the buildings. For now they should be avoided because of their dilapidated and unsafe condition.

**Directions:** The trail is located on CR 905, 0.5 mile north of the intersection of CR 905 and US 1.

**Dates:** Open daily.

**For more information:** Key Largo Hammocks State Botanical Site/Crocodile Lake National Wildlife Refuge, PO Box 370, Key Largo, FL 33037. Phone (305) 451-4223.

## CROCODILE LAKE NATIONAL WILDLIFE REFUGE

[Fig. 5(4)] Adjoining the Key Largo Hammocks State Botanical Site, Crocodile Lake National Wildlife Refuge was created in 1980 to protect the endangered American crocodile. Humans are crocodiles' only predator. Poaching and widespread destruction of their habitats has reduced the crocodiles' population to fewer than 500. They feed primarily on fish, snakes, turtles, crabs, birds, raccoons, and other small animals unfortunate enough to be within their reach.

Because of the crocodiles' sensitivity to human disturbance, the national wildlife refuge is off-limits to the public, except by special permit. Refuge management is studying ways of offering public use that will safeguard the visitors and inhabitants. An elevated boardwalk and/or a wildlife observation tower are possibilities.

Adjacent inshore waters are managed as part of the Florida Keys National Marine Sanctuary. Between March 1 and October 1, when crocodiles are mating and hatching their young, there is a 100-foot, no-access buffer zone on the entire refuge shoreline.

Key Largo and neighboring areas on the extreme South Florida mainland are the crocodiles' northernmost range. The mangrove wetlands in the refuge and exposed canal banks in the abandoned Port Bouganville development provide habitat, solitude, and nesting areas for the shy, secretive reptiles.

The saltwater crocodiles' only other refuges are in Everglades National Park and the Florida Power and Light Company's Turkey Point Nuclear Power Plant, near Homestead.

**Directions:** Highway CR 905, north of the abandoned Port Bouganville Development.

# Endangered Beauties

One of the famous, and most elusive, of endangered butterflies is the Schaus' swallowtail, which was once common from Miami to the Middle Keys. The large brown and yellow butterfly, with orange and blue spots and brown and blue patches, was named for Dr. William Schaus, a physician who observed it and collected specimens in the early 1900s in a Miami area known as Brickell Hammock. Urban development eventually destroyed most of the swallowtails' hammock habitat and reduced the amount of food available. Mosquito control pesticides have also contributed to the butterfly's decline.

In the 1930s, a Schaus' swallowtail colony was discovered in Islamorada. Its habitat was destroyed by the 1935 Labor Day hurricane. Rediscovered in the Upper Keys in the 1960s, the species now is found in the lush, tropical landscape of Elliott Key in Biscayne National Park and North Key Largo. It is also infrequently seen in Everglades National Park. The State of Florida and the federal government put the Schaus' swallowtail on the endangered species list in 1975.

The tail-less atala hairstreak (*Eumaeus atala*), also endangered, lives in hardwood hammocks and adjacent open areas. The iridescent black, red, and white member of the gossamer wing family averages about 1.5 to 2 inches high. At Crane Point Hammock in Marathon, naturalists are attempting to sustain the atala hairstreak by planting Florida coontie (*Zamia integrifolia*), a primary food source for the butterfly. A bushy fern-like woodland member of the sago palm family, the Florida coontie is also becoming rare.

**Activities:** Closed to the public.

**Closest town:** Key Largo.

**For more information:** Crocodile Lake National Wildlife Refuge, PO Box 370, 211 Charlemagne Road, Key Largo, FL 33037. Phone (305) 451-4223.

### DOLPHINS PLUS

[Fig. 5(2)] This is one of four places in the Keys where you can encounter playful, intelligent dolphins on their own turf. Structured and nonstructured programs are designed for those who want to do much more than sit in an amphitheater and watch dolphins leap for fish and dive through hoops. Each program begins with an hour-long orientation session on dolphins' natural history, intelligence, anatomy, communications abilities, social structure, and environmental issues that affect them.

Small-toothed mammals that are related to whales, dolphins' long, sleek, torpedo-shaped bodies and elongated snouts are easily recognized. They nurse their young, often with the aid of a female wet nurse, and care for their calves for up to four or five years.

They use about 90 percent of their lung capacity (humans use only 15 to 20 percent) and can remain submerged for 15 to 20 minutes at a time. They can shut down either side of their 5-pound brain, while the other side continues to take care of metabolic processes, blood flow, breathing, and other vital functions.

The eyes of a dolphin operate independently, so that even when they are resting they can be continuously aware of what is happening around them. They have no olfactory glands, and thus no sense of smell, but they have a heightened sense of taste, which accounts for their mouths usually being held open in a happy face smile.

Dolphins have several stomach chambers and don't chew or bite down on their food. They communicate with each other with clicking sounds. In the wild, they search for food, potential enemies, and other objects by use of echolocation, an incredible sonar that allows them to transmit clicks, whistles, and screams and interpret the returning echoes. Blowholes on the top of their heads are nostrils with internal passages for each lung.

There are three prevalent species of dolphins in Florida's nearshore waters: the Atlantic bottle-nosed dolphin, striped dolphin, and spotted dolphin. The bluish gray bottlenose has a bump on its forehead and can grow to 10 feet or larger. A fully grown blue-black striped dolphin can reach up to 8 feet in length. The slat-black Atlantic spotted dolphin grows to be 7 feet long. All three species have whitish bellies.

Highly social animals, dolphins travel in large herds, divided into family groups called pods. They love to ride ships' bow waves and gracefully leap far out of the water, as if to entertain awestruck humans.

Often confused with porpoises, dolphins have a conspicuous beak and a dorsal fin that arcs toward the tail; porpoises have a less prominent beak and all but one porpoise species has a triangle-shaped dorsal fin. Also, dolphins have cone-shaped teeth, and porpoises' are spade-shaped.

If you see dolphin on a restaurant menu, don't be concerned that you're being asked to eat Flipper. What's being prepared is the dolphin game fish, a commonly caught, cold-blooded ocean fish, unrelated to mammalian dolphins. Restaurants aware of the confusion frequently list it by its other names such as mahimahi and dorado.

At Dolphins Plus and other encounter places in the Keys, the structured program guarantees contact with dolphins. Constantly choreographed by the instructor, the friendly mammals will playfully bump you, roll over, and invite you to rub their bellies, and invite you to grasp their pectoral fins and take a joy ride across the pool. The nonstructured program is a free-swim, for about an hour, with no guarantee of contact. With no instructor to direct them, the dolphins may playfully interact, or exert their independence and choose to ignore you altogether. Their unique personalities are evident after only a few minutes in the water with them.

**Directions:** MM 99.5 Oceanside, Key Largo.

**Activities:** Structured and nonstructured swimming with dolphins; rehabilitation therapy for persons with mental and physical disabilities.

**Facilities:** Fenced-in pools, restrooms, changing rooms, gift shop.

## Crocodiles Find an Unlikely Home

A nuclear power plant provides the American crocodile with an unusual, but protected and comfortable, habitat. The reptiles have been attracted to Florida Power and Light Company's Turkey Point Nuclear Power Plant south of Miami near Homestead for more than 20 years. Chased away from their ancient habitats on Florida's sunny, sandy beaches, hundreds of crocodiles have found a home in man-made canals that are part of the plant's latticework of cooling ponds.

The warm water discharged from the plant is not radioactive and has no ill effects on the reptiles, which are contentedly breeding within sight of the giant cooling towers. Each year, biologists tag more than 100 newborn babies. It's a small, and hopeful sign, but still less than 10 percent of hatchlings reach maturity.

**Dates:** Open year round.

**Fees:** There is a charge for swimming with dolphins. Reservations required. Participants under 18 years old must be accompanied by an adult.

**Closest town:** Key Largo.

**For more information:** Dolphins Plus Marine Mammal Research and Education Center, PO Box 2728, Key Largo, FL 33037. Phone (305) 451-1993. Fax (305) 451-3710. Web Site www.pennekamp.com/dolphins-plus.

### KEY LARGO RESTAURANTS

Seafood dominates Key Largo restaurant menus. You'll also find Italian, Mexican, Thai, and other cuisines and all your favorite fast-food emporiums.

### BALLYHOO'S SEAFOOD GRILL

MM 98 Median, Key Largo. Breakfast regulars swear by the pancakes and seafood omelets at this Old Florida-style eatery in a 1930s conch house. Many come back for seafood, chicken, and steak at lunch and dinner. Very casual. No reservations. *Moderate. Phone (305) 852-0822.*

### THE FISH HOUSE

MM 102 Oceanside, Key Largo. Big servings of fish, steak, and chicken keep this New England-type seafood house packed at lunch and dinner. The Fish House will also ship fresh and precooked seafood anywhere in the U.S. Casual. No reservations. *Moderate. Phone (305) 451-HOOK (4665) or (888) 451-4665.*

### THE ITALIAN FISHERMAN

MM 104 Bayside, Key Largo. This longtime favorite of locals and visitors serves generous portions of pastas, veal, chicken, and seafood dishes. Conch prepared as chowder and several other ways is a specialty. Enjoy the sunset from the outdoor terrace. Casual. Reservations for large groups. *Moderate. Phone (305) 451-4471.*

## MRS. MAC'S KITCHEN

MM 99.4 Overseas Highway, Key Largo. Friendly, unpretentious roadside shack serves terrific chili, pita bread sandwiches, steaks, seafood, burgers, basic Italian dishes, and Key lime pie. Very casual. No reservations. *Inexpensive. Phone (305) 451-3722.*

## NUM THAI RESTAURANT AND SUSHI BAR

MM 103 Overseas Highway, Key Largo. Small, friendly shopping center restaurant serves excellent Thai cuisine and sushi. Casual. Reservations for groups of six or more. *Inexpensive to moderate. Phone (305) 451-5955.*

## KEY LARGO LODGING

Lodgings range from ultraexpensive resorts to small, privately owned motels. In-season and out-of-season rates vary greatly. For a full list of accommodations contact the Key Largo Chamber of Commerce, MM 106, 105950 Overseas Highway, Key Largo, FL 33037. Phone (800) 822-1088. Local phone (305) 451-1414.

### HOLIDAY INN KEY LARGO SUNSPREE RESORT

MM 100 Oceanside, Key Largo. This big, splashy chain hotel has just about everything: 135 guest rooms and suites, a large marina and boat ramp, a freshwater swimming pool, restaurants and bars, shops, and diving and snorkeling excursions. Plus it's the home port of the *African Queen. Expensive. Phone (305) 451-2121 or (800) THE-KEYS.*

### JULES' UNDERSEA LODGE

Koblick Marine Center, 51 Shoreland Drive, MM 103.2 Oceanside, Key Largo. Guaranteed—you won't wake up in your room, look out the window, and wonder what city you're in, not with fish swimming nonchalantly past your windows, 30 feet below the surface of a lagoon, about 100 feet from shore. If you aren't a certified scuba diver, the staff can give you a quickie course that will ease you down into your air-conditioned quarters, where you'll have the comforts of a bathroom, TV, VCR, and phone. The price includes a full dinner and breakfast. *Very expensive. Phone (305) 451-2353. Fax (305) 451-4789. Web site www.jul.com.*

### LARGO LODGE

MM 101.7 Bayside, Key Largo. Located 0.5 mile south of John Pennekamp park, this small, quiet, immaculately kept resort is set among tall palms and lush tropical foliage. Six cottages with screened porch, living room, and kitchen can sleep up to four. If there are youngsters in your party, you'll have to look elsewhere. To maintain the adult decorum, no one under age 16 is allowed. *Moderate. (305) 451-0424 or (800) IN-THE-SUN.*

### WESTIN BEACH RESORT KEY LARGO

MM 97 Bayside, Key Largo. If you're looking for a full-service, all-the-bells-and-whistles resort, the Westin is the nicest Key Largo has to offer. Fitted into a buttonwood grove on the shore of Florida Bay, the low-rise buildings house 200 guest rooms, two restaurants, pools, a beach, tennis, nature trails, and a boat dock. *Very expensive.*

*Phone (305) 852-5553 or (800) KEY-LARGO. Fax (305) 852-8669. Web site www.888tellnet.com/keylargo.html.*

### STONE LEDGE RESORT

MM 95.3 Bayside, Key Largo. A nicely run stucco motel with 19 guest rooms. All have refrigerators and 10 have kitchens. Amenities include a dock and sandy beach. *Inexpensive to moderate. Phone (305) 852-8114.*

### ▓ KEY LARGO CAMPGROUNDS

Key Largo and many of the Keys are popular destinations for the winter RV crowd. Reservations should always be made in advance during colder months.

### AMERICAN OUTDOORS

MM 97.5 Bayside, Key Largo. RV sites, boat dock, ramp, marina, laundry, and showers. Pets allowed. *Inexpensive. Phone (305) 852-8054. Fax (305) 853-0509.*

### KEY LARGO KAMPGROUND AND MARINA

MM 101.5 Oceanside, Key Largo. RV and tent sites, showers, pool, laundry, boat dock and ramp. Pets allowed. *Inexpensive. Phone (305) 451-1431 or (800) KAMPOUT.*

# Tavernier

[Fig. 4] If bird-watching is your interest, then your vacation begins in earnest in Tavernier, a small settlement of about 3,000 residents on the lower end of Key Largo.

If the center is open, you'll want to pick up a copy of the booklet *Birding the Florida Keys* from the National Audubon Society Tavernier Science Center at 115 Indian Mound Trail, Tavernier, FL 33070. Phone (305) 852-5092. (Indian Mound Trail turns off US 1 Bayside near MM 89.) The booklet is available for a small donation. It's an insider's guide to some of the hottest birding spots throughout the Keys.

From below Key Largo to Key West birding enthusiasts should look for birds everywhere—on the wires and poles along the road, on the mud flats visible at the ends of bridges, and at the end of side roads that go to the bay. The best birding will almost always be at low tide.

Binoculars or a spotting scope will vastly enhance your trip. Many birds on mud flats or in mangrove rookeries are some distance from the road, or difficult to walk out to.

### ▓ FLORIDA KEYS WILD BIRD REHABILITATION CENTER

[Fig. 4(1)] A walk through the Wild Bird Center isn't a Disney World kind of experience. It's all too real and disturbing. But for those concerned about the plight of Florida's diminishing wild creatures, a visit to the facility between Tavernier and Key Largo can be both heartening and thought provoking.

The 5.5-acre complex was opened in June 1991, by retired teacher Laura Quinn. Quinn is the director, and she and the other volunteers are happy to discuss the center's goals with visitors. Don't be offended by the natural odors or be concerned about pollution of Florida Bay. Officials say environmental studies have determined that runoff from the center hasn't polluted the bay and actually may be promoting the growth of sea grasses.

The center's fourfold mission is to reduce the suffering of sick and injured wild birds, reduce the occasions of injury by better educating the public, reduce environmental hazards that place the birds at risk, and increase the number of birds, both common and endangered, released to live in the wild again. The center's components consist of treatment and laboratory facilities, natural habitats, and educational exhibits.

Birds receiving care at the facility range from least terns to magnificent frigatebirds and red-footed boobies (*Sula sula*). The injured include a variety of sea gulls, pelicans, hawks, owls, herons, and egrets. Bald eagles, ospreys, turkey vultures (*Cathartes aura*), and double-crested cormorants are regularly cared for.

Most injured birds have run afoul of humans. Many are snagged by fishermen or get wrapped up in monofilament fishing line. Others are struck by automobiles and boats, and some are even deliberately shot and maimed.

Loss of habitat is the most serious ongoing problem facing the Keys bird populations. The surging human population is rapidly eradicating shallow-water

# How Divers Can Protect the Underwater Environment

These tips are taken from Project AWARE, Aquatic World Awareness and Education, a corporate environmental program of International PADI, Inc. (Professional Association of Diving Instructors), the PADI Retail Association, PADI Travel Network, and PADI International Resort Association.

—Dive carefully in fragile aquatic ecosystems, such as coral reefs. Many aquatic organisms are fragile creatures that can be killed by the bump of a tank, knee, or camera, a swipe of a fin, or the touch of a hand. Some organisms are very slow-growing and destruction of even a small piece can cause long-lasting damage to dive sites.

—Be aware of your body and equipment placement when diving. Much environmental damage is done unknowingly. Keep gauges and alternate air sources secured so they don't drag over reefs or the sea bottom.

—Keep your diving skills sharp with continuing education.

—Consider your impact on aquatic life through your interactions. Touching, handling, feeding, even hitching rides on certain aquatic creatures may cause stress to the animal, interrupt feeding and mating, and introduce food not healthy to the species, and can even provoke aggressive behavior in normally unaggressive species.

# Tips for Boaters and Fishermen

—Practice good seamanship and safe boating. Keep safe distances from other boats and fisherman. Observe size and catch limits. Release all fish you can't consume.

—Don't disturb wildlife. Stay at least 200 feet offshore. Keep speed, noise, and wakes to a minimum near mangroves.

—Dumping trash at sea is illegal. Plastic bags and other debris can injure or kill marine animals. Try to retrieve fishing gear and equipment, especially monofilament line.

—Accidental boat groundings damage the reef. Prop damage destroys shallow seagrass beds. Consult tide and navigational charts and steer away from shallow areas. Keep in mind: "Brown, brown run aground. Blue, blue sail on through."

—Use reef mooring buoys or anchor in sandy areas away from coral and seagrasses so that anchor and chain do not damage the coral or seagrass beds.

—Use sewage pump-out facilities and biodegradable bilge cleaner, and never discharge bilge water at the reef.

mangrove swamps, transitional wetlands, freshwater ponds, and hardwood hammocks. Over 40 percent of shallow-water mangrove pools in the Upper Keys were destroyed for housing and other human uses between 1955 and 1985 and the problem has only accelerated since then.

Birds are brought to the rehabilitation center from throughout the Keys and South Florida. About 30 to 40 percent of the more than 1,000 admitted in a typical year are successfully treated and released. Others with catastrophic injuries remain permanent residents.

Visitors follow a zigzagging wooden boardwalk past 25 natural habitats. Each shelters birds that have sustained crippling injuries. Signs tell their sad stories. Broad-winged hawks "Spike" and "Stumpy" have amputated wings. "Gary," a Cooper's hawk brought here from Key West, is permanently disabled by a broken wing. "Harriet," a large female osprey with one wing that has been amputated at the wrist has been here since 1993. Volunteers say she helps the other ospreys adjust to living in an enclosure and being dependent on humans for survival.

The largest enclosure houses dozens of injured brown pelicans. It's the only habitat visitors are allowed to walk into. Stay behind the yellow line and watch the birds interact with each another.

The center augments the diets of wild, free-flying, healthy birds that perch in trees and the roofs of habitats around the center, but only for a two-hour period each day. A sign explains: "Humans have encroached on their habitats and feeding areas and it is difficult for them to find enough food. We supplement their diets, but don't provide them with all they'd gladly eat. So, they're still compelled to hunt for food in the wild and not become dependent on humans."

On the boardwalk, the first area you'll come to is a transitional wetland—a salt marsh and buttonwood habitat found between the dry hammock and the swampy wetlands. Plants from both these areas include ground-covering sea oxeye daisy (*Borrichia frutescens*) and saltwort (*Batis maritima*), as well as buttonwood, Spanish stopper, blackbead (*Pithecellobium guadalupense*), and saffron-plum (*Bumelia celastrina*), a food source for the threatened white-crowned pigeon. Succulents include prickly pear and barbed-wire cactus (*Cereus pentagonus*). The exposed rock is Key Largo Limestone, the ancient coral reef that the Keys are built on.

The boardwalk next passes into a mangrove-dominated wetland typical of

## Birding Ethics

These guidelines are provided by the National Audubon Society.

—Avoid chasing or repeatedly flushing birds.

—Avoid excessive use of recordings.

—Avoid approaching too close to nests and colonies.

—Do not handle birds or eggs except if engaged in rehabilitation activities.

—Avoid trampling the vegetation and breaking branches.

—Do not litter or otherwise introduce foreign materials into natural environments.

—Do not trespass.

—Follow all regulations in using public land.

the shoreline along Florida Bay. The mangrove trees form the first rung on the food chain in this nutritionally rich ecosystem. Leaves and other organic debris collected in the wetlands are broken down by bacteria and fungi, which provides nutrients to small organisms. In turn, these organisms serve as a food source for larger birds and mammals.

The ground cover is saltwort, sea lavender (*Tournefortia gnaphalodes*), and sea purslane. Farther on, two solution holes were formed when cap rock broke up and began to sink. The holes' rich nutrients support black mangrove and white mangrove trees and numerous wetland creatures including the mosquito-eating gambusia fish. Many species of birds and other marsh inhabitants feed at the holes.

Near the solution holes, rocky, saline terrain stunts the growth of mangroves and other trees. The trail ends at a slightly elevated, bayside berm where trees root in a nutritious environment and grow to normal size.

**Directions:** MM 93.6 Bayside. It's between Tavernier and Key Largo.

**Activities:** Viewing injured wild birds and mangrove wetlands.

**Facilities:** Boardwalks, screened habitats holding permanently injured birds, gift shop, educational center, and restroom.

**Dates:** Open daily, year-round.

**Fees:** Admission is free, but the center receives no public funding and depends on donations for its survival.

**For more information:** 93600 Overseas Highway, Tavernier, FL 33070. Phone (305) 852-4486.

### TAVERNIER LODGING
### FRANK'S KEY HAVEN

MM 92 Bayside, Tavernier. If you're looking for a quiet, unfussy, off-the-beaten-path place to while away a few days, one not listed in most tourist guides, Key Haven could be your kind of place. Although not well known even by the locals, divers, fishermen, and budget-conscious Europeans and Australians have faithfully stayed at the haven year after year.

Parts of the resort date back to the 1930s. In the mid-1980s, the current owners Frank Johnson and his wife spent more than three years restoring the motel.

Simply furnished guest rooms have kitchenettes, cable TV, air conditioning, and in-room phones for local calls. The Johnsons have added landscaping, a fishing dock, and a pool. Special diving/training packages are available. There is no restaurant or bar, but the Copper Kettle on the Overseas Highway is an excellent place for breakfast and first-rate conch chowder at lunch and dinner. *Moderate to expensive. Web site www.fkeyhaven.com. Phone (305) 852-3017. Fax (305) 852-3880.*

# Islamorada

[Fig. 4] It takes a degree of confidence to profess to be the "Sport-fishing Capital of the World," but Islamorada's claim to the title would be hard to dispute. A perennial mecca for anglers since the early part of the twentieth century, it draws those who have always dreamed of casting a fly to a ghostly bonefish, or of leaning back in a fighting chair, hooked one-on-one to a leaping sailfish.

The sight of a fishing guide poling a small skiff slowly along a backcountry flat is a common one; as is the silver flash of a 100-pound tarpon rocketing out of the water with a thrashing, lure-tossing shake of its head. No wonder famous sportsmen like Ernest Hemingway, Zane Grey, and Harry Truman, who could choose to fish anywhere, chose Islamorada.

Waiting to greet arriving anglers is an army of experienced fishing guides and charter boat captains, a selection of accommodations and world-class resorts, unparalleled choices of fishing opportunities, and one of the most beautiful settings in all of the Keys.

Sixteenth-century Spanish explorers were so enthralled by the purple sunset haze hanging over the beaches that they called the area *Islas Moradas*, which means Purple Isles. The Islamorada area (MM 90 through MM 77) includes Plantation Key, Windley Key, Upper Matecumbe Key, Lower Matecumbe Key, and Long Key. The town of

# What To Do With an Injured Bird

—Keep your safety in mind when approaching an injured bird. Lead it into a safe area, away from traffic or water, before attempting to catch it.

—Eye protection is essential when approaching herons and egrets. These birds instinctively lunge at their prey, and when injured may lunge at you.

—Cover the bird's head with a towel or T-shirt. This will often have a calming effect.

—Don't tape or tie a bird's bill shut. Some birds do not have nostrils, some nostrils may be clogged with blood, some injured birds may regurgitate recently eaten food, and some cool themselves by panting.

—Transport the injured or hooked bird to the nearest rehabilitation center, either the Wild Bird Center in Tavernier, or one of these other locations: Marathon Wild Bird Rescue, MM 47, Marathon. Phone (305) 743-8382. Wildlife Rescue of the Florida Keys, Key West. Phone (305) 294-1441. If you're not near a bird rescue center, contact a local veterinary clinic.

Islamorada, one of the largest in the Keys with 8,287 residents, is located on Upper Matecumbe Key.

Traveling south from Key Largo to Islamorada, you cross the first series of 42 bridges connecting the Florida Keys. This is where the beauty of the islands becomes evident from the highway. Unless you've taken one of the boat trips out of Key Largo, this may be your first glimpse of the multihued waters that surround the islands.

The waters of the Keys come in a stunning variety of shades of blue and green extending as wide, uneven bands out from the shoreline. A change in depth means a change in color. From light pastels in the shallowest water, through a series of blues and greens, to the dark royal blue depths offshore, there are more colors than in a giant box of crayons—powder blue, sky blue, lime green, aqua marine, steel blue, and azure.

Many of the bridges have an area at either end where you can pull off and park. These are some of the nicest places to stop just to stretch and take in a little of the feel of the Keys; smell the salt air and feel the heavy moisture on your skin. You can usually walk down to a seawall by the water, or in some cases out onto portions of the old bridges.

Most of the highway bridges in use today throughout the Keys are second generation. The first highway bridges, which were built across Flagler's original railroad tresses, have been abandoned, destroyed, or in some cases turned into fishing piers and bicycle trails. These are great places to watch the sunset! And in a few minutes you won't even hear the cars whizzing by on the other bridge.

Like many of the Keys, the islands of Islamorada have a storied past. Calusa Indians, pirates, wreckers, and treasure hunters have called these islands home (or hideout).

## Rescuing Hooked Brown Pelicans

Every year scores of brown pelicans are accidentally hooked by fishermen who fail to remove the hook and line from the injured bird. When the bird flies away, the line is frequently entangled in trees and bushes, ensnaring the bird in a trap from which it can't escape. It eventually dies of starvation. The Florida Keys Wild Bird Rehabilitation Center offers these guidelines to rescue hooked pelicans.

—First, reel in the pelican hooked on your line. Be careful not to break the line. Although the bird will be struggling and flapping its wings, it weighs only about 6 pounds and can be handled if done properly.

—Next, grab part or all of the bird's bill. Close it and hold it securely in one hand. The inside edges of the bill, and the tip, are sharp, but unless you rub your hand up and down the edge, a pelican's bite shouldn't hurt you.

—Next, fold the wings into their normal closed position and hold them there. This quiets the bird and it should stop struggling enough to be transported to the nearest wildlife rehabilitation center.

—Transport the injured or hooked bird to the nearest rehabilitation center, either the Wild Bird Center in Tavernier, or one of these other locations: Marathon Wild Bird Rescue, MM 47, Marathon. Phone (305) 743-8382. Wildlife Rescue of the Florida Keys, Key West. Phone (305) 294-1441. If you're not near a bird rescue center, contact a local veterinary clinic.

The most historically significant event in modern times, however, was the killer hurricane of 1935. The monstrous storm struck with winds over 200 miles per hour, driving a 17-foot tidal wave across the islands and killing hundreds of residents and laborers working for the Florida East Coast Railroad. A late-arriving evacuation train sent from Miami was washed off the tracks. A mass grave of hurricane victims is marked by the Islamorada Hurricane Monument at MM 81.5.

Islamorada's tourism-catering core is on Upper Matecumbe Key, where the Overseas Highway is elbow-to-elbow on both sides with resort hotels, motels, shell shops, fast-food eateries, shopping centers, and, above all, places to latch onto a boat and a guide to head off fishing.

Outdoor centers like Holiday Isle Resort and Marina at MM 84 Oceanside and Bud n' Mary's Fishing Marina at MM 79.8 Oceanside, have both offshore and inshore guides available. Check in with the booking offices to find out what type of trips are available and what fish are in season. Holiday Isle Resort and Marina, 84001 Overseas Highway, Islamorada, FL 33036. Web site www.theisle.com. Phone (800) 327-7070 or (305) 664-2321. For information on Bud n' Mary's Fishing Marina, see page 62.

Bud n' Mary's is the place with the giant plastic white shark hanging in front. As you drive through the Keys, you'll see all types of giant plastic and concrete creatures—lobsters, crabs, sailfish, and dolphins to name a few. They go well with manatee, whale, and red snapper mail boxes you'll see along the highway.

A remarkably long list of major game fish can be caught year-round from waters surrounding Islamorada—including marlin, kingfish, wahoo, shark, barracuda, blackfin tuna, dolphin, sailfish, snapper, grouper, bonefish, redfish, snook, tarpon, and permit. Catching a "grand slam"—a permit, tarpon, and bonefish all on the same day—is a once-in-a-lifetime thrill sought by many dedicated anglers. Catching even one of these common yet incredibly elusive species sometimes takes years.

Shallow-water guides fish in the Florida Bay backcountry for snook, redfish, seatrout, and tarpon. Standing on a high platform mounted over the engine they pole their clients along in the clear water, pointing out fish with casting directions like "redfish, three o'clock" or "tarpon moving left to right, one o'clock, 20 yards."

Other times they'll ease the boat silently along a mangrove-covered shoreline while clients cast plugs or flies next to the tangled prop roots, tricking snook and redfish into giving up their hiding places for a chance at a meal.

The search for bonefish and permit takes place on wide sandy flats. The common approach is to leave the boat behind and stalk the game fish on foot while keeping a low profile. The guide will go with you to help spot fish in the clear water.

**BROWN PELICAN**
(Pelecanus occidentalis)
This bird dives into the water with its bill closed, lifts its upper mandible, and opens its pouch outward to scoop up its prey. The fish, and water twice the weight of the bird, enters the bill.

Offshore charter boats venture into the deep, dark-blue waters of the Atlantic Ocean. Charters usually have a maximum of six passengers. You can sometimes split charters with another small group.

Dolphin (the fish) and sailfish are the most popular targets. Dolphin fishing peaks

# Florida Keys Bridges

In the Florida Keys there are 42 bridges, connecting more than 100 islands over a 126-mile distance. The bridges total 18.8 miles in length, and travelers spend about 15 percent of the total travel time between the mainland and Key West on them. Three bridges have been named National Historic Sites—old Seven Mile, Bahia Honda, and Long Key.

| Bridge | Mile Marker | Length In Feet | Bridge | Mile Marker | Length In Feet |
|---|---|---|---|---|---|
| Jewfish Draw Bridge | 106 | 223 | North Pine | 29.5 | 660 |
| Key Largo Cut | 103.5 | 360 | South Pine | 28.5 | 850 |
| Tavernier Creek | 91 | 320 | Torch Key Viaduct | 28 | 880 |
| Snake Creek | 86 | 230 | Torch-Ramrod | 27.5 | 720 |
| Whale Harbor | 84 | 270 | Nile Channel | 26 | 4,490 |
| Tea Table Relief | 80 | 270 | Kemp's Channel | 23.5 | 1,030 |
| Tea Table | 79 | 700 | Bow Channel | 20 | 1,340 |
| Indian Key | 78 | 2,460 | Park | 185 | 1,340 |
| Lignumvitae | 77.8 | 860 | North Harri | 18 | 430 |
| Channel 2 | 73 | 1,760 | Harris Gap | 17.5 | 140 |
| Channel 5 | 71 | 4,580 | Harris | 16 | 430 |
| Long Key | 65 | 12,040 | Lower Sugar Loaf | 15.5 | 1,260 |
| Tom's Harbor 3 | 61 | 1,270 | Saddle Bunch 2 | 14.5 | 660 |
| Tom's Harbor 4 | 60 | 1,460 | Saddle Bunch 3 | 14 | 760 |
| Vaca Cut | 53 | 300 | Saddle Bunch 4 | 13 | 900 |
| Seven Mile | 47 | 35,830 | Saddle Bunch 5 | 12.5 | 900 |
| Little Duck Missouri | 39.5 | 840 | Shark Channel | 11.8 | 2,090 |
| Missouri-Ohio | 39 | 1,440 | Rockland Channel | 10 | 1,280 |
| Ohio-Bahia Honda | 38 | 1,050 | Boca Chica | 6 | 2,730 |
| Bahia Honda | 36 | 6,734 | Stock Island | 5 | 360 |
| Spanish Harbor | 33.5 | 3,380 | Key West | 4 | 159 |

in the summer, and sailfish fishing is best in fall and early winter, which is also a good time for catching king mackerel and blackfin tuna. Anglers even catch a couple great white sharks every year.

For the land-bound angler, many of the older Keys bridges that are no longer being used for traffic have been turned into fishing piers. A rod and reel, a minimum of fishing tackle, and some live or frozen shrimp from the nearest tackle store are all it takes to get started. Some tackle stores rent fishing tackle.

Snapper, grouper, sheepshead, and jack crevalle (*Caranx hippos*) are commonly caught from the bridges. On occasion, bridge anglers are surprised by a tarpon that was moving through the pass and spotted their bait. Because of their hard mouths and incredible strength, tarpon are rarely landed. Snook like to hang out around bridge structures and are caught at night on feathers, shrimp, or small live baits fished on the bottom.

Florida nonresidents are required to have saltwater fishing licenses when fishing from bridges. Charter boat and guide boat licenses cover their clients. (*See* Appendix E, page 297, for more information on fishing license regulations.)

**For more information:** Stop at the Islamorada Chamber of Commerce located in a bright red Florida East Coast Railroad caboose at MM 82.5 Bayside, PO Box 915, Islamorada, FL 33036. Web site www.florida-keys.fl.us/islamorada/index.htm. Phone (800) 322-5397 or (305) 664-4503.

### WORLD WIDE SPORTSMAN

[Fig. 4(2)] It's hardly surprising that one of the most popular attractions in the "Sport Fishing Capital of the World" would be one of the world's largest tackle stores. Then again, calling World Wide Sportsman just a fishing tackle shop is like calling Moby Dick just another whale. A regional favorite for 30 years, the store expanded to this new location in 1997. It attracts between 15,000 and 20,000 visitors a day to its cavernous, two-story, 27,000-square-foot former boat barn at MM 81.5 Bayside, on the Overseas Highway.

Those who live to fish and those who wouldn't know a fishing hook from a picture hook can enjoy wandering along aisles of fishing gear and lures of all sizes and descriptions. There's a 6,000-gallon aquarium with good-sized tarpon, bonefish, redfish, and snook; a large selection of sportswear and outdoor clothing; a fully stocked selection of fishing books; a fully staffed booking service specializing in deep-sea fishing trips around the world; and a marine art gallery. On the water, behind the store, there's a marina, seafood market, bait shop, and headquarters for charter fishing guides.

The owners have done much more than provide a place to buy fishing-related wares; they have preserved a bit of the history associated with Islamorada fishing. In the second floor Zane Grey Lounge—a reproduction of the original Long Key Fishing Lodge—you can lunch on the terrace with a magnificent view of Florida Bay with its varied shades of blue and green, decorated with a scattering of mangrove islands.

Zane Grey popularized fishing in Islamorada and was president of the Long Key Fishing Club, established in 1906. A display case in the lounge contains original tackle used by both Zane Grey and Ernest Hemingway, including handcrafted deep-sea fishing reels from as early as 1927. There are also original writings on display, along with old photos of the famous novelists standing with great catches.

The centerpiece of the store, however, is a 43-foot cabin cruiser that sits right in the middle. Built in 1933, the elegant craft has been restored to its original condition right down to the wooden fighting chair.

This cabin cruiser is an identical sister ship (built the same year in the same boat yard) to the boat, *Pilar*, that Ernest Hemingway used in these waters. Photos inside show Hemingway on his boat with various famous people. An old typewriter on a small table speaks for itself.

**Directions:** MM 81.5 Bayside on the Overseas Highway.

**Activities:** Shopping, dining, and browsing.

**Facilities:** Restaurant and bar, marina, deep-sea fishing charters.

**Dates:** Open daily.

**Fees:** None.

**Closest town:** Islamorada.

**For more information:** World Wide Sportsman, 81576 Overseas Highway, Islamorada, FL 33036. Phone (305) 664-4615 or (800) 327-2880. Web site www.worldwidesportsmantravel.com.

### THEATER OF THE SEA

[Fig. 4(3)] Opened in the 1940s, in a quarry blasted and dug out of the fossilized

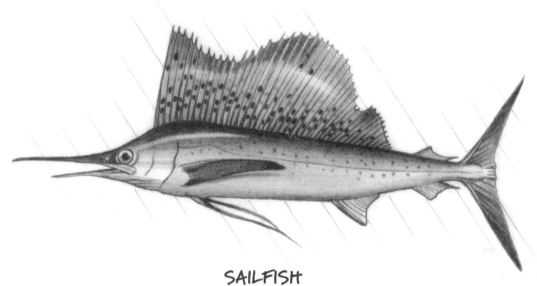

## SAILFISH
### (Istiophorus platypterus)
This prized game fish may be seen leaping repeatedly from the sea. When it's hooked, the fish shakes violently and can also evert its stomach in an attempt to dislodge the hook.

coral by the Florida East Coast Railroad, Theater of the Sea is one of the world's oldest marine parks. It's easy to spot at MM 84.5 by the splendid landscaping of full-sized, leaping dolphin topiaries along the highway.

Inside you'll find a friendly, "early Florida" kind of place, where families can watch smiley-faced dolphins and sea lions jumping through hoops, leaping for fish and beach balls, and giving spectators sitting too close to the pool some good-natured splashes. With advance reservations, you can participate in a structured swim with the dolphins, sea lions, or stingrays, be a trainer for a day, or take a boat cruise.

**Directions:** MM 84.5 Oceanside on the Overseas Highway.

**Activities:** Dolphin and sea lion performances, marine animal encounters, guided marine life show, bottomless boat rides.

**Facilities:** Covered seating to view shows, snack bars.

**Dates:** Open daily, year-round.

**Fees:** There is a charge for admission and dolphin encounters.

**Closest town:** Islamorada.

**For more information:** Theater of the Sea, PO Box 407, Islamorada, FL 33036. Phone (305) 664-2431.

### WINDLEY KEY FOSSIL REEF STATE GEOLOGICAL SITE

[Fig. 4(4)] At 18.5 feet above sea level, Windley Key is one of the highest in the chain of islands. Formed of Key Largo Limestone, the key was created from coral reef formations during the Sangamon interglacial period about 125,000 years ago. About 25,000 years later, when the Pamlico Sea subsided during the Wisconsin ice age, the reef was exposed to form the Florida Keys. Calusa Indian tribes inhabited the area centuries before the first European explorers arrived. Their shell middens and other remains can be found in the northern boundary of Windley Key's Quarry Tract.

Before the early 1900s, Windley Key was called the Umbrella Key. Its elevation made it a practical place for Henry Flagler's construction crews to quarry fill and rock for the railroad bed. When the railroad construction was finished in 1912, fossilized coral rock, called keystone, was quarried from this site for the decorative exteriors of public buildings and wealthy estates in Florida and elsewhere. Islamorada's memorial to the 1935 hurricane victims was also fashioned from Windley Key's polished fossilized coral.

Commercial quarrying continued through the 1960s. Environmentalists and concerned Keys citizens, with support from scientists and geology buffs who study the fossilized coral, eventually prompted the State of Florida to purchase the site in 1985 and save the important resource from proposed development. Windley Key Fossil Reef State Geological Site was created in 1989.

Five interlocking trails take you around three former quarries, and through tropical hardwood hammocks and wetlands.

Flagler Quarry Trail, approximately 948 feet long, is an easy introductory walk through a thick hardwood hammock above the quarry. Signatures of ancient microorganisms can be seen on the fossilized coral walls. Rare, and quite impressive mahogany, joe-wood (*Jacquinia keyensis*), torchwood (*Amyris elemifera*), and white ironwood trees (*Hypelate trifoliata*) can be seen. Black ironwood, known for its very hard and heavy wood, is a small tree with gray bark, light green leaves, black fruit, and white flowers.

Quarry Station Trail, about 525 feet long, branches away from Flagler Quarry Trail and passes the quarry station area, where the railroad spur line brought fresh water to the area and carried the quarried stone away.

Quarry Walls Walk, around 340 feet long, gives visitors a rare opportunity to stand inside a fossilized coral reef that died tens of thousands of years ago.

Sunset Trail, approximately 1,650 feet long, traverses the high hammock, wetlands, salt marsh, and mangrove ecosystem and concludes with a view of Florida Bay.

Hammock Trail, 2,682 feet long, offers views of contrasting environments: rare and endangered palms and cacti, a high tropical hammock, and wetlands and their connecting transitional areas.

**Directions:** MM 85.5 Bayside on the Overseas Highway, near Snake Creek bridge.

**Activities:** Hiking.

**Facilities:** Five hiking trails, from easy to moderately strenuous; visitor center; restrooms; and self-guided tours.

**Fees:** There is a small fee for self-guided tours.

**Dates:** Open year-round, Thursday through Monday. Contact the number below for hours of operation.

**Closest town:** Islamorada.

**For more information:** Long Key State Parks, PO Box 1052, Islamorada, FL 33036. Phone (305) 664-2540.

## ISLAMORADA LODGING

### BUD N' MARY'S FISHING MARINA AND DIVE CENTER

MM 79.5 Oceanside, Islamorada. As the name suggests, Bud n' Mary's is the place to park your boat or rent one, or to arrange a backcountry or deep-sea fishing trip, a snorkeling and diving adventure, a sight-seeing cruise, or even a trip to Indian Key State Historic Site and Lignumvitae State Botanical Site. It's also the place if you want to sleep a few yards from all those activities or to enjoy a private beach. Six motel units (one above the tackle shop) have kitchenettes, phone, and TV. *Moderate. Phone (305) 664-2461 or (800) 742-7945. Fax (305) 664-5592. Web site www.budnmarys.com.*

### CHEECA LODGE

MM 82 Oceanside, Islamorada. Opened in 1946 and continuously modernized and upgraded, Cheeca Lodge is among the Keys' classiest acts. It fronts 1,000 feet on the Atlantic and has 27 acres of gardens, 203 large rooms and suites, and the usual array of deluxe resort recreation, dining, and entertainment options. The lodge boasts the longest fishing pier in the Keys, and is also the home of the George Bush/Cheeca Lodge Bonefish Tournament, which raises money for charities and conservation causes. There's also a saltwater lagoon full of native fish and perfect for kids that want to learn to use a mask and snorkel, and Camp Cheeca, an environmental awareness program for kids ages 6 to 12. *Expensive. Phone (800) 327-2888 or (305) 664-465. Fax (305) 664-2893. Web site www.cheeca.com.*

### CORAL BAY RESORT

MM 75.5 Bayside, Islamorada. Former North Carolinians Selby and Michele Blair welcome families with children, couples, retirees, and other guests seeking a quiet, well-run destination set well back from the highway. Modern, attractively furnished motel-type rooms and efficiencies with kitchens are close to a freshwater pool, private bayside beach, marina and boat ramp, and tidal saltwater pool with fish and lobsters. *Moderate to expensive. Phone (305) 664-5568. Web site www.thefloridakeys.com/coralbay.*

### FIESTA KEY KOA CAMPGROUND

MM 70 Bayside, Long Key. This is an upscale campground, with 300 full-service RV sites on a 28-acre island. Many sites face the Gulf of Mexico. Amenities include a boat ramp and marina, a restaurant and bar, hot tubs, a swimming pool, a convenience store, and 24-hour gated security. Fishing boats, kayaks, and bikes are available for rent. *Inexpensive. Phone (305) 664-4922.*

## ISLAMORADA DINING

### MANNY & ISA'S KITCHEN

MM 81.6 Oceanside, Overseas Highway, Islamorada. This is one of those places that have become a part of the fabric of the Keys. Without a recommendation, you probably won't be tempted to stop, and you might not even see it set back off the road next to the Hurricane Monument. Everything served here is wonderful, especially Cuban palomilla steak, picadillo, ropa vieja with black beans and rice, broiled and fried fish, and lobster. There are also steaks, hamburgers, and sandwiches. If you have only one slice of Key lime pie while you're in the Keys, have it here. Manny grows his limes in the orchard behind the restaurant, squeezes them himself, and makes the pies every morning. You can take along a whole one to enjoy down the road. Open for lunch and dinner. Closed Tuesday. *Inexpensive to moderate. Phone (305) 664-5019.*

### THE GREEN TURTLE INN

MM 81.5 Oceanside, Islamorada. The restaurant got its name in the 1940s, when saltwater green turtle soup and steaks processed at a cannery across the road were the house specialties. Since the government banned the harvesting of green sea turtles in the 1970s, the Green Turtle gets its supply from freshwater, farm-raised turtles. If you don't care for the restaurant's namesake, the menu also includes fish, shrimp, lobster, and steaks. Smiling photos of celebrities past and present cover the wooden walls. A piano player helps keep everybody happy. Closed on Mondays. *Moderate. Phone (305) 664-9031.*

### PAPA JOE'S RESTAURANT AND MARINA

MM 80, Islamorada. A Keys landmark for many years, Papa's packs them in for lunch and dinner in an old Keys ambience of worn wooden floors, cypress walls, friendly servers, and good food. The menu includes fish served a myriad of ways, Italian dishes, and steaks. Behind the restaurant, the walk-up bar, overlooking the marina, is a convivial place to enjoy a refreshment, watch the sunset, and meet some of the local personalities. While you're here, you can arrange a backcountry fishing trip or rent a boat. *Moderate. Phone (305) 664-8109 or 664-8756. Marina phone (305) 664-5005.*

### SQUID ROW RESTAURANT

MM 82 Oceanside, Islamorada. The award for the least appetizing name for a Key's restaurant could go to Squid Row, but the fine food and fabulous bouillabaisse found inside is undeniably most appetizing. Homemade soups, dressings, and desserts make choices difficult. Try the yellowtail snapper meuniere, which is dipped in flour, egg-wash, and flour again before it's lightly sautéed and served with citrus butter. They also serve fish and chicken in a Saint Croix style, which is rolled in Japanese bread crumbs, sautéed, and served with black pepper and citrus butter. *Moderate. Phone (305) 664-9865.*

### UNCLE'S RESTAURANT

MM 80 Oceanside, Islamorada. Uncle's serves a full selection of excellent Keys seafood plus a number of Italian specialties, wild game including venison and quail, and "Heart Healthy" meals. Patio dining. Open Monday through Saturday for dinner. *Moderate. Phone (305) 664-4402.*

### LIGNUMVITAE KEY STATE BOTANICAL SITE

[Fig. 4(5)] Lignumvitae Key State Botanical Site preserves one of the last of the virgin tropical forests that once covered much of the Upper Keys. The 280-acre island was formed thousands of years ago as a living coral reef. When the sea level dropped the top of the reef was exposed, forming an island of fossilized coral rock.

Through subsequent eons, storm tides deposited seaweed, driftwood, and organic detritus on the bare rock. The material decayed and formed small pockets of soil in the coral rock depressions. Seeds from tropical islands floated ashore or were carried by the winds or in the digestive tracts of migrating birds. The seeds sprouted and plants began to grow, dropping leaves, producing flowers and seeds, maturing, dying, and decaying. As more centuries passed, a complex and diverse tropical hammock covered the ancient coral reef. The land was never burned or cleared for farming or to flush wildlife from their habitats.

John James Audubon visited the island in 1832. From 1919 to 1953, the island was owned by the family of Miami pioneer W. J. Matheson, who cleared a site for their limestone house. A cistern filled by rain falling from the roof supplied drinking water, and a windmill furnished power. They also put in an airstrip, bulldozed a trail, and brought in ducks, geese, peafowl, goats, burros, and Galapagos Island tortoises. An unwanted guest, the Key Largo wood rat, either swam to the island or hitched a ride in on boats bringing supplies.

The State of Florida purchased the island and neighboring Indian Key and Shell Key in 1971. At 16.5 feet above sea level, it's one of the Keys' highest islands. Twice a day, Thursday through Monday, state park rangers conduct tours of the forest and Matheson house, which contains nature artifacts. Parts of the tombstone of Indian Key pioneer Jacob Housman and six cannons from the British frigate HMS *Winchester*, grounded on Carysfort Reef in 1695, are on the grounds by the house.

On your boat ride to the key watch for terns, gulls, double-crested cormorants, brown pelicans, and osprey. Great white herons are often seen on the flats near the islands.

While on Lignumvitae, look for a variety of butterflies, migratory warblers in the spring and fall, and white-crowned pigeons. Look for the pigeons in the tops of the trees. They are in the Keys year-round but can be hard to find during cold winter days. There have also been sightings of black-whiskered vireos and mangrove cuckoos on the island. The best time to see both is mid-May when the vireos are nesting and the cuckoos are calling.

The island is named for the lignum vitae tree (*Guaiacum sanctum*), the so-called "tree of life." Its wood is so extremely dense and the resin so thick and oily, it's impervious to pests and destructive organisms, and it can outlast steel, bronze, and other materials. Columbus took some of the trees back to Europe from the Caribbean.

The wood is still used for wooden propeller shaft bearings. Some residents of the Bahamas and other Caribbean islands claim it has curative powers. In the spring, the trees produce blue flowers and yellow seed pods. Botanists say that zealous collecting and a decline in major hurricanes that scatter the seeds and promote reproduction are important reasons why slow-growing lignum vitae trees are now on the endangered list.

All of the island's exotic animals and most of the strange plants have vanished on their own. The Key Largo wood rat, now on the endangered species list, mysteriously disappeared after about two decades.

The tropical forest includes some 132 other varieties of trees and plants. When it comes to wood density, the champion is the black ironwood, at 95 pounds per cubic foot. Gumbo-limbos are easily recognizable tropical trees. They have a thin, reddish-brown bark that peels in paperlike sheets from the twisted trunks. Gumbo-limbos are also nicknamed "sunburned tourist trees," "naked Indian trees," and "living fence post trees" because when cut into sections and stuck in the ground they grow back rapidly.

Interestingly, they frequently grow alongside poisonwood trees and are believed to be an antidote for the virulent rash caused by contact with the poisonwood leaves and sap. (Park rangers and others who frequent poisonwood habitats prefer more modern,

# Choosing the Right Pair of Sunglasses

A necessary piece of equipment for any trip to the Florida Keys is a good pair of sunglasses. The right kind will protect your eyes from a tropical glare they are unaccustomed to, and will vastly improve the entire visual experience.

There is no question about the importance of UV (ultraviolet radiation) protection. Although invisible to the naked eye, it's present in all natural and fluorescent light. Short-term effects of UV radiation, which occur from exposure to excessive amounts over a short period of time, such as from a welder's arc or a full day at the beach, are similar to a sunburn: They can be painful but are usually temporary and rarely cause permanent damage.

Long-term effects of UV radiation, on the other hand, happen slowly and painlessly. Research has found that UV rays are involved in many serious eye disorders people experience today, including cataracts. Because of reflection, people who spend time around the water are exposed to levels of UV radiation two to three times that which is normally experienced. The Keys' latitude, lovely white reflecting sands, and shining seas make the potential for damage greater here than anywhere else in the country.

The solution is to wear sunglasses that have polarized lenses. They will block 100 percent of the UV radiation and cut the glare coming off the water so you can see beneath the surface. The next step is to choose a lens color, and for that take a tip from fishing enthusiasts. When they want to spot fish in clear, shallow water, serious anglers use high contrast lenses that have a tan, amber, brown, or vermillion component. These colors will cause the warm colors to pop out—the yellows, greens, and reds which are the colors of things you'll want to see such as reefs and grasses.

Being able to see through the glare and pick out colors on the bay and ocean bottom will enhance every view, every scene. From bridges and boats you'll see more fish and wildlife, and more of the Florida Keys.

FDA-approved medications). The gumbo-limbo's light wood, similar to balsa, was once used to make bobbers and corks for fishing lines.

Before commercial waterproofing products were developed, the thick gumbo-limbo sap was used to protect the bottom of boats. Wildlife entrepreneurs in the nineteenth century had a more specialized use for the gummy gumbo-limbo sap: They used it to snare songbirds, which were sold as entertainment.

The sweet fruits of sapodilla (*Sideroxylon tenax*) and pigeon plum trees are favorites of the island's raccoons. Park rangers say the raccoons sometimes become so intoxicated by the heavy sugar they fall right out of the trees. Raccoons and birds also feed on Florida tree snails, which are found in large numbers on the island. A tea brewed from the black stopper tree is an old reliable cure for diarrhea. The common white stopper (*Eugenia axillaris*) has a skunklike aroma that is hard to miss.

The island also has remains of an Indian burial mound and a coral rock wall 0.5 mile long and 4 feet high, possibly built by Calusas or earlier inhabitants. Black and red mangroves are massed along the eastern shorelines by the dock.

**Directions:** In Florida Bay, 1.5 miles northeast of Lower Matecumbe Key. Arrange boat transportation or rent a boat from Robbie's Marina, MM 77.5, phone (305) 664-9814, or Bud n' Mary's Fishing Marina and Dive Center, MM 79.5, phone (305) 664-2461 or (800) 742-7945. For those who bring their own small boat, there is a public boat ramp on Indian Key Fill at MM 78.5 Bayside. Look for the sign for Indian Key Fill as you are headed south.

**Activities:** Guided tours of a virgin tropical hammock and early 1900s house two or three times a day at designated times. Reservations are not required but are suggested during season. No unescorted exploration is permitted. Visitors should wear comfortable walking shoes, long pants, and a long-sleeve shirt, and bring insect repellent.

**Facilities:** Historic 1919 four-bedroom home, nature trail, restrooms. Most facilities aren't accessible to the disabled.

**Dates:** Open Thursday through Monday.

**Fees:** There is a charge for boat transportation and a small fee for the tour.

**Closest town:** Islamorada is about 2 miles north on the Overseas Highway.

**For more information:** Lignumvitae Key State Botanical Site, PO Box 1052, Islamorada, FL 33036. Phone (305) 664-2540.

## INDIAN KEY STATE HISTORIC SITE

[Fig. 4(6)] Prophetically, it seems, sixteenth-century Spanish explorers called Indian Key *Matanzas*, or slaughter, after a historically unsubstantiated massacre of shipwrecked French sailors by Calusa Indians. Legend has it that on moonlit nights you can encounter the spirits of French sailors, Spanish soldiers, hanged pirates, and victims of an 1840s Indian battle that wiped out the Keys' most thriving community.

The 11-acre island, separated from Lower Matecumbe Key and the Overseas Highway by open water, scarcely seems like a place that played an important role in early Florida history. But it did. Archaeological excavations suggest aboriginals lived on the island as far back as 1200 B.C. They were succeeded by Calusas, who lived here until about the mid-to-late 1700s. Next came Seminole Indians, who were pursued into the Everglades and the Keys by the United States government.

When the Spanish began exploring the Keys in the early 1500s, they discovered that the Straits of Florida and the Gulf Stream were a convenient route for treasure ships returning home from Central and South America. But this quick route was hardly a safe one. Calusa, English, and Bahamian pirates plundered ships wrecked by hurricanes and shallow coral reefs.

The United States' acquisition of Florida in 1819 put the pirates out of business and initiated the legalized business of "wrecking." Wrecking was a licensed business

*Aboriginals, then Calusa Indians, and finally Seminole Indians inhabited Indian Key. Pictured here is one of 3,000 Seminole descendants who live in the Florida Everglades today.*

intended to rescue passengers and salvage cargoes that ran aground on reefs and sandbars. Under the law, wreckers were entitled to a percentage of everything they salvaged.

Nevertheless, many shipwrecked captains claimed the wreckers were no more than licensed pirates who deliberately lured their ships to destruction. Some stories hold that wreckers intentionally set fires in certain places on the islands during bad weather to trick ships into entering dangerous waters.

In 1830, New Yorker Jacob Housman purchased Indian Key and set about turning it into a town that would rival Key West as the center of the shipping industry. He also hoped to break the Key West monopoly on the wrecking business, and make himself the wealthiest, most powerful man in the Keys.

To assure his independence from the courts in Key West's Monroe County, in 1836 Housman pressed Florida's territorial legislature to create Dade County (now Metro Miami) with Indian Key as its seat and himself as its majordomo. (The *New World Dictionary* defines majordomo as, "a man in charge of a great, royal or noble household.") He offered settlers something scarce in the rest of the Keys—fresh water on nearby Matecumbe Key—and to accommodate them he created a prosperous small town.

Around a spacious central square and wide, hard-packed streets, he built homes for 40 to 50 permanent inhabitants, a general store, a hotel with a bowling alley, a bar and a ballroom, a saloon, cisterns, a post office, wharves, and warehouses to store goods salvaged from wrecking. John James Audubon was a guest of the hotel. Topsoil was shipped in and sown with tropical trees and plants.

In 1838, Dr. Henry Perrine, a physician with a scholarly and very practical interest in tropical plants, moved to the island to cultivate agave, a sisal hemp plant with a tough, durable fiber used in the manufacture of rope and canvas. He also introduced tea, coffee, mangoes, bananas, and scores of other plants to the Keys and South Florida.

During the Seminole War of the mid-1830s, Housman's wealthy island empire became increasingly threatened by Indians who were at war with the United States over forced removal policies. Fears were realized on the morning of August 7, 1840, when a large, armed force of Seminoles attacked, burned, and looted the island. Dr. Perrine and many others were killed, but Housman and his wife managed to escape.

Housman never returned to Indian Key, but instead went to Key West and in 1841 was killed in an accident while working on a wrecking ship.

Small populations of farmers, boat builders, and smugglers lived on Indian Key through the early 1900s. The state purchased it and Lignumvitae and Shell Key in 1970 and a year later it became Indian Key State Historic Site.

Guided and self-guided tours lead to interpretive markers by the foundations of the hotel, warehouse, hospital, dwellings, and Housman's empty burial site. His remains and most of his tombstone were destroyed by plunderers in the early 1900s. Parts of the tombstone are on Lignumvitae Key.

Of more interest to naturalists are the wild-growing agave and other tropical plants that Dr. Perrine cultivated. A grove of umbrella-like tamarind trees (*Lysiloma lastisilquum*) is a cool, shady place to stop and contemplate the little island's turbulent history. Beside the grove is an observation tower where you can get a comprehensive overview.

**Directions:** In the ocean, 0.75 mile southeast of the north shore of Lower Matecumbe Key. Arrange boat transportation or rent a boat at Robbie's Marina, MM 77.5, phone (305) 664-9814, or Bud n' Mary's Fishing Marina and Dive Center, MM 79.5, phone (305) 664-2461 or (800) 742-7945. For those who bring their own small boat, canoe, or kayak there is a boat ramp on Indian Key Fill at MM 78.5 Bayside. Look for the sign for Indian Key Fill as you are headed south.

**Activities:** Guided and self-guided tours of 1830s historic site and natural and exotic trees and plants. Park rangers lead scheduled guided tours. Call for reservations.

**Facilities:** Boat dock, observation tower, open-sided shelter, walking trail, remains of 1830s town. No restrooms or picnic areas. Most facilities aren't accessible to the disabled.

**Dates:** Open daily sunrise to sunset. The guided tours are held Thursday through Monday at designated times.

**Fees:** There is a small charge for ranger tours.

**Closest town:** Islamorada is 1.5 miles north.

**For more information:** Indian Key State Historic Site, PO Box 1052, Islamorada, FL 33036. Phone (305) 664-2540.

### ROBBIE'S MARINA

[Fig. 4(7)] Located at Lignumvitae Bridge, Lower Matecumbe Key, Robbie's is one of the departure points for Lignumvitae and Indian Key. Practically under the bridge, Robbie's packages the raffish old Keys spirit in a cluttered shop and wooden dock and offers some of the best entertainment you can get for a few bucks. It's a boat rental, charter fishing, and Keys touring center, but just about anybody will tell you the main attraction is the huge tarpon that hang around the dock.

For a small fee, you can walk onto Robbie's 90-foot dock and look down in the dark green water at a hundred or more silver kings weighing—if you could ever get them on a scale—from 10 to 150 pounds. You can also purchase a bucket of herring and sardines to toss into the feeding frenzy. Don't try to hand-feed the tarpon. Their sandpapery mouths can give you a nasty rasp and strip your watch and jewelry like a rapacious gang of thieves.

Annie Reckwerdt, who co-owns the place with her husband Michael, calls it, "My own little aquarium." Tarpon first became a fixture and feature attraction in the early 1980s, when Michael's parents, Robbie and Mona Reckwerdt, ran the dock and a small restaurant. One morning a small, injured tarpon showed up for the food scraps they tossed off the end of the dock.

The fish had facial lacerations, so they called him Scarface, and put him in a holding tank where he could safely recuperate. When he regained his health, Scarface became a pampered pet around the dock. Fed by handouts from fishermen and tourists, he grew and grew and must have put out the word to his fellow tarpon. They came and stayed after the 150-pound Scarface went back to sea and never returned.

**Directions:** MM 77.5.

**For more information:** Robbie's Marina, Islamorada, FL 33036. Phone (305) 664-9814.

### THE HUNGRY TARPON

MM 77.5, Islamorada. The Hungry Tarpon is situated right next to Robbie's. Built in the 1940s, the old-timey diner, with counter stools and a few tables, is done up to an old Keys "T" with neon beer signs, year-round Christmas lights, and photos of proud anglers with their trophy catches. "Good Food and Lots of It," as the menu boasts, is prepared at a busy grill right in front of diners' eyes. Fishermen and others who show up as early as 6 a.m. pack in the protein for the day with the house special, Grits and Grunts: two eggs, biscuits, grits or hashbrowns, and fried fish.

"The Hungry Tarpon" is a generous plate of hashbrowns with eggs, sausage gravy, and Monterey jack cheese. Other morning specialties are breakfast burritos, huevos rancheros, and Durango eggs—three eggs with ham, scallions, Monterey jack, and ranchero sauce. Dinner favorites are a seven-rib rack of lamb, blackened hogfish, yellowfin tuna, mahimahi, and grilled Florida lobster in the shell. There is also an outstanding hamburger and shrimp salad sandwich at lunch and dinner. Lunch only Monday through Friday, lunch and dinner on weekends. *Inexpensive. (305) 664-0535.*

### SAN PEDRO UNDERWATER ARCHAEOLOGICAL PRESERVE

[Fig. 4(8)] An underwater nature trail, opened in 1989 by the State of Florida, attracts snorkelers and divers to the remains of the *San Pedro*. A Spanish galleon wrecked by a hurricane, the *San Pedro* was part of the 1733 Spanish treasure fleet. Twenty-one galleons from the fleet were driven onto Florida's shores. The *San Pedro* went down in 18 feet of water a short time after leaving Havana. Some of the ballast stones have been used in John Pennekamp Coral Reef State Park's Cannon Beach snorkeling area.

Ballast stones are large rocks carried by sailing vessels to provide weight and counterbalance to empty or partially loaded vessels. The stones were discarded as needed when ships took on cargo.

Despite the history of the site, the corals, the schools of colorful tropical fish, and the crustaceans are more fascinating than the ship's remains. A scattering of ballast stones and bricks are all that remain of the 290-ton ship. Replicas of an anchor and cannons have been placed at the site by state archaeologists to enhance the feel of an eighteenth-century shipwreck.

State park rules: To protect the site, visitors are requested to tie-up to the available mooring buoys instead of using an anchor. Spearfishing, fishing, and collection of artifacts and use of metal detectors is prohibited.

**Directions:** Located 1.3 nautical miles offshore of Indian Key, just about due south of MM 76. GPS 24° 51′ 802 N, 080° 401′ 795 W.

**Activities:** Diving, snorkeling, boat trip to remains of eighteenth century Dutch-built treasure ship.

**Facilities:** Underwater nature trail.

**Dates:** Open daily year-round.

**Closest town:** Islamorada is about 3 miles north.

**For more information:** San Pedro Underwater Archaeological Preserve, PO Box 1052, Islamorada, FL 33036. Phone (305) 664-2540.

## LONG KEY STATE RECREATION AREA

[Fig. 4(10)] Imagine sleeping with the Atlantic Ocean right outside your tent flap or RV door, the small waves gently lapping against the shore. In the morning you're greeted by the splash of a skittish mullet, or the whoosh from the wings of a great blue heron flying low along the water's edge. This perfectly located state recreation area has camping sites right on the beach and also offers picnic areas and two nice nature trails.

The Golden Orb Trail is a 1-mile loop trail with a wooden boardwalk that blends into natural paths. The trail crosses mangrove swamps and hammocks with thick forests of gumbo-limbo, West Indian mahogany, Jamaica dogwood (also known as the fish poison tree), and other tropical trees. Plaques explain the natural history. It also skirts the usually tranquil Atlantic shoreline, where egrets, herons, and other wading birds can usually be sighted, especially at low tide in the winter.

The trail is named for the golden orb spider (*Nephilia clavipes*). You can often see this spider's heavy webs from the boardwalk. The large red and gold female will frequently be stationed in the center of the web, on the lookout for unwary insects that fly too close. Males are small and drab and usually die of exhaustion and starvation shortly after mating.

With a rental canoe, you can cruise the tidal lagoons on the self-guided Long Key Lakes Canoe Trail. Snorkelers can see lobster, octopus, and tropical fish in the shallow waters. A creek that runs through the recreation area was named for Zane Grey. The

Western novelist was once the president of the Long Key Fishing Club, which Henry Flagler opened in 1912 with Grey's encouragement. While working on his books, Grey popularized sailfish fishing and, as a dedicated conservationist, sometimes startled his companions by releasing his trophy catches.

The beach is a good place for small children because the water is so shallow. Sixty campsites are shaded by Australian pines. Thirty have RV electrical and water hookups. As in all state parks, half may be reserved no more than 60 days in advance; the rest are first-come, first-served. This is a very popular park in the winter so make reservations early.

**Directions:** MM 67.5 Oceanside.

**Activities:** Hiking, canoeing, camping, swimming, birding, and fishing.

**Facilities:** A short nature trail and a canoe trail, campgrounds, canoe rentals, picnic area.

**Dates:** Open year-round daily until sundown.

**Fees:** There is an admission fee and a charge for camping and canoe rentals.

**Closest town:** Islamorada is 14 miles north of the state park.

**For more information:** Long Key State Recreation Area, PO Box 776, Long Key, FL 33001. Web site www.dep.state.fl.us/parks/LongKey/longkey.html. Phone (305) 664-4815.

### LAYTON NATURE TRAIL

[Fig. 4(9)] Most references to this trail suggest it as a good place to stretch your legs and take a break from driving and watching the scenery slide by. But more than that, this little-known trail is another chance to walk through a thick hammock of tropical trees such as gumbo-limbo, wild coffee, torch, and pigeon plum. The state park has provided interpretive signs along the trail. The trailhead is located about 0.5 mile above the Long Key Bridge, and the trail forms a 0.5-mile loop from the highway to the Gulf of Mexico. At a casual pace you can walk it in about 20 minutes.

**Directions:** MM 66, near the small community of Layton.

**Facilities:** 0.5-mile nature trail.

**Dates:** Open year-round.

**Fees:** None.

**Closest towns:** Marathon and Islamorada.

### LONG KEY BRIDGE

[Fig. 6(1)] Completed in 1907, the original 2.25-mile Long Key Bridge at MM 65.5 is the second longest bridge on the Overseas Highway (after the Seven Mile Bridge). It's certainly the most majestic. Flagler so admired its classical lines and arches, reminiscent of a Roman bridge or aqueduct, he used photographs of passenger trains crossing over it in advertisements touting the railroad's spirit of romance and adventure. It required 186 reinforced arches standing 35 feet high to span the distance between Long Key and Little Conch Key. The bridge's completion in the

# Overseas Heritage Trail

The original Long Key Bridge has been maintained for use as a fishing pier, walking trail, and bicycling path. It's one of seven sections now open of the planned Overseas Heritage Trail, which will stretch from Key Largo to Key West. The seven sections make up the first 17.5 miles of the trail. Eventually 90 miles of trail will be available. Whenever possible, old bridges will be used, and in some cases reconnected, to carry the trail from key to key. The Florida Rails to Trails Conservancy is working with Monroe County to establish the trail.

Initial open sections of the Overseas Heritage Trail include the following:

—Long Key to Conch Key Section. Long Key to Conch Key, 2.3 miles, asphalt.

—Channel 5 Section. Fiesta Key to Craig Key, 1 mile, asphalt.

—Cudjoe Key Section. Cudjoe Key, 2 miles, dirt.

—Lower Matecumbe Section. Lower Matecumbe Key, 4.4 miles, asphalt.

—Marathon Key to Pigeon Key Section. Marathon Key to Pigeon Key, 2.3 miles, asphalt.

—Missouri Key to Ohio Key Section. Missouri Key to Ohio Key, 0.5 mile, asphalt.

—Tom's Harbor Section. Grass Key to Walker's Island, 5 miles, asphalt and dirt.

For more information: Bicycle/Pedestrian Coordinator, Monroe County Planning Department, 2798 Overseas Highway, Marathon, FL 33050. Rails to Trails Conservancy of Florida, 2545 Blairstone Pines Drive, Tallahassee, FL 32301. Phone (850) 942-2379.

wake of difficult construction, engineering problems, and a 1906 hurricane that drowned dozens of workmen gave hope that if these challenges could be overcome, surely the railroad could be built all the way to Key West.

When the bridge was completed, Flagler converted the work camp into the Long Key Fishing Club, a resort for the wealthy who came by train and yacht drawn by the tremendous fishing opportunities. Western novelist Zane Grey was a frequent guest and for awhile served as the club's president. The building was destroyed by the 1935 hurricane that also devastated the railroad.

For 45 years or so, the picturesque arches carried the Overseas Highway across these waters where the Gulf of Mexico meets the Atlantic Ocean. The train rails were converted to guard rails, and the road was paved right on top of the old rail bed.

Replaced by the new highway bridge in 1982, the old bridge still makes a fetching photograph. Turn off the highway to the left, just before driving onto the new bridge. Walk down the embankment and gaze at the weathered old arches against the blue sky and emerald seas.

**Directions:** MM 65.5.

# Middle Keys

*The Middle Keys include Marathon, the "Heart of the Keys."*

| | |
|---|---|
| 1 | Long Key Bridge |
| 2 | Dolphin Research Center |
| 3 | Tropical Crane Point Hammock Museums |
| 4 | Bahia Honda State Recreation Area |

FLORIDA BAY

ATLANTIC OCEAN

HAWK CHANNEL

HAWK CHANNEL

GREAT WHITE HERON NATIONAL WILDLIFE REFUGE

Channel Key
Walkers Island
Conch Keys
Duck Key
Toms Harbor Keys
Long Point Key
Burnt Point
Grassy Key
Crawl Key
Little Crawl Key
Fat Deer Key
Stirrup Key
Russel Key
Sandy Point
Key Colony Beach
Marathon Shores
Tingler Island
Vaca Key
Marathon
Boot Key
931
931
Pigeon Key
Sevenmile Bridge
Molasses Key
Little Duck Key
Missouri Key
Ohio Key
Bahia Honda Key
Spanish Harbor Keys
No Name Key
West Summerland Key
Spanish Harbor
Southeast Point

**Ref: Delorme Florida Atlas and Gazetteer**

# The Middle Florida Keys

T he Middle Keys, as their name implies, are in the middle of the Keys' chain. They
include Conch Key, Duck Key, Grassy Key, Boot Key, Vaca Key, Key Colony Beach,
and Pigeon Key at the north of the Seven Mile Bridge. The entire area is considered part of the unincorporated City of Marathon, which has the geographically truthful
motto, "Heart of the Keys." (For more information on the natural and human history of
the Keys, see the introduction to the Upper Florida Keys, page 27.)

[Fig. 6] Marathon's midway location makes it a convenient base for exploring the rest
of the Keys. No key or attraction is more than an hour's drive away. But with a full realm
of keys-type activities right at your doorstep, you may not want to leave the area.

With 12,000 residents spread along both sides of the Overseas Highway between
MM 50 and 65, Marathon is the third most populous community in the Keys after
Key West and Key Largo. Nevertheless, for all its outwardly urban appearance—large

[ *Above:* Marathon is considered the heart of the Florida Keys ] shopping centers, fast-food outlets, golf courses, a commercial airport next to US 1, motels, restaurants, subdivisions, and busy traffic—it provides every quality experience the Keys can offer.

Marathon also features a selection of self-contained resorts—places that have everything you need for a Keys vacation on the premises. Resorts on the Atlantic side often have fishing piers and white, sandy beaches, while those on the Gulf of Mexico offer marinas with an array of water sports opportunities. Your choice also depends on whether you want to watch the sunrise over the Gulf of Mexico or the sunset over the Atlantic.

The Marathon area was settled more than 500 years ago by Indian tribes. Spanish explorers in the 1500s called it Key Vaca, for the manatees, or sea cows, that were plentiful in this part of the Middle Keys. *Vaca* is the Spanish word for cow. In the eighteenth and early nineteenth centuries, the small islands were a haven for pirates, who used them as a base for plundering merchant vessels in the Atlantic and Gulf of Mexico.

Marathon's modern history began in the early 1900s railroad era, when the area was a central supply depot for construction of the Seven Mile Bridge. Some say the community got its name from a weary construction worker, who griped that building the railroad had become a never-ending marathon.

Perhaps a more plausible source for the name was American playwright and poet Witter Bynner. During an early 1900s yachting trip in the Keys with a Florida East Coast Railroad official, Bynner quoted a passage written by Lord Byron during his idyll in Greece: "The mountains look on Marathon, and Marathon looks on the sea." Lord Byron would have been hard-pressed to conjure any mountains hereabouts, but he'd very likely have been mesmerized by the beauty of the tropical seas.

After the Seven Mile Bridge was completed in 1912, some members of the railroad crew remained as maintenance workers and fishermen. Nowadays, Marathon is a popular year-round sport-

## WEST INDIAN MANATEE
(Trichechus manatus)
Manatees are born underwater, and immediately after birth, the mother brings the calf to the surface and dunks it repeatedly until it can submerge on its own. To nurse, the mother holds the calf against her breast with her flippers.

# Mind Your Manatee Manners

It's estimated that there are about 2,000 sea cows, or West Indian manatees, left in the United States. About 43 percent of the endangered animals die of human-induced causes, many by collisions with boats.

Full-grown manatees reach lengths of 10 feet and weigh about 1,000 pounds. They can be found in fresh, brackish, or salt water, as long as it's above 68 degrees Fahrenheit.

While in the Florida Keys, and especially if you bring your own boat, here are a few things to know about protecting manatees, compliments of the Save the Manatee Club.

—Practice "passive observation" by watching manatees from a distance.

—Obey boating speed limits, especially in designated manatee protection zones.

—Resist the urge to feed manatees or give them water.

—When swimming or diving, look, but don't touch.

—Stash your trash. Discard monofilament line, hooks, and other trash properly.

—If you see an injured, dead, tagged, or orphaned manatee, or if you see a manatee being harassed, Call 1-800-DIAL-FMP (1-800-342-5367), or *FMP from a cellular phone, or VHF Channel 16 on your marine radio. For more information on West Indian manatees, see page 16.

fishing destination for anglers seeking inshore and offshore action. To accommodate any fishing interests, the area boasts a large fleet of charter boats, party boats, and backcountry guides.

Tarpon have become one of the most popular angling attractions both for anglers and spectators. Big silver kings averaging between 50 and 80 pounds are caught in the passes beneath the Seven Mile Bridge, Bahia Honda Bridge, and Long Key Bridge. For a treat, visit the east end of the Seven Mile Bridge one evening. Not only will you enjoy a beautiful sunset, but chances are you'll also see tarpon, drawn by the swirling currents caused by the bridge pilings, feeding and crashing into schools of baitfish in their evening feeding frenzy.

Marathon also offers miles of oceanside flats fishing where bonefish and even the more wily permit are found in the gin-clear waters. In the spring large tarpon invade the flats, creating fantastic sight-fishing opportunities on light-tackle. A number of guides also specialize in backcountry fishing north into Florida Bay and Everglades National Park, all the way to Cape Sable, for redfish, snook, seatrout, and (smaller) tarpon.

Reef fishing near Marathon is similar to other parts of the Keys, with party boats scoring on grouper, snapper, Spanish mackerel, and king mackerel. What the area does boast, however, is a large number of artificial reefs created from dismantled bridges and sunken barges. The deep-water artificial reefs tend to attract greater numbers of amberjack (*Seriola dumerili*) and barracuda, in addition to the regular array of bottom fish.

## Florida Lobster

The Florida lobster, or spiny lobster, unlike its northeastern relative has no claws, but it is just as popular and tasty. You'll find lobster on almost every menu, and maybe on your grill if you're lucky enough to catch one or buy one from a local seafood outlet.

The Keys have a very large commercial lobster industry that sets 500,000 traps in the water every year. Penalties for molesting traps are very stiff.

Sport diving for lobster is also very popular, but pursuing it requires a certain amount of skill and knowledge to locate the lobster and then coax the wily creature from the cracks and crevices of the coral reef. Equipment includes gloves, "tickle sticks," and small nets to entrap the animals.

Regular lobster season for commercial and recreational harvest begins in early August and ends in late March. There is a two-day Sport Lobster Season every July for recreational divers only. The chance to get first shot at the lobsters before the traps are put out draws a huge crowd, filling every hotel, motel, and campground in the Keys.

Lobster harvest regulations are available at most dive shops and where fishing licenses are sold.

The waters on the Gulf of Mexico side of Marathon are much deeper and more open than those of its eastern neighbor Islamorada. A series of natural ledges and artificial reefs extend from the island for 15 miles. Similar to the Atlantic side, bottom fishing is productive for grouper, snapper, and on occasion, cobia.

Marathon also hosts a number of charter boats that specialize in long-range trips out to wreck sites in deep water. The deep-water bottom structure produces large grouper, cobia, mangrove (gray) snapper, and permit. A large freshwater spring known as Blue Hole is found 47 miles into the Gulf of Mexico, where it sits in the bottom of a hole 100 feet deeper than the surrounding bottom. The area supports excellent bottom fishing for grouper and snapper and attracts a large number of tarpon, but the spring is most renowned for offering fishermen the chance to catch giant permit in the 20- to 30-pound range.

The Atlantic side has its own unique attraction. The Marathon West Hump rises from depths of 1,100 feet to a peak 480 feet below the surface. The structure sits squarely in the Gulf Stream, and attracts such targeted game fish as blue and white marlin (*Tetrapturus albidus*), mako shark, blackfin tuna (*Thunnus atlanticus*), and amberjack. Great white sharks weighing more than 1,000 pounds have been caught here in past years.

Diving opportunities are as varied as the fishing in Marathon. Coral reefs abound in the area and are easily accessible to both snorkelers and divers. The most popular destination is Sombrero Reef where towering coral fingers or "spurs" rise up from the 25-foot depths. Known as a "spur and groove" reef system, the grooves are parallel channels of reef.

Sombrero Reef sits about 4 miles offshore (about a 30-minute boat ride out of Marathon) and is marked by the antique Sombrero Reef Light, a tower that straddles some of the more dramatic coral formations. Snorkelers can drift along in the clear water and get a bird's eye view of multihued parrotfish, angelfish, yellowtail snapper, jacks, and clouds of sergeant majors swimming among the red, yellow, and green coral formations and the decorative, branching soft corals and sponges. Divers will be able to peer at eye level into nooks and crannies where lobsters, crabs, and maybe even a grouper will be peering back at them.

Many of the dive shops can provide quick and safe diving courses that will get you out on the reef the same day. They'll also provide snorkeling advice and rental equipment. A vast number of dive and snorkel tours are available from the area's dive shops and resorts. Glass-bottom boats are also available for drier trips to the reefs. They still provide an excellent opportunity to clearly see the reef and its inhabitants.

Between the main line of coral reefs and Marathon's shore are a number of patch reefs too numerous to count. Each patch nurtures its own family of fish, shells, crabs, and corals. Should you meet a reclusive lobster, don't take it home to dinner unless it's in season.

Wreck diving is also popular in the waters surrounding Marathon where there are more than 50 sites to choose from, including sunken Spanish treasure ships and the 189-foot research vessel *Thunderbolt*, which was intentionally sunk in 120 feet of water. With the doors, hatches, and windows removed, divers are free to swim through and explore the five-story ship and see the community of sea life that has been established.

Bird watchers staying in Marathon will be rewarded for exploring even the developed parts of Marathon. Scissor-tailed flycatchers (*Tyrannus forficatus*)

**FLORIDA SPINY LOBSTER** (Panulirus argus)
Spiny lobsters hide in crevices in reefs by day and come out at night to feed. They have no claws, but they have long antennae that produce a rattling or squeaking sound when they are moved up and down. This sound warns other lobsters to stay out of their territory.

# Safe Boating Tips

These tips are provided by the Florida Keys National Marine Sanctuary.

—Avoid areas that appear brown in color. Shallow reef areas and seagrass beds will appear brown. Brown, brown run aground.

—If you run aground immediately turn the engine off. Do not try to motor off. Wait until high tide to remove the vessel. Call for assistance when necessary.

—Fines are imposed for damaging seagrasses and coral by running aground.

—Motor slowly parallel to the reef, in deep water, until a mooring buoy is selected. Turn and idle directly to the buoy without meandering among other boats. Reverse this procedure when motoring to another site.

—When in a dive area, slow down to an idle speed. Make sure your bow is down and the motor or stern is not digging down deep into the water.

—Use extra caution when boating near charter vessels. The concentration of divers off these vessels poses a greater potential for accidents.

—Fishermen, do not troll over or near divers. Stay at least 100 yards from a red and white "diver's down" flag and watch for bubbles.

—Regulations prohibit littering. Do not discard your chum box, fishing line, or other trash into the water.

—Hand feeding of fish is discouraged. Such activity changes the natural behavior and diet of the fish.

—Other rules and regulations apply in various areas of the Florida Keys. Check with the appropriate governing agencies for current regulations.

For more information: Florida Keys National Marine Sanctuary, PO Box 500368, Marathon, FL 33050. Phones: Administration (305) 743-2437, Upper Region (305) 852-7717, Lower Region (305) 292-0311.

and western kingbirds (*Tyrannus verticalis*) can often be seen on the power lines along US 1 in the late fall, winter, and early spring. The section of highway next to the airport can be the most rewarding.

Burrowing owls (*Athene cunicularia*) nest on the fairways of the Sombrero Country Club and on hot days can often be seen in trees along the road next to the course. Turn left at MM 50 onto CR 931. The road passes the country club and ends at Sombrero Beach Park. Burrowing owls also nest in the park.

Black-necked stilts (*Himantopus mexicanus*) and reddish egrets (*Egretta rufescens*) can be seen among other wading birds in the winter around a series of brackish ponds in the Lake Edna area of Grassy Key. You might also spot an American avocet (*Recurvirostra americana*) in the summer. Turn toward the bayside at MM 57.8 on Peachtree Avenue to reach the ponds.

Boot Key near the southern end of Marathon is one of the best spots in the Keys

*Sport-fishing is big business in the Florida Keys. Charter services and fishing guides are available to increase visitors' chances of hooking the catch of a lifetime.*

to see raptors in the fall when the Keys become a bottleneck for migrating birds. Turn toward the Atlantic at MM 48.1 onto CR 931. Peregrine falcons and merlins (*Falco columbarius*) are common in the Australian pines along the road from mid-September into November. In 1995, scientists documented a higher concentration of migrating peregrine falcons here than anywhere else on the Eastern seaboard, except Cape May, New Jersey. American kestrels (*Falco sparverius*), northern harriers (*Circus cyaneus*), sharp-shinned hawks (*Accipiter striatus*), and broad-winged hawks (*Buteo platypterus*) are sometimes reported in large numbers.

A gathering of wading and diving birds that includes brown pelicans, double-crested cormorants, and great white herons can be seen near the east end of the old Seven Mile Bridge. Pull off the road near the end of the old bridge and look back toward the mangroves.

**For more information:** Marathon Chamber of Commerce, 12222 Overseas Highway, Marathon, FL 33050. Phone (800) 262-7284 or (305) 743-5417. MM 53.5 Bayside. The chamber of commerce has a current list of guides, charter boats, dive boat operators, resorts, and motels. Also see Appendix D, page 296 for marina and dive center information. Public boat ramps are located at MM 49 Bayside and MM 54 Bayside. The Marathon Airport has regularly scheduled commercial flights from Miami.

# Marathon

### MARATHON AREA LODGING
### CONCH KEY COTTAGES

MM 62.3 Oceanside. 62250 Overseas Highway, Walkers Island. "Come and stay on our private island in one of our oceanfront cottages," entices the brochure for Conch Key. Like tourist cabins of the 1940s and 1950s, the five, two-bedroom and three, one-bedroom cottages have screened porches, hammocks, pine walls, ceiling fans, full kitchens, air conditioning, and cable TV. The complex also has efficiencies and apartments. Easy access to a quiet beach, dock, fishing charters, private marina and dockage, boat ramp, and heated swimming pool. Conch Key Cottages are off the highway between MM 62 and 63. *Expensive. Web site www.florid-keys.net/conchkeycottages Phone (305) 289-1377, (800) 330-1577. Fax (305) 743-8207.*

### BANANA BAY RESORT AND MARINA

MM 49.5 Bayside, Marathon. The resort and marina stands on the site of the original Marathon Tarpon Lodge, developed in the 1950s, which was a respected name as a world-class sport-fishing club. Ten lush, tropical-landscaped acres shelter this full-service resort with new buildings and thus a new name. A marina on the bay has dock space and sailing tours, including a sunset sail. There's also a sailing school on the property and learn-to-sail package vacations. A Tiki bar on the bay boasts the best place to watch the sunset in Marathon. Tennis courts, restaurant, whirlpool, complete water sports rentals. *Expensive. Web site www.bananabay.com. Phone (800) 226-2621 or (305) 743-3500. Fax (305) 743-2670.*

### FARO BLANCO MARINE RESORT

MM 48 Bayside and Oceanside, Marathon. The white and red four-story faux lighthouse, built in the 1940s, is the centerpiece of a resort complex with facilities on both the Atlantic and the Gulf of Mexico. You can stay in lighthouse apartments, on a houseboat, or in landside condos. Pets may stay with you in houseboats and cottages, but not the condos. Amenities include four restaurants, a freshwater pool, a bar, a diving center, a full-service marina, and a ships store. Kelsey's, the resort's main restaurant, is a relaxed, pleasant room overlooking the marina, with a dressy menu of seafood, beef, duck, and lamb. *Expensive. Phone (305) 743-9018 or (800) 759-3276. Fax (305) 289-7599.*

### HAWK'S CAY RESORT

MM 61 Oceanside, Duck Key. This is the Middle Keys' most deluxe and all-encompassing resort complex, and it's on its own 60-acre tropical island. Just name it, and it's a few steps from your deluxe guest room, suite, or two-bedroom villa. The choices include a lagoon, pools, tennis, access to a nearby golf course, deep sea and backcountry fishing, diving, Jet Skiing, children's programs, parasailing, glass bottom boat and snorkeling trips, sunset cruises, a 110-slip marina and dive shop, an array of dining from casual to dress-up, bars, and nightclubs. The resort also has its own dolphin encounter programs. Casual,

yet elegant. *Very expensive.*
*Phone (305) 743-7000 or*
*(800) 432- 2242. Fax (305)*
*743-0641. Web site*
*www.hawkscay.com*

**RAINBOW BEND
FISHING RESORT**

MM 58 Oceanside,
Marathon. This small,
intimate resort complex is
4 miles north of Mara-
thon with a private beach,
dock, pool, and spa. There
is a bait and tackle shop
and you can arrange boat
charters and tours and
diving trips. Guests in
suites and efficiencies
have free use of motor
boats, kayaks, spyaks,
paddleboats, and sail-
boats, as well as compli-
mentary full breakfast
daily. The Hideaway
Restaurant includes an
open-air second-floor area
overlooking the beach, and
is surprisingly upscale.
Entrees include seafood,

# Conched Out

The conch in the conch chowder and fritters you get
in the Keys probably came from South America, Jamaica,
or the Bahamas. The queen conch was once heavily
harvested in waters around the Keys. In 1965, 250,000
conchs were brought into Key West alone.

Today only a small, protected fraction of the once
plentiful mollusks remains in local waters. Commercial
harvest was stopped in 1975, and recreational harvest was
outlawed in 1986. The depletion of the species was as
much a result of its shell as for the meat that is so popular
in local recipes. The pink and white shells were used for
roadbeds, as a building material, and as a very beautiful
souvenir to sell to tourists.

By 1991, it was apparent that conchs were not
recovering and a state-run hatchery was opened on Long
Pine Key. The scientists are raising and releasing baby
conchs and then following their progress in the wild. So
far, 6,000 of the young mollusks have been released.
Scientists are also experimenting with moving them into
deeper waters away from predators, to allow for natural
reproduction and re-seeding in the waters.

If you see a conch shell, don't pick it up. Even one
animal is important in repopulating the species. Under
state law it's illegal to collect or even disturb queen
conchs.

duck, prime rib, and steaks. *Very expensive. Phone (305) 289-1505 or (800) 929-1505.*
*Fax (305) 743-0257.*

**SEASCAPE OCEAN RESORT**

MM 52 Oceanside, Marathon. Former New England professional photographer
Bill Stites and his wife Sara, an artist, are hosts of this casually elegant small resort
located in a quiet residential neighborhood off the Overseas Highway near the
Marathon Airport. Bright, cheerful guest rooms are decorated with Sara's artwork.
Some rooms have kitchenettes. Facilities include a freshwater pool, deep-water
marina, walled garden with tropical plants and herbs, complimentary afternoon wine
and hors d'oeuvres, and an elaborate continental breakfast buffet. Snorkeling and
kayaking to a nearby bird rookery is also available. *Expensive. Phone (305) 743-6455,*
*(800) 332-7327. Fax (305) 743-8469. Web site www.floridakeys.net/seascape*

### MARATHON AREA DINING
#### BARRACUDA GRILL
MM 49.5, Marathon. If your idea of Keys dining is a shacky place hung over the water, with nets, beer signs, stuffed fish, and photos of grinning anglers and their catches on the walls, the Barracuda Grill definitely is not it. With its minimalist interior, stark white walls, unobtrusive art, functional little bar, and eclectic menu, this small, urbane room could as well be in Key West's Old Town or Miami's Coconut Grove instead of the Marathon strip. The varied appetizer selections include tuna sashimi, conch cakes, and "painfully hot" columnar (take home a bottle of the house Barracuda Bite Hot Sauce for masochistic friends who brag that no sauce yet devised by man is too hot for them). Entrees include dolphin, black grouper, grilled yellowfin tuna, rack of lamb, and grilled beef tenderloin. Dinner Monday through Saturday. *Expensive. Phone (305) 743-3314.*

#### THE CRACKED CONCH
MM 49.5, Marathon. Next door to the Barracuda Grill, but worlds apart in style, this is perhaps the casual "typical Keys" place you're looking for, especially if you crave conch. The restaurant's namesake is prepared fried, frittered, stewed, and other basic ways. Other choices include grouper, yellowfin tuna, steak, and chicken. *Moderate. Phone (305) 743-2233.*

#### HERBIES
MM 50.5, Marathon. This may be the most traditional Keys restaurant you dine at, popular with locals and visitors alike. Longtime visitors to the Keys won't remember a time when Herbies wasn't here. A basic facility with a counter and screened dining area, air conditioning was only recently added to a portion of the restaurant. Try the homemade fish and conch chowders, cracked conch, and conch or lobster fritters. No checks or credit cards. *Inexpensive. Phone (305) 743-6373.*

#### PANDA HOUSE CHINESE RESTAURANT
MM 50, Marathon. If you're ready for a temporary break from a constant seafood diet, the Panda has a basic, but pretty well-prepared selection of Hunan, Szechuan, and Cantonese standards for dining in and carting out. *Inexpensive. Phone (305) 743-3417.*

### DOLPHIN RESEARCH CENTER
[Fig. 6(2)] This multifaceted complex on Grassy Key offers visitors another opportunity for an encounter with intelligent, social, often playful bottle-nosed dolphins. Many will remember the TV show *Flipper*, which originated from this facility.

The Dolphin Encounter is a 2.5-hour educational program that begins with an orientation session about the dolphins and what to expect when you're in the water together. That's followed by a 20-minute structured swim in a pool and a nonstructured session in the Gulf of Mexico. Children must be at least 5 years old and those under age 13 must be accompanied by a participating adult.

Those who would rather watch and not get into the water can take an Educational Walking Tour, where they can observe training sessions and research and look in on Dolphin Encounter swimming sessions. Serious students can sign up for two in-depth programs. DolphinLab is a week-long course that includes seminars and a variety of observational and hands-on activities, as well as swim sessions, training sessions, and food preparation. The minimum age is 18, although students 15 to 17 may participate in offered youth sessions.

DolphinInsight is a three-hour program. Aimed at anyone who has ever wondered what it might be like to be a dolphin trainer, it includes instruction on dolphin physiology and echolocation (dolphins' biological sonar that lets them find food and other objects by sending out sound waves that are reflected back to them). "Gradua-tion" is a hands-on chance to communicate directly with dolphins with verbal and hand signals. Recommended for those at least 12 years old.

**Directions:** MM 59 Bayside of the Overseas Highway.

**Activities:** Swimming with dolphins, attending seminars about dolphins.

**Facilities:** Orientation area, pools and Gulf of Mexico lagoons for dolphin encounters, seminar classrooms, treatment center for burned-out performing dolphins and injured manatees.

**Dates:** Open daily, except holidays.

**Fees:** There is a charge for all activities and reservations are required.

**Closest town:** Marathon.

**For more information:** PO Box 522875, Marathon Shores, FL 33052. Web site www.dolphins.org Phone (305) 289-1121 or (305) 289-0002.

## TROPICAL CRANE POINT HAMMOCK MUSEUMS

[Fig. 6(3)] The Museums of Tropical Crane Point Hammock are located in a 64-acre hardwood hammock, parts of which have been largely untouched by human hands. This beautiful forest, known as Tropical Crane Point Hammock, is the home of the Museum of Natural History, the Florida Keys Children's Museum, the Adder-ley Village Historic Site, and an extensive system of trails that lead to a spectacular view of Florida Bay.

This one stop will provide you with a complete background in the cultural and natural history of the Florida Keys. There's a display of replica artifacts such as masks and art pieces from the Frank Cushing archeological dig in 1896 on Marco Island that reveals the rich maritime culture of the Calusa Indians.

The Calusa story is told from early occupation in the Keys, through European contact, to a time in 1763 when, after thousands of years, the last 80 or so families of Calusa Indians left Florida forever. Key Vaca (Marathon) and Key West were the sites of their final settlements.

You'll learn the story of Hernando d'Escalante Fontaneada, a 13-year-old Spanish crew member who survived a shipwreck off the Keys and was raised by Calusa Indians for 17 years. His memoirs stand as one of the most descriptive sources of information on the Indians of the Florida Keys.

There are also displays of artifacts like shell hammers and paleo points from peoples that preceded the Calusa Indians. These people arrived in the Keys around 3,000 B.C. but left very little record. There's also a walk-through replica of a coral reef where you walk along the ocean floor and look at reproductions of reef inhabitants while a tape explains the coral reef system. Dioramas display wildlife of the Everglades backcountry and many Keys habitats.

There is a beautiful display of sea turtle shells and the skull of a mink whale that was stranded on No-Name Key in 1979. But the most intriguing item is the skull of a pygmy sperm whale that still has the tip of a swordfish bill buried in it that apparently was the cause of its death. It was found washed up on a beach in 1992.

Outside the Museum of Natural History, a short walkway to the Children's Museum passes an iguana display and crosses a 15,000-gallon saltwater Tropical Lagoon containing varieties of local reef fish. The backdrop for the lagoon is an incredible mural by the famous environmental artist, Wyland. The wall is #27 in a series of 100 murals Wyland has pledged to complete to increase awareness of whales and marine life. There's also a supervised marine life introduction tank that allows children to touch harmless marine animals.

The small Children's Museum building is a Flagler-era cottage moved to the site in 1992. For a smaller kid there's an interactive pirate vessel, *Los Ninos de Los Cayos*, complete with cannon, wheel, skeletons, and treasure. There's even a chest of pirate clothes for the kids to dress up in. One of the largest shell collections on public display is also on exhibit.

Once the inside touring is over, the site offers a system of short nature trails that wind through the hardwood hammock and end at a fantastic view of Florida Bay. Check to be sure that you have insect repellant before heading out. You may also wish to carry water and a snack.

While in the hammock, watch for endangered white-crowned pigeons, which resemble domestic pigeons but have distinct white crowns and longer tails. They eat the fruit from many of the hammock plants, including pigeon plum and poison-wood.

You might also see white ibis, little green herons, little blue herons, black-whiskered vireos, American kestrels, broad-winged hawks, a Florida box turtle (*Terrapene carolina*), mangrove cuckoos, raccoons, Florida tree snails, mangrove skippers (*Phocides pigmallon*), and even an occasional alligator around the pond.

Also watch for the peeling red bark of a gumbo limbo tree, and the barbed-wire cactus, which has climbing branches that can reach 15 feet and produces a white and yellow flower that only blooms at night. Look also look for Spanish stopper, a small evergreen plant that can grow as a shrub or a tree and has dark-colored fruit favored by many of the hammock's birds. All three plants are native to South Florida, the Florida Keys, and the West Indies.

This bayside property in the heart of Marathon was purchased by Francis and Mary Crane, who came to the Keys from Massachusetts in the late 1940s. Dedicated conservationists, the Cranes carefully built their own home in a way that preserved the tropical hammock. Today the land is owned by the Florida Keys Land and Sea Trust, a nonprofit, private conservation organization.

Another site along the trail is an important part of the property—an early 1900s Bahamas House.

## Coral Spawning

Every summer around the August full moon, a remarkable and little understood phenomenon takes place on the coral reefs. All at one time, a number of species of branching and stony corals spawn, filling the waters with tiny round eggs and a cloud of sperm. Although generally asexual in their reproduction, meaning that during the year they simply divide into exact genetic replicas, the corals have apparently set aside this one night of the year for sexual reproduction.

The fact that corals even had such a night life wasn't discovered until the 1980s in Australia. It was first documented in North America in 1990 at the Flower Gardens National Marine Sanctuary in the Gulf of Mexico. Since then, the spectacle has been observed at reefs throughout the Keys, and has even become a well-attended event. Apparently other species take a cue from the coral because sponges, brittle stars, gorgonians, and Christmas tree worms are known to spawn at the same time.

Dive shops throughout the Keys offer night dive trips to observe the coral spawn. Although the activity is geared around the August full moon, it can vary according to the reef and the species.

Elkhorn and staghorn branching corals tend to spawn with the full moon while star corals spawn eight days later.

The Adderley Village Historical Site protects the location of a small settlement created by Bahamian immigrants in 1903. For a while, the village was the home of about 20 families.

The Adderley house, built by George Adderley, is the only structure remaining. The walls were constructed of tabby, a concretelike material consisting mainly of ground conch shells, which was used frequently for building by early Bahamian settlers in the Keys. It's believed to be one of the oldest houses in the Keys and has been placed on the National Register of Historic Places.

The simple white house with blue shutters stands as a somewhat incongruous structure surrounded by the junglelike vegetation. But it's also easy to imagine busy family members, tending to their garden and livestock in between fishing and hunting and gathering wild foods.

Past the Adderley house, the nature trail winds along beautiful Florida Bay. Dark blue waters close to shore are bordered by a deeper green band offshore. White buoys reveal the location of crab traps. Also on the trail is the Marathon Wild Bird Rescue, where visitors can observe injured birds in their rehabilitation environment.

The trail ends where a short bridge crosses the opening to a small saltwater lagoon that's full of sea life. This is one of the places you'll need a pair of polarized sunglasses to see all the life beneath the surface.

A maroon-colored nurse shark swims slowly by. In the clear water you can see crabs, sea anemones, schools of baitfish, and small groups of blue and red parrotfish. In the clear water flowing underneath the bridge look for nearly motionless mangrove snapper.

The longer you stay the more you'll see. It's a gorgeous spot—a great place to sit for awhile, have a snack, and just take in the scene. In addition to the lagoon, the peaceful surroundings present a panoramic view of Florida Bay and a number of small mangrove islands. But be careful, time (which is a tenuous thing in the Keys anyway) may seem to actually stop while you're there.

**Directions:** MM 50.5 Bayside in Marathon.

**Activities:** Hiking, educational programs.

**Facilities:** Gift shop, nature trail, displays.

**Dates:** Open daily year-round. Hours vary seasonally.

**Fees:** One admission charge gives access to both museums, seasonal presentations, and trail system.

**Closest town:** Marathon.

**For more information:** Tropical Crane Point Hammock, 5550 Overseas Highway, Marathon, FL 33050. Phone (305) 743-9100. Fax (305) 743-0429.

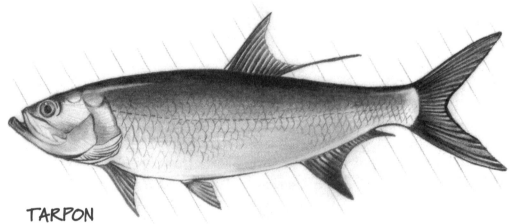

## TARPON
(Megalops atlantica)
The bullish tarpon, which usually weighs less than 50 pounds but may weigh as much as 300, ranks high as a game fish because of it's fast runs and twisting leaps when its hooked.

## PIGEON KEY

[Fig. 6] Pigeon Key, a historical visitor site, is a 5-acre island that lies between the new Seven Mile Bridge and the old Seven Mile Bridge. The old bridge connects to Pigeon Key by way of a short ramp that turns off the bridge 2 miles from the mainland. The new bridge bypasses the little island but does provide a scenic view of swaying palm trees and historic buildings.

The small island teemed with activity between 1908 and 1912, when it was the construction camp for the original railroad bridge. At the island's peak of activity, more than 400 workers lived in hastily constructed bunkhouse buildings and tent communities.

When the bridge was completed, the buildings were taken down and used elsewhere on the line. A more permanent village that appeared much as it does today was built between 1912 and 1920 to house bridge tenders and maintenance workers. When the railroad was converted into a highway, the turn down the ramp onto Pigeon Key was the only break in the guardrail of the Seven Mile bridge.

The Pigeon Key Foundation, based in Marathon, is restoring and maintaining about a dozen buildings as part of the Pigeon Key National Historic District. A motorized tram takes visitors over the old bridge to the village from the visitor center on Knights Key (MM 48 Oceanside) about every hour. You're also free to walk, roller skate, roller blade, or ride your bike, but no auto traffic is allowed on the old bridge. It's 2 miles out to Pigeon Key from the visitor center.

On the island, volunteer guides are sometimes on hand to lead tours, but more often, visitors enjoy self-guided exploration. The tram lets passengers off at the Old Section Gang Quarters. One of two remaining buildings from the 1908 to 1912 era, the Section Gang Quarters became a dormitory and dining hall for maintenance workers after 1912. A video tells Flagler's rags-to-riches story and the history of the railroad. The building's 1,800-square-foot former dining hall is now a meeting room for young people taking part in environmental workshops offered by the Pigeon Key Foundation.

The Assistant Bridge Tender's House houses the Pigeon Key Museum. Many of the artifacts on display were retrieved from the trash and garbage thrown into the water during the bridge construction.

The Bridge Tender's House is said by some to be haunted by the wife of the bridge tender. She was reportedly having an affair with an assistant bridge tender—an almost risk-free matter in those days because husbands traveled to work over the railroad trestle in noisy gasoline-powered handcars that could be easily heard in plenty of time for all parties to return to their proper places.

All the same, the lady in question was apparently so guilt-ridden she committed suicide by hanging herself from a rafter on the second floor of the house. Her weeping and wailing spirit is reportedly heard by students using the house as a dormitory.

The Mote Marine Laboratory (off-limits to visitors), a yellow house with an

## Bird Protection Tips

—Slow down if you see a bird standing in or near a road.

—Don't feed wild birds filleted fish carcasses. The sharp, exposed bones get caught on pouches or in throats and it's impossible for the bird to shake them loose or swallow them. If swallowed, the sharp bones can fatally puncture the bird's stomach and vital organs.

—Properly dispose of fish hooks, fishing line, plastic six-pack holders, plastic bags, and other trash.

—Pick up and properly dispose of any trash you see in the water, on the beach, and on roadsides.

adjacent covered area of white tanks, is conducting research with live coral for possible use in bone transplants and artificial eyes and as possible cures for cancer, arthritis, and other diseases.

Researchers say replacing damaged and diseased bones with coral seems particularly promising as an alternative to taking pieces of a patient's hip bone. In Europe, the skeletons of certain species of coral have been used successfully. Pharmaceutical companies in the United States have begun the same procedures used in Europe.

The Negro Quarters formerly housed cooks and other black workers. Now a dormitory for educational programs, the small house is one of the southernmost points on the National Black Heritage Trail.

While walking the grounds, stop and look up under the old Seven Mile Bridge. The blue metal spans are part of the original railroad bridge built nearly 100 years old. As trains slowly crossed the narrow bridge, passengers could have imagined themselves floating on air when they looked down and saw nothing but blue-green water far below them.

**Directions:** Visitors can see the island on guided and self-guided tours that begin at the Pigeon Key Visitor Center located in a red and silver railroad car on the Overseas Highway at Knights Key, MM 47. Books about Pigeon Key's role in the construction of the railroad are on sale.

**Activities:** Historical tour.

**Dates:** Open daily year-round. The tram is closed on Mondays during the summer.

**Fees:** There is a charge for the tram ride and the village tour.

**Closest town:** Marathon is 2 miles to the north.

**For more information:** Dave Whitney, Executive Director, Pigeon Key Foundation, PO Box 500130, Marathon, FL 33050. Phone (305) 289-0025. Pigeon Key Visitor Center, phone (305) 743-5999. Education Center, phone (305) 289-9632. Web site www.pigeonkey.org

## THE SEVEN MILE BRIDGE

[Fig. 6] If you saw the 1990s movie *True Lies*, you'll recognize the Seven Mile Bridge as the site of the climatic scene where Jamie Lee Curtis is pulled from a runaway limousine, and the bad guys are blown up with missiles launched from British Harriers. Actually, Arnold Schwarzenegger and company didn't really blow up the Seven Mile Bridge. If the catastrophic Labor Day hurricane of 1935 couldn't destroy it, the bridge can withstand a few computer-generated missile strikes as well.

Including its approaches, the largest segmented bridge in the world spans 9 miles from Knights Key to Bahia Honda Channel. The views of the Atlantic Ocean and Gulf of Mexico on either side are so beguiling, you may be tempted to stop and take a picture. Please don't.

Henry Flagler was already 75 years old when preliminary construction began in 1906 on this incredible engineering feat that would giant-step his railroad toward Key West. The project was divided into four parts. The first three segments were constructed of steel-girder sections anchored on top of 550 concrete foundation piers connected to bedrock nearly 30 feet underwater. The fourth segment, a swinging 255-foot-long span, enabled boat traffic to pass unhindered between the Atlantic and the Gulf of Mexico.

Flagler's engineers intended the bridge to withstand anything that nature could throw at it. Devastating hurricanes in 1906 and 1909 took a terrible toll of human life and wiped out part of the ongoing work. But despite the setbacks, and the problems with plagues of mosquitoes, fever, heat, and drought, the work proceeded.

Five years after the first pilings were laid, the Seven Mile Bridge—the costliest in the system—was opened to the first trains. The "Railroad That Went to Sea" finally reached Key West in January 1912.

In 1936, a year after final rites were said over "The Railroad that Died at Sea," the State of Florida began converting the defunct railway into the Overseas Highway. I-beams widened the bridge from 14 feet to 22 feet and many of the old iron tracks were put back to use as highway guardrails. The revamped bridge stayed in service until 1982, when a higher, wider, more modern bridge was opened.

The 65-foot-high span over Moser Channel is one of the finest scenic views in the Keys for everyone but the driver. Like many other Keys bridges, the old bridge has been put to use as a fishing pier and recreational trail.

Here's a way to get a good look at the scenery on the bridge. Every April over 1,000 runners participate in the Seven Mile Bridge Run on the new bridge. Entries are limited and US 1 is closed for the event. For more information on the run call (305) 743-8513.

**Directions:** MM 47 through 40.
**Activities:** Fishing, hiking, biking, walking on old bridge.
**Dates:** Open year-round.
**Fees:** None.
**Closest town:** Marathon is 2 miles north of Knights Key.

# Lower Keys

*The Lower Keys are home to the endangered Key Deer.*

Ref: Delorme Florida Atlas and Gazetteer

| 1 | Looe Key Marine Sanctuary |
| 2 | The Bat Tower |
| 3 | Key West Botanical Gardens |
| | National Key Deer Refuge |
| | Great White Heron NWR |
| | Key West NWR |

# The Lower Florida Keys

T he Lower Keys begin at the end of the Seven Mile Bridge and include Little Duck Key, Big Pine Key, the Torch Keys, Bahia Honda Key, Cudjoe Key, Sugarloaf Key, Summerland Key, the Saddlebunch Keys, Big Coppitt Key, Stock Island, and Key West. Highlights of the Lower Keys [Fig. 7] include some of the finest beaches in the world, great diving and fishing opportunities and a chance to see wild miniature deer. (For more information on the natural and human history of the Keys, see the introduction to the Upper Florida Keys, page 27.)

The Lower Keys were sparsely settled in the mid-1800s. The few who stayed in this isolated land made their living from making charcoal, fishing, farming, and sponging. By comparison, Key West at that time had 18,000 residents and was the largest city in Florida.

When Flagler's railroad came through in 1912, the isolation was over and for the

[ *Above:* No trip to the Lower Keys is complete without viewing a sunset from Mallory Square in Key West ]

next 23 years, trains ran daily through the lower Keys on the way to and from Key West. When the railroad was destroyed in 1935, the Overseas Highway kept the link open. Even today, however, the Lower Keys population, minus that of Key West, is around 16,500. The population of Key West is about 25,000.

One interesting sight you'll pass is the Flagler Bridge off the southern peninsula of Bahia Honda at MM 36. From the highway, look over at the top of the old trestle-type railroad bridge to the south. When the Overseas Highway was constructed, the railbed of the bridge wasn't wide enough for a highway, so the designers reinforced the superstructure and ran the road right across the top, high over the railroad track.

# Bahia Honda Key and State Park

[Fig. 6(4)] Bahia Honda rivals John Pennekamp as the Keys' most outstanding state park. Granted, the 524-acre park, which includes the entire Bahia Honda Key, can't match John Pennekamp's coral reefs, but its beaches are without challenge, the overwhelming choice as the best in the Keys. In fact, they are among the finest anywhere in Florida and regularly rank among the best in the nation. This could well be the most beautiful beach you'll ever see—long, luxurious white strands of soft, sugary sands bordered by clear, blue-green waters and fringed with tall, graceful, swaying palms—and there's one on each side of the island.

Crystal-clear and deep close to shore, the Gulf of Mexico and Atlantic waters on both sides of this tropical island are ideal for swimming and snorkeling for the thousands of visitors who pass through the park's gates on peak days. Snorkeling off the beach in the shallow waters where the seagrass grows you'll encounter a rich and colorful variety of marine life.

The grass beds are home to shrimp, crabs, and a myriad of small fish. You might see a hermit crab creeping along beneath its borrowed shell, or sea anemones anchored in place waving their tentacles in the current. A small octopus might swim by, or you may spot a live queen conch nestled in the grass. But don't touch, conchs are protected, as is all the marine life within the park.

The island was formed from Key Largo Limestone derived from a coral reef similar to the living reefs elsewhere in the Keys. Along with other Keys, the island emerged after a dramatic drop in the sea level millions of years ago. Its rock foundation has been overlaid with a thick cover of loose carbonate sands.

In the early 1900s, when Henry Flagler's Florida East Coast Railroad crews were digging the foundations for the original Bahia Honda Bridge, it took them week after week of arduous, frustrating labor to finally hit bedrock. The 5,005-foot long bridge was damaged by hurricanes, but like the Seven Mile Bridge and others on the line, it stood up valiantly to nature's fury, including the 1935 Labor Day hurricane. The bridge was refashioned for the Overseas Highway in the late 1930s.

## Hurricane Georges

When Hurricane Georges passed over Key West in September of 1998, it changed the landscape of the Lower Keys. The farther you travel along the string of islands towards Key West, the more evident the damage caused by the storm becomes. You'll see trees leaning in one direction with their tops missing, yards with little or no landscaping, and campgrounds with a lack of shade.

Many Keys residents lost their homes to wind or flooding. Many houses suffered severe roof damage. Electricity was out for weeks. State parks and recreation areas were closed for months.

Although hurricanes are part of the natural environment and the damage they cause to flora and fauna of the islands in seldom permanent, it still can take years to recover. On land, acres and acres of mangroves and tropical hammock trees were knocked down by Georges. On the reefs, some large structures were pushed over and branching corals were heavily damaged in some areas. Before and after photos of patches of elk-horn corals show a pile of rubble where a beautiful branching garden once stood.

Volunteers with the nonprofit reef protection organization, Reef Relief, have been righting, stabilizing, and reattaching hundreds and hundreds of living coral formations throughout the Lower Keys.

The old bridge, with two sections removed from the ends, is part of the view of the beaches. In the 1980s, it was mothballed for a modern four-lane bridge that now carries US 1. You can walk out on a portion of the old bridge for panoramic views of the Gulf of Mexico and Atlantic.

In Spanish, *Bahia Honda* means "deep bay," and the channel between the new and old Bahia Honda bridges is one of the deepest natural channels in the Keys. In some places it goes down 35 to 40 feet.

Bahia Honda State Park is also a botanical treasure. Since the late nineteenth century, botanists from around the world have traveled here to study its remarkable plant life. Many of the plants found were carried from the West Indies and Caribbean by birds, winds, sea tides, and hurricanes.

The park's Silver Palm Nature Trail passes through one of the state's last remaining stands of silver palms (*Coccothrinax argentata*). Also known as silver thatch palm, the graceful tree grows to 20 to 35 feet high, with a slender trunk about 6 inches in circumference and smooth, fan-shaped fronds about 3 inches long. Also look for gumbo limbo, satinwood (*Zanthoxylum flavum*), and seagrape (*Coccoloba uvifera*). Specimens of silver palm and yellow satinwood have been certified as national champion trees.

Many bird ranges overlap or reach their farthest ranges here. Roseate spoonbills, white-crowned pigeons, great egrets, great blue herons, great white herons, white ibis, laughing gulls (*Larus atricilla*), brown pelicans, and smooth-billed anis can be observed most of the year. Watch along the shoreline for ruddy turnstones, willits, short-billed dowitchers (*Limnodromus griseus*), and semipalmated plovers. In the winter, ring-billed gulls (*Larus delawarnensis*), common terns (*Sterna hirundo*), and royal terns join the party.

Migratory warblers visit in April and October on their way between North American and South America. Black-whiskered vireos and mangrove cuckoo can be seen in the tropical vegetation in the summer and fall.

While walking along the beach, which is always an enjoyable thing to do, look for moving, shadowy schools of black mullet (*Mugil cephalus*) or silver mullet (*Mugil cephalus*) in the shallow areas. Black mullet are dark on top and light on the bottom. Silver mullet are light colored all over. You can also see both species jumping into the air, sometimes two or three times in a row, in an attempt to elude a real or imagined predator. In fact, anytime you see a small fish jumping in Florida's nearshore or inshore waters, first think mullet, because that's probably what it is.

One of Florida's most important inshore forage fish, mullet is a source of protein for a wide range of game fish including tarpon and snook. Mullet also make up a good deal of the diet of brown pelicans and osprey.

Mullet roe is prized as a delicacy in the Far East. Long years of overharvest of spawning mullet to supply that market led to a depletion of the species throughout Florida. A net ban passed in 1994 by statewide vote eliminated the use of gill nets in Florida, which in turn reduced the harvest of mullet. The species is on the comeback in all parts of the state.

Along with beaches and nature trails, the park has numerous other facilities you can learn about at the visitor center. There is a snack bar and book and gift shop. The observation deck on the bridge offers dramatic views of the park, the water, and neighboring Keys.

The park's concessionaire has snorkeling gear for rent and offers daily snorkeling trips to Looe Key National Marine Sanctuary (*see* page 106). You can also rent sea kayaks. The park also has a 19-slip marina and two ramps for trailered boats.

**Directions:** MM 36.9 Oceanside.

**Activities:** Swimming, sunbathing, fishing, boating, camping, bird-watching, snorkeling and diving, kayaking, parasailing, and hiking.

**Facilities:** Campsites, furnished cottages, picnic areas, educational center, marina, boat ramps, nature trails, beaches.

**Dates:** Open daily year-round.

**Fees:** There is a charge for park admission, campgrounds, cabins, and most activities.

**Closest town:** Big Pine Key is 6 miles to the south on the Overseas Highway.

**For more information:** Bahia Honda State Park, 36850 Overseas Highway, Big Pine Key, FL 33043. Phone (305) 872-2353.

### LODGING ON BAHIA HONDA

The state park maintains six very nice waterfront cabins, each with two double beds and two bunk beds. Dishes, cookware, towels, and bed linens are provided. The cabins are accessible by boat. Guests must stay at least two nights, but may stay no longer than two weeks. Moderate rates are highest in winter and spring, lowest in summer and fall. Limit six persons per cabin. Phone (305) 872-2353.

### CAMPING ON BAHIA HONDA

Like the beaches, Bahia Honda's 80 campsites are the class of the Keys. There are well-spaced, well-kept, scenic bayside and oceanside locations that are less expensive than many commercial campgrounds. There are showers and restrooms. All the sites may be reserved up to 11 months in advance. Those not reserved are first-come, first-served.

# Big Pine Key

[Fig. 7] Big Pine Key, 8 miles long and 2 miles wide, with about 6,000 acres, is second in size only to Key Largo. Pinelands cover much of the island, except for pockets of hardwood hammocks and a fringe of mangroves. The island is the center of a cluster of smaller keys that include Ramrod, Summerland, Big and Little Torch, No Name, and Newfound Harbor keys.

Big Pine has resorts, restaurants, and rental homes (some with boat access). Looe Key Marine Sanctuary, just 5 miles offshore, is the most poplar dive spot in the Lower Keys, and the Key Deer National Wildlife Refuge protects one of America's most unusual mammals, the tiny Key deer.

Approaching Big Pine Key, roadside signs ask you to slow down to help protect the Key deer. Many of these very endangered animals are hit by automobiles every year. The speed limit is 45 mph daytime and 35 mph at night on US 1, and usually 35 mph or lower on the back roads. You risk a stiff fine for speeding. The local police and the Florida Fish and Wildlife Conservation Commission go to great lengths to enforce the law and protect the deer.

When you first come onto Big Pine Key take a left at Long Beach Drive. On your left is the Big Pine Key Fishing Lodge and Campground. Inside the lodge on the counter, the proprietors have assembled an interesting scrapbook of photos and articles about Hurricane Georges, including some shots taken of the rising water during the storm.

Continuing on Long Beach Drive you'll pass a number of small salt ponds that often hold wading birds, including roseate spoonbills and a variety of herons. As you drive out Long Beach Road you'll notice hurricane damage to the vegetation. Many of the trees that weren't uprooted now lean in one direction.

Salt ponds, scattered throughout the Lower Keys and surrounded by mangroves, attract a variety of birds. Many salt ponds and even some freshwater ponds can be discovered by simply following the few side roads on the narrow island. Great blue herons, great white herons, and ducks in winter use these ponds. Both immature (white phase) and mature reddish egrets can also be spotted stalking small fish by raising their wings and casting a shadow on the water that makes it easier for them to see their prey.

**Activities:** Camping, hiking, scenic drives, boating, diving, snorkeling, fishing, cycling, kayaking, bird-watching.

**For more information:** Big Pine Key Fishing Lodge, PO Box 430513, Big Pine Key, FL 33043. Phone (305) 872-2351.

# Key Deer National Wildlife Refuge

[Fig. 7] A developed trail through pine rockland forest in the lower Keys, and a chance to see one of nature's wonders, the tiny Key deer, are the reasons most visitors head for the Key Deer National Wildlife Refuge.

The refuge encompasses about 8,000 acres on Big Pine Key, No Name Key, other lower Keys, and some smaller outer islands. Many of the parcels on Big Pine are separated by wide tracts of land in private ownership. The refuge's main goal is the protection of the endangered Key deer by seeking ways to increase and stabilize its numbers.

A subspecies of Virginia white-tailed deer, Key deer are the smallest of all white-tailed deer. With a shoulder height between 24-32 inches, Key deer are about the size of a German shepherd. Females weigh 45 to 60 pounds, bucks 55 to 80 pounds.

Key deer mate between September and December. Gestation is 204 days and fawns are about the size of a house cat. Generally born between April and May, they weigh between 2 to 4 pounds. Females reproduce after two years. First-time mothers usually give birth to a single fawn and after that occasionally more than one. Males rarely take part in breeding after their third year. Even under the best of circumstances, males and females rarely live beyond eight years.

The upper part of the deer's body is light reddish brown. The underside is white, as is the underside of its tail. Faces have a dark, V-shaped marking.

Believed to be originally about the same size as other North American white-tailed deer, the Key deer probably migrated to this area from the Florida mainland tens of thousands of years ago, when what is now Florida Bay and the Keys were dry land. As the earth warmed, seas rose creating Florida Bay and a chain of small islands.

Isolated from the mainland, with limited food sources, smaller deer survived, while the larger deer perished. The deer adapted to their environment and reached

# How to Drive "Deerfensively"

One big danger facing the endangered Key deer is getting hit by a car. When driving on Big Pine Key, following a few simple rules will help you be part of the answer, not the problem.

1. Obey the speed limit.

2. Be alert for deer on the sides of the road.

3. Be aware of color. Key deer are a light brown that blends into the roadside vegetation.

4. Buckle up. Put young children in car seats and secure your packages. Be prepared to brake without worrying about your passengers or packages.

5. If you see a deer crossing the road, look for another. They tend to travel in pairs or groups.

6. When a deer in the road acts erratically, slow down and stop. Turn on your hazard lights to warn surrounding cars of a dangerous situation. Wait for the deer to cross the road safely.

7. If you see a deer and want a photo, slow down, use your turn signal, be aware of cars around you, and pull off the road.

8. Be extra careful from May to July. Fawns, yearlings, and does are moving.

9. Be extra careful from October to December. Bucks are moving and the breeding season is under way.

10. If you see, or have, a deer/vehicle accident, call the Sheriff dispatcher at (305) 872-3311 or Emergency at 911. He or she will contact the Key Deer Refuge staff. Your information is important.

their present size about 1,000 years ago. They were an important food source for Indian tribes. European explorers in the sixteenth century found them in large numbers. Hernando d'Escalante Fontaneada, a Spaniard taken prisoner by Calusa Indians in the 1570s, was the first European to call attention to them. He called them "a great wonder" in a diary he kept during 17 years of captivity. Word of the deer reached Caribbean sailors, who hunted them for meat and hides.

As the human population in the Keys increased in the mid-1800s to late-1800s, much of the deer's wooded habitat was cleared for timber and farming. Hunters with dogs often burned thick vegetation to drive the deer from their habitat into the water where they could easily be shot and clubbed.

By the early 1930s, the deer were close to extinction. In 1934, Jay N. "Ding" Darling, a conservationist, cartoonist, and chief of the U.S. Bureau of Biological Survey (which later became the U.S. Fish and Wildlife Service), was horrified by a deer slaughter he witnessed from a fishing boat. His nationally syndicated cartoon, "The Last of the Toy Deer," helped convince the Florida legislature to ban hunting of Key

**GREAT EGRET**
(Casmerodius albus)
Also known as the common egret
and American egret, this bird nests
in trees, frequently in mixed colonies
that include cormorants and ibis.

deer in 1939. Nonetheless, with little or no enforcement, the destruction continued unchecked.

By the early 1950s, surveys found the deer population had dwindled to less than 50. In 1957, Congress established the Key Deer National Refuge, and through the zealous efforts of a game warden named Jack Watson the deer began a revival. The deer were further protected under the 1967 Endangered Species Act. By the mid-1970s, their numbers increased to an estimated 300 to 400.

Their numbers declined again over the next two decades. However, in the past five years, their population has risen dramatically, and today there are believed to be between 580 and 680 on Big Pine and No Name keys and less than 100 on smaller islands included in the refuge.

Like many of Florida's other endangered species, the deer's march toward extinction is hastened by a growing human population, which is encroaching on the refuge with subdivisions and other facilities. Collisions with vehicles are also taking a toll. Each year several dozen grazing on roadside grasses wander innocently, and fatally, into harm's way. The number of road kills has been steadily rising since 1995, culminating in 90 in 1998, which is 68 percent of all known deer deaths for that year. Some deer drown while attempting to swim between keys. This frequently occurs during dry seasons when the animals attempt to swim to other islands in search of fresh water. Some Key deer fawns and does fall into mosquito control ditches and drown when water levels rise.

To visit the refuge, turn off US 1 at Key Deer Boulevard (MM 30.5) and look for the U.S. Fish and Wildlife Service Headquarters in the Big Pine Shopping Center on the right. Pick up information on nature trails and areas where you're most likely to see the deer. Like most wildlife, the deer are most easily seen early in the morning and in early evening when they come out of the forests to eat and drink at ponds and water holes.

Take heed of the dos and don'ts. Obey posted speed limits, and carefully watch the roadsides for any deer that might be on the verge of darting into the path of your vehicle. Another important rule is don't feed the deer, either by hand, or by leaving food on the ground for them to find. Deer accustomed to human food are more likely to wander onto highways and onto private property, where they're frequently attacked by dogs while feeding on shrubbery and gardens. Interacting with them also entices them to continue to approach people and roads, where they are more likely to be struck by vehicles.

After leaving the refuge headquarters, turn right and drive 2.25 miles on Key Deer Boulevard to Blue Hole. This former oolitic rock quarry, blasted out during the railroad days and filled with fresh water is the largest body of fresh water, in the Keys, and is a primary place for Key deer to drink.

Deer feed primarily on fruit and leafy plants, including red and black mangrove, Indian mulberry (*Morinda royoc*), pineland acacia (*Acacia farnesiana*), thatch palm fruits, blackbead, grasses, pencil flower (*Stylocanthes hamata*), and wild dilly fruits. At Blue Hole's wooden viewing platform you can observe alligators, turtles, wading birds, and fish, including exotics like koi and goldfish that people have dumped into the lake. A humorous sign by the water hole carries a serious message about the dangers of not respecting alligators:

*There once was a gator named Allig,*
*Who lived in a place called Blue Hole,*
*Some people fed him, while others they swam,*
*But most of the water was his dinner bowl,*
*So, Allig grew braver with each passing week,*
*And no longer called his visitors sir,*
*He mistook a young miss for his usual fish,*
*And one morning before breakfast,*
*Allig-ate-her.*

The Blue Hole observation platform can bring you face-to-face with deer, raccoons, and other creatures. You can also see them in Watson's Hammock, a hardwood hammock off Higgs Lane just beyond Blue Hole. A lofty tree canopy includes a massive gumbo-limbo tree, although this hammock was hit hard in 1998 by Hurricane Georges. From Blue Hole, drive or hike 0.25-mile up the road to the paved parking area at the Jack Watson and Frederick C. Manillo wheelchair accessible nature trails. Check to see if any refuge brochures are in the boxes by the trailheads.

The Jack Watson Trail is a 0.66-mile loop developed in partnership between the U.S. Fish and Wildlife Service and the nonprofit Florida Keys Land Trust. "Watchful Steward of the Key Deer Refuge," Jack Watson was a game management agent for the U.S. Fish and Wildlife Service in the 1940s and 1950s and an early manager of the refuge. He spent nearly 25 years working to protect the deer and is given much of the credit for fostering their step away from extinction.

Pause and read the trail-side markers. Heed the warnings about poisonwood plants. A member of the cashew family, the poison tree grows from shrub size to 30 to 40 feet tall. The slightest touch of the sap from its reddish-brown, scaly bark and shiny green leaves, dotted with black spots, can set off a virulent, itchy rash similar to poison ivy, poison oak, and poison sumac. The tree's fruit is a main food source for white-crowned pigeons.

Although it is rarely seen and not found on the nature trails, be extra cautious of the manchineel tree (*Hippomane mancinella*). One of the world's most poisonous trees, the small trees with oval, sharp-pointed leaves and yellow and green flowers carry a double whammy. The tree looks similar to guava and other tropicals, but the plumlike fruit is highly toxic to anyone unfortunate enough to bite into it. In addition, the manchineel's milky sap burns human skin like the most caustic battery acid. Calusa Indians used it for torture and fatally shot sixteenth-century Spanish explorer Juan Ponce de Leon with an arrow dipped in manchineel sap.

Benign plants include buttonwood trees. Found in the lower areas, where the soil is wetter, the ridged gray-brown buttonwood bark has medicinal properties and is used in tanning hides. A member of the white mangrove family, buttonwood can reach a height of 40 to 50 feet and has a narrow rounded crown, elliptical evergreen leaves, and small, green, oval-shaped flowers. Around the turn of the century the wood was commercially harvested for charcoal.

The pine woodlands are also home to several species of snakes. Among the most venomous are Eastern coral snakes but they are rarely seen. Up to 2 feet in length, with alternating black, red, and orange bands, and a broad yellow band on its head, the coral snake is usually not aggressive, but its bite can be deadly if antivenom is not quickly applied. Keys hospitals are well equipped and staffs are trained to respond quickly to snake bites. Nonvenomous scarlet kingsnakes and scarlet snakes have similar bands and are often mistaken for coral snakes.

The Eastern diamondback rattler has distinctive black diamond patterns, outlined in black and yellow. If you hear its rattle, stand still and allow it to pass you by. Some can grow as long as 6 to 8 feet.

As a general rule, snakes are wary of humans and don't look for trouble. If you stay on the trails and out of the underbrush, you can enjoy your hike free of fear of snakes.

Walk into the Watson Trail's pine rockland forest, a green canopy that grows out of caprock and oolite substrate. In the U.S., pine rocklands are found only in southern Florida, and only 5 percent still survive. Over 80 percent of those are in the National Key Deer Refuge. There's underbrush in the pine rockland, but a look inside a small solution hole reveals native orchids and ferns, tiny fruits and flowers, frogs, insects, snakes, and fish.

Next on the Jack Watson Trail pass through one of the best examples of a tropical hardwood hammock remaining in the Lower Keys. Tropical hardwood hammocks are prevalent here and elsewhere in the Keys and other areas of southern Florida. Hammocks (a variation of hummock) are groves of tropical hardwood trees, shrubs, and plants that grow on ridges and islands of ground elevated above the level of surrounding marshes and other wet areas. From 80 to 100 species can flourish in a single hammock. They include mahogany, gumbo-limbo, pigeon plum, poisonwood, and many types of vines, mosses, and lichens. Hammocks are also habitats for many species of tree snails and butterflies, including the rare Schaus' swallowtail butterfly.

A marker advises us to connect with our surroundings: "You're in the midst of one of the natural habitats of the Keys...Focusing one's senses can create a sense of place. Allow yourself to become part of what you're experiencing. Look up at the tall pines, the color of the tropical sky, the openness of the tree canopy. Look down at the ground, focus on the tiny plants, the spare soil, exposed and abundant rock, small holes filled with water. Look for evidence of fire at the bases of palms and pines and observe the difference in leaves that reveal a great variety of plants.

**WAX MYRTLE**
(*Myrica cerifera*)
Candles can be made from the waxy coating of this plant's fruit, although it would require several bushels of fruit to produce one candle.

"Now smell the pine rocklands, the wax myrtle (*Myrica cerifera*), slash pines, white stopper and possibly the odor of the last fire. Listen to the insects, the call of birds, the rattle of thatched palms, and the intervals of silence..."

Farther on, another marker tells us this: "What you're seeing is essentially what Native Americans would have seen before the rush of civilization. The pine rockland forest contains more than 250 species of plants, but the dominant feature is the slash pine, so-called because they were slashed for turpentine. They're extremely fire resistant, and are so deep rooted even a dead tree can stand for many years. They serve as feeding areas for woodpeckers and roosting places for hawks, ospreys, and turkey vultures."

Another marker points out that fire is a beneficial natural phenomenon that plays a major role in shaping Florida's ecosystems. Pinelands depend on periodic fires, frequently ignited by lightning during summer thunderstorms. Saw palmetto, longleaf (*Pinus palustris*), and slash pines have developed a resistance to fires. Their outer bark may be burned, but their inner core stays protected. Some may live for several hundred years. Fires clear away low branches and dead and unhealthy trees and enable sunlight to reach the forest floor. Ashes from the trees and grasses and low shrubbery nourish the soil. Pine cone seeds that fall onto this fertile bed quickly germinate.

The Frederick C. Manillo Jr. Nature Trail is a smooth, flat, disabled-accessible 250-yard forest trail that leads to a platform overlooking a small wetland. Markers identify trees and plants. Manillo (1948-1996) was a strong advocate of environmental conservation.

**Directions:** The Key Deer National Wildlife Refuge Headquarters is located in the shopping center off Key Deer Boulevard, north of the traffic light (the only traffic light) on Big Pine Key.

**Activities:** Wildlife watching, hiking.

**Facilities:** Nature trails, observation platform, visitor center.

**Dates:** Open year-round. Refuge headquarters is open Monday through Friday.

**Fees:** None.

**Closest town:** Big Pine Key.

**For more information:** Refuge Manager, Florida Keys National Wildlife Refuges, PO Box 430510, Big Pine Key, FL 33043-0510. Phone (305) 872-2239.

### TIPS ON SEEING KEY DEER

If you fail to happen upon Key deer on the Watson Trail, you may need to go looking for them. The deer are common in some parts of Big Pine, and can often be spotted in the daytime along roadsides and in some of the neighborhoods on Big Pine. One of the best ways to see deer is to drive slowly through the neighborhoods branching off of Watson Boulevard, being careful not to disturb the residents.

A very likely spot is the very end of Key Deer Boulevard (CR 940), which goes north from US 1 at the only traffic light on the island. Follow the road all the way to the end, about 4.5 miles. The road passes a subdivision and dead ends at some land managed by the National Key Deer Refuge.

Park and wait for a few minutes. By looking back down the last 0.5 mile or so of straight road you'll be able to see when a Key deer ventures out on the road shoulder, something they do all the time. Many of the deer have radio tracking collars on as part of a study to determine their numbers and movements.

A few yards past the end of the road, you'll see one of the hundreds of miles of mosquito ditches that were dug into the hard limestone throughout the island. The idea was to drain the land and lower the population of saltwater mosquitoes. Only about a foot wide and a couple feet deep, the ditches unfortunately became death traps for Key deer fawns and even adults who couldn't climb back up the steep sides.

Although the residents of the nearby subdivision aren't necessarily fond of a constant flow of tourist traffic winding up and down their streets, the deer do hang around in their yards, in part because of a now limited practice of people feeding them everything from heads of lettuce to table scraps.

Another reliable deer sighting spot is on No Name Key. Head back down Key Deer

Boulevard and turn left (east) on Watson Boulevard. Turn left at the stop sign on Avenue B, cross a small bridge, and continue through the subdivision. The road crosses another longer bridge onto No Name Key.

Key deer are commonly seen along this road. Follow it to the end where you can walk out for a look at the Gulf of Mexico waters. Keys residents once regularly fed the deer at this spot, and many deer still come around. Unfortunately, it's also an area that collects a lot of trash and garbage. It's important to resist the urge to feed the small deer. It only hurts their chances for survival.

## DIVING IN THE LOWER KEYS

Diving in the Lower Keys consists of an outstanding array of possibilities enhanced by reliable water clarity and warm weather. Dive shops cater to a variety of experience and offer a wide choice of dive trips including custom trips and night dives.

By far the most popular dive spots are in the Looe Key Marine Sanctuary (*see* page 106). Hundreds of other dive spots from patch reefs very close to shore to ledges in 90 feet of water are waiting to be explored.

The Gulf of Mexico side of the islands has its own interesting diving sites. The Rock Pile north of Content Keys is a unique site in 15 to 20 feet of water that displays hundreds of attractive coral heads. Ledges of coquina rock only 50 yards off some of the islands are worth seeing.

A serious amount of damage at popular reef diving sites is caused by boat anchors striking the fragile coral, or the rope or chain attached to the anchor chafing coral or breaking off coral branches. A mooring buoy system has been developed to reduce anchor damage and to provide convenient means for securing boats.

At many reefs, mooring buoys encircle the shallowest reef areas or are located on the ocean side of the reef. Shallow reef areas are distinguished by brownish-colored water. Circle around either side of these shallow areas—always steering to the outside of a ring of buoys—and never motor directly across a shallow reef to get to a buoy!

Following are basic steps for using mooring buoys provided by the Florida Keys National Marine Sanctuary.

1. Buoys are available on a first-come, first-served basis to everyone.

2. To avoid grounding, use caution when approaching and while tied to a buoy.

3. Watch carefully for swimmers, snorkelers, divers' bubbles, and fishing lines. When in a dive area, slow down to an idle speed. Make sure your bow is down and the motor or stern is not digging down deep into the water.

4. Motor slowly parallel to the reef, in deep water, until you select a mooring buoy. Turn and idle directly to the buoy without meandering among other boats. Reverse this procedure when leaving.

5. Approach the buoy very slowly from downwind or down current. Always keep the buoy in sight. The biggest problem with maintaining the buoys occurs when boaters approach the buoy too fast, run over it, and slice the line or buoy with their propeller.

# Reef Etiquette

Florida Keys National Marine Sanctuary provides the following guidelines and regulations to protect the coral reefs and provide for a safe trip.

—Just touching coral may cause damage to this fragile animal; therefore, do not allow your hands, knees, fins, gauges, or tank to touch the coral.

—When anchoring, the anchor, anchor chain, or line should not be in contact with coral. Use mooring buoys that are provided. If one is not available, ask to tie off to another boat's stern. If neither option is available, carefully anchor in sand.

—Corals, shells, sea biscuits and other animals, living or dead, cannot be removed from the Key Largo or Looe Key national marine sanctuaries.

—The red and white divers down flag must be flown while diving or snorkeling. Boats should slow to a no-wake speed within 100 yards of a dive flag. Divers should stay within 100 feet of their dive flag.

—Spearfishing and possession of spearfishing equipment or of speared fish is not allowed within the boundaries of the Key Largo National Marine Sanctuary. Within the Looe Key National Marine Sanctuary, spearfishing is not allowed; however, equipment may be stowed and not readily available on board. Call the Florida Marine Patrol concerning other closed areas (800-DIAL-FMP).

—Florida law requires a fishing license. Special stamps are required for lobster, snook, and tarpon. Applicable size, bag limits, and seasons must be observed when harvesting seafood products. Consult state and federal authorities for current regulations.

6. To secure your boat to a mooring buoy, run your line through the loop of the floating pick-up line and cleat both ends to the bow of your boat. On rough days and for larger boats, increase the length of your line. This will improve the ride of your vessel and reduce wear and tear on the buoy system.

7. Inspect the mooring buoy your boat is tied to—you are still responsible for your vessel. Check to be certain that the mooring buoy is holding the vessel as intended, and inspect the buoy for functional integrity. Please report any problems, such as broken or frayed lines, to the Sanctuary Office at (305) 743-2437 or to Sanctuary Patrol on VHF channel 16.

8. If a mooring buoy is not available, anchor only in sand—never in coral. Always check to be sure your anchor is not dragging and your anchor chain or line is not contacting coral.

### LOOE KEY MARINE SANCTUARY

[Fig. 7(1)] A spectacular coral reef track, 5 nautical miles offshore from Ramrod Key, the 5.3-square mile sanctuary is a sub-unit of the Florida Keys National Marine

Sanctuary. It gets its name from the British frigate HMS *Looe* that sank there in 1744. Ballast stones from the ship can still be seen at the reef.

Although small compared to other Keys reefs, many seasoned divers give Looe Key top ranking. The wish-bone-shaped diving area, about 200 yards wide and 800 yards long, descends through gin-clear waters some 35 feet down to a sand bottom. Snorkelers and scuba divers alike float through caves and canyons, surrounded by countless and colorful varieties of fish, lobsters, and stingrays that swim among the brain coral, pillar coral, soft coral, sea fans, and sea whips.

Only 5 nautical miles from shore the reef is a good choice for those not-too-experienced divers that want to captain their own snorkeling trip to a reef. Boats and snorkeling equipment can be rented on Big Pine and Little Torch Key.

The trip begins with a few simple directions on following a marked channel to the Atlantic Ocean. From there it's a straight shot out to the reef. Mooring buoys are provided to avoid damage to the reef from anchoring.

Once safely tied off you're ready to slip over the side into a world that nearly defies description. The reef's majestic ledges of living corals on the fore (the side facing the ocean) stand upon 7,000 years of coral growth. A classic spur and groove formation, it sports fingerlike spurs of coral separated by grooves of sand and rubble.

Every July the Lower Keys Chamber of Commerce holds an annual Underwater Music Festival at Looe Key. Microphones are dropped onto the water, and divers can explore the reef to the sounds of rock and roll.

If you rent a boat, before leaving the dock discuss weather and sea conditions with the marina personnel and be sure to have a complete understanding of the boat's operation and safety equipment. Although close to shore, Looe Key is still in the open sea, which can become very rough under certain wind conditions.

**Directions:** Looe Key Marine Sanctuary is 7 miles offshore.

**Activities:** Diving, snorkeling, boating.

**Facilities:** Mooring buoys available for dive visits. Boats and equipment can be rented at Big Pine Key Fishing Lodge, MM 33 Oceanside, phone (305) 872-2351. Dolphin Marina Resort MM 28.5 Oceanside, phone (305) 872-2685 or (800) 553-0308.

**Dates:** Open year-round.

**Closest town:** Big Pine Key.

**For more information:** Florida Keys, National Marine Sanctuary, Lower Keys Regional Office, 216 Ann Street, Key West, FL 33040. Phone (305) 292-0311.

## FISHING IN THE LOWER KEYS

Fishing is hugely popular in the Lower Keys as it is throughout the chain of islands. Charter boats and fishing guides stand ready to fulfill your fishing dreams, whether that entails fighting a leaping sailfish, making the perfect cast to a large bonefish, or struggling to pull a grouper from the bottom.

In summer, offshore action on the Atlantic side of the Lower Keys is largely focused on dolphin. Also known as dorado or mahimahi, these blue, green, and yellow fish put up a great fight, and are excellent table fare.

With the arrival of the first cold fronts come the first sailfish of the year. Unlike the catch and kill approach to trophy billfishing in the past, most sport-fish enthusiasts release the sailfish they catch and have a plastic replica created to commemorate their catch. Trolling the deep offshore waters also means a chance to catch blue and white marlin, wahoo, king mackerel, blackfin tuna, and barracuda.

Inshore reef fishing means targeting large groupers and a variety of snapper including lane, gray, and yellowtail. Other species commonly caught over the reefs are king mackerel, jacks, cobia, and barracuda. Some of the best fishing takes place in 60 to 100 feet of water.

The channels between the keys offer excellent fishing for grouper, snapper, and jacks. In the spring, lots of effort turns toward the almighty tarpon. Giant silver kings, up to 200 pounds, settle in for a few months of feeding in the churning waters caused by tidal currents flowing through the bridge pilings in the passes.

Tarpon also hang out on the wide sandy flats along both the Atlantic and Gulf of Mexico sides. The other flats inhabitants, permit and bonefish, have become the popular targets of fly-fishermen and other shallow water, light-tackle advocates.

In the Gulf of Mexico, fishing centers around reef and wreck fishing. The goal is to locate structure on an otherwise smooth bottom. That's where grouper, snapper, permit, cobia and shark will be waiting.

## BIG PINE KEY DINING
### BIG PINE COFFEE SHOP
MM 30, Big Pine Key. Fishermen, divers, and other early birds get ready for the day with a substantial, no-frills breakfast, starting at 6 a.m. Many return during the day for fish plates, sandwiches, soups, and other good, basic fare. Open daily. *Inexpensive. Phone (305) 872-2790.*

### CHINA GARDEN
MM 30.2 Bayside, Big Pine Key. Located in the Big Pine Shopping Center, at Overseas Highway and Key Deer Boulevard. This restaurant serves okay Hunan, Szechuan, and Cantonese food and is located in the same shopping center as the U.S. Fish and Wildlife Visitor Center. Takeouts and free delivery from Bahia Honda to Summerland Key. Lunch and dinner daily. *Inexpensive. Phone (305) 872-8861.*

### NO NAME PUB
North Watson Boulevard, 0.25 mile south of No Name Bridge. This excellent, very local restaurant and bar boasts that it's "A Nice Place, If You Can Find It." Locating it isn't really very difficult. On Big Pine, turn right at the traffic light on Watson Boulevard (you can't miss it, it's the only one) and bear to the right fork on Wilder Road. Look for the small frame building in a clump of trees on the left just before you cross the No Name Bridge from Big Pine Key.

If you're looking for real food in a real place, it's like finding a small treasure. Whether the pizza is "The Best in the Known Universe" is a subjective opinion, but it's mighty good, all the same. You can have your pizza the tried-and-true way, with pepperoni, Italian sausage, mushrooms, and other regular stuff, or go for the Keys shrimp style, Caribbean chicken, Hawaiian (with ham and pineapple), vegetarian, Mexican, and other more exotic versions. Domestic and imported beers and a few basic wines are served. The decor is also striking. A few decades back, patrons with a few brews under their belts decided to write their names on dollar bills and post them on the walls. In case they ever came in short of cash, they could pluck their bill off the wall and pay for lunch and beer. Nowadays, every inch of wall and ceiling is covered with autographed dollars, as well as English pounds, German marks, and even a few food stamps. Open daily late morning to late at night. *Inexpensive. Phone (305) 872-9115.*

### BIG PINE KEY LODGING
#### BIG PINE KEY RESORT MOTEL
MM 30.5 Bayside, Big Pine Key. This bayside motel has 32 rooms and apartments with kitchens, a restaurant, and a freshwater pool. A dive shop is across the highway. *Inexpensive. Phone (305) 872-9090 or (888) 872-9191. Web site www.bigpinekeymotel.com*

#### DOLPHIN MARINA RESORT
MM 28.5 Oceanside, Little Torch Key. Twelve basic motel rooms, some with kitchens. Close to Looe Key Marine Sanctuary. *Inexpensive. Phone (305) 872-2685 or (800) 553-0308. Web site www.thefloridakeys.com/dolphinmarina*

#### LOOE KEY RESORT AND DIVE CENTER
MM 27.5 Oceanside, Ramrod Key. Twenty rooms, freshwater pool, dive shop, boats, dive/snorkel instruction. *Inexpensive. Phone (305) 872-2215 or (800) 942-5397. Web site www.diveflakeys.com*

#### OLD WOODEN BRIDGE FISHING CAMP
MM 30.5 Bayside, Big Pine Key. Thirteen simple units with kitchen facilities, bait shop, and private fishing bridge. Boat dockage available for lodgers. Pets accepted. *Inexpensive. Phone (305) 872-2241.*

#### PARMER'S PLACE
MM 28.5 Bayside, Little Torch Key. Forty rooms, cottages, and apartments, kitchen facilities, free continental breakfast, marina, freshwater pool. *Inexpensive to moderate. Phone (305) 872-2157. Fax (305) 872-2014. Web site www.parmersplace.com*

#### ERA LOWER KEYS REALTY
MM 30, Big Pine Key. Rental oceanfront homes. Monthly rates available. *Inexpensive to expensive. Phone (305) 872-2258 or (800) 859-7642. Fax (305) 872-2438. Web site www.eralowerkeysrealty.com*

# Key West and Great White Heron National Wildlife Refuges

[Fig. 7] Key West and Great White Heron national wildlife refuges, with offices located on Big Pine Key, include hundreds of islands in the Gulf of Mexico and Florida Bay. Known locally as the backcountry, and accessible only by boat, the refuges protect more than 600 nautical square miles and about 10,000 acres of land in the Lower Keys. The islands have names such as the Marquesas, Woman, Joe Ingram, Barracuda, Crawfish, Mule, Big Spanish, Snipe, and Crane Key, and range in size from a few square yards to several hundred acres. Both refuges are of tremendous environmental importance. They protect about two dozen endangered species of birds and thousands of marine species.

West of Key West, Key West National Wildlife Refuge is the Keys' oldest national wildlife sanctuary. It was established by President Theodore Roosevelt in 1908 to curtail the mass slaughter and near-eradication of egrets, herons, and other birds for their feathers used in hat and clothing decorations. The refuge encompasses 375 square miles of open water and 2,019 acres of land, and it provides habitat for a wide variety of birds, including nesting or wintering populations of terns, frigatebirds, white-crowned pigeons, ospreys, and great white herons. Sand beaches serve as nesting areas for endangered Atlantic green and loggerhead sea turtles.

Great White Heron National Wildlife Refuge includes a huge array of pristine islands extending over 264 square miles in the Gulf of Mexico, including about 7,400 acres of land. Established in 1938, the refuge's red and black mangroves offer protection to the great white heron, America's largest wading bird. Other rare birds that nest here are white-crowned pigeon, roseate spoonbill, and the only known colony of laughing gulls in the Lower

## SNOWY EGRET
(Egretta thula)
The snowy egret's showy breeding plumage almost caused it to be hunted to extinction. Luckily, this bird, with its quick, darting motions and golden "slippers," may still be seen near shallow fresh or brackish water.

Keys. Endangered American crocodiles hide away in the tangled mangrove islands in northwestern and northeastern Florida Bay.

Until fairly recently, few people visited the backcountry. But as the mainline keys have become more congested, more boaters, fishermen, Jet Skiers, and other recreation seekers have been attracted to the small islands and shallow waters. Boat propellers have been especially devastating to shallow seagrass meadows. The use of personal watercraft, airboats, hover craft, sea plane landings, and water skiing are prohibited within Key West and Great White Heron national wildlife refuges.

Among the world's most productive ecosystems, seagrass meadows are nurseries for spiny lobster, crab, red drum, mangrove snapper, tarpon, snook, trout, jack crevalles, and many other marine species. Herons, egrets, bald eagles, terns, plovers, and other wildlife species also depend upon this important foundation of the aquatic food chain.

Most of the backcountry waters are only a few feet deep. Navigable channels that wind, usually unmarked, through intertidal flats are often difficult to follow. Without a knowledgeable guide to steer them through, hundreds of boats every year plow up the shallow bottom, uprooting the seagrass and leaving vast areas of scarred, unproductive habitat.

Damaged areas heal slowly, if at all, and are more vulnerable to erosive waves and currents. Boaters can reduce this senseless destruction, and avoid fines, by staying out of the shallows, which are a protected resource.

In the Lower Keys, the hardbottom community is a vital habitat of soft corals, sponges, and other invertebrates. Driving a boat over shallow hardbottom can destroy fragile sea life and seriously damage a boat's propeller. A quick guide to reading water depth goes like this: "Brown, brown, you'll run aground; white, white, you might; green, green, nice and clean; blue, blue, go on through."

Polarized sunglasses can also be helpful in reading the water depth. However, when riding into bright, glaring sunlight or on overcast or windy days, detecting water color and depth can be more difficult. Under those conditions, boaters are urged to slow down and stay in marked channels.

Those who run aground may find it necessary to walk or pole their boat to deeper water, or wait for the incoming tide. A lengthy push-pole with an oar-shaped blade is an almost mandatory piece of backcountry boating gear.

Boaters should wear sturdy sneakers or other footwear as protection against sharp coral and spiny sea urchins, and take along a hat and long-sleeve shirt. Also take insect repellent, sunglasses, water, food, rain gear, sunblock with at least 30 SPF, and a VHF radio. The U.S. Fish and Wildlife Service recommends other equipment such as binoculars, a compass, tide tables, and navigation charts. The service also recommends that boaters take a course in seamanship or boating safety and leave a float plan with a responsible person.

Increasing boat traffic is also having a detrimental effect on the backcountry's bird populations. Nesting birds' sensitivity to boat noises varies from species to species. The frequency, duration, proximity, and type of disturbance, as well as birds' past experience with humans, are other contributing factors. Many species are especially sensitive to disturbance during the breeding season, particularly just before or during incubation. An approaching boat can frighten a bird from its nest, leaving the eggs or hatchlings exposed to predators or intense deadly sunlight.

**Directions:** Great White Heron National Wildlife Refuge encompasses 264 square miles just north of the Lower Keys. The Key West National Wildlife Refuge manages 375 square miles west of Key West.

**Activities:** Fishing, boating, and bird watching.

**Facilities:** None. Camping is allowed, by permit, on Little Rabbit, North Nest, and Carl Ross keys in the Florida Bay portion of Everglades National Park. For more camping information contact Everglades National Park, PO Box 279, Homestead, FL 33030. Phone (350) 247-6211.

**For more information:** Refuge Manager, Florida Keys National Wildlife Refuges, PO Box 430510, Big Pine Key, FL 33043-0510. Phone (305) 872-2239.

# Sugarloaf Key

### ▒ THE BAT TOWER

[Fig. 7(2)] Sugarloaf Key got its name from sugarloaf pineapples, which were grown there in the late nineteenth and early twentieth centuries. In 1929, a real estate developer named Richter Clyde Perky envisioned a luxury resort, complete with a first-class hotel, restaurants, and a gambling casino on Sugarloaf Key. Unfortunately for him, Sugarloaf Key was well established as a breeding ground for voracious hordes of mosquitoes.

Perky took a page from Dr. Charles Campbell, a health official in San Antonio, Texas, who advanced the theory that bats, which feed eagerly on mosquitoes, were the answer to his dilemma. He built a 35-foot-high, cypress-shingled Bat Tower, and filled it with odorous bat guano, which, theoretically, would attract the bats, which would devour the mosquitoes.

Alas, the bats didn't buy it. A colony installed in the tower apparently didn't care for the accommodations or the odor, and promptly flew away with Perky's investment money. The mosquitoes swarmed unabated and eventually the devastated Perky went bankrupt and died. (Some people have suggested the mosquitos ate the bats.)

Looking for all the world like a bladeless windmill awaiting Don Quixote, the tower still stands behind the Sugarloaf Lodge, next to the island's small airport. While you're at the airport, check out Fantasy Dan's Airplane Rides, which offers half-hour flight-seeing tours of the Lower Keys.

**Directions:** MM 17, next to Sugarloaf Airport, behind Sugarloaf Lodge.

**Activities:** Photographing the tower, sight-seeing tours from Sugarloaf Airport.

**Facilities:** Restrooms are in the airport.

**Dates:** The tower can be viewed in daylight hours year-round.

**Fees:** There is no charge for viewing the tower; fees are charged for sight-seeing tours.

**Closest town:** Key West is 17 miles south.

**For more information:** Fantasy Dan's Airplane Rides, phone (305) 745-2217.

## LODGINGS ON SUGARLOAF KEY
### SUGARLOAF LODGE

MM 17 Bayside, Sugarloaf Key. Well-run, old Keys-style resort complex has comfortable guest rooms and efficiencies with kitchen facilities, ocean views, a freshwater swimming pool, tennis courts, and a good restaurant and bar. Pets accepted. Happily, modern mosquito eradication methods have largely accomplished what the Bat Tower couldn't, but insect repellent should be part of your gear. *Inexpensive to moderate. Phone (305) 745-3211 or (800) 553-6097 Fax (305) 745-3389.*

### SUGARLOAF KEY RESORT KOA KAMPGROUND

MM 20, Sugarloaf Key. Campsites on 14 acres, with marina, boat, and canoe rentals, swimming pool, grocery store, pool, beach, laundry, restaurant, and hot tub. *Inexpensive. Phone (305) 745-3549 or (800) 562-7731. Web site* *www.thefloridakeys.com/koasugarloaf*

## DINING ON SUGARLOAF KEY
### MANGROVE MAMA'S

MM 20, at the Bow Channel Bridge, Sugarloaf Key. If you've gotten up the nerve to venture into Mangrove Mama's, it's probably because a local touted you on to it. Like a hole-in-the-wall on a Caribbean island roadside, Mama's boasts a spare, open-air decor, a concrete floor, brick fireplace (for those chilly Keys winter nights), mismatched furniture and utensils, an eccentric, eclectic clientele, and pretty good versions of Keys favorite foods. Baked stuffed shrimp, grilled local fish, and exemplary Key lime pie are big favorites. There's live music on weekends. *Moderate. Phone (305) 745-3030.*

# Stock Island

Stock Island is an unpromising gateway to Key West. Both sides of the highway are lined with gas stations, mini marts, trailer parks, fairly uninviting restaurants, and bars. There is also a jail and landfill and an unofficial Keys visitor center, where you can sign up for timeshare visits, parasailing, and other activities.

# Key West

*Depending on how you hold your map, Key West is the beginning or end of the Florida Keys.*

**1** Mallory Square
**2** Key West Aquarium
**3** Audubon House & Tropical Gardens
**4** Mel Fisher's Maritime Heritage Society Museum
**5** Truman Little White House & Botanical Garden
**6** Oldest House Museum
**7** City Cemetery
**8** Key West Lighthouse
**9** Ernest Hemingway House Museum
**10** Fort Zachary Taylor State Historic Site & Park
**11** Southernmost Point in Continental U.S.
**12** East Martello Museum & Art Gallery
**13** Nancy Forrester's Secret Garden
**14** Charles "Sonny" McCoy Indigenous Park

Ref: Sail Fury Catamarans Key West Map

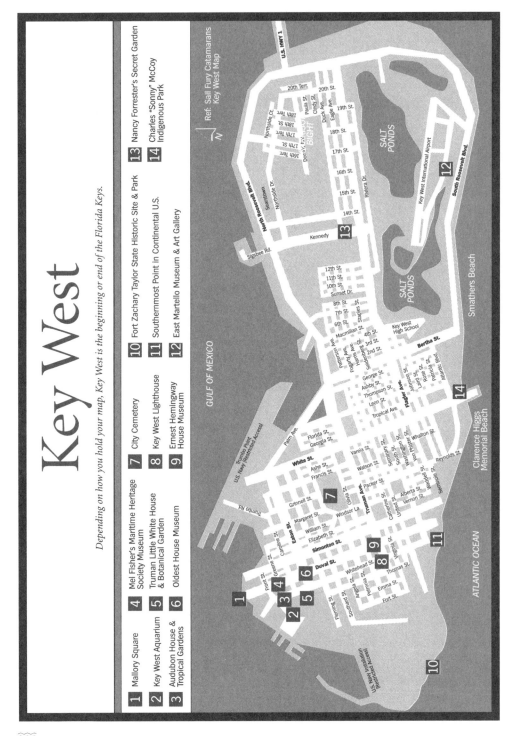

## KEY WEST BOTANICAL GARDENS

[Fig. 7(3)] The Key West Botanical Gardens is a 55-acre sanctuary, in a natural hammock, originally developed as a federally funded preserve in the 1930s. Turn right before crossing the bridge over Cow Key Channel and continue to the botanical gardens.

Partially destroyed by hurricanes and abandoned for many years, it was revived in the 1960s and 1970s by a consortium of civic groups. The tropical garden contains more than 90 species of native and imported plants. Noteworthy are national champion lignum vitae, Arjan almond, and Barringtonia trees. Some species of trees and plants are found nowhere else in the Keys.

White-crowned pigeons are frequent summer visitors and scissor-tailed flycatchers come in the winter. Gray kingbirds and black-whiskered vireos also visit the area. The garden is also home to the endangered Stock Island tree snail.

**Directions:** Driving south, turn left at the traffic light at College Road, pass a health club and nursing home, keep bearing right until you see the gate.

**Dates:** Open daily.

**Fees:** There is an admission charge.

**For more information:** Key West Botanical Garden Society, PO Box 2436, Key West, FL 33045. Phone (305) 296-1504.


# Key West

[Fig. 8] In a way, Key West defines the spirit, the history, and the mythology of the Florida Keys. If you missed something during the drive down through the islands, you'll find it in Key West.

If you flew into Key West, you can find everything the Florida Keys have to offer within the island's 2,987 acres, except maybe solitude. And even that can be found when you take to the water, or plunge beneath the surface into another world.

The island is here for you, the tourist. Your visit, and that of millions of others each year, is *the* industry of Key West. Museums, scuba diving, deep-sea fishing, eco-tours, historic buildings, street entertainers, fine restaurants, shopping and more shopping, parasailing, boating, and bird-watching—it's all here, at your doorstep.

You can spend days just walking around Old Town, from one marvelous spot to another. From the Hemingway House to Sloppy Joe's, from Mallory Square to the Hard Rock Cafe, there's an endless number of sights, and shops, and great treats to sample along the way.

While you're here you may have to learn drink names like a Sloppy Rita or a Pan Am Panic, or you may find yourself out of costume during the world famous fantasy fest, or you might have to face an irresistible urge to never leave this tropical paradise. But these are the risks you take on a visit to Key West.

After crossing Cow Key Channel (MM 4), you're on the brink of Key West. The first thing you'll encounter is a major intersection where the road forks left and right. Most of the attractions including the Southernmost Point and Mallory Square lie at the other end of the island.

If you bear to the left at the junction, you'll be on South Roosevelt Boulevard (A1A), which takes you past Atlantic Ocean beaches and the airport. If you continue to bear to the left at the next few intersections and follow US A1A, you'll eventually come to the Southernmost Point in the continental United States.

If you turn right when you first come onto the island, you'll remain on U.S. 1, which continues as North Roosevelt Boulevard, a multilane commercial strip skirting the Gulf of Mexico. (If you do plan to turn to the right, all the locals know you should get in the right-hand lane before crossing the bridge.) After dozens of traffic lights and hundreds of neon signs, the boulevard eventually narrows into Truman Avenue and takes you into Key West's Old Town.

At Whitehead Street turn left to go to the Southernmost Point or right to Mallory Square and two public parking areas. There's also plenty of metered street parking available; the farther away from the square you get, the more likely you are to find a spot. But take note of which street you're on, and which turns you take when walking; the old narrow streets can tend to look alike to the newcomer.

Like Savannah, New Orleans, and Charleston, Key West is one of those special American cities that feel so different, so foreign, so out-of-synch with the mainstream, you wonder whether you should have brought your passport and a phrase book.

Depending on which way you hold your map, Key West is the beginning or the end of the Florida Keys. If you've been driving the length of the Keys you'll want to know that the Overseas Highway's Mile Marker 0 is at Fleming and Whitehead streets, near the Hemingway House in Old Town. From here it's 126 miles north to Florida City on the Overseas Highway. The Mile Markers are the original Mile Markers from the Flagler Railroad.

The road brings millions of visitors to the Keys every year. They may stop and dally awhile at Key Largo, Islamorada, Marathon, Bahia Honda, and Big Pine Key, and some may not make it to Key West. But as the sign in front of City Hall proclaims, Key West is "The End of the Rainbow," and although it may be a zany, eccentric, let-it-all-hang-out pot of gold, those who seek it are rewarded.

Key West's international stewpot has been simmering for hundreds of years. When the first Europeans set foot here, the island was covered mainly by low, dense bushes. The tall palm trees, fruit trees, flowering plants, and lush vegetation that now characterize the city were brought in from the Caribbean. Dr. Henry Perrine introduced many of these plants to the Keys in the late 1830s.

The island's original settlers were Calusa Indians, who lived here more or less peacefully until Spanish explorers showed up in the early 1500s. The Spaniards discovered piles of human bones littering the island and named it *Cayo Hueso*, "Island of Bones."

By the mid-1700s, European contact, which brought disease and slave traders, had

*Stories of Ernest Hemingway's days in the Keys are legendary.*
*His home in Key West is a popular tourist attraction.*

decimated the Calusa population. Key West was reported to be one of their last settlements. It was abandoned in 1763 when England gained control of Florida from Spain.

When the English arrived in the 1700s, they anglicized the morbid *Cayo Hueso* to the more inviting Key West, although the Keys' most westerly islands are actually the Dry Tortugas, 70 miles over open water from Key West.

Key Westers are fond of calling themselves Conchs (pronounced konks), after the magnificent pink-shelled mollusks that tourists love to haul home. By some accounts, the original Conchs were British Loyalists who fled the 13 colonies during the American Revolution. Under the pledge, "We'd rather eat conchs than fight Mother England," they settled in the Bahamas and later migrated to Key West.

The appellation was often used in derision. In more recent times, however, Conch has come to mean a lifelong resident of the Keys, although Key West sticklers insist it's a badge that can be worn only by someone actually born on their island. In the meantime, conchs (the mollusk) are served in salads, frittered, stewed, and steaked.

In 1822, a Spanish nobleman who'd been awarded the island by his government in 1815 was so disillusioned with its heat, mosquitoes, fevers, and lack of fresh water, he sold it for $2,000 to Alabamian John Simonton. (A major Old Town street is named for Simonton.) A United States Navy presence was established and Key West was chartered as a city.

At the time pirates operating out of safe havens in the Caribbean were a serious menace to the fledgling town's existence, preying on merchant ships traveling the Florida Straits. In their swift, low-draft boats, they ambushed heavier ships wallowing in the shallow waters. Virtually uncontested, they seized goods, plundered, and murdered.

By the mid-1820s, the situation had become so critical that President John Quincy Adams sent Commander David Porter to rid the shipping lanes of the menace. Porter employed a fleet of mobile, light-draft schooners and a ferry boat requisitioned from New York City and was able to put the buccaneers out of business. However, *sic transit gloria*, so fleeting is fame, Porter was later court-martialed for chasing the pirates all the way into Spanish territory in Cuba and the Caribbean.

The pirates were replaced by "wreckers," members of a legalized industry that rescued passengers and salvaged the cargoes of ships that ran aground on the reefs and sand bars. According to the law, wreckers were entitled to 25 percent of everything they salvaged, but apparently they didn't always come by their cut on the up-and-up. Many ship captains claimed their saviours were no more than licensed pirates who even set strategically located fires to lure storm-threatened ships into dangerous waters.

From the early 1830s to the mid-1850s there were so many shipwrecks that Key West grew and prospered from the wrecking trade. The population increased to nearly 3,000 as New Englanders and British from the nearby Bahamas rushed in to take part in the lucrative enterprise. Key West became Florida's largest city and for a brief time one of the wealthiest per capita in the entire country.

Wrecking's heyday was over by about 1860. Lighthouses had finally been erected throughout the Keys and, along with improved navigation charts, were keeping new steam-powered ships out of harm's way. In wrecking's wake, other industries were spawned. Green turtles abundant in the Gulf of Mexico were harvested, canned, made into soup, and shipped from the island, to the point of near-extinction.

Harvesting sponges from the sea bottoms also put a jingle in the islanders' pockets. But, by the early 1900s, the overzealous spongers had nearly wiped out the supply. The divers moved on to Tarpon Springs, on Florida's west coast, where they prospered until the late 1930s, when a blight killed off most of the sponges and reduced the industry to a tourist attraction.

After the Civil War, thousands of Cubans fleeing their homeland's struggle for independence from Spain brought the cigar-making industry with them to Key West. By the turn of the century, more than 150 operations on the island were supplying much of the world's demand for quality cigars. But, like the sponging industry, cigar makers pulled up stakes and moved on to the west coast and made Tampa's Ybor City America's cigar city. Cubans who stayed behind have left their indelible mark on Key West.

On January 22, 1912, Key West's isolation from the rest of the world ended with a festival of marching bands, ship whistles, overblown rhetoric, and shouts of adoration from the townsfolk.

Henry Flagler's Florida East Coast Railroad, with the venerable, 82-year-old, almost blind and deaf, great man himself riding in triumph in his private car, entered the city. To the wildly cheering populace he proclaimed, "We have been trying to anchor Key West to the mainland, and anchor it we have."

With his dream fully realized, Flagler died peacefully in May 1913. His railroad brought boom times to Key West. Passengers and freight could now travel in two days between New York and Key West and continue to Havana on ferries that carried the cars across 90 miles of open water. The catastrophic Labor Day Hurricane of 1935 blew away the railroad, but three years later the Overseas Highway (US 1), built on the railroad's bones, was opened to tourist-bearing automobiles.

Tourist numbers remained small, however, and the island's businesses suffered the same bankruptcy problems suffered elsewhere during the Great Depression. Over the years the island has also attracted a number of literary lions: Ernest Hemingway, Tennessee Williams, Truman Capote, John Hersey, Gore Vidal, and Carson McCullers sought inspiration from the tropic vibes.

The early nineteenth century island of Key West was probably one-third to one-half the size it is today. As the population grew, ponds and lagoons were filled in for houses, businesses, and docks. Periodic hurricanes have had a hand in reconfiguring the island. So did Henry Flagler. When Flagler learned that there was no dry land in the city for a terminal for his approaching railroad, he ordered the filling of about 140 acres on what is now Trumbo Point.

Before World War II, Key West was a city of small wooden houses in a forest of exotic trees and red, yellow, pink, and white jacaranda, poinciana, frangipani, and bougainvillea flowers. There was no freshwater pipeline from the Florida mainland until early in the war, when increased military presence gave it a high priority, so each house had a cistern to collect rain water to supplement ground wells. The city had no sewer system, only a few houses had indoor plumbing, and outhouses and cesspits were the rule for most of the population.

Self-reliant Conchs depended on fishing and usually had at least one Key lime tree in their yard. The fruit was used for the Keys' famous pie, and the juice went into drinks and marinades for poultry, fish, and meat. Key Westers also grew Spanish limes, sapodilla, sour oranges, bananas, Jamaica apple, avocados, and mangos.

With the economic benefits from the Navy's heightened presence during World War II, the island began to modernize its infrastructure, a process that continues today. Tourists who began arriving in a trickle in the 1950s now arrive like a year-round tidal wave from around the world.

Drug smugglers also found the Keys a lucrative place to ply their trade. In response, in April 1982 the U.S. Border Patrol set up a blockade on US 1 at Florida City in order to trap drug smugglers using the Overseas Highway. Every vehicle approaching the roadblock was stopped and searched. The small number of arrests and confiscations was mitigated by a horrendous traffic jam that had thousands of cars and trucks backed up for miles.

Key West citizens, declaring that they were being treated like a different country, seized upon the road block as an opportunity for some fun and a party. A mock-secession conclave was called, and a flag with a big, lustrous conch shell as its centerpiece was created and raised in Mallory Square. The Conch Republic was born and quickly surrendered, making itself eligible for "foreign aid" from the notoriously generous U.S. government. "Conch Republic Days" is now an annual April happening.

Nowadays, visitors on extended holiday, taking in the island at a properly tropical, leisurely pace, are joined by daily throngs of cruise ship passengers, who rush down the gangways on a frantic mission to see it all in the few hours before the *Royal "Whatever"* sails onto Nassau or Cozumel.

Most of them never stray very far from Duval Street. From the Gulfside Pier House to South Beach and the Southernmost House on the Atlantic, Duval is one of the most eclectic, nonstop, energized miles in America (also, some say, one of the tackiest and tawdriest).

It's a neverending carnival, a sensual fiesta, a pedestrian river that flows at high tide around the clock. Posh apparel boutiques, art galleries, gift shops, and hip department stores like Fast Buck Freddie's stand side-by-side among an endless number of shops selling the same T-shirts. Remodeled Conch houses, cigar makers' cottages, and new little malls sell yogurt, ice cream, conch fritters, sponges, racy lingerie, books, dive trips, kayak trips, fishing trips, parasailing, excursions to the Dry Tortugas, bagels and cappuccino, real estate, pizza, pottery, Key lime pie, and Peking duck.

There are small hotels like the revamped Cuban Club, and the La Concha, a seven-story skyscraper now flying the Holiday Inn flag, that has seen the street through boom, bust, and boom since 1924. Some of the island's very oldest homes and churches, like the blinding-white St. Paul's, also knew the old town when it was just a town at the end of the railroad, not a tourist haven.

Attractions include The Wreckers Museum in the town's oldest house and the more recently established Ripley's Believe It Or Not! Odditorium. At restaurants by the score you can sit at a raw bar overlooking the street and gulp oysters by the dozen, or up the ante in more formal rooms and lushly planted courtyards with pricey French and Italian cuisines, plus steaks and seafood fixed every way imaginable.

Menus are often conveniently posted by the sidewalk. You can stroll along, enjoying the shops and the crowds, while choosing the perfect meal from dozens of offerings.

Of course, there are bars, bars, and more bars. Gay bars and mixed bars. Darkly lit bars with alluring corners and racy shows. Open-air bars, where music, hawkers, and wafts of cool air lure you from the hot crowded sidewalks. Old-time favorites like Sloppy Joe's, Captain Tony's, and the Green Parrot, where Papa Hemingway boozed and brawled. Jimmy Buffett sometimes does a surprise drop-in to the delight of patrons at his Margaritaville Cafe.

Tourists glad to see a familiar face and other elements rush to Planet Hollywood, Hooters, and the Hard Rock Cafe. If you don't want to walk, rent a bike, a moped, or roller blades. The streets are filled with a constant traffic jam, and parking is usually limited to somewhere not close to where you want to be.

A few steps off Duval Street and you're at Mallory Square, Mel Fisher's Maritime Museum, Harry Truman's Little White House, the Key West Aquarium, the Sponge Market, Hemingway's House, the Lighthouse, and the Southernmost Point.

After a few days of encountering fellow travelers from Alabama,

*The Conch Tour Train offers visitors an overview of Key West and its attractions.*

Australia, and points in between, you might begin to wonder where all the bartenders, shopkeepers, hawkers, and other permanent residents live. The answer lies in the residential areas on either side of Duval. On Fleming, William, Petronia, Angela, Thomas, Olivia and dozens of other quiet streets, where tourist feet seldom tread and where residents are busily rehabbing the decreasing number of fixer-up Conch and gingerbread Caribbean houses. Many of the residents frequent their own restaurants, Cuban and Bahamian grocery stores, bars, and hangouts.

Bahama Village is one of the best places to encounter the real, old Key West. On the island's southwest side, bounded by Duval, Angela, and Louisa streets, it's like an old untouristed neighborhood in Nassau. Dogs, children, chickens, and roosters run in the streets and in swept-dirt yards in front of wooden houses painted turquoise and white. People dress up for Sunday services in simple white frame churches, patronize small grocery and merchandise shops, play cards, and gossip, seemingly oblivious to the tourist hubbub just around the corner. If you need a goal, go for breakfast, lunch, or dinner at Blue Heaven, at Thomas and Petronia.

Dozens of Old Town's most attractive Conch homes are on the small streets and alleys bordering the City Cemetery. Pick up the *Pelican Path*, a free descriptive folder of many of these houses produced by the Old Island Restoration Foundation, at the Chamber of Commerce Visitor Center in Mallory Square at 402 Wall Street. Phone (305) 294-2587.

By most accounts, Key West is cleaner and more prosperous than at any time in its history. A modern sewer system has virtually eliminated cesspits. But observers also say that the root of that prosperity may also be causing the city to lose much of its unique, appealing character.

The city's economy depends almost solely on tourism. Each year the resident population of 27,000 is impacted by more than 1 million visitors. Unwittingly, the golden goose of tourism is degrading the quality of the environment by using resources and triggering construction of hotels, shopping areas, and other developments that erase more of the city's dwindling green spaces. With land at a premium, much of the island's garbage is hauled to landfills on the mainland. The city's middle class is becoming a threatened species. With an average wage of about $7 an hour, thousands of service workers find it difficult to locate affordable housing. Even small apartments rent for $900 to $1,000 a month, and Conch houses that sold for $30,000 to $40,000 a decade or so ago now go on the market for upwards of $200,000. Surging development, coupled with skyrocketing property values, is endangering traditional older neighborhoods like Bahama Village. The cost of food, gasoline, and other necessities is also above the national average.

The city's liberal, live-and-let-live attitude has welcomed a gay community that makes up about 25 percent of the population. Tourism efforts include promoting Key West to domestic and overseas gay markets as well as to traditional outlets.

No matter when you visit Key West, there's bound to be a festival just ending or coming up soon. In winter, the big events are house and garden tours, literary seminars, and the really big Old Island Days Festival. Spring means the Conch Republic Independence Celebration, Key West and Lower Keys Fishing Tournament, and Key West Music Festival. Fireworks explode on the Fourth of July, the same month that Hemingway Days fills the streets with lots of "Papas." Cooler weather ushers in the theater and cigar festivals and Christmas celebrations.

**For more information:** Key West Chamber of Commerce, 402 Wall Street, Key West, FL 33040. At Old Mallory Square. Phone (800) 527-8539 or local (305) 294-2587.

# Key West Attractions

### SUNSET CELEBRATION AT MALLORY SQUARE

[Fig. 8(1)] There's one festival that takes place every evening: the Sunset Celebration at Mallory Square. You haven't really been to Key West until you've taken part in the ritual. Crowds gather early on the old dock that's been recently dressed up with brick paving and other amenities.

It's easy to tell when it's time to head for the square. People all over Old Town will begin drifting in that direction. Before long the streets fill with people flowing into the square and out onto the dock.

The nightly entertainment includes the Iguana Man: In exchange for a tip you can pet his scaly green friend (decked out in a scarf and jaunty palm frond hat) and have your picture taken with it draped across your shoulders. The Cookie Lady pedals her bike and sings the wonders of her chocolate chips and fudge brownies.

Street performers, food vendors, and crafts dealers line the dock. Performing dogs, cats, and humans entertain the crowds. Jugglers twirl machetes and Indian clubs, fire-eaters and sword swallowers test their tonsils, mimes mime, musicians play, and a longtime performing tight rope walker mixes comedy with a well-polished balancing act. Everyone works for dollars dropped into a hat or can.

You can also buy jewelry, hand-painted T-shirts, straw hats, and watercolors, and refresh yourself with conch fritters, hot dogs, popcorn, fish sandwiches, and lemonade squeezed while you watch. In the vernacular of the 1960s, it's a happening, and it happens every night at sunset.

And as someone once said, "Everywhere else in the world, the sun is merely expected to rise, shine all day, and set again. In Key West, it's expected to perform." As the sun begins to touch the horizon, the crowd quiets a little and turns to the sea. Most take a moment just to watch nature at its finest. If it's been a good sunset, then the last of the blazing orange sliver of fire disappearing into the sea prompts a spontaneous applause. But if it's a cloudy night, no matter, another encore is just 24 hours away.

**Directions:** Mallory Square, on the waterfront at the end of Whitehead Street.
**Dates:** Every evening.
**Fees:** None.

### AUDUBON HOUSE AND TROPICAL GARDENS

[Fig. 8(3)] John James Audubon reportedly was a guest of Captain John H. Geiger, a retired boat pilot and wrecker, during his 1832 visit to Key West. Audubon makes no mention of his host in any of his writings, but nonetheless, the story persists that the world-renowned ornithologist did grace the stately white-frame mansion with his presence.

On one of his many voyages, Captain Geiger brought back from the West Indies the Geiger tree *(Cordia sebestena)*, which fascinated him with its brilliant 1.5-inch trumpet-shaped orange-red blossoms and white berrylike fruit, and because it coincidentally had his own name. A magnificent Geiger in the front yard is one of Key West's most photographed sights.

In the 1950s, the house was in such deplorable disrepair, it was on the verge of being demolished for a parking lot. In stepped Key West native Mitchell Wolfson and his wife Frances, then of Miami, who restored it to nineteenth century glory and furnished it with period antiques and Audubon's complete, original Birds of America Double Elephant Folios. A film depicts many of the birds Audubon saw and painted during his Florida explorations. The restoration was the catalyst for an ongoing rejuvenation of Key West's Old Town.

**Directions:** 205 Whitehead Street, near the corner of Whitehead and Greene.

**Fees:** There is an admission charge.

**Dates:** Open daily.

**For more information:** Audubon House and Tropical Gardens, 205 Whitehead Street, Key West, FL 33040. Phone (305) 294-2116.

### CITY CEMETERY

[Fig. 8(7)] This carefully tended 16-acre spot in the center of Old Town is one of the best places to get away from the crowds for some quiet contemplation. It's also one of the best birding spots in town. Some unusual sightings have occurred over the years, including one of the Antillean palm swift *(Tachornis phoenicobia)*.

Open every day from sunrise to sunset, it's a popular place for Key Westers to walk, ride bikes, jog, and find a shady place under a tree or beside a tombstone to read and muse on the vagaries of life. Since 1847, the cemetery has been the final resting place for the town's illustrious citizens, eccentrics, ordinary citizens, a few beloved dogs, and even a pet Key deer.

An attractive, fenced plot, with a bronze statue of a sailor holding an oar, is the final resting spot for the seamen who died when the battleship *Maine* exploded in Havana harbor in 1898. Although evidence, still not conclusive, pointed to an accidental explosion, William Randolph Hearst and other "yellow journalists" of the time blamed the Spanish Empire, which was then fighting Cuba's independence movement. The influential newspapers exploited the disaster, pushing the U.S. into the war with the Spanish Empire and netting Uncle Sam an empire of his own, which included Puerto Rico and the Virgin Islands.

Today, more than 70,000 graves fill the cemetery and spaces were long ago sold out. Bring your camera because you'll probably want a photo of BP Robert's crypt with the inscription, "I told You I was Sick."

**Directions:** Bordered by Angela, Frances, William, and Olivia streets. The main entrance is on Margaret Street.

**Activities:** Guided tours 2 days a week.

**Dates:** Open daily sunrise to sunset.

**Fees:** There is a small fee for the tours, which begin at the Margaret Street entrance.

**For more information:** Phone (305) 292-6829.

### CONCH TOUR TRAIN

If this is your first visit to Key West, hop on the Conch Train, at the terminal near Sloppy Joe's and other locations, for a 90-minute orientation. The motorized tram, a series of open-sided cars pulled by a Jeep disguised as an old-timey locomotive, covers the town from the Atlantic to the Gulf of Mexico. Along the way, the driver delivers a nonstop spiel about every street and landmark, with commentary on local personalities, scandals, gossip, and ongoing controversies—all salted with far too many corny jokes.

A lot of it can and should be tuned out, but the tour does give you an opportunity to see things you'd probably miss on your own, and places you might want to come back to another time. It operates nonstop every day. The same company also operates more comfortable Trolley Tours on the same route. The tram can be boarded at most of the major hotels and motels.

**Directions:** Conch Train has 2 boarding locations, Mallory Square at 301 Front Street and Lands End Village at Margaret and Caroline streets.

**Dates:** Operates every day.

**Fees:** There is a charge for the tour.

**For more information:** Phone (305) 294-5161 or (800) 868-7482. Web site www.historictours.com.

### EAST MARTELLO MUSEUM AND ART GALLERY

[Fig. 8(12)] Built before the Civil War as part of Fort Zachary Taylor's coastal defenses, the brick and mortar building was never completed. By the late 1950s, when the local art and historical society began restoration, the structure was in a dreadful state of dilapidation. Now it serves as an excellent window on Key West's past. Permanent exhibits focus on pirates, Indians, Civil War artifacts, and the turtling, fishing, cigar making, and sponge harvesting industries. The art gallery displays a series of changing shows by local artists.

Jerry-rigged and flimsy rafts, some little more than blocks of styrofoam tied together, serve as reminders of the waves of Cuban refugees that for more then 30 years have been risking their lives in an against-all-odds attempt to float across the hazardous Straits of Florida. Many washed ashore in the Keys, others were picked up by the U.S. Coast Guard and private vessels, and some didn't make it across.

**Directions:** 3501 South Roosevelt Boulevard, across from the airport.

**Dates:** Open daily.

**Fees:** There is an admission charge for self-guided tours.

**For more information:** Phone (305) 296-3913.

## FORT ZACHARY TAYLOR STATE HISTORIC SITE AND PARK

[Fig. 8(10)] Built in the 1840s as a link in Florida's coastal defense system, the massive brick fortress was named for President Zachary Taylor, who died in office in 1850. On the day Florida seceded from the Union, troops loyal to the Union seized the fort and held it throughout the war. New rifled cannons that developed during the war and were capable of knocking out chunks of bricks with every shot rendered the fort obsolete. During the Spanish-American War of 1898, the fort was temporarily reactivated and its walls were lowered to accommodate installation of modern armaments.

It was subsequently abandoned, all but buried in debris and rubble, and largely forgotten for about half a century. Rediscovered and restored, it's now part of an 87-acre park administered by the Florida State Park System. The museum contains Civil War weaponry, including one of the country's largest cannon collections, and exhibits that tell the fort's history. Park rangers conduct guided tours. Many people come not for the history, but for the shaded picnic grounds, one of Key West's best beaches, and to celebrate the sunset from one of the best viewpoints on the island.

**Directions:** Enter on Southard Street, through the Truman Annex Gates, at the southwest end of the island.

**Dates:** Open daily until sunset.

**Fees:** There is an admission charge.

**For more information:** Fort Zachary Taylor State Historic Site, PO Box 6560, Key West, FL 33041. Phone (305) 292-6713.

## ERNEST HEMINGWAY HOUSE MUSEUM

[Fig. 8(9)] Today a registered national historic landmark, the house was bought by Ernest Hemingway and his wife Pauline in 1931. Built in 1851 by Connecticut ship-builder Asa Tift, from rock hewn from the grounds, the Spanish Colonial-style house was once the finest in town. However, the Hemingways and their two sons found it in disrepair and spent considerably more than their $8,000 purchase price making it a suitable living and creative space for one of the world's most esteemed authors.

In the midst of the Great Depression, when most of Key West was flat broke and bankrupt, the house was staffed by a team of servants and equipped with one of Key West's rare indoor bathrooms. While Hemingway was away on one of his adventures, Pauline had a 60-foot-long swimming pool built as a homecoming surprise. When Papa learned it cost the princely sum of $20,000—an amount guides always point out as the equivalent of about $230,000 today—his surprise purportedly turned into his famous fury. He took a penny from his pocket and shouted, "Here, take the last penny I've got!" throwing the coin onto the pool deck, where it's now impressed in cement for all to see.

The tiled "fountain" in the back garden is actually a urinal Hemingway ripped out of the men's room of the original Sloppy Joe's (now Captain Tony's) during a drunken brawl.

Between big-game hunting and fishing expeditions in the Keys, Africa, the American West, and elsewhere—and rowdy drinking bouts in Key West saloons—Hemingway stayed at his desk long enough to produce an astounding body of work, including *A Farewell to Arms, The Green Hills of Africa, The Snows of Kilimanjaro,* and *To Have and to Have Not,* a novel (made into Humphrey Bogart's first film with Lauren Bacall with the famous line, "You know how to whistle, don't you? Just pucker up and blow") that showcased Key West's sad plight during the Great Depression.

To assure his concentration, and keep his family and legions of fans at bay, he built a catwalk from the main house to his studio above the former carriage house. And God help anybody who attempted to walk the catwalk while the great man was in the creative clouds. Speaking of cats, dozens of them, including many descended from his exotic six-toed clan, still have the run of the grounds.

Hemingway remained at the house until 1940, when he divorced Pauline and moved to Cuba. He owned the house until his suicide in 1961 in Ketchum, Idaho.

Papa's everlasting impression on his adopted city's psyche comes full flower during mid-July's Hemingway Days Festival, a 10-day blowout with a Caribbean street festival, fishing tournament, writers conference, walking tours, a 5K sunset run, readings of Hemingway's works, and the popular Papa Look-Alike Contest at Sloppy Joe's. One of the newest wrinkles is Sloppy Joe's "Running of the Bulls," a wacky no-bull takeoff on the annual event in Pamplona, Spain, which Hemingway immortalized in *The Sun Also Rises.*

**Directions:** 907 Whitehead Street. Close to Truman Avenue. Look for the Key West Lighthouse across the street.

**Dates:** Open daily.

**Fees:** There is an admission charge.

**For more information:** Phone (305) 294-1136.

### KEY WEST AQUARIUM

[Fig. 8(2)] Opened in 1934, this pleasant little aquarium is one of the few places in this adult Disney World that seems tailored for kids. At the Touch Tank, children will giggle as they pick up starfish, clams, oysters, shrimp, and squid and squeeze a squirt out of the sea cucumbers.

At regular intervals, guides feed the resident sharks. There is also a turtle pool, live coral, and a mangrove ecosystem. You can observe a smorgasbord of Keys marine life that resides in glass tanks: colorful, coral-eating parrotfish, porcupine fish, monkfish, sawfish, barracuda, turtles, squid, jellyfish, and many others. Fish feeding takes place at 11 a.m. everyday.

**Directions:** One Whitehead Street, on the waterfront at Mallory Square.
**Dates:** Open daily.
**Fees:** There is an admission charge.
**For more information:** Phone (305) 296-2051.

### KEY WEST LIGHTHOUSE MUSEUM

[Fig. 8(8)] You can climb 88 steps to the top of Florida's third oldest brick lighthouse for one of the best views around of Key West, the Atlantic Ocean, and the Gulf of Mexico. When it was built in 1847, it was only 58 feet high. But as trees grew and buildings blocked the lightkeeper's view, the sentinel's height was increased to keep ahead, finally topping out at 78 feet. The light was turned off in 1969, and the lighthouse was deactivated. Displays in the museum include relics from the battleship *Maine,* which mysteriously exploded in Havana harbor in 1898. The current lens is from the Sombrero Lighthouse. The lighthouse keeper's quarters has undergone an award-winning restoration.
**Directions:** 938 Whitehead Street, across from the Hemingway House.
**Dates:** Open daily.
**Fees:** There is an admission charge.
**For more information:** Phone (305) 294-0012.

### CHARLES "SONNY" MCCOY INDIGENOUS PARK

[Fig. 8(14)] Named for Key West's early 1980s mayor, the 3-acre city park contains over 125 species of trees and shrubs, purportedly the largest public collection of tropical native plants in the Keys. All are identified and include many endangered and rare plants such as torchwood, crabwood, satinwood, soldierwood, Darling plum, pitch apple, pond apple, lignum vitae, Jamaica caper, silver and buccaneer palms, satinleaf, silver buttonwood, and black ironwood.

Among the park's tropical fruit trees are sour orange, Spanish lime, breadfruit, governor's plum, and Key lime. Medicinal trees include stoppers—a group of six related trees Keys pioneers brewed into tea that stopped diarrhea.

All this plant life attracts migrating songbirds; buntings, tanagers, vireos, 20 species of warblers and wintering ducks and shorebirds have been spotted in the trees. The park is also a habitat for butterflies, including giant swallowtails, red admirals, queens, and zebra longwings. An observation platform offers views of salt marshes and bird life.

Wildlife Rescue of the Florida Keys is also on the grounds. This group of dedicated individuals cares for and rehabilitates injured birds and releases them back to the wild when possible. The park also houses the city nursery where native and imported plants are raised for landscaping around the city.
**Directions:** Atlantic Boulevard (US Highway A1A) between White Street and Steven Avenue. Near the White Street Pier.

**Fees:** There is no admission charge.

**Dates:** Open Monday through Friday.

**For more information:** Key West Recreation Director, phone (305) 292-8190.

### MEL FISHER'S MARITIME HERITAGE SOCIETY MUSEUM

[Fig. 8(4)] A portion of the booty Fisher and his intrepid team of divers uncovered from the Spanish treasure ships *Santa Margarita* and *Nuestra Senora de Atocha* is displayed in a big stone building near the waterfront. The gold-laden sister ships were sent to the bottom by a hurricane on September 6, 1622, shortly after setting sail from Havana. The ships carried gold and silver bullion, magnificent jewelry, and a fortune in emeralds—a small fraction of the riches Spain was bleeding from the New World.

After long years of research and treasure hunting, Fisher's crew discovered the wrecks about 40 miles off Key West.

Expect to be stunned: This is a real treasure, one that even Long John Silver would be proud of. Chests of silver coins and gold bars, heavy gold chains you could pull a truck with, and emerald-encrusted gold jewelry are there. One of the more bizarre pieces is a poison cup, which has an embedded bezoar stone that changed colors when it came in contact with toxic substances. Weapons and navigational tools from the two ships are also on display.

You can also see a film about the discovery and the difficulties of locating and extracting sunken treasure. The *Arbutus*, one of Fisher's work vessels, sank in 1980, with no loss of life, in the Dry Tortugas. Much of the treasure discovered between 1970 and the early 1990s is still being cleaned and cataloged elsewhere in the huge building.

**Directions:** 200 Greene Street, near Mallory Square.

**Dates:** Open daily.

**Fees:** There is an admission charge.

**For more information:** Phone (305) 294-2633.

### NANCY FORRESTER'S SECRET GARDEN

[Fig. 8(13)] Since 1994, artist and nature-lover Nancy Forrester and her friends have transformed her 1-acre parcel of land into one of Key West's natural treasures. The diverse assortment of trees, flowers, and plants includes many that are endangered and some no longer in existence in their native habitat. Under a deep green canopy, spangled by filtered sunlight, thrive hundreds of orchids, bromeliads, ferns, palms, and bog plants. The dirt paths skirt 150 species of palms—including equatorials from the Pacific Marquesas Islands, deep forest species from South America's Amazon Basin and Orinoco River, and near-extinct palms from Cuba.

Here and there are open spaces with garden chairs where you can sit and contemplate awhile. Squawking parrots and other tropical birds, in cages around the grounds, enhance the sensation that you have, indeed, wandered into a tropical rain forest. Wandering the paths, it's easy to get happily turned around and temporarily lose track of the way out. Unfortunately, like many of the Keys' wild areas, the garden is threatened by developers, hoping to turn this valuable property into more lucrative residential real estate.

Botanical prints are on sale in the art gallery.

**Directions:** One Free School Lane, off Simonton Street behind the Marquesa Hotel.

**Dates:** Open daily.

**Fees:** There is an admission charge.

**For more information:** Phone (305) 294-0015.

### HARRY TRUMAN'S LITTLE WHITE HOUSE AND BOTANICAL GARDEN

[Fig. 8(5)] President Harry S Truman made the first of 10 winter vacation trips to Key West in 1946. His place of lodging, which came to be known as "The Little White House," was the former home of the commandant of the Key West Naval Base. Built in 1890, the two-story house is noted for its tropical gardens and wide verandas enclosed by wooden louvers.

Away from the presidential grind of Washington, and the prying eyes of the press and public, folksy Harry enjoyed strolling around town in outlandish Hawaiian shirts, chatting with locals and tourists, fishing, swimming, drinking bourbon, and playing the piano and poker with his cronies. Truman reportedly invited potential appointees to see how they held up under the pressures of the poker table.

Guides point out that Truman's middle initial is just that. His parents didn't give him a middle name, so to stifle questions about it, he adopted the letter S, which is correctly spelled without a period.

After touring the house, take a self-guided walk through the surrounding botanical garden. More than two dozen types of tropical trees, grasses, and shrubs have been identified and marked by the Key West Garden Club. They include bougainvillea and fishtail fern; fiji fan, coconut, Manila, Madagascar, thatch, and Washingtonia palms; monkey and St. Augustine grasses; avocado, banyan, gumbo-limbo, mahogany, royal poinciana, tropical almond, jacaranda, and Spanish lime trees.

Down-to-earth, man-of-the-people Harry S would probably be astonished to learn that his house and garden are now in the middle of a very expensive real estate community. In 1986, the Navy declared the 43-acre Truman Annex surplus property and sold it at auction. The Truman Annex Real Estate Co. has sold the former officers' homes to fortunate private citizens. Other buildings, including the U.S. Marine Hospital, built in 1844, have become pricey condominiums. Architecturally compatible new condos and townhouses have joined the housing mix.

**Directions:** 111 Front Street.

**Dates:** Open daily.

**Fees:** There is an admission charge.
**For more information:** Phone (305) 294-9911.

### SOUTHERNMOST POINT IN THE CONTINENTAL UNITED STATES

[Fig. 8(11)] A large black, yellow, and red missile-shaped buoy marks the most southerly place you can go and still be in the continental confines of the United States. "Continental" is the key word, because the actual most southerly place in all the 50 states is on the Big Island of Hawaii. "America Begins Here" is painted on the curb. It could just as well say, "America Ends Here."

Hundreds of tourists come everyday by Conch Train, bicycle, foot, and rental car to have their pictures taken by the buoy. Nearby vendors staff tables laden with conch shells and all manner of trinkets, T-shirts, and souvenirs fashioned from shells. They are here every day.

**Directions:** Whitehead and South streets at the ocean.
**Fees:** None.

### OLDEST HOUSE MUSEUM

[Fig. 8(6)] Built around 1829, and believed to be Key West's oldest house, the museum is a window on the Keys' early maritime history. Once the home of harbor pilot Captain Francis B. Watlington, you can learn the "Rules of Wrecking" and its history through photographs, ship models, and wrecking documents. A locator map shows the location of 50 nineteenth century wrecks.

The house still has a back porch cistern and a separate cook house—the town's last remaining outside kitchen. Kids are usually fascinated by the built-to-scale Victorian-style doll house with a mural of old Key West in the dining room. Be sure to take a stroll through the Rosemary Austin Memorial Garden.

**Directions:** 322 Duval Street.
**Dates:** Open daily.
**Fees:** There is an admission charge.
**For more information:** Phone (305) 294-9502.

# Key West Beaches

For the majority of visitors to Key West, beach-going is not at the top of their list. And if it is, Bahia Honda State Park (*see* page 94), north on the Overseas Highway at MM 37 is where they should go. Around Key West the waters are shallow, and the beaches are small and narrow and usually crowded. But none of that takes away from the beauty of the water, or the feel of the sun's warmth on your skin after a swim. In the summer, an occasional dip in the water is a good way to pass a hot afternoon, but don't forget your sunscreen.

There's also an endless number of water sport opportunities available. Jet Skis, parasailing, water skiing, tubing, boating, windsurfing, and sailing concessions are easy enough to find by simply driving around the perimeter of the island. There's even something called a Banana Boat, which looks for all the world like a great big banana that you sit on while another boat tows it around.

### FORT ZACHARY TAYLOR STATE PARK

[Fig. 8(10)] This park is the consensus choice for the town's best beach. You'll want to wear some old sneakers, sandals, or some other type of footwear as protection against the rough coral sand. When the sun gets too scorching, you can take respite under a group of trees. It's a good place to watch the sunset and pleasure boats skimming by on the gentle surf.

Fishing for snapper and other bottom species is good on the west side of the park because of a deep ship channel near shore.

**Directions:** Go through the Truman Annex gates on Southard Street, through the state park gates, and onto the beach.

**Activities:** Swimming, sunning, fishing.

**Facilities:** Picnic areas, restrooms, food and drink concessions, grills, outside showers and bathhouses.

**Dates:** Open daily.

**Fees:** There is an admission charge.

**For more information:** Phone (305) 292-6713.

### CLARENCE HIGGS MEMORIAL BEACH

[Fig. 8] This small, clean beach is popular with families and just about everybody else. There is a playground and free tennis courts across the street. The adjacent White Street Pier is a popular fishing spot and a good bird-watching spot for gulls, terns, and other shorebirds.

**Directions:** Atlantic Boulevard between White and Reynolds streets.

**Activities:** Swimming, sunbathing, fishing.

**Facilities:** Restrooms, picnic areas, tennis courts, concession stands, water sports equipment rentals, fishing pier.

**Dates:** Open year-round.

**Fees:** None.

### SMATHERS BEACH

[Fig. 8] This is the city's longest stretch of sand. It's where the action is. You can join beach volleyball games, rent Jet Skis, and sign up for a parasailing ride over the beach. There are plenty of places to buy snacks, drinks, and suntan lotion.

**Directions:** Off South Roosevelt Boulevard (US A1A), west of the airport.

**Activities:** Swimming, sunbathing, water skiing, picnic grounds.

**Facilities:** Picnic areas, restrooms, bathhouses, water sport equipment rentals, food and drink concessions.
**Dates:** Open year-round.
**Fees:** None.

## ON-THE-WATER ACTIVITIES

With all the places to see and things to do on the island of Key West, it's easy to forget that it's really the surrounding waters that define its qualities. The life-rich, blue-green Caribbean waters brought the first Indians, the first Europeans, the pirates and wreckers. It's the water that defines the available space on the island, that creates the eclectic jumble of buildings, and crowds the people together that squeeze onto the island. And its the water that will allow you to escape the island when all of this becomes too much.

For the stay-dry crowd, there's a vast choice of boating and sailing opportunities. Great tall-masted schooners will carry you on a leisurely voyage around the island. Or you can choose a sleeker, faster catamaran for a trip to the reef or just a spray-filled ride through the waves. Glass bottom boat rides will give you a clear, close-up view of the coral reef in its full splendor. Large ferries and high-speed catamarans make full day runs to the Dry Tortugas.

Some of the finest snorkeling and diving opportunities in the world are available in Key West. This far from the mainland, the waters are always crystal clear, and the selection of reef and wreck diving in the Atlantic and the Gulf of Mexico is unsurpassed.

Sand Key, just 2.5 miles away from Key West, is one of the most popular dive sites. The small island and adjacent reef are marked by a lighthouse built in 1853. Perfect for snorkelers, the reef's fingerlike rock outcroppings in less than 20 feet of water support staghorn and elkhorn coral, a variety of sponges, and anemones. A place called Western Dry Rocks has caves and crevices teeming with life; crabs, lobsters, stingrays, and sea turtles roam the natural structure. Or you can spend an entire vacation exploring sunken ships like the *Alexander's Wreck*, a former Navy destroyer escort sunk in 30 feet of water, or the *Aquanaut*, a wooden salvage tug in 75 feet of water.

Any of the many Key West dive shops offer trips to the best sites. They'll also provide equipment, advice, directions, and lessons. Many of the dive sites are susceptible to strong currents and winds. Using a professional dive operation is the safest choice for first-time visitors. (*See* Appendix D for a list of dive operations).

Deep-sea fishing in the waters around Key West is another can't-miss adventure. The best way to find out what your choices are is to stop by Charter Boat Row near the intersection of Palm Avenue and North Roosevelt Avenue (US Highway 1). The entrance is off Palm Avenue, a short distance north of the intersection.

A stroll along the dock past dozens of charter boats and party boats will give you a quick lesson in the fishing experiences available. Go in the late afternoon and you can check out the boats, see the day's catches, talk to the captains or the first mates, and decide what kind of fishing challenge strikes your fancy.

Charter boats venture into the Gulf Stream where they troll for trophy sailfish and marlin, wahoo, dolphin, king mackerel, bonita, yellowfin tuna, and blackfin tuna. Most species are around all year, but sailfish, wahoo, and the tunas are more abundant in the fall and winter.

Cobia, amberjack, snapper, and grouper are available all year, gathered at the wrecks and reefs where they occupy a lofty place on the food chain and provide targets for the big and small party boats and bottom fishing charters. Many of the boats offer one-, two-, or three-day trips to the Dry Tortugas and back. On the way they fish for all the great saltwater species—marlin, tarpon, sailfish, and wahoo—and they provide their clients with a chance to see the last keys in the string.

Backcountry fishing here is as fine as anywhere in the Keys. Shallow-water flats guides will lead the way to a world of permit, bonefish, and barracuda. In the spring and summer, the dark shapes of tarpon cruise the flats and can be a challenge on flyrod or conventional tackle. Most guides will cater a trip to your level of experience and the fish you hope to catch.

**For more information:** Most diving and eco-tour operations have brochures and information sheets you can pick up around town and look over later when making your choices. Or you can stop by the Key West Chamber of Commerce (which is also located at Old Mallory Square) at 402 Wall Street. Phone (800) LAST-KEY or (305) 294-2587. For more information on dive shops and fishing charters see Appendix D, page 296.

# Key West Lodging

A town that lives and dies by the constant flow of tourist dollars naturally has the widest possible spectrum of places to keep tourists comfortably housed—from chain motels similar to the thousands that line America's roadways, to lavish resort hotels, to quaint guest houses and bed and breakfast inns in restored Caribbean and Victorian homes.

For a prolonged stay, you might want to rent a house or a condo from a local realtor. Chain motels—Days Inn, Howard Johnson, Holiday Inn, Best Western, Fairfield Inn, Hampton Inn, etc.—are lined along North Roosevelt Boulevard (US 1), a four-lane traffic-crazy artery that brings you into town from the Lower Keys.

Most of the motels offer at least limited Gulf of Mexico views, although the beaches and waterfront views are much better on South Roosevelt Boulevard (US A1A) where the lodging is more expensive. Crowded among the motels are all the most common fast-food outlets. And there are plenty of shopping malls with familiar stores like Kmart and Sears. You can also stop at the Key West Welcome Center, 3840 North Roosevelt Boulevard for maps, brochures, and information. Phone (305) 296-4444 or (800) 284-4482.

If you're looking for charm with a capital C, however, you'll have to head to quiet residential streets like Fleming, Simonton, William, Angela, Olivia, Caroline, and Southard. There you'll find comfortable bed and breakfast inns, guesthouses, and small hotels that welcome you with private gardens, pools, continental breakfast with piles of tropical fruit, complimentary afternoon wine, and a friendly, welcome-to-our-happy-home spirit. The innkeepers cheerfully share their cache of hidden away eateries and bars, known only to locals (and other tourists steered there by their hosts).

Some Old Town guest houses are exclusively gay. Innkeepers will probably inform you if that's the case, but if that's not your preference, and there's a doubt, be sure to inquire. If you're looking for a full-service resort on the ocean, South Roosevelt Boulevard (A1A) should be your address. Hotels that front Atlantic beaches are so close to the airport, you'll be in the water, musing smugly about what the poor folks at home are doing, a few minutes after picking up your luggage in the terminal. There are also many moderately priced motels in the closer-in South Street-Simonton Street beach area.

Prices are highest during the December through May winter season, when hotels may require a nonrefundable two- to three-day deposit. Rates are usually jacked up a few more notches during holidays and big local festivals, when many places require a multiple-day minimum stay. Prices drop dramatically in summer and fall.

**For more information:** The Key West Chamber of Commerce will send you an accommodation guide, with thumbnail descriptions. PO Box 984, Key West, FL 33041. Phone (305) 294-2587 or (800) LAST-KEY (527-8539). Fax (305) 294-7806.

## GUEST HOUSES, INNS, RESORTS, AND HOTELS
### ALEXANDER'S GUEST HOUSE
1118 Fleming Street. Award-winning exclusively gay accommodations. There are 17 deluxe guest rooms, some with kitchens, freshwater pool, complimentary continental breakfast. *Expensive. Phone (305) 294-9919 or (800) 654-9919.*
### ANDREWS INN
Zero Whalton Lane. On a shaded lane, off the 900 block of Duval Street. There are 8 tropical-style rooms. Pool, off-street parking. Breakfast, evening cocktails. *Moderate to expensive. Phone (305) 294-7730.*
### ATLANTIC SHORES RESORT
510 South Street. An Art Deco motel, with 72 rooms right on the ocean, a half-block from Duval. Restaurant, lively, very popular bar, 150-foot pier, and clothing-optional pool. *Moderate to expensive. Phone (305) 296-2491 or (800) 526-3559.*
### BANANA BAY RESORT
2319 North Roosevelt Boulevard. Located on a historic piece of property. Once the site of Flagler's Key West railroad terminal. Later the first post-war motor lodge was built on the site. Today the Banana Bay Resort has 48 deluxe rooms including 12

suites. It also has a Gulf-front beach, sun deck, water sports, pool, whirlpool, beach-side Tiki bar, and a marina with dock space. *Moderate. Phone (800) 226-2621, ext 2.*

### BEST WESTERN KEY AMBASSADOR RESORT INN

3755 South Roosevelt Boulevard. There are 100 guest rooms, many with porches, balconies, and refrigerators, across from the ocean. Pool, continental breakfast, airport shuttle. *Expensive. Phone (305) 296-3500 or (800) 432-4315.*

### CURRY MANSION INN

511 Caroline Street. Features 15 elegant old Keys-style rooms and more modern rooms by the pool. Breakfast, lavish gardens, beach privileges at the Pier House and Casa Marina. *Expensive. Phone (800) 253-3460.*

### CYPRESS HOUSE

601 Caroline Street. Built in 1888, the grand Conch mansion, a block off Duval, is one of Key West's best examples of nineteenth century Bahamian architecture. Large air conditioned guest rooms, with high ceilings and ceiling fans, open onto gardens and a 40-foot heated lap pool. *Expensive. Phone (305) 294-6969 or (800) 525-2488.*

### GARDENS HOTEL

526 Angela Street. A block off Duval, 17 deluxe rooms and suites are in four Bahamian-style houses, grouped around a garden courtyard and swimming pool. The sumptuous gardens are the legacy of the late Peggy Mills, a Key West nature enthusiast who began her botanical collection in the 1930s and grew fantastic things until her death in the 1980s. Royal poinciana, palm and mango trees, orchids, hibiscus, and bougainvillea create a secluded haven that attracts visiting celebrities and many weddings. Among the nonbotanical treasures are *tinajones,* enormous earthenware jars that originally brought oil and other products from Cuba. The amiable pool-side bartender is a wealth of inside tips about local favorite restaurants and bars. The breakfast buffet is laden with fresh-baked breads and pastries and tropical fruit. *Very expensive. Phone (800) 526-2664 or (305) 294-2661.*

### HOLIDAY INN LA CONCHA RESORT HOTEL

430 Duval Street. The seven-story 1920s landmark, modernized in 1986, towers over the Duval Street entertainment area. The comfortable lobby with cushy chairs and sofas is a good place to meet friends and call timeout for a spell. Walk out the front door, and you're in the middle of the day-and-night action. The inn also includes 160 guest rooms, rooftop restaurant (The Top) with all-encompassing views, stylish streetside Celebrities restaurant, shops, tour services, bar, and pool. *Expensive. Phone (800) 745-2191 or (305) 296-2991.*

### KEY WEST HILTON RESORT & MARINA

245 Front Street. Contemporary resort complex opened in 1995. Guests can walk around the corner for sunset on Mallory Square, or watch it from their rooms or the marina. Also includes oceanfront dining, full service marina, water sports, and secluded beach. *Very expensive. Phone (800) 445-8667 or (305) 294-4000.*

### KEY WESTER RESORT

3675 South Roosevelt Boulevard. A 100-room resort on 9 Atlantic-facing acres. Tennis courts, pool, Tiki bar, and restaurant. *Very expensive. Phone (800) 477-8888 or (305) 296-5671.*

### LA PENSIONE INN

809 Truman Avenue. Classic Revival mansion on the edge of Old Town. Built in 1891, with 7 luxurious guest rooms with distinctive Key West-Caribbean decor. Pool, continental breakfast, off-street parking. *Expensive. Phone (305) 292-9923 or (800) 893-1193.*

### MARQUESA HOTEL

600 Fleming Street. Small, elegant hotel in a restored 1880s boardinghouse and two companion buildings a short walk from Duval. There are 27 deluxe rooms and suites. Upscale restaurant with Caribbean and American cuisine, bar, pool. *Expensive. Phone (800) 869-4631 or (305) 292-1919.*

### MARRIOTT'S CASA MARINA RESORT

1500 Reynolds Street. Henry Flagler planned this Spanish Renaissance-style Xanadu as a plush exclamation point at the end of the Florida East Coast Railroad. He died before it was built, but its languid Old World charm lured affluent pre-WWII travelers all the same. Marriott saved it from the bulldozers in 1978, did a total makeover, and nowadays, it's Key West's largest oceanfront resort, with 314 rooms, 2 pools, a 1,100-foot beach, water sports, bikes, a health club, Flagler's Restaurant, bars, and entertainment. The only drawback is it's a bit of a hike or bike from downtown. *Very expensive. Phone (305) 296-3535.*

### NASSAU HOUSE

1016 Fleming Street. Hospitable B&B in quiet Old Town residential area. There are 6 rooms and suites, some with kitchens. The spacious, third-floor Treetop Suites and Nassau Cottage offer the ultimate privacy. Continental breakfast, pool, pets allowed. *Moderate. Phone (800) 296-8513 or (305) 296-8513.*

### OCEAN KEY HOUSE SUITE RESORT AND MARINA

Zero Duval Street. On the edge of Mallory Square. Deluxe suites with kitchens, jacuzzi, balconies with views of water and sunset. *Very expensive. Phone (800) 231-9864 or (305) 296-7701.*

### PIER HOUSE RESORT HOTEL AND CARIBBEAN SPA

One Duval Street. A longtime favorite of Key West regulars. The 142 rooms and suites with private terraces are in a tropical garden setting. At the gateway to the Duval activities, its got just about everything you could require—a private beach, shops, health spa, outdoor pools, 5 restaurants, and 5 bars. *Very expensive. Phone (800) 327-8340 or (305) 296-4600.*

### SOUTHERNMOST POINT GUESTHOUSE

1327 Duval Street. Across from South Beach. There are 6 rooms in a revamped 1885 Victorian mansion. Ocean view, continental breakfast, BBQ grills, whirlpool, jacuzzi, parking. Pets, children welcome. *Inexpensive to moderate. Phone (305) 294-0715.*

## ▓ CHAIN MOTELS
### DAYS INN
3852 North Roosevelt Boulevard. 133 rooms, 18 suites with full kitchens, pool, breakfast restaurant, pets welcome. *Inexpensive to moderate. Phone (305) 294-3742 or (800) 325-2525.*

### ECONO LODGE RESORT
3820 North Roosevelt Boulevard. 145 rooms, some with kitchens, 24-hour Denny's Restaurant, Tiki bar, lounge, parking. *Moderate to expensive. Phone (305) 294-5511 or (800) 999-7277.*

### FAIRFIELD INN BY MARRIOTT
2400 North Roosevelt Boulevard. 100 guest rooms, 32 suites. Free continental breakfast, pool. *Moderate to expensive. Phone (305) 296-5700 or (800) 228-2800.*

### HAMPTON INN
2801 North Roosevelt Boulevard. 158 rooms, pool, continental breakfast, jacuzzis, Tiki bar. *Inexpensive to expensive. Phone (305) 294-2917 or (800)-HAMPTON.*

### HOLIDAY INN BEACHSIDE
1111 North Roosevelt Boulevard. 222 rooms, 79 with Gulf of Mexico views. Freshwater pool, water sports, diving and snorkeling trips arranged, restaurant, bar, gift shop, lighted tennis courts. *Expensive. Phone (305) 294-2571 or (800) 292-7706.*

### HOWARD JOHNSON LODGE
3031 North Roosevelt Boulevard. Midscale resort with 64 rooms, restaurant, bar, pool, Jet Ski and bicycle rentals. *Expensive. Phone (305) 296-6595 or (800) 654-2000.*

### QUALITY INN
3850 North Roosevelt Boulevard. 148 rooms and efficiencies, some with kitchens. Pool, in-room coffee makers. *Moderate to expensive. Phone (305) 294-6681 or (800) 228-5151.*

### RAMADA INN
3420 North Roosevelt Boulevard. 104 rooms. Full service restaurant, lounge with entertainment. Pool. Pets welcome. *Inexpensive to moderate. Phone (305) 294-5541 or (800) 330-5541.*

## ▓ CAMPGROUNDS/RV PARKS
### BOYD'S KEY WEST CAMPGROUND
MM 5, 6401 Maloney Avenue, Stock Island. 203 RV camping sites, freshwater pool, camp store, water, electricity, sewer hookups, cable TV, 24-hour security, boat ramp and dock. Pets welcome. *Inexpensive. Phone (305) 294-1465, fax (305) 293-9301.*

### JABOUR'S TRAILER COURT AND CAMPGROUND
223 Elizabeth Street, Old Town. Waterfront campground is in walking or short driving distance of everything in town. 74 tent, van, RV, and trailer sites. Pets are welcome. *Inexpensive. Phone (305) 294-5723.*

### 🖼 VACATION RENTALS

**AT HOME IN KEY WEST**

3201 Flagler Avenue. *Moderate to expensive. Phone (305) 296-7975.*

**KEY WEST REALTY**

1109 Duval Street. *Moderate to expensive. Phone (305) 294-7253 OR (800) 654-5131.*

**OLDE ISLAND REALTY**

525 Simonton Street. *Moderate to expensive. Phone (800) 621-9405.*

**RENT KEY WEST VACATIONS**

1107 Truman Avenue. *Moderate to expensive. Phone (800) 833-7368.*

# Key West Dining

Seafood naturally dominates Key West restaurant menus. Some of it is fresh from local waters, as advertised, but a lot of it is shipped in frozen from other coasts. You'll also find Cuban, Mexican, Chinese, Italian, Thai, and other cuisines. Duval Street is lined with restaurants. Some are quite good and popular with locals. Many are tourist restaurants in the worst sense, indistinguishable, one from the other. Some of the best food and most interesting dining experiences are in residential neighborhoods off Duval. You can leave your ties and dressy clothes at home. Even the best restaurants only ask is that you wear shoes and otherwise come decently clothed. "Dressy casual" usually means a shirt with sleeves and a collar.

**ANTONIA'S**

615 Duval Street. In this fickle here-today-gone-tomorrow town, Antonio's is something of a landmark. After it was destroyed by fire in 1995, it was quickly rebuilt by popular demand. Locals and tourists happily mingle and enjoy Antonio's rich Southern Italian fare and excellent wines. Casual to dressy. Dinner nightly. Reservations accepted. *Expensive. Phone (305) 294-6565.*

**BLUE HEAVEN**

729 Thomas Street at the corner of Thomas and Petronia streets. As the signs advises, "You don't have to die to get here." All you have to do is walk a couple of blocks off Duval Street into the colorful Bahama Village neighborhood. Enter the spacious, fenced, tree-shaded, dirt-and-sawdust floored patio and wait for one of the colorfully painted tables to open up.

While you're perusing the menu, look under the table. Chances are, a mother hen and brood of chicks are earnestly scratching in the dirt for their breakfast. The free-range chickens are in keeping with the neighborhood, where in Caribbean tradition, they wander unfettered in yards and streets. We're assured that none of the restaurant's chicks end up on dinner plates.

At one corner of the patio, there's a Rooster Cemetery. Craftsmen sell jewelry, tarot cards, and Caribbean art. All this and the food is terrific, which explains the usual wait for a table. "Breakfast with the Roosters" is highlighted by "Richard's Very Good Pancakes," seafood Benedict, omelettes, a breakfast tortilla, big bowls of fruit, and homemade banana bread. Caribbean-slanted lunch brings forth vegetarian black bean soup, jerk chicken, local fish, and black beans and rice. "Dinner with Chef Dan" starts with carrot and curry soup or Caribbean BBQ shrimp (also an entree), and includes jerk chicken, fish, pork tenderloin, and New York strip steak. Shrimp and grits and the avocado omelette are among the Sunday brunch specials. The companion Blue Heaven Bakery has Key lime pies, croissants, breads, and quiches to take out or enjoy at sidewalk tables on Petronia. Both are open everyday. Very casual. No reservations. *Inexpensive. Phone (305) 296-8666.*

### EL SIBONEY

900 Catherine Street. When Conchs crave Cuban they usually head for this reliable old favorite. Traditional Cuban favorites like *ropa vieja* (a shredded beef dish with a rumpled appearance that resembles "old clothes"), picadillo, fried plantains, black beans and rice, roast pork, and sangria. Casual, no reservations. Lunch, dinner daily, closed Sunday. *Inexpensive. Phone (305) 296-4184.*

### HALF SHELL RAW BAR

231 Margaret Street. No visit to Key West seems complete without boiled shrimp, oysters on the half shell, fried and grilled fish, stone crabs, and lobster in the screened dining room overlooking West Key Bight. Casual, reservations for large parties. Lunch and dinner daily. *Inexpensive to moderate. Phone (305) 294-7496.*

### LOUIE'S BACK YARD

700 Waddell Street, at the corner of Waddell and Vernon streets. One of Key West's oldest, and without doubt, one of its best-known restaurants. First-rate Caribbean and American food in a romantic setting. Sit outside on the seaside dining deck, under the tropical trees and feel smug that you were able to garner one of the hard-to-come-by reservations. Lunch and dinner daily. *Expensive. Phone (305) 294-1061.*

### MANGIA MANGIA

900 Southard Street, at Margaret Street. That's Italian for "Eat, Eat," and that's what legions of local and visiting faithful do at this cheerful Old Town favorite. What they mostly come to devour are a half dozen pastas, made fresh daily, topped with a variety of sauces. The menu also includes seafood, grilled meats, and salads, and an award-winning, 300-selection wine list. Casual to dressy. Reservations suggested. Open nightly. *Moderate to expensive. Phone (305 )294-2469.*

### MICHAEL'S

532 Margaret Street. In this seafood-oriented town, Michael's is where meat-lovers come to eat beef. In the formal dining room or at umbrella tables by the fountain, they tuck into USDA prime, Midwestern grain beef—ribeyes, T-bones, New York strip, prime rib, filet mignon—served in very generous portions. The menu also offers seafood and game dishes. Dressy. Reservations suggested. Open nightly. *Expensive. Phone (305) 295-1300.*

### SEVEN FISH

632 Olivia Street at Elizabeth Street. This small, squeaky-clean dining room in a rehabbed Old Town residential area is a big favorite with the locals, who patiently wait outside and around the tiny bar for a chance to devour wild mushroom quesadilla, crab cake, and spicy tuna roll appetizers, and main courses such as shrimp scampi, pasta, grouper, sea scallops, and other fresh seafood. As noted, be prepared to wait, especially on weekends. Dinner every day except Tuesday. Casual. No reservations. *Inexpensive to moderate. Phone (305) 296-2777.*

# Key West Night Life

In Key West, every hour is happy hour. Finding a place to settle awhile and enjoy a brew or favorite beverage is as simple as looking around and making a choice among bars that are almost as numerous as the island's T-shirt shops.

### CAPTAIN TONY'S SALOON

428 Greene Street. As the sign over the front door announces, this dark saloon a few steps off Duval was "The First and Original Sloppy Joe's." Between 1933 and 1937, it was Hemingway's favorite hangout. Papered with business cards and fading posters, it claims to be Florida's oldest bar. There's raucous live entertainment nightly. *Phone (305) 294-1838.*

### SLOPPY JOE'S

201 Duval Street, at the corner of Duval and Greene streets. When the rent on Captain Tony's was increased in 1937, the owner picked up his wares, his patrons (Hemingway among them), and moved down the street to a former restaurant, where the bar has become as huge a Key West tradition as homage to Hemingway and sunset on Mallory Square. Absolutely nobody comes to Key West without at least stepping inside the always-wide-open doors and seeing what the fuss is all about. It's as big as a barn, colorful, plastered with Papa's images, loud, and positively vibrating with hundreds of energy sources and rock bands that play from early morn to the wee hours. The beer's cold, the margaritas potent, and you can't go back to Ohio or Liverpool without a T-shirt with Hemingway's stern image. *Phone (305) 294-5717.*

### HOG'S BREATH SALOON

400 Front Street. This laid-back old saloon sells almost as many T-shirts as Sloppy Joe's ("Hog's Breath is Better than No Breath At All"). And it packs 'em in just as tightly. Open daily. Live entertainment from early afternoon to at least 2 a.m. *Phone (305) 296-2032.*

### THE GREEN PARROT

601 Whitehead Street, at the corner of Whitehead and Southard streets. A lot of locals come to this old-time neighborhood saloon to escape the tourists at Captain Tony's and Sloppy Joe's. Intrepid tourists find it anyway, on the way to and from Hemingway's House. Good drinks, a pool table, darts. *Phone (305) 294-6133.*

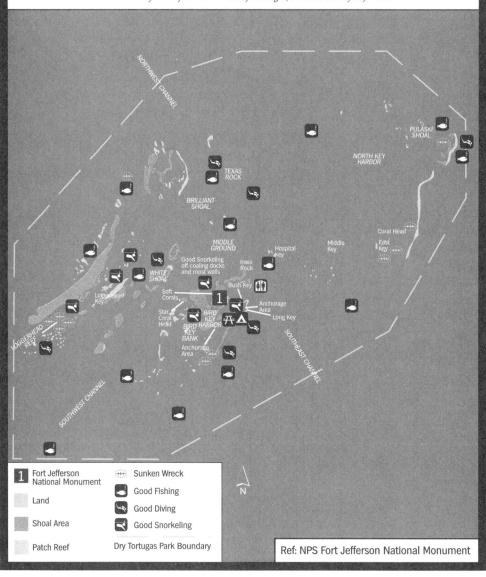

# Dry Tortugas National Park

*The real end of the Keys chain is the Dry Tortugas, 70 miles west of Key West.*

### MARGARITAVILLE CAFÉ

500 Duval Street. There you are, sipping your second or third margarita, munching your cheeseburger, grooving to the music, when, wow, wait till we tell the folks back home they'll never believe it the man Buffett himself walked in and stopped by our table and asked us were we having a good time. In Key West, all dreams are possible. *Phone (305) 292-1435.*

# Dry Tortugas National Park

[Fig. 9] Although Key West is often considered the end of the Keys chain, that real honor belongs to the Dry Tortugas, a group of seven coral islands 70 miles west of Key West. The islands' coral reefs are among the best and least disturbed in the Keys.

The islands were first discovered in 1513 by Ponce de Leon, who named them the Tortugas because of all the sea turtles he found breeding there. The word "dry" was added later to warn sailors of the lack of water.

Following Ponce de Leon's visit, Spanish vessels continued to stop at the Tortugas to collect turtles, seabirds, and eggs for their ships' stores. Pirates later used the islands as a strategic base from which to prey upon ships in the Straits of Florida. After Florida became a United States territory in 1821, the islands were garrisoned and fortified to protect navigation between ports on the East Coast and New Orleans and the Mississippi River.

The Tortugas' tropical vegetation includes red-barked gumbo-limbo trees, coconut palm (*Cocos nucifera*), date palms (*Phoenix dactylifera*), seagrape, prickly pear cactus, and ancient buttonwood trees that were probably mature when Ponce de Leon set eyes on them in 1513.

Today, divers, anglers, and sightseers converge on the Tortugas every day, drawn by the natural wonders of a true tropical paradise. Yet, it's an incongruous, nineteenth century fort that is the main attraction. There in the middle of nowhere, covering almost all of a 16-acre island, stands Fort Jefferson, the largest brick structure in the Northern Hemisphere.

### 🦑 TRAVEL TO FORT JEFFERSON AND THE DRY TORTUGAS

Travel to the fort is by seaplane or boat. A one-day round-trip boat ride from Key West can take up to eight or nine hours, depending on the boat and sea conditions.

A seaplane on the other hand takes about 35 minutes and is definitely one of the premier experiences in the Florida Keys. Although moderately expensive, it's a day that will fill many pages in your vacation journal, your photo scrapbook, and your memory file.

There's the lift off into the wind, then a turn over the city of Key West as the pilot turns and heads west. From the bird's-eye view of the seaplane, you can easily spot sea turtles, sharks, stingrays, dolphins, and schools of smaller fish swimming in the clear, shallow waters of Florida Bay. Flocks of seabirds cast fleeting shadows on the sea 500 feet below.

Next, passing below are the Marquesas Keys—an irregular ring of seven coral islands that resembles a coral atoll type usually found only in the South Pacific where a ring of coral islands surrounds a central lagoon. The Marquesas are also one of very few North American nesting sites for the magnificent frigatebird. Sometimes the pilot will drop down low enough over the islands to spot some of the large, black fork-tailed birds. Large fish and sharks are easy to spot in the shallow water surrounding the islands.

Another part of the flight passes over an area of shifting undersea sand dunes called the Quicksands. The dunes are at the mercy of strong tide and storm currents. A white mast poking out of the water marks the clearly visible outline of a sunken ship.

The *Arbutus* was treasure-hunter Mel Fisher's work vessel. The 70-foot ship sank from hull deterioration, with no loss of life, during Fisher's expedition to salvage Spanish treasure that tropical storms had strewn across the sea bottom. Fisher's successful efforts to liberate millions of dollars in booty from the *Nuestra Senora de Atocha* and *Santa Margarita* have inspired other adventurers to plumb the depths for other caches of South American gold, silver, and emeralds that never completed their voyage to Spain's royal coffers.

The pilot will also point out the ghostly shadows of the World War II destroyer escort *Patricia.* The Navy intentionally scuttled her as a bombing practice target.

Thirty-five minutes and 70 miles after leaving Key West, the seaplane banks sharply over the morning's destination, star-shaped Fort Jefferson, which occupies virtually all of 16-acre Garden Key. From the air, this huge, out-of-place, out-of-time structure is a surrealistic sight, a giant incongruity in a land of blue-green waters and emerald islands.

From the moment the plane begins to descend begin watching for unusual birds. Out the airplane's window you might easily spot a magnificent frigatebird or a white-tailed tropicbird (*Phaethon lepturus*) with its long white flowing tail.

After landing in the protected harbor next to the key, and the plane bumps onto the beach of Garden Key, only a few yards from the entrance into the red-brick ramparts of Fort Jefferson.

**Directions:** 70 miles west of Key West. Seaplanes of Key West is the easiest, fastest, and most expensive way to get there. The 35-minute morning and afternoon flights, with about 3 to 6 hours at Fort Jefferson, include a cooler of soft drinks and water and snorkeling equipment. Phone (800) 950-2359 or (305) 294-0709. Yankee Fleet's Dry Tortugas Ferry has an all-day package that includes a 2.5-hour cruise each way, breakfast, lunch, and snorkeling gear. Phone (800) 634-0939.

**Activities:** Touring historic Fort Jefferson, swimming, snorkeling, nature walks, bird-watching.

**Facilities:** Small gift shop, orientation film, restrooms, campsite, picnic areas. Most areas are not accessible to the handicapped.

**Dates:** Open daily.

**Fees:** There is a small charge for camping.

**Closest town:** Key West, 70 miles over open water.

**For more information:** Dry Tortugas National Park, PO Box 6208, Key West, FL 33041. Phone (305) 242-7700. Web site www.nps.gov/drto

### ▓ FORT JEFFERSON

[Fig. 9(1)] "All who enter here, lose all hope," are the words that grace the entrance to Dr. Samuel Mudd's prison cell at Fort Jefferson in Florida's Dry Tortugas Islands. For a little history reminder, Mudd was the physician who set John Wilkes Booth's broken leg during his escape after shooting Abraham Lincoln. Mudd was later tried for conspiracy in Lincoln's murder, sentenced to life in prison, and shipped off to Fort Jefferson.

He must have been just as astounded as modern-day visitors to see the massive red fort rising up from the horizon and towering over the shallow waters, earning it the nickname "Gibraltar of the Gulf."

The six-sided structure has 50-foot-high walls that are 8 feet thick. It's over 0.5 mile around the fort's walls. Complete with ramparts, bastions, a moat, and a drawbridge it might look more at home guarding an important seaport.

When Thomas Jefferson conceived of a string of forts protecting the United States' coast from Maine to Texas, the Tortugas were again considered for their strategic location. Eventually Garden Key was picked as the site of the largest of these coastal fortifications, which was named for Jefferson.

The military minds of the time determined the fort's location would allow for control of the shipping lanes between the Atlantic and the Gulf of Mexico, including the commerce beginning to flow from the Mississippi Valley and the Panama Canal Railroad. The fort could harbor a defensive fleet that would patrol the Florida Straits, engage the enemy, then duck inside the protection of the fort's cannons.

Standing upon the ramparts you can sense the domination hundreds of cannons would have over the surrounding waters. The fort's bastions, which are rounded extensions at each corner, made it possible to train a crossfire upon any point outside the walls. It was the ultimate defensive structure of its time.

Under the direction of the U.S. Army Corps of Engineers, construction began in 1846 and continued on and off for 30 years. Forty-two million bricks were hauled to the island and after the foundation was completed, the walls slowly began to rise, reaching only 10 feet by 1856 and 20 feet by 1858. The fort's current height was reached in 1862 but construction on much of the fort's interior was never completed.

It no longer mattered. The fort took so long to build its impervious defenses were overcome by improvements in weaponry. At the time construction began, thick walls were the accepted defense to stop cannonballs that would simply get stuck in the bricks or bounce off. The Civil War, however, saw the invention of the rifled cannon, capable of sending a projectile that would penetrate and knock out huge chunks of bricks. A fleet of ships could simply lie off the fort and reduce it to rubble.

As a result only 141 guns were ever placed in the 420 designed gun emplacements, and they were never fired in a confrontation.

Under the control of Union forces, Fort Jefferson had been a deserters' prison for four years when Samuel Mudd arrived on the docks in midsummer of 1865, one of four Lincoln-assassination conspirators sentenced in life in prison at Fort Jefferson. Upon his first acquaintance with the isolated fort, towering four stories above the dock, he must have found it easy to "lose all hope."

At home, Mudd's wife worked for his release based on his innocence. Even today, Mudd's relatives continue to campaign to clear his name.

When Mudd was thwarted in an attempt to escape on a ship returning to the mainland, he was confined to a dank dungeon. His departure would be hastened by an enemy the fort builders never predicted. Yellow fever attacked the garrison. It struck quickly, spreading through prison guard and prisoner alike.

Mudd arose from his chains and solitary confinement to become the healing angel to these devastated men. Part of his treatment was to have the men pound holes through the walls to let in the fresh sea air. He is credited with saving the lives of all who survived.

Thirty-eight died including officers and their spouses and children, but Mudd was credited with saving the lives of many others. Grateful officers petitioned President Andrew Johnson to pardon Dr. Mudd. However, Johnson had serious troubles of his own. Congress was in the midst of impeachment proceedings against him, and he dared not provide his enemies additional artillery by releasing such a notorious prisoner.

President Johnson avoided conviction by a single vote in the Senate, and on his last day in the White House issued the order freeing Dr. Mudd from the hell where he'd languished for three years, seven months, and 12 days.

The fort was closed in the 1870s. Years later, near the turn of the century, it was reopened as a quarantine station for ships contaminated with cholera, yellow fever, or small pox. The entire ship would be unloaded. Everything portable was stacked in an oven and treated with heat and steam. The ship itself was sealed and filled with sulphur gas. Afterwards the crew was safe to land at any American port.

Fort Jefferson was proclaimed the Tortugas Keys Reservation in 1908 to protect the bountiful bird life. In 1935 it was declared a National Monument by Franklin Roosevelt. In 1992 the fort and the surrounding islands were redesignated as Dry Tortugas National Park.

An orientation film in the fort's visitor center will give you some background on the site. A small gift shop has books, film and postcards, but no food or drinks. The self-guided tour takes you through the soldiers' barracks, officers' quarters, brick colonnades, parade grounds, lighthouse, dungeons, and along the seawall that girds

*Six-sided Fort Jefferson has 50-foot-high walls that are 8 feet thick. It was used during the Civil War and later as a quarantine station for sailors with cholera, yellow fever, and small pox.*

the more than 150-year-old fortress.

Within the 7-acre interior of the fort is a vast green lawn dotted with tropical trees and plants. There is also an ammunition dump inside, and a cannonball furnace. Red hot cannonballs was used at the time to set fire to enemy ships.

A surrounding seawall encloses a moat, which contains a perpetually calm marine environment that resembles waters on the leeward (protected) side of a reef. Even on stormy days, when strong winds and waves churn up the seas outside the wall, a variety of life inside the moat goes about its business unperturbed. Nondiving and non-snorkeling visitors can see a sampling of the coral reef's sea life while taking a casual stroll. Swimming and fishing are prohibited in the moat.

One of the inhabitants is the gray mangrove snapper, an excellent edible fish that's also plentiful in the waters off the dock. Yellow stingrays (*Urolophus jamiecensis*) burrow themselves into the sand, poking the sharp spine at the base of their tail at anything or anybody that comes within range. Green and yellow parrotfish search the bottom for food.

A sea squirt resembles a squeeze bottle with a pair of siphons. It feeds by drawing water through one siphon, filtering out the edible organisms, and ejecting the water through the other siphon. Also common are sea cucumbers, which feed on small creatures on the bottom of the moat. The queen conch, enclosed in its magnificent pink shell, looks as cumbersome as a landbound tortoise, but in search of algae and sea grasses, it can move up to 100 yards a day. Its tracks can sometimes be seen in the clear waters of the moat.

Sweltering in the tropical heat and humidity, most visitors welcome the opportunity to cool down with a swim in shallow water lapping a pristine sandy beach. Snorkeling is excellent in 4- to 7-foot waters, marked by one of Florida's finest living coral reefs.

The depths are alight with yellow, brown, and green corals. Sea fans, staghorn coral, sea whips, and sponges stand out from the bottom. Sea anemones poke rose and lavender tentacles upward for a chance to catch a small fish. Lobsters, sea cucumbers, and queen conch bury themselves in the sand. Toothy, territorial barracudas cruise at a safe distance. The visitor's guide advises, "If you can count their teeth, you've gotten too close."

Besides the plentiful species of undersea life you might see an occasional loggerhead sea turtle or green sea turtle swimming by between the waving, wide-bladed turtle grass and the surface. Snorkelers and swimmers should also be wary of spiny green and black sea urchins and the sharp, fine spikes of bristle worms. And, as always, don't touch the coral. Humans constitute the greatest danger to the fragile reefs. Contact with the reefs kills the tiny polyps and can also leave the perpetrator with a nasty cut, or an offending boat with serious damage.

The incredible bird life brings many visitors to the islands. The Dry Tortugas are the only place in the contiguous United States where several species of tropical birds can be seen regularly, including white-tailed tropicbird, masked booby (*Sula dactylatra*), brown booby (*Sula leucogaster*), red-footed booby, and magnificent frigatebirds, to name a few. Nearly 300 species have been recorded on the small islands, many as storm-driven accidentals and others that just stop over for a rest during migration. The islands are in the path of one of the principal flyways between North and South America.

The big event occurs each year beginning in late March and continuing for the next few weeks with the arrival of an estimated 100,000 sooty terns. The birds take up nesting sites in the sand on Bush Key, just a few hundred yards from the fort.

Except for Hawaii, Bush Key is home to the sooty tern's only major United States breeding colony. Up to 100,000 black and white sooties wing in from the Caribbean and west-central Atlantic, some from as far away as the West Coast of Africa. They mate while in flight, and when they finally land, females immediately lay their single egg in the sand. Parents take turns shading the egg from sunlight and protecting it from predators. They care for the hatched chick for 8 to 10 weeks.

People are prohibited on Bush Island from March through September—a blessing for all concerned. Sooties are fiercely protective and will attack anything, no matter how large, which poses a real or imagined threat to their young. However, the rookery's swarming activity can be easily observed through binoculars from Fort Jefferson. A much smaller number of brown noddies (*Anous stolidus*), roseate terns, and magnificent frigatebirds also nest on Bush Key. (The brown noddy and other noddies got their name, which can mean sleepy head, because they were so tame and easy to approach and kill, almost as if they were nodding off.)

By June, all the eggs have hatched and Bush Key's beaches are alive with juvenile sooty terns in full raucous cry. Magnificent frigatebirds, with their 7-foot wingspans and the males' distinctive puffed-up red chest pouches, can appear in numbers as high as 500. They frequently prey on the fledgling terns.

When the young terns are able to fly and fend for themselves, the colony takes flight and spends most of its time at sea, living on fish and squid caught at the surface of the water. The adult birds return every year, but the young ones will journey across the Atlantic and not return for four or five years.

Spring is height of migration for a wide and unpredictable variety of migrating warblers, vireos, and songbirds. Although some northbound early birds arrive as early as mid-February, most appear from the end of March to about the third week of May. White-tailed tropicbirds are regulars in late April and early May.

During September and October, the Tortugas' most regular migrants are raptors, particularly sharp-shinned and broad-winged hawks, merlins, and peregrine falcons, which prey on smaller land birds. In winter, the most prevalent birds are gulls and terns that follow the fishing fleets and a few land birds such as American kestrels, belted kingfishers (*Ceryle alcyon*), gray catbirds (*Dumetella carolinensis*), yellow-rumped warblers (*Dendroica coronata*), palm warblers, and Savannah sparrows (*Passerculus sandwichensis*).

One way to describe the fishing in the Dry Tortugas would be to say it's the same as anywhere else in the Florida Keys, only better. Fishing charters out of Key West regularly ply these waters for amberjack, grouper, snapper, wahoo, tarpon, and shark.

If you're camping, you can catch gray snapper from under the dock for use on that grill in the campground. A live bait free-lined into the harbor just at sunrise has the chance of attracting one of the big tarpon that hang around the harbor. That is, if the sharks and barracuda don't find it first.

The game fish activity is excellent both inside and outside of the park. Snapper are the most sought after species. Mutton snapper (*Lutjanus analis*) have a spawning run in the spring. And mangrove snapper arrive in big numbers during a summer spawning period. Catches of yellowtail snapper have been on the increase the last few years.

Ten tree-shaded, first-come, first-served campgrounds next to the fort have picnic tables, grills, and access to saltwater toilets, but no fresh water. You must bring your own fresh water and all supplies when camping. Except for a drinking fountain inside the visitor center, there's no water available to the public, even in the restrooms on the dock. Campers may not have the comforts of a hot shower at day's end, but they have amenities day visitors miss: They can sit on the deserted beach and savor their own sunset celebration and take romantic moonlight walks around the seawall. In the spring the buttonwood trees in the campground fill with migrating warblers, giving campers the luxury of identifying a dozen or more species without stirring from their sleeping bags.

Tours of the fort are led by National Park Service personnel, or you can wander around by yourself watching for enemy ships on the horizon to train your cannon on.

**Directions:** Located 70 miles west of Key West. Accessible by boat and seaplane.

**Activities:** Touring historic Fort Jefferson, swimming, snorkeling, nature walks, bird-watching, fishing.

**Facilities:** Small gift shop, orientation film, restrooms, campgrounds, picnic areas.

**Dates:** Open daily sunrise to sunset.

**Fees:** There is a small charge for camping.

**Closest town:** Key West, 70 miles over open water.

**For more information:** Dry Tortugas National Park, PO Box 6208, Key West, FL 33041. Phone (305) 242-7700. Web site www.nps.gov/drto

## RED-TAILED HAWK
(Buteo jamaicensis)
Red-tailed hawks hunt for small mammals from the air or exposed perches such as dead trees.

# Loggerhead Key

[Fig. 9] In addition to snorkeling off Fort Jefferson and Garden Island, visitors can also snorkel and dive around reefs and shipwrecks off the other small islands. Hospital Key and Long Key are closed year-round, but day visits are permitted on Loggerhead Key. Two-and-a half miles west of Garden Key, 1 mile long and nearly 30 acres, nature-blessed Loggerhead is by far the largest of the Tortugas.

As remote as it is, Loggerhead is a prime example of the dictum "Don't mess with Mother Nature." In the midnineteenth century, its only noteworthy vegetation was a ring of bay cedar bushes and beach and dune plants such as sea oats, sea lavender, and cactus. But tall Australian pines imported for shade succeeded in shading out most of the sun-loving natives. The spreading roots of the Australian pines discourage sea turtles, which dig their nests around the island. The Park Service is trying to eliminate the stubborn, rapidly multiplying pines, but is leaving some of the trees, which can grow to 100 feet, as roosting places for hawks, osprey, and other birds.

Most visitors come for Loggerhead's excellent snorkeling and diving. A reef tract called *Little Africa* is a favorite destination. Marked by spar buoys off the island's west side, the reef gets its name from its Africa-like shape visible from the top of the lighthouse. The wreck of the windjammer *Avanti* is another fascinating place to explore. The iron-hulled sailing vessel sank in 1907 on its way from Pensacola to Montevideo, Uruguay, with a cargo of lumber. It's 1 mile southwest of Loggerhead's southwest tip.

Those who'd really like to get to know the Dry Tortugas, and take a break from real life for a month or so, can apply for the Loggerhead Key Maintenance Volunteer Program. Those accepted are housed, free of charge, in an air-conditioned, one-bedroom, two-story brick house. It's anything but a desert island vacation, however. In return, they're required to stay a minimum of 30 full days and put in at least 32 hours a week of volunteer work that includes cleaning grounds and beaches, transferring fuel, changing generators, mowing and trimming lawns, burning trash, and doing plumbing, carpentry, electrical, and other maintenance and mechanical work. Apply to Dry Tortugas National Park, PO Box 6208, Key West, FL 33041.

The island has no visitor facilities. The 150-foot Loggerhead Lighthouse, first lighted in July 1858 to guide ships away from the reefs, is off-limits to visitors. The island's dock is also reserved for park employees. Visitors are required to anchor offshore and come onto the beach in small boats.

**Directions:** 72.5 miles west of Key West. Accessible by boat.

**Activities:** Swimming, snorkeling, bird-watching.

**Facilities:** None.

**Dates:** Open daily sunrise to sunset.

**Closest town:** Key West, 72.5 miles over open water.

**For more information:** Dry Tortugas National Park, PO Box 6208, Key West, FL 33041. Phone (305) 242-7700. Web site www.nps.gov/drto

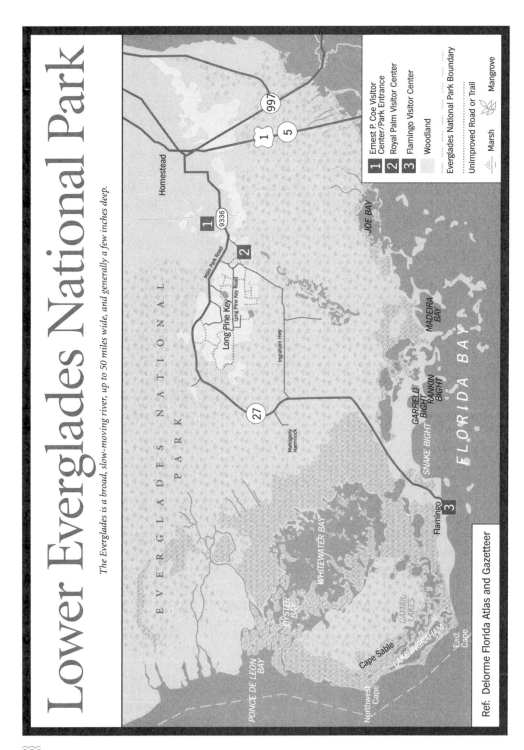

# Lower Everglades National Park

*The Everglades is a broad, slow-moving river, up to 50 miles wide, and generally a few inches deep.*

Ref: Delorme Florida Atlas and Gazetteer

| | Ernest P. Coe Visitor Center/Park Entrance |
| **1** | |
| **2** | Royal Palm Visitor Center |
| **3** | Flamingo Visitor Center |
| | Woodland |
| | Everglades National Park Boundary |
| | Unimproved Road or Trail |
| | Marsh    Mangrove |

Homestead

997

1

5

JOE BAY

**1**  9336

Main Park Road

**2**

Long Pine Key

Long Pine Key Road

Ingraham Hwy

MADEIRA BAY

27

Mahogany Hammock

GARFIELD BIGHT

RANKIN BIGHT

SNAKE BIGHT

F L O R I D A   B A Y

E V E R G L A D E S   N A T I O N A L   P A R K

WHITEWATER BAY

OYSTER BAY

CATTAIL LAKES

**3**

Flamingo

LAKE INGRAHAM

Cape Sable

East Cape

PONCE DE LEON BAY

Northwest Cape

# Florida Everglades: Everglades National Park to Shark Valley

"*The Everglades is a test, if we pass, we get to keep the planet.*"—From a plaque in the Everglades National Park visitor center.

When Ross Winne drove a notched stake into a small creek on Torry Island in September of 1928, he already had a suspicion of what to expect. A monstrous, late-summer hurricane had spawned somewhere in the tropics and was bearing down on Florida's east coast. The north wind preceding the storm was pushing the shallow water into the southern end of Lake Okeechobee.

Ross, his wife Gertrude, and their children had been only the second family to settle in this inhospitable but fast-changing land 18 years earlier. And although Ross and Gertrude's only goal was to survive and make a new life for themselves, they witnessed and took part in many of the major events of the first half of the twentieth century—events that would reshape the Everglades. One of these was the hurricane of 1928.

[ *Above:* Mangrove islands are one type of habitat found in the Florida Everglades ]

*Airboats rides are offered outside of the park to Everglades visitors who want to explore the river of grass.*

When the wind-driven water that day rose 6 inches in 15 minutes, Ross and Gertrude loaded their four children into the old pickup truck, warned their neighbors it was time to leave, and headed east towards West Palm Beach, straight into the teeth of the approaching hurricane. Twenty years later Gertrude would write that with the wind before them and the water behind, they chose the wind.

The Winne family survived that terrifying journey, making a stand against the storm while still in their truck on the outskirts of West Palm Beach. They were the lucky ones.

The people that stayed behind didn't fare as well. Nearly 2,000 people died that terrible night when the lake's waters piled high, then crashed through a low earthen dike at the southern end of the lake, sending a wall of water across the countryside, carrying away entire farming communities, scattering buildings and people for miles into the Everglades.

That single, disastrous event and the unimaginable loss of life energized an effort to gain total control over Florida's waterworks. Dovetailing nicely with an approaching Depression-era call for huge public works projects, the Army Corps of Engineers was soon busy creating the largest drainage and flood-control project in the world.

Prior to man's tampering, the Florida water system was a marvel of natural engineering. A giant watershed extended for 250 miles from as far north as current-day Orlando to the tip of the peninsula. During the rainy months each year, between June and October, water falling throughout Central Florida flowed down creeks and through swamps into the Kissimmee River.

From its headwaters, the Kissimmee then meandered 90 miles through wide marshy switchbacks, eventually delivering its precious cargo into the northern end of Lake Okeechobee. The wide, shallow lake covers more than 600,000 acres and is billed as the second largest freshwater lake entirely within the boundaries of the United States.

Other tributaries brought additional water to the lake from the wetlands east and west of the lake. As the water level rose during the annual rainy season, excess water spilled over the lake's southern rim. A small portion of the water soaked through the ground, helping to recharge the Biscayne Aquifer, which supplies water to most of the population of southeast Florida. The remainder formed a sheet-flow that followed an almost imperceptible slope of 2 to 3 inches per mile southwest to the Gulf of Mexico.

This is the heart and the lifeblood of the Everglades, a great, slow-moving river, up to 50 miles wide, but only a few inches deep. Held to the west by an unimposing, but sufficient Atlantic Coastal Ridge, the water swept slowly across 100 miles of a wet grassy prairie, flowing through Taylor Slough into Florida Bay and bending toward the west into the Gulf of Mexico through the Shark River Slough.

The predominant plant in this land, sawgrass, formed a great grassy plain, a river of grass flowing to the sea. Where the water was deeper it formed sloughs, slow-moving channels that held water most of the year and became a refuge for wildlife during dry times. Where the water was shallow tree islands formed, in elongated shapes reflecting the direction and flow of the water.

The system delivered a slow but steady supply of water to the plants and wildlife of the Everglades. By building a head of water in Lake Okeechobee, the system provided life-giving water to the Everglades long past the end of the rainy season, decreasing the length of time each year that Everglades wildlife had to deal with low water conditions.

The land along the southern rim of Lake Okeechobee was also covered by a thick tangled forest of pond apple trees, which slowed the flow of water out of the lake. In addition, the thick vegetation, predominantly sawgrass, further slowed the flow of water. It has been estimated that a drop of water falling near the upper end of the system might reach the Gulf of Mexico a year later.

Although timeless is often one of the adjectives that come to mind when you look out across the green and gold sea of sawgrass, it inaccurately describes this relatively young land. Ten thousand years ago, during the last Ice Age, and when Paleolithic Indians are first thought to have entered the Florida peninsula, Florida was mostly a dry, arid land.

With huge amounts of the world's water locked up in the earth's glaciers, the exposed portion of the Florida peninsula was roughly twice the size it is today. A porous layer of limestone rock held little surface water.

As the climate began to warm and the glaciers retreated, sea levels rose. The peninsula shrank, and underground aquifers, hemmed in by the seas, began to fill. With nowhere else to go, the water could only flow slowly across the mostly flat surface. Wetlands and cypress swamps soon began to develop in South Florida, and sometime around 5,000 years ago the Everglades began to form.

Paleolithic Indians adapted their culture to the changing climate. They learned to hunt alligators and deer, and to rely on the bountiful sea life close at hand. When Europeans first arrived in Florida in the 1500s, they encountered well-developed civilizations. The Calusa lived along the southwestern Florida coast, and the Tequestas along the southeast. By the mid-1700s, European contact, which included both diseases and slave raids, had led to the near extinction of both tribes.

Bands of Creek Indians, collectively known as Seminoles, fleeing first pioneer settlement, and then harassment by the United States Army, were next to arrive in the region. They named the land *Pah-hay-okee* (grassy water), and quickly learned to live and thrive in the harsh environment. By the late 1800s only a few hundred of these brave people survived in the Everglades; their descendants live here today.

The story of the modern Everglades era more or less began when a late nineteenth century canal builder and land speculator named Hamilton Disston inherited enough money to pursue his long-held dream of draining Florida's swamplands. It was an idea he picked up years earlier while on a fishing trip in Florida. There was a prize for such an endeavor—some of the richest farmland in the world, land the state would gladly give away to anyone who could drain it and put it to "good" use.

Thousands of generations of sawgrass living and dying in the Florida sun had deposited a thick layer of black muck, more than 15 feet deep in some places. Combined with the warm climate, the rich organic soil could grow multiple crops year after year.

Disston's plan was to drain all of the land north of Lake Okeechobee into the lake, then lower the lake by dredging canals to the east and west coasts of Florida, cutting off the flow of water to the Everglades. One of his first acts was to dredge the Caloosahatchee River from Fort Myers and connect it to Lake Okeechobee. This opened up a waterway from the southwest coast, through Lake Okeechobee, and on into the Kissimmee Valley. In 1882, a company-owned steamboat made the first trip from Fort Myers to the Kissimmee River.

After Disston abandoned the scene, his dreams largely unfulfilled, the State of Florida continued to stumble forward with one drainage project after another, always determined to turn what it perceived as a wasteland into viable agricultural lands. By the early 1900s, 440 miles of canals had been dug for drainage and to provide transportation to the inaccessible Florida interior.

It was about that time that Ross Winne brought his family from Ohio to their Everglades homestead. They rode a steamboat from Fort Myers up the winding Caloosahatchee River and into Lake Okeechobee. The family of three landed on Torry Island and settled in a 10-by-10 tent, next to a creek today known as Winne Creek, and on the shore of a small cove called Winne Cove. The rich lands that would later spawn an agricultural boom still lay hidden beneath the sawgrass and pond apple forest south of the lake.

Ross became one of a number of commercial catfish fishermen scattered around Lake Okeechobee during the early part of the twentieth century. Catfish were caught on trot lines and kept alive in wire pens until a run-boat came along to buy them or trade for supplies.

When the North New River Canal was opened in 1912 connecting Lake

Okeechobee to Fort Lauderdale, it fell to Ross Winne, who had experience in the coastal waters, to pilot the first load of catfish down the 56-mile-long canal to the Miami fish docks.

While Ross fished, Gertrude Winne grew a vegetable garden in the muck around their homestead. As the story is told, land speculators brought prospective buyers to see her garden and the bountiful harvest that could be produced in the rich soil.

By 1928, Ross was the local sheriff and agricultural agent for a growing farming community centered around the small town of Belle Glade. The low, state-built dike that failed to hold back the hurricane-driven lake waters that year had been thrown-up to protect the farmlands from the natural sheet flow, not hurricanes.

Construction continued for decades following the great storm. Today a hurricane-proof dike surrounds Lake Okeechobee while more than 1,000 miles of canals crisscross the state, moving water back and forth with the help of 150 water-control structures and 16 major pumping stations. A 700,000-acre swath of farmland, known as the Everglades Agricultural Area (EAA), now exists below Lake Okeechobee where Everglades once existed.

Although once known for its winter vegetable production, the EAA is today largely dominated by a politically strong sugar-producing industry. The rapid expansion of sugarcane as a crop of choice came about because of federally support-ed sugar subsidies that guarantee a profitable price for the growers and producers.

In addition, a levee was built along the eastern edge of the Everglades to protect advancing urban development from flooding. Three state-owned water conservation areas south of the current agricultural area covering 1,300 square miles of Everglades were enclosed by levees so water could be stored for times of drought.

Lost forever, however, was the natural water delivery system. Instead, a water system that was designed to protect agriculture and urban development at the expense of the natural ecosystem continues to take its toll. Rain falling in the historic watershed that once guaranteed an extended wet season is now carried away by canal in the name of flood protection and dumped into the Atlantic Ocean and Gulf of Mexico.

Even under the best of conditions the Everglades were, and still are, treated to shorter wet seasons and longer dry seasons. In addition, increased nutrient runoff from agricultural operations has changed the native vegetation. Bull rushes (cattails) are undergoing rapid expansion in the place of sawgrass in the conservation areas.

At the same time an ongoing controversy has been waging for decades between conservationists, Native American Tribes, the State of Florida, and the sugar farming industry over such questions as Who is responsible for polluting the Everglades? Who should pay to restore the Everglades? Who should get the water during droughts? And who should have to take the water during floods? Many conservation organizations believe that agricultural lands should no longer be protected from either drought or flood when the alternative, either excessively flooding the Everglades, or diverting badly needed water for irrigation, is so devastating to native habitats and wildlife.

The only remaining natural Everglades system is now found mostly within the boundaries of Everglades National Park. Once a portion of the water is finally allowed to enter the northern boundary of the park through a system of culverts, it spreads out and reverts to the natural sheet flow that once characterized the entire Everglades.

Clearly though, except for its ability to protect farming interests, the system isn't working. During severe droughts in the early 1960s, the park's water supply was cut off, and disaster was only averted with the timely arrival of drought-breaking rains. In the 1970s, flood waters that threatened urban and agricultural areas were pumped into the Everglades conservation areas, drowning deer and other wildlife. By the early 1990s, without its normal freshwater input, Florida Bay at the end of the system began a gradual transition from pristine estuary to a hyper-saline saltwater lagoon.

Although urban growth and agricultural pressures continue into the twenty-first century, the Everglades isn't defenseless. Efforts to preserve a portion of the ecosystem began in the early 1900s. The conservation movement was permanently galvanized, however, when Marjory Stoneman Douglas published her famous treatise. *The Everglades: River of Grass* in 1947 (revised 1987). Of the book, Majorie Kinnan Rawlings wrote, "This beautiful and bitter, sweet and savage book may be recommended not only to all residents and tourists of Florida, but to all readers concerned with American life and the great relations of man to nature."

Born in 1890 in Minneapolis, Minnesota, Marjory Stoneman Douglas arrived in Miami in 1915 and began working at the *Miami Herald*. Beginning as a society reporter, then an editorial page columnist, she campaigned for yet-to-be popular causes such as feminism, racial justice, and conservation.

Her book, published the same year that Everglades National Park was established, has for decades convinced people who have never seen the Everglades of the importance of its preservation. In 1970 Marjory Stoneman Douglas established the Friends of the Everglades, a nonprofit organization supporting protection of the river of grass. Today, the Everglades Coalition, a broad-based union of more than 30 state and national conservation and environmental organizations, is working for the land's protection and eventual restoration. But it remains a difficult task.

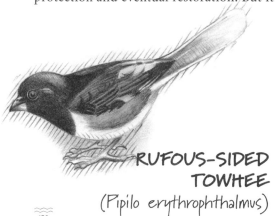

In 1993 a controversial settlement of litigation took place between the U.S. government, the State of Florida, and the sugar industry that addressed the discharge of polluted water into Everglades National Park. That was followed in 1994 when the Florida legislature took up the Marjory Stoneman Douglas Everglades Forever Act.

Despite its title, the act was roundly criticized by environmental organiza-

**RUFOUS-SIDED TOWHEE**
(*Pipilo erythrophthalmus*)

## Storms, Stings, and Sun

Mosquitos can be fierce at times in Everglades National Park, especially during the summer rainy season. It's a good idea to carry an extra supply of your favorite repellant, and consider wearing lightweight, long-sleeve shirts and long pants.

Be sure to pack a lightweight rain suit or poncho. In spring, summer, and early fall, thunderstorms can seemingly appear out of nowhere, sweeping across the landscape and delivering a solid drenching to everything below.

Summer temperatures and humidity can reach extremes. Refreshments and drinking water are scarce within the park, but picnic sites are plentiful. A cooler with cold beverages, water, snacks, and a picnic lunch will come in very handy. The use of sunscreen and a wide-brimmed hat are also recommended.

tions which claimed that lobbying efforts by the sugar industry had successfully weakened the act to the point that is was an actual setback in the efforts to restore the Everglades. A feisty, 104-year-old Ms. Douglas, disappointed by changes made to the original legislation that she supported, demanded that her name be removed from the legislation before its final passage. It was.

In 1997 the United States Congress passed legislation designating Everglades National Park as the Marjory Stoneman Douglas Wilderness. In 1998, Marjory Stoneman Douglas died in her Coconut Grove home at the age of 108, but the struggle she began to restore this remarkable natural resource continues.

The latest effort to confront and accommodate the continuing pressures on the system is the development of a comprehensive multibillion-dollar plan by the U.S. Army Corps of Engineers, environmentalists, and water managers that is designed to lead to the creation of a healthier, more natural Everglades and at the same time meet the long-term water demands of Central and South Florida's booming human population.

The redesign effort is expected to be the most complex ecological project ever undertaken. Engineers would build 286 square miles of reservoirs and filter marshes on all sides of Lake Okeechobee and along the eastern boundaries of the Everglades. The reservoirs would store up to 465 billion gallons of water, which otherwise would flow into the Gulf of Mexico and the Atlantic. During rainy years, hundreds of storage wells would also be used to hold additional billions of gallons for use during dry seasons to create a more natural wet/dry season.

Some environmentalists believe the survival of the Everglades, as well as South and Central Florida's quality of life, depends on the success of the proposal. Others think it still leaves too many areas of the Everglades susceptible to excessive water or excessive droughts. Only time will tell who is right, and whether or not future generations will be able to visit this unique and magnificent land.

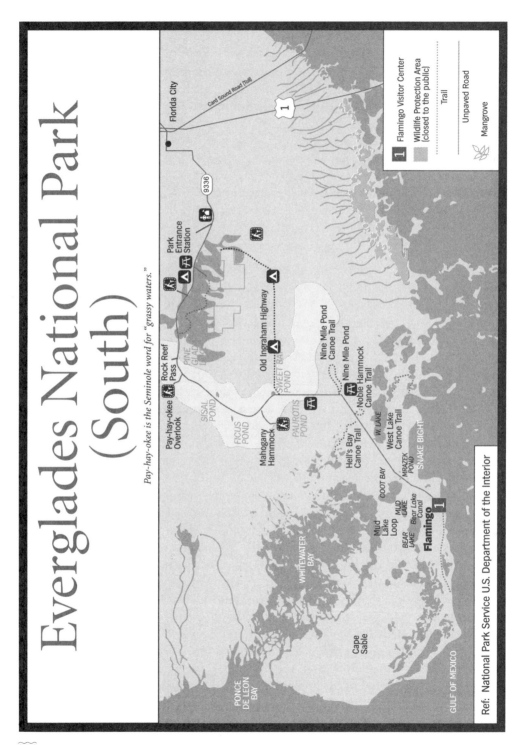

# Everglades National Park (South)

*Pay-hay-okee is the Seminole word for "grassy waters."*

Florida City

Card Sound Road (Toll)

1

9336

Park Entrance Station

Pay-hay-okee Overlook

Rock Reef Pass

PINE GLADE LAKE

Old Ingraham Highway

SWEET BAY POND

SISAL POND

FICUS POND

PAUROTIS POND

Mahogany Hammock

Nine Mile Pond Canoe Trail

Nine Mile Pond

Noble Hammock Canoe Trail

W. LAKE

West Lake Canoe Trail

SNAKE BIGHT

Hell's Bay Canoe Trail

MRAZEK POND

COOT BAY

Mud Lake Loop

MUD LAKE

BEAR LAKE

Bear Lake Canal

Flamingo

1

WHITEWATER BAY

Cape Sable

PONCE DE LEON BAY

GULF OF MEXICO

| 1 | Flamingo Visitor Center |
| | Wildlife Protection Area (closed to the public) |

Trail

Unpaved Road

Mangrove

Ref: National Park Service U.S. Department of the Interior

# Everglades National Park

*"Here are no lofty peaks seeking the sky, no mighty glaciers or rushing streams worrying away the uplifted land. Here is land tranquil in its quietude, serving not as the source of water but as the last receiver of it. To its natural abundance we owe this spectacular plant and animal life that distinguishes this place from all others in our country."*— President Harry S. Truman's address at the dedication of Everglades National Park, December 6, 1947.

[Figs. 10, 11, 12, 15] As President Truman pointed out to the crowd gathered to dedicate Everglades National Park more than 50 years ago, it's the rich diversity and profusion of plants and animals found in the Florida Everglades that make it a land worthy of preservation.

The country's third largest national park behind Yellowstone and Death Valley, Everglades National Park encompasses more than a 1.5 million acres of sawgrass prairies, hardwood hammocks, pinelands, mangrove forests, open waterways, and the park's centerpiece, a 50-mile-wide "River of Grass."

Stretching from the outskirts of Miami to the Gulf of Mexico, it's an area 20 percent larger than the state of Delaware that is reserved almost exclusively for wildlife and plant life. Thousands of species of plants and animals, some rare and exotic, are found here including such varied and remarkable creatures as saltwater crocodiles, alligators, panthers, manatees, wood storks, and roseate spoonbills.

The park's climate accounts for much of the variety of life found here. Located at the northernmost point in the tropical belt and the southernmost point in the temperate belt, the Everglades is a land where unusual combinations of trees and plants overlap. Temperate plants such as live oak (*Quercus virginiana*), willow, and myrtle migrated overland to the Everglades, while tropical varieties such as gumbo-limbo, royal palms (*Roystonea elata*), tree orchids, and airplants were carried from the West Indies by winds, waves, and migrating birds. About 70 percent of the 700 native plant species in the park are of tropical origin.

Everglades National Park has also been recognized as a World Heritage Site and an International Biosphere Reserve serving as one of a network of protected samples of the world's major ecosystem types. Without the efforts of a few determined individuals, however, there may not have ever been a park.

Many who came to South Florida during the late nineteenth and early twentieth centuries viewed the Everglades as worthless land that cried out to be drained and put to good use. Others came, however, who saw the beauty of this unique land and the value of preserving it in its natural state. These early conservationists recognized the complexity of the Everglades ecosystem and they struggled to alert the public of the threats to the land's existence.

Ironically, the park's creation can be traced back to the devastation that was wrought upon the area's bird populations by plume hunters in the early 1900s. At the time there was a demand for bird feathers to adorn ladies' hats. As a result of overhunting, wading bird populations declined until local conservation groups hired wardens to protect bird rookeries. The murder of Audubon Warden Guy Bradley in 1905 led directly to legislation that outlawed plume hunting. This was the first conservation measure applied to the Everglades area.

In 1914 the Florida Federation of Women's Clubs successfully sought the establishment of a state park to protect Paradise Key, a large tropical hammock in the southeastern portion of what is now Everglades National Park. At the same time, efforts continued by others to penetrate and drain the rest of the Everglades.

When Henry Flagler was awarded much of the land in the Cape Sable area on the extreme southwestern tip of the peninsula in return for pushing his railroad all the way to Key West, his first instincts were to drain and develop the area. Although Flagler died in 1913, the effort continued. Canals were dug near the coast to help drain the low-lying land, and in 1916 the Ingraham Highway, named after Florida East Coast Railroad Vice President J.E. Ingraham, was pushed across the Everglades from Miami all the way to Cape Sable.

The company's goal of developing the cape proved largely unsuccessful, however, and in 1934, largely due to the park's foremost supporter, Ernest F. Coe, Congress passed the Everglades National Park bill. Following delays caused by the Great Depression and World War II, Everglades National Park was dedicated on December 6, 1947. Both Paradise Key and Flagler's Cape Sable land became part of the new park. Flagler's company parted with its holdings for $295,000.

Sometimes called the "Father of the Everglades," Ernest F. Coe was a native of New Haven, Connecticut, and a graduate of Yale University's School of Fine Arts in 1887. He and his wife Anna moved to Coconut Grove near Miami, in 1925, where he did landscape work and developed a penchant for exploring the Everglades.

His concern over the killing of birds and the removal of rare plants started him on a course of action that began in 1928 with a simple letter to Stephen T. Mather, first director of the National Park Service, outlining a proposal for a new national park. That same year he formed the Tropical Everglades National Park Association (later Everglades National Park Association) to push for the park's creation.

Interestingly, in 1930, a government-appointed inspection party came to Miami to tour the area and decide on lands for inclusion in the proposed park. Joining the group was Miami Herald journalist Marjory Stoneman Douglas, who would 17 years later write *The Everglades: River of Grass*, the classic treatise on the Everglades that galvanized national support for the park and the Everglades ecosystem.

Nevertheless, Everglades National Park only protects a portion of the historic Everglades system, which exists at the end of a vast watershed that has been forever changed. Today the health of the park, and of its plant and animal communities, is still dependent upon a man-made system of canals, levees, and huge pumping stations that move water around South Florida.

For many years the need to maintain a natural regime of sheet-flow vital to the health of the Everglades ecosystem within the park was largely sacrificed to provide either farmland irrigation water or urban flood protection to other parts of South Florida. A constant outcry from state and national conservation organizations, along with a handful of lawsuits, has succeeded in at least improving the level of importance placed by politicians on restoring a natural flow to the remaining Everglades within the park.

The Everglades is a place where slight changes in elevation or salinity can create entirely different and distinct habitats, each with its own community of plants and animals. In a similar manner, changes in the historic wet and dry seasonal flows can, and have, altered the types of wildlife and plant life that survive here.

But don't visit the Everglades with a sad heart. Changes are under way for the better, and the wildlife and plant life survives—perhaps not as plentiful as in earlier times, but still in numbers to awe even the most veteran nature lover.

Birders and other wildlife enthusiasts will find a new wonder at every turn. Anglers can hire a guide or rent a boat and stalk redfish, snook, or tarpon. Hikers will find themselves walking through magnificent tropical hammocks, while canoeists and kayakers can explore mangrove creeks, hidden ponds, and deserted beaches.

To get the most out of the park, you may wish to extend your trip beyond the more well-worn visitor facilities. That can include a ride on one of the tour boats available at Flamingo, or a bicycle trip on the Snake Bight Trail. It can mean loading your canoe for a two-day to two-week adventure into the backcountry, or a half-day spent tooling along endless miles of twisted waterway and broad inland bays by motorboat.

The park can be sampled at many levels, with something new to offer at each one. If you take time to learn while you play, and to look a little more closely at the land, you'll be rewarded with a fresh understanding of the wonders nature can produce.

Visitor centers are located near the main entrance, in Royal Palm (within the park), in Flamingo, in Shark Valley, and at the Gulf Coast Ranger Station in Everglades City. The main entrance is open daily, 24 hours a day.

The only lodging and food service in the park is in Flamingo. Campgrounds are located at Long Pine Key and Flamingo within the main park and at Chekika, a disconnected portion of the park 26 miles north of the main entrance on State Road 997.

The Everglades backcountry is open for primitive camping at any of 43 designated sites. Reservations must be made in person no more than 24 hours before entering the backcountry. There is a fee for backcountry camping.

There are no service stations in the park. Gasoline only is available at the Flamingo Marina. It's a good idea to enter the park with a full tank of gas. Cars, trucks, RVs, campers, and vans can travel easily on the paved roads within the park. Airboats, swamp buggies, and ATVs are prohibited. Airboat and swamp buggy rides are available at several private concessions outside the park.

Universally accessible facilities and trails can be found throughout the park. All of

# Everglades National Park (Long Pine Key)

*Everglades National Park is the country's third largest national park behind Yellowstone and Death Valley.*

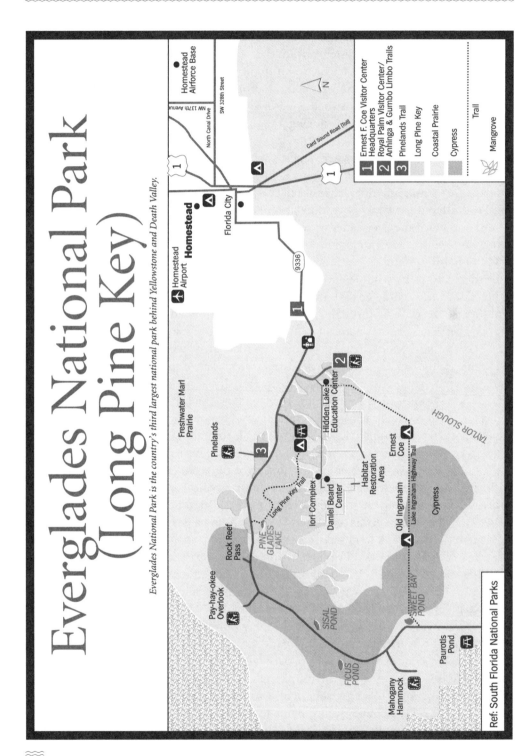

Ref: South Florida National Parks

the park's visitor centers, most interpretive trails, some of the Flamingo boat tours, and the Shark Valley tram tours are wheelchair accessible. There are accessible campsites at all three campgrounds in the park, and one primitive backcountry campsite, at Pearl Bay, is accessible to people with mobility impairments. Audio programs and captioned movies are available at most visitor centers.

**Directions:** From Miami and points north take the Florida Turnpike (Route 821) south until it ends, merging with US 1 at Florida City. Turn right at the first traffic light onto Palm Drive (SR 9336/SW 344th Street) and follow the signs to the park. Visitors driving north from the Florida Keys should turn left on Palm Drive (SR 9336/344th Street) in Florida City and follow the signs to the park.

**Activities:** Hiking, bicycling, wildlife watching, camping, picnicking, photography, canoeing, boating, fishing. Ranger-led activities include canoe and hiking trips, slogging, off-road hiking, and wildlife and campfire programs.

**Facilities:** Visitor centers, museums, campgrounds, lodging, restaurant, marina.

**Dates:** Open year-round. Only limited food service available in the summer. Peak season is Dec. through Apr. Ranger-led activities are also limited from Apr. to Dec.

**Fees:** A per-vehicle fee is charged at the main entrance near Homestead.

**Closest town:** Homestead is 10 miles north on SR 9336.

**For more information:** Everglades National Park Headquarters, 40001 State Road 9336, Homestead, FL 33034. Phone (305) 242-7700. Web site www.nps.gov/ever

# Ernest F. Coe Visitor Center

[Fig. 12(1)] The destruction of the park's original visitor center by Hurricane Andrew in 1992 provided the Park Service with an opportunity to construct a brand new, state-of-the-art facility. Located just outside the main entrance to the park, the visitor center is the beginning of your connection to the Everglades.

The bright, airy facility, dedicated in December 1996, educates with wall-sized murals, interactive video monitors, and small alcoves that surround the visitor with both the sounds and sights of the Everglades. An intriguing, 15-minute film introduces the visitor to some of the wildlife, and provides a brief history of the park's relationship to the rest of South Florida and the millions of people who now make it their home.

A large 360-degree diorama tells one of the most important stories of the Everglades—the role of the alligator as water-hole custodian. During the dry season, these ancient reptiles settle into small, water-filled solution holes in the limerock. With their great tails they sweep out the mud and debris, keeping the gator hole clear and maintaining a place of refuge for the area's wildlife until the rains return.

The visitor center also provides an easy introduction to the varied and distinct habitat types found within the borders of the park. There's the Florida Bay estuary with its 800 square miles of seagrass and marine bottom, which shelters the small fish and shellfish that in turn, support the higher invertebrates in the bay.

Coastal prairies are located just above the tidal flats of Florida Bay. Arid regions of salt-tolerant vegetation, the prairies are shaped by periodic hurricane-caused flooding. This land is characterized by succulents and other low-growing desert-type plants that can withstand the harsh conditions.

Mangrove forests are found in tidal estuaries where fresh water from the Everglades mixes with salt water from the Gulf of Mexico. The estuary system is a valuable nursery for pink shrimp and fish. During dry months an increased number of birds rely on the estuary for a place to feed. Many species also nest in the mangroves.

Freshwater marl prairies, which tend to border the deeper sloughs, are large areas characterized by marl sediments, a calcareous material that settles on the limestone. The marl allows slow seepage of the water in to the aquifer below, but not drainage.

Sloughs are the deeper and faster-flowing centers of a broad marshy river. Even the fast flow moves at a turtle pace of 100 feet per day. Dotted with tree islands called hammocks or heads, sloughs channel life-protecting waters from north to south. Everglades National Park contains two distinct sloughs, the Shark Valley Slough, which is the true "River of Grass" and Taylor Slough, a narrow eastern branch of the river.

Cypress domes are dense clusters of cypress trees growing in water-filled depressions in the landscape. Deciduous conifers, cypress trees can survive in standing water. The dome shape results from trees in the deeper soil at the center of a depression growing taller than those on the outside. Also, scattered throughout the park are stunted cypress trees, called dwarf cypress, that are a result of poor soil and dry land. While they are only a few feet tall, they can be as old as their stately brothers.

Hardwood hammocks are dense stands of hardwood trees that grow on natural rises of only a few inches. The flowing water in the slough causes many of the islands to have a teardrop shape. In hammocks, many tropical plants such as the West Indian mahogany, gumbo-limbo, and cocoplum (*Chrysobalanus icaco*) grow alongside more temperate species such as live oak and red maple (*Acer rubrum*).

Because of their slight elevation, hammocks rarely flood. Over many years, acids from decaying plants dissolve the limestone around each tree island, forming a natural moat and thus further protecting the trees from fire. Shaded from the sun by the tall trees, ferns and airplants thrive in the moisture-laden air inside the canopy of the hammock.

Slash pines are the dominant plants in the pine forest, which sits on top of limestone ridges running into the eastern side of the park. More than 200 varieties of tropical plants inhabit the pinelands understory, making it the most diverse habitat in the Everglades.

The pines root in the dirt-filled cracks and crevices found in the jagged bedrock. Fire, often caused by lightning strikes, is another essential condition for the survival of the pine community. It controls the spread of hardwoods that, if left unchecked, would eventually shade the forest floor, preventing the growth of new pine trees. The multilayered bark of the pine trees allows them to survive all but the hottest fires with little more than a scorching.

Be sure to check the "What to see. Where to Look" display before heading into the park. The regularly updated display uses symbol magnets on a map of the park to report recent sightings of such species as alligators, wading birds, panthers, crocodiles, roseate spoonbills, manatees, woodstorks, and osprey. Another "Everglades Update" located in the small alcove in front of the visitor center discloses the best places for wildlife viewing for each season.

You can even begin your wildlife watching right on the grounds of the visitor center. Look for tricolored herons

## Sneaky Feeders

Some of the wildlife in Everglades National Park has become a bit too bold when it comes to helping themselves to your picnic supplies. Don't leave food exposed anywhere in the park and especially not in any of the parking areas. Turning your back for even a moment on an open bag of potato chips or cookies can result in a visit from an unwelcome diner. Black birds, crows, blue jays, and sea gulls have learned that thievery sometimes pays off better than foraging.

At night, raccoons will crawl through any car window left open. They'll also rummage through coolers and baitwells in boats on trailers and docked in the marina. Don't leave any food outside at night, and don't assume that food kept in a cooler is safe.

and great blue herons showing an interest in the fish-filled waters. Largemouth bass and other sunfish, including bluegills and redear sunfish (*Lepomis microlophus*), are easy to see from the footbridge leading into the visitor center.

Before leaving the visitor center you may wish to take moment to look at the extraordinary bronze statue of a Florida panther standing next to the parking lot. It's dedicated to the park's strongest champion, and the namesake of the visitor center, Ernest F. Coe.

**Directions:** Located 500 yards outside of the main entrance to Everglades National Park.

**Activities:** Interactive information displays, wildlife viewing.

**Facilities:** Information counter, bookstore, restrooms.

**Dates:** Open year-round.

**Fees:** None.

**Closest town:** Homestead is 10 miles north on SR 9336.

**For more information:** Everglades National Park Headquarters, 40001 State Road 9336, Homestead, FL 33034. Phone (305) 242-7700.

# Road To Flamingo

It's only a 48-mile drive from Homestead to Flamingo, at the very tip of mainland Florida in Everglades National Park, but the trip takes you from a fast-paced urban environment of concrete and traffic lights, to a serene, yet wild land called the Everglades. Along the way you'll be treated to a number of astonishing points of interest.

The road passes through a land like none other in the world. This is a place where time, weather, geography, fire, and water have created a varied landscape—some of which man has altered, and some of which man is trying desperately to repair.

A number of stops along the road in Everglades National Park have been made accessible to the average visitor by the National Park Service. There are well-constructed trails and boardwalks that pass through dark, primitive hammocks and cross wildlife-filled sloughs and sawgrass prairies. Roadside ponds and overlooks provide exciting opportunities for wildlife viewing. Each stop reveals a different habitat and a different connection to the overall Everglades ecosystem.

But the park experience will not always come to your car. You should get out and take a closer look, listen a little more carefully, and maybe walk a little farther. If you do, you'll see enough to come away with a steadfast appreciation for this unique and intricate ecosystem.

### HOMESTEAD TO EVERGLADES NATIONAL PARK MAIN ENTRANCE

[Fig. 12] From the end of the Florida Turnpike, the road to Everglades National Park (SR 9336) heads west than south, passing first through Florida City, a small agricultural community. Watch for Roberts Fruit Stand just outside of Florida City. It's a great place to sample locally grown tropical fruits, including sapodilla, egg fruit, papaya, limes, and oranges that you might want to add to your picnic cooler.

Heading south on SR 9336 (SW 192 Avenue), the signs you'll see for airboat rides are part of a commercial operation on the edge of the park called Everglades Alligator Farm. Located 4 miles south of SW 344th Street on SW 192 Avenue, it features airboat rides, alligator and nonpoisonous snake demonstrations, wildlife lectures, and a gator farm.

During a walk around the alligator pen, only a chainlink fence separates you from hundreds of the big brutes. In addition, the wildlife lectures sometimes include captive black bears, bobcats, and even Florida panthers that have been injured and rehabilitated but cannot be returned to the wild because the permanent disabilities they suffered would prevent them from surviving.

Continuing toward the park you'll begin passing through the middle of a widespread farming district. Known as the Rocky Glades, the dusty white and rocky fields belie their nonfertile appearance with bountiful crops of green beans, peppers, and lots of tomatoes. Often long strips of plastic are used as mulch in these intensely farmed lands and there's not a weed in sight.

# Did You See a Large White Bird?

There are a number of large white birds commonly seen in the Everglades that are easily confused by the first-time observer. After a little study, however, the differences become clear.

**Great White Heron** (*Ardea herodias*). At 50 inches in height, the great white heron, the largest heron in the Everglades, is actually considered a "morph" or color variation of the great blue heron. It's distinguished by yellow legs and a yellow bill. Some experts believe it may one day again be given separate species status.

**Great Egret** (*Casmerodius albus*). Often mistaken as a great white heron, great egrets stand about 40 inches tall. They have a yellow bill but are most easily distinguished from the larger heron by their black legs.

**Wood Stork** (*Mycteria americana*). This bird is easily distinguished by its slate colored head and neck. Wood storks also have black wing tips and stand about 40 inches tall.

**White Ibis** (*Eudocimus albus*). About 25 inches tall, white ibis are easily distinguished by their long, down-curved red bill and red legs. They also have black wing tips.

**Snowy Egret** (*Egretta thula*). Standing 24 inches tall, snowy egrets have a black bill and black legs with yellow feet sometimes referred to as golden slippers.

**Cattle Egret** (*Bubulcus ibis*). Only 20 inches tall, cattle egrets are buff colored on their head, chest, and back. They have yellowish legs and a short yellow beak.

**Little Blue Heron** (*Egretta caerulea*) (white phase). Immature little blue herons are all white with dull, olive-colored legs and a pale bluish bill tipped in black. They stand about 24 inches tall.

**Reddish Egret** (*Egretta rufescens*) (white phase). Less commonly seen, immature reddish egrets stand about 30 inches tall. They are all white with bluish legs and a pink bill with a black tip.

And then without warning there's a nearly instant transition from monocultured farmland, to the multihabitat, multispecies land of the Everglades. All of a sudden the wildlife outnumbers people and cars, and the glare of the bright, treeless farmland is replaced by a restful scene of green and yellow pastels. You've entered Everglades National Park.

**Directions:** Turn west from US 1 in Florida City onto State Road 9336 (SW 344th Street). Follow the signs to Everglades National Park.

**Fees:** A per-car fee is charged at Everglades National Park. There is a charge for admission to the Everglades Alligator Farm.

**Closest town:** Homestead is 10 miles northeast of the park entrance on SR 9336.

**For more information:** Everglades National Park Headquarters, 40001 State Road 9336, Homestead, FL 33034. Phone (305) 242-7700. Everglades Alligator Farm, PO Box 907, Homestead, FL 33090. Phone (800) 644-9711, local (305) 247-2628.

### ▦ PARK ENTRANCE TO ROYAL PALM VISITOR CENTER

[Fig. 10] The first thing you may notice upon entering the park is the hundreds of pine trees that have been broken off 15 to 20 feet above the ground. This is the first evidence you'll see of the passing of Hurricane Andrew, but not the last. Fortunately, in even the most damaged pineland areas, only about 35 to 40 percent of the trees were felled.

Forests of South Florida slash pines, similar to what you see here, once covered all the limestone ridges of southeastern Florida. Since they tend to grow on high ground, the pines covered the most desired building sites and were the first to go when the building boom hit South Florida in the 1940s and 1950s. Before that logging took a heavy toll; even in the park most of the pine trees are second growth.

You'll also soon begin passing through the first of many sections of sawgrass prairies. The golden-green grass extends on the flat land as far as the horizon, interspersed with only the rounded domes of tree hammocks. The scattered, spidery white flowers of the water-loving swamp lily (*Crinum americanum*) are easy to spot when it is in bloom.

Also, watch for wading birds scattered about in the grass. Great egrets, snowy egrets, cattle egrets (*Bubulcus ibis*), white ibis, wood storks, and great blue herons are likely to be anywhere, but they may only be visible for an instant if you drive by too quickly.

About 1.5 miles from the main entrance, begin looking to the left. You'll see a stand of royal palm trees extending their lofty clump of fronds high above a large hardwood hammock. The trees stand as sentinels over Royal Palm Hammock. Once called Paradise Key, this area was the first part of the park to be protected.

Although Hurricane Andrew downed many of the great hardwoods in the hammocks, most of the royal palms bent with the winds, then reclaimed their lofty positions after the storm passed.

The turn to Royal Palm Hammock, which features the trailhead for the Anhinga and Gumbo Limbo trails, is 2 miles from the main entrance. As you enter the hammock, look in the woods on the left where you can still see the remains of gumbo-limbo and bay trees toppled by Hurricane Andrew. Notice that many of the smaller trees that survived the storm had many of their branches stripped away.

## ANHINGA
(Anhinga anhinga)
This bird, also called the snakebird and water turkey, may often be seen perching with its wings outstretched, possibly trying to dry them.

The small visitor center at Royal Palm includes a bookstore and a small museum in which original artworks by wildlife artist Charles Harper depict life in a freshwater slough. With three-dimensional, overlapping layers of sharp-edged wildlife cutouts, the artist has reduced the surrounding environment to basic outlines and angles. His stylized murals seem to strip away all but the stark reality of the web of life— alligators eating possums, birds eating snails, snakes eating frogs, fish eating smaller fish, alligators eating lizards and fish, frogs eating lizards, anhingas eating everything but alligators.

**Directions:** Follow the road south from the main entrance for 2 miles. Turn left at the sign to Royal Palm Visitor Center.

**Activities:** Hiking, wildlife viewing, photography.

**Facilities:** Information, bookstore, drinking water, vending machines, restrooms.

**Dates:** Open year-round.

**Closest town:** Homestead is 12 miles to the northeast on Route 9336.

**For more information:** Everglades National Park Headquarters, 40001 State Road 9336, Homestead, FL 33034. Phone (305) 242-7700.

### ANHINGA TRAIL

[Fig. 12(2)] With its always-fulfilled promise of wildlife encounters, the Anhinga Trail is one of the most famous trails in America. It offers a close-up view of Taylor Slough, a miniature, but complete version of the larger Shark River Slough that anchors the river of grass to the west.

## Anhinga or Cormorant

People commonly confuse anhingas and double-crested cormorants. Although anhingas prefer freshwater habitats, cormorants are likely to show up in freshwater or saltwater areas, wherever the fishing is good. In some places, like along the Anhinga Trail, anhingas and cormorants can be seen both fishing and roosting nearly side-by-side.

In general the anhinga has a longer tail, a thinner, snakelike neck, and a smaller body than a cormorant. Cormorants often fly low to the ground with rapid, ducklike wing beats. Anhingas, on the other hand, soar high over the marshes with their necks and wings straight out.

Male anhingas, which grow to 33 inches tall, are all black. The females have a brown neck and head. Both sexes have large silvery wing patches. They also have a pointed bill that they use to spear fish, which are brought to the surface, flipped up, and swallowed head first.

Both sexes of the double-crested cormorant are dark all over with orange throat patches. This 34-inch-tall bird has a thicker body than the anhinga, and although cormorants also swim with only their head and neck above the water, they are easy to distinguish by the down-turned hook at the end of their bill. They capture small fish by grabbing them with their strong bills.

The best wildlife viewing along this 0.5-mile paved trail and boardwalk takes place during the winter dry season when the area's wildlife comes to the remaining water in the slough. Fish concentrated in the clear waters become easy prey for the birds and alligators that gather.

The trail begins next to the borrow pond behind the small visitor center. Look in the water for alligators and one of their favorite foods, the log-shaped Florida gar (*Lepisosteus platyrhincus*), which is easy to distinguish in the clear water by its long body and long snout. This light brown, spotted fish is seldom eaten today but was popular fare for Indians.

From the pond the trail follows part of the roadbed of the old Ingraham Highway, which was constructed in 1916 in an early attempt to develop part of the region. The road also provided a way for early visitors to discover the natural values of the Everglades, which in turn led to the protection of this area. The Florida Federation of Women's Clubs preserved and dedicated the area as Royal Palm State Park in 1916.

The shallow borrow canal next to the trail was dug when the highway was originally constructed. Birds and fish have found it to be as useful as any pond.

Florida softshell turtles are commonly spotted in the clear water. The large turtle spends most of its time underwater, even hiding its entire body in the mud to wait for prey, and occasionally using its long neck to raise its tubular snout to the surface for a breath of air.

Look in the water beneath the first little bridge you come to for huge largemouth bass lying almost motionless in the slow current. Look in the reeds near the bridge for a resident great blue heron and a green-backed heron. In the sawgrass beyond the canal look for great egrets, snowy egrets, great blue herons, and great white herons.

Although it is considered a color variation of the great blue heron, the great white is the largest of all the herons. Great white herons are frequently seen in the Anhinga Trail area and around Florida Bay. They stalk a great variety of large prey, including rodents and other birds. Both great white and great blue herons feed by standing nearly motionless waiting for their prey to come within the strike radius of their lightning-fast neck and beak.

Turning left onto the boardwalk, the trail next takes you out over a mature sawgrass prairie. Notice how tall the sawgrass is here, reaching heights of 8 feet or more. The triple-edged sawgrass is actually an ancient sedge and is the most abundant land plant in the Everglades.

Passing on through a thicket of willow trees (*Salix caroliniana*), the boardwalk extends out over the open, pondlike heart of Taylor Slough where visitors encounter what can only be described as a living mural of wildlife. Anhingas (*Anhinga anhinga*) and double-crested cormorants adorn the clumps of pond apple (*Annona goabra*) and willow trees surrounding the slough.

When hungry, both anhingas and cormorants dive into the clear water in pursuit of sunfish species such as bluegills and shellcrackers. Often putting on a show for the visitors gathered along the boardwalk, they swim around until sighting their prey, then move in for the kill.

The purple gallinule, one of the most strikingly beautiful birds in the Everglades, can often be seen walking gingerly on spatterdock (*Nuphar luteum*) leaves using its very long toes to lift the leaves in search of insects. Nearby, common moorhens (*Gallinula chloropus*) (also known as Florida gallinules) and coots can usually be seen floating on the water's surface, reaching down for an occasional mouthful of underwater salad.

Alligators, along with an occasional Florida brown water snake (*Storeria dekayi victa*) or Florida cottonmouth, will drag themselves onto the muddy bank below the boardwalk to absorb warmth from the afternoon sun. If you see a big green frog, it's probably a pig frog (*Rana sphenocephala*). This is the largest frog in South Florida and the most common frog in the Everglades.

A number of exotic species that have escaped from the Florida aquarium trade can also be spotted in Taylor Sough. They include blue tilapia (*Tilapia aurea*), Mayan cichlid (*Cichlasoma urophtalmus*), oscar (*Astronotus ocellatus*), and the unusual walking catfish, which actually uses its fins to walk from pond to pond.

All of these species rely on a food web that begins with a sun-nurtured, heavy growth of algae, which feeds and shelters tiny insects and animals. These in turn are eaten by mosquito fish, sailfin mollies (*Mollienisia latipinna*), and other small fish that also feed upon the plentiful mosquito larvae. These small fish are eaten by everything from sunfish to wading birds.

Pond apple trees (*Annona glabra*), also known as alligator apple or custard apple, grow in the shallower areas of the slough. When ripe, the yellow fruit is edible but has the taste of turpentine. Turtles and alligators feed on the fruit when it falls. Great thickets of these water-loving trees once grew in a wide band along the southern end of Lake Okeechobee. The trees were removed long ago to make way for farming.

Many of the trees around the slough are decorated with an array of air plants. Resembling pineapple tops, these bromeliads aren't parasites, but merely use the tree as support. They get their nourishment from the rain and debris that falls into little pockets at the base of the plant. Frogs, snakes, and insects add their droppings to the nutrient pool. Spanish moss (*Tillandsia usneoides*) and tree orchids are air plants found in the park.

**Trail:** 0.5 mile.

### GUMBO LIMBO TROPICAL HAMMOCK TRAIL

[Fig. 12(2)] This paved, 0.3-mile loop trail passes through the junglelike vegetation of Royal Palm Hammock. Royal palms, gumbo-limbo trees, wild coffee, strangler figs (*Ficus aurea*), and lush aerial gardens of ferns and orchids grow in this dense lush hammock, an island only 1 foot higher than the surrounding land.

Before Hurricane Andrew in 1992, the forest floor was dark and shaded by a thick tree canopy. After the storm toppled many of the mature trees, sunlight found the ground and the understory began to grow rapidly. Within 10 days of the storm, the

**GUMBO LIMBO**
(Bursera simaruba)
This hammock tree
is easily identified
by its peeling red
bark.

leaves began to sprout. And as is the way in the tropics, plants began growing on plants in their search for sunlight. It was a scene that was repeated in hammocks throughout the Everglades.

The hammock today is healthy and growing, and it is alive with insects, reptiles, birds, and small mammals. But the dense vegetation makes all but the biting insects difficult to find. One species that is quite visible because of its bold yellow stripes is the zebra butterfly. A tropical species from the West Indies, small groups of this butterfly can often be seen wandering slowly along the trail visiting with the vegetation. It is a prolific species in part because during its caterpillar stage it feeds on passion flowers, which give it a bitter taste, discouraging predators.

By growing close together in a hammock, plants help each other retain moisture and resist fire and frost. There is also a pronounced similarity of leaf shapes among the various trees in hammocks. Almost all the leaves are elliptical with smooth margins and waxy surfaces. A pointed "drip tip" allows excessive rain and dew to quickly drip off the leaf, and the waxy surface slows evaporation during the dry season.

At one point the paved trail crosses a wide grassy track leading into the hammock. This is a 0.8-mile section of the old Ingraham Highway that leads to the Hidden Lake Research Center.

Leave the Gumbo Limbo Trail and follow the old highway for a short distance. After a couple of hundred yards you'll enter a grove of royal palms, at more than 100 feet tall, standing high above the rest of the vegetation. A little farther and you'll see plants that look familiar.

Common house plants such as variegated philodendrum and elephant ear philodendrum (*Monstera deliciosa*) can be seen growing up and over the other plants along both sides of the trail and winding up the trunks of some of the royal palms. A few yards farther and you'll find a grove of wild orange trees that are mixed in with the hammock vegetation.

Somewhere off the trail a short distance to the north, through almost impassable foliage, is the site where the Royal Palm Lodge once stood and where early visitors could enjoy the tropical environment. The unusual plants were part of the original landscaping. The lodge, which was completed in 1919, was moved to Homestead in 1954.

**Trail:** 0.3-mile loop.

## LAKE INGRAHAM HIGHWAY TRAIL

[Fig. 12] A portion of the old Lake Ingraham Highway that once connected Miami with Cape Sable has been opened as a hiking trail. The trail follows the old limestone roadbed for 11 miles.

To find the beginning of the trailhead, go back toward the main road from the Royal Palm parking lot and turn left (southwest) down the paved road leading to the Daniel Beard Research Center. Continue straight at the point where the road takes a hard curve to the right. Watch out for potholes in the unimproved road. When you pass the gate to the Hidden Lake Research Center you'll actually be driving on the Old Ingraham Highway.

The road ends at Gate 15, which bars vehicle traffic but allows hikers and off-road bicyclists to continue. There are two campsites on the trail: the Ernest F. Coe Campsite is 4 miles out, and the Old Ingraham Campsite is 10 miles down the roadbed. Backcountry camping permits are required and the road can be flooded during the wet season.

The trail crosses the sawgrass prairie, and because it parallels the Homestead Canal it provides wildlife viewing opportunities similar to those found in Taylor Slough.

Even if you don't plan a hike, a drive down the old road is a chance to experience a little history. This somewhat circular area is known as the "Hole-in-the-Doughnut" because it's surrounded by undeveloped wetlands. Most of the area had been turned into crop and pasture land before the park was created. Brazilian pepper, which lines much of the road open to automobiles, is an unwelcomed exotic plant that has taken

# Is it a Panther or Bobcat?

Maybe you were driving or walking a trail near sunset, and you looked just in time to see a large cat disappearing into the bushes. Maybe it was a Florida panther (*Felis concolor coryi*), but chances are far greater it was a bobcat (*Lynx rufus*).

A very small number of Florida panthers, less than 10, spend part of their time within the boundaries of Everglades National Park. They are very reclusive and seldom spotted by even park service employees who live in the park.

An almost identical subspecies of the western cougar, adult male panthers grow up to 8 feet in length and can weigh up to 125 pounds. They have a tawny brown coat and a long tail that almost drags the ground.

Bobcats have black spots on a reddish, buff, or gray-colored coat. They seldom exceed 30 inches in length or weigh more that 35 pounds. They have short, triangular-shaped ears and a very short tail and are occasionally seen dashing across a road or trail.

As one park ranger put it, "If you see a Florida panther, you'll know it's a panther. There will be no doubt in your mind."

advantage of the disturbed lands. Scientists at the Daniel Beard Research Center are working to find ways to restore native vegetation.

Before leaving, drive down the road to the research center and to the restoration plots beyond. The road passes through a very nice pine and palmetto forest. Watch the wires along the road for hawks and other birds. During the late evening you have a chance of seeing a white-tailed deer (*Odocoileus virginianus*) or a gray fox (*Urocyon cinereoargenteus*).

**Directions:** Drive from the Royal Palm parking lot towards the main road and turn southwest towards the Daniel Beard Research Center. When the road curves to the right continue straight on the one-lane to Gate 15.

**Activities:** Hiking, bicycling, camping, wildlife viewing.

**Trail:** 11 miles one way. Campsites at 4 miles and 10 miles.

### LONG PINE KEY

[Fig. 10] Back on the main road and headed toward Flamingo again, you'll notice an occasional panther crossing sign. With very few of these big cats remaining in the area, and their penchant for travelling mostly at dusk and after dark, the chances of seeing one are very slim.

Two miles below the Royal Palm Road on the main road is the turn to Long Pine Key, a popular center for camping, hiking, and bicycling. The key is a continuation of the Atlantic Coastal Ridge that runs along the southeastern Florida coast.

Hiking trails of 3, 5, and 8 miles are interconnected to form more than 28 miles of trails through the pine forest. The longest loop trail follows an old auto trail that is now restricted to hiking or biking. Pick up a map of the trails at the visitor center before starting out.

The pine forest on Long Pine Key is the most diverse in the park, with between 100 and 200 species of plants recorded. About 20 are found here and nowhere else, and among them are milk pea (*Galactia pinetorum*) and narrow-leaved poinsettia (*Poinsettia pinetorum*).

While hiking look for species such as rough velvetseed (*Guettarda scabra*), willow bustic (*Dipholis salicifolia*), tetrazygia (*Tetrazygia bicolor*), and satinleaf trees (*Chrysophyllum oliviforme*). Leaves of the satinleaf are dark green on top and shiny bronze underneath, and they appear to shine and shimmer when the wind blows.

The Long Pine Key picnic grounds are comfortable and bug-bearable in the cooler months. Picnic sites with tables are scattered throughout the pine forest and connected by narrow paths. A nearby lake always seems to hold an alligator or two. During hot weather the tall pine trees offer very little shade.

Flocks of red-winged blackbirds (*Agelaius phoeniceus*) are common in the picnic area, as are the smaller pine warbler (*Dendroica pinus*), and red-bellied woodpecker (*Melanerpes carolinus,*) which actually has red on its head, not its belly. Just before dark look for three different species of owls, Eastern screech owls (*Otus asio*), barn owls (*Tyto alba*), and barred owls (*Strix varia*), on tree branches or actively hunting in the campgrounds and picnic grounds.

The Long Pine Key Campground has 103 tent and RV sites and pull-through sites for vehicles up to 35 feet. Each site has a picnic table and grill. There are restrooms, and water is available, but there are no hook-ups. The sites are well spaced, which is nice because the vegetation in the pine woods between sites isn't very tall.

**Directions:** The turnoff to Long Pine Key is 4.8 miles from the main entrance.

**Activities:** Picnicking, hiking, camping, bird-watching.

**Facilities:** Campground sites, water, grills, tables, hiking trails, restrooms.

**Dates:** Trails are open year-round. Campground is seasonal.

**Fees:** There is a fee charged for camping.

**Closest town:** Homestead is 15 miles to the northeast on SR 9336.

**For more information:** Everglades National Park Headquarters, 40001 State Road 9336, Homestead, FL 33034. Phone (305) 242-7700. Reservations may be made through the National Park Reservation Service at (800) 365-2267 in the U.S., (301) 722-1257 outside the U.S., or (888) 530-9796 with a TDD for the hearing-impaired.

## PINELANDS TRAIL

[Fig. 12(3)] A short, paved, and interpreted trail winds through another portion of pine forest about 2 miles down the main road at the Pinelands Trail pull-off. The 0.5-mile paved trail is wheelchair accessible.

On the way to the Pineland Trail notice how the landscape alternates from pine forest to sawgrass prairie and back again. These sections of forest are called keys (a South Florida name for islands) because they are surrounded by sawgrass prairie wetlands.

Hurricane Andrew left many pines in this area snapped off. Many of the largest trees were blown completely over. Many trees, however, survived because of their ability to bend. The dominant plant in these lands, the South Florida slash pine, is a native species adapted to a hurricane-prone climate.

Unfortunately, the 20,000 acres of the pineland community in the park represents nearly all that remains in North America of this unique habitat, making it one of the continent's most endangered pine communities.

The pine forest is also a fire forest, which means the habitat has evolved to depend upon periodic wildfire. When fire, often caused by lightning, sweeps though the area, hardwoods that try to invade the pinelands are destroyed while the pine trees' thick bark insulates them from all but the hottest fires. If hardwoods are able to grow, they will eventually shade the forest floor, which prevents young pine seedlings from germinating.

Various other plants have developed alternative fire-resistant mechanisms. The fernlike coontie, which has large underground stems, can burn to ground level, then quickly sprout again. Another common pinelands plant, saw palmetto (*Serenoa repens*) wrap its buds in layers of protective tissues.

Today, controlled burns are performed by the Park Service in an attempt to duplicate the role of natural fires. On the Pinelands Trail, at the base of some of the trees, you can see charring from earlier fires. Whenever possible, wildfires caused by lightning storms are allowed to follow their natural course and burn out on their own.

Watch out for poisonwood (*Metropium toxiferum*) along the Pinelands Trail. A close relative of poison ivy, the poisonwood tree can cause a severe rash. The tree has drooping compound leaves with five to seven leaflets. The shiny leaves and reddish-brown bark often have dark splotches on them. Animals can eat the berries with no ill effects.

**Directions:** The Pinelands Trail parking lot is 7 miles from the main entrance.

**Trail:** 0.5 mile.

**Closest town:** Homestead is 17 miles to the northeast on SR 9336.

**For more information:** Everglades National Park Headquarters, 40001 State Road 9336, Homestead, FL 33034. Phone (305) 242-7700.

### PINELANDS TRAILS TO PAY-HAY-OKEE

Continuing south along the main road from the turnoff for the Pinelands Trail, the pine forest begins to die out and the road again passes across the edge of the river of grass. The sawgrass extends from horizon to horizon like an Oklahoma wheat field, broken only by the occasional domed-shaped silhouette of a hardwood hammock or cypress head.

Red-tailed hawks (*Buteo jamaicensis*) and American kestrels are commonly seen in the short cypress trees and small hammocks near the road. Wood storks, great egrets, white ibis, and snowy egrets can be seen in wet areas along the road.

In the summer, puffy white clouds with flat anvil bottoms form almost every afternoon over the Everglades. The clouds soon grow into thunderheads reaching great heights. When the rain begins and the thunder starts rumbling across the sawgrass, they almost seem to lean forward as they sweep across the landscape trailing a dark downpour behind. Because of the flat landscape, you can see these great storms from many miles away, and appreciate how fast they move if they are heading your way.

Don't stay to watch for too long, however. Florida is known as the nation's thunderstorm capitol and leads the nation in deaths from lightning. Researchers have also pointed out that Florida lightning is particularly powerful because the tall storm clouds that it comes from are more highly charged than the average thunderhead.

Although the rainstorms can be intense, they seldom last more than two hours, and often pass by in only a few minutes. The sauna-like conditions that persist for hours after these storms pass give true meaning to the statement, "It's not the heat it's the humidity."

If there's not too much traffic, consider pulling over to the side somewhere along the main road. Step out of your car and appreciate the quiet of the Everglades. If you stand with your back to the road and look out across the sawgrass, you can feel the

Everglades the way you might feel a great desert or mountain range. See the wind blow across the grass, listen to the sounds of birds and insects. Feel the life of a place that may have seemed lifeless through a car window.

Step closer, look at an individual strand of sawgrass. Notice how it has three edges, each with an impressive row of serrated teeth. Look up again and imagine what it must have been like for the first explorers, or the Native Americans who turned to this harsh land for refuge from an unjust government.

At one point the road passes through a dwarf cypress forest. The miniature cypress trees, although as old as their taller cousins, are merely stunted because they grow where there is only a thin layer of top soil and a short supply of nutrients.

**Directions:** From the main entrance travel 7 miles down the main road.

**Activities:** Wildlife and habitat observation.

**Facilities:** None.

**Dates:** Open year-round.

**Closest town:** Homestead is 17 miles to the northeast on SR 9336.

**For more information:** Everglades National Park Headquarters, 40001 State Road 9336, Homestead, FL 33034. Phone (305) 242-7700.

## PAY-HAY-OKEE OVERLOOK

[Fig. 11, Fig. 12] Thirteen miles south of the main entrance, Pay-hay-okee, which is the Seminole word for "grassy waters," is an overlook worth looking over. A short road takes you to the edge of the Shark River Slough where the park has built a tower, which provides a exceptional view of the river of grass.

A very short boardwalk (0.2 mile) leading out to an observation tower passes close to a small stand of pond apple trees. This is an area where visitors are likely to see red-shouldered hawks (*Buteo lineatus*) in the treetops and wood storks feeding in the shallow water around the bases of the cypress trees. Bald eagles are also often sighted in the area.

Look at the base of the tall sawgrass next to the boardwalk. That thick mat of brown ooze floating on the shallow water is periphyton, which is made up of several different types of algae and is one of the most important components of the sawgrass prairie. Serving as the base of the food web, periphyton hosts a variety of tiny insects and crustaceans and makes up much of the soil in which the sawgrass grows. During drought the thick mats help to seal moisture in the ground.

This overlook provides one of the best views of the sawgrass. Even from the vantage point of the tower, the yellow and green sawgrass extends to the horizon in a uniform sheet broken only by the occasional cypress dome. The water in this river began its journey hundreds of miles to the north and may have taken nearly a year to get this far. The Pay-hay-okee Overlook is also one of the best spots in the park to watch the sunset over the sawgrass. In fact, someone even put a bench in just the right location for watching the sun fall into the sawgrass.

As darkness slides over the land, many of the animals seem to come alive with a desire to communicate. Croaking, squawking, chattering, squealing, chirping, and buzzing sounds fill the air.

At the same time, the dark blue evening sky fades into a bright orange band that runs along the horizon and reflects through the thin cypress in the water below. Slowly, faint green and yellow bands appear above the deep orange, forming a horizontal rainbow that lasts for only the final few minutes of nature's daily show.

**Directions:** 13 miles south of the main entrance on the main road.

**Activities:** Scenic view, wildlife watching.

**Facilities:** Accessible overlook tower.

**Dates:** Open year-round.

**Closest town:** Flamingo is 25 miles to the south along the Main Park Road.

**For more information:** Everglades National Park Headquarters, 40001 State Road 9336, Homestead, FL 33034. Phone (305) 242-7700.

### MAHOGANY HAMMOCK

[Fig. 12] Seven miles farther down the road to Flamingo, and 20 miles from the main entrance, Mahogany Hammock provides a revealing look into a unique Everglades habitat. A circular, elevated 0.5 mile boardwalk has been constructed and passes through the heart of a mature hardwood hammock dominated by huge mahogany trees.

Even the short road out to the hammock offers an excellent scenic view of a sawgrass prairie dotted with swamp lilies and stunted cypress trees. Look for red-shouldered hawks and kestrels in the short, skimpy trees. The hammock is also a good place to see barred owls *(Strix varia).* Look for their dark shapes in the upper branches.

Just to the right of the point where the boardwalk enters the hammock is a large clump of rare paurotis palms *(Aeoelorr haphe wrightii).* These skinny palms can also be found in urban developments around Miami where they have been used

## STRANGLER FIG (Ficus aurea)
The seeds of this tree usually germinate in the bark crevices of other trees. The strangler fig sends out aerial roots that may wrap around or "strangle" the host tree. The roots eventually reach the ground and develop an independent root system.

extensively for landscaping.

Inside the hammock, a couple hundred feet down the right-hand fork, is a plaque that reads, "The oldest living [West Indies] mahogany tree in the United States." The tree is an astounding sight. According to the National Registry of Big Trees, it has a girth of 128 feet and a height of 51 feet. The old giant has branches bigger than the trunks of the other mature mahogany trees in the hammock. Like a great grandfather watching over his brood, it towers far above the other trees.

Since this tree was nominated for champion status in the 1975, however, a couple of larger trees have been discovered, including a Key West tree that has a girth of 175 feet and a height of 79 feet.

Prior to 1960 this isolated hammock was largely composed of giant mahogany trees and a very few plants that could grow beneath the dark canopy. That was before the 180 mph winds of Hurricane Donna toppled many of the largest trees, allowing sunlight to penetrate to the forest floor.

## Strangler Fig

The strangler fig is an unusual tree. It can grow as a normal tree from a seed dropping on ground, or it can begin life as an epiphyte after finding a foothold high in the branches of another tree. After securing a hold on a host tree, a strangler fig grows upward until it can set a crown of leaves above its host. At the same time, it sends down strangling aerial roots that wrap around the host tree on their way to the ground, eventually killing the host and leaving the strangler fig standing in its place.

The leaves of the strangler fig are leathery to the touch and dark green with yellow midribs. Fruits are true figs and have hollow centers that are eaten by birds. The fig seeds are then dispersed, sometimes into the tops of other trees, through bird droppings. The strangler figs are often seen strangling a cabbage palm or other tree but will also climb up abandoned cars and even chimneys.

Almost immediately, new species began competing for the sunlight. Today the hammock features a thick growth of tropical plants, cabbage palms, royal palms, strangler figs, and gumbo-limbo trees.

At one point along the walk, giant leather ferns (*Acrostichum danaeifolium*) growing up and around the boardwalk add to the primeval feeling of the junglelike environment. Also look high in the trees for resurrection fern (*Polypodium polypodioides*), a plant known for turning brown and drying up as if dead, only to revive within minutes of the first rain. Tree orchids found in the hammock include cowhorn orchid (*Cyrtopodium punctatum*), butterfly orchid (*Encyclia tampensis*), clam shell orchid (*Encyclia cochleata*), twisted air plant (*Tillandsia flexuosa*), and needle leaf air plant (*Tillandsia setacea*).

**Directions:** 20 miles south of the main entrance on the main road.

**Activities:** Hiking, wildlife and habitat observation.

**Dates:** Open year-round.

**Closest town:** Flamingo is 18 miles to the south along the main road.

**For more information:** Everglades National Park Headquarters, 40001 State Road 9336, Homestead, FL 33034. Phone (305) 242-7700.

## ▩ MAHOGANY HAMMOCK TO FLAMINGO

The rest of the road to Flamingo features a number of spots worth a two-hour picnic, or a 10-minute stop over, depending upon your mood and schedule. Each stop has the potential to present a special surprise, another discovery.

A few miles below Mahogany Hammock, near the turnoff to Paurotis Pond, mangroves begin to dominate the roadside vegetation. Mostly red mangroves, the trees on the west side of the road grow in a borrow canal created when the road was built. In the summer watch the sky just above the trees for the tilting and dipping flight of a swallow-tailed kite (*Elanoides forficatus*). The startling black and white birds have long forked tails that make them easy to identify.

Any time of the year, the canal behind the mangroves offers some terrific birding opportunities. Wading birds of all types—great blue herons, wood storks, white ibis, roseate spoonbills, great egrets and snowy egrets, tricolored herons—gather in large numbers in open spots in the old canal. As you drive by, watch for gaps in the trees where you can see back into open water. If you spot an accumulation of birds, you can carefully pull off and walk back for a closer look.

Paurotis Pond is a picnic area overlooking a small borrow pond. It's a fair place to spot wood storks and some wading birds.

A few picnic tables and a scenic view of a freshwater pond highlight the pull-off at Nine Mile Pond. Actually a series of connected spots, this is the starting point for the Nine Mile Pond canoe trail. Look for alligators and the regular assortment of wading birds. It's also a good place to see bald eagles, osprey, and wintering waterfowl. In summer look for small flocks of white-crowned pigeon and swallow-tailed kites.

West Lake is another stop that offers some excellent birding opportunities. In winter, depending upon the severity of the weather, look for migrating waterfowl in the lake behind the boat launch. Northern shoveler (*Anas clypeata*), blue-winged teal (*Anas discors*), green-winged teal (*Anas crecca*), American widgeon (*Anas americana*), ring-necked duck (*Aythya collaris*), and lesser scaup (*Aythya affinis*) have been sighted there. The boardwalk through the mangroves and out to the main lake often reveals rafts of American coots, and some wading birds along the shore.

Wildlife calendars all over the country contain photos of birds taken at Mrazek Pond, the next stop on the road. It's a Jekyll and Hyde kind of spot. When the water is high the wildlife is scarce, but when the water is low it earns its reputation as the most highly photographed spot in the park.

On most days in the winter, there's a constant crowd of photographers and bird watchers posted at the water's edge. Binoculars, spotting scopes, and telephoto lenses steadily record the changing picture of the pond's wildlife.

## Are There Flamingos in Flamingo?

Despite its name, there has long been debate as to whether flamingos ever spent much time in Flamingo. It seems evident that they once did, although many sightings over the years have been attributed to birds that escaped from Miami attractions.

Until the turn of the century, several hundred flamingos migrated from summer breeding grounds in the Bahamas and wintered in Florida Bay. Old accounts exist of hunting flamingos for meat in the Florida Keys and the Bahamas, although habitat losses at vital nesting sights most likely contributed to the birds' disappearance from these waters.

Today, however, flamingos are again occasionally sighted in their historic haunts near Flamingo. In recent years flocks of up to 30 have been sighted in Florida Bay, and occasionally in Snake Bight. The origin of these birds is not known. Speculation ranges from possible escapees from a free-flying flock at the Hialeah Race Track to truly wild birds wandering in from remaining protected breeding grounds in the Bahamas.

One day may find hundreds of great egrets stationed in the trees and shallow water. Another day might find rafts of white pelicans performing their feeding ballet. Working shoulder to shoulder as a group they drive schools of minnows up against the shore. Then at some unknown signal, all the birds dip their large pouches at once, then raise them high to let the water run out before gobbling down the filtered contents.

On any visit to the pond, you might also see roseate spoonbills, common moorhen (also known as a Florida gallinules), American bitterns (*Botaurus lentiginosus*), least bitterns (*Ixobrychus exilis*), anhingas, double-crested cormorants, great blue herons, white ibis, pied-billed grebes, little blue herons (*Florida caerulea*), and tricolored herons.

Another mile down the road, Coot Bay Pond, which is surrounded by a thick growth of red mangroves, is a nice place for a picnic, but seldom contains much in the way of visible wildlife. The pond is connected by a small waterway to the much larger Coot Bay.

For a brief time before the area became a park, a fishing lodge sat at this spot next to Coot Bay Pond. American coots, which were once plentiful on Coot Bay, have a gizzard much like a chicken. Apparently the rest of the bird wasn't much to brag on, but the lodge was known for a special dish of coot gizzards and rice.

Along the final few miles to Flamingo the road passes between high walls of red mangroves and Brazilian pepper. Again watch for openings in the almost solid walls of vegetation where wading birds will be gathered.

**Directions:** From 20 miles south of the main entrance to Flamingo on the main park road.

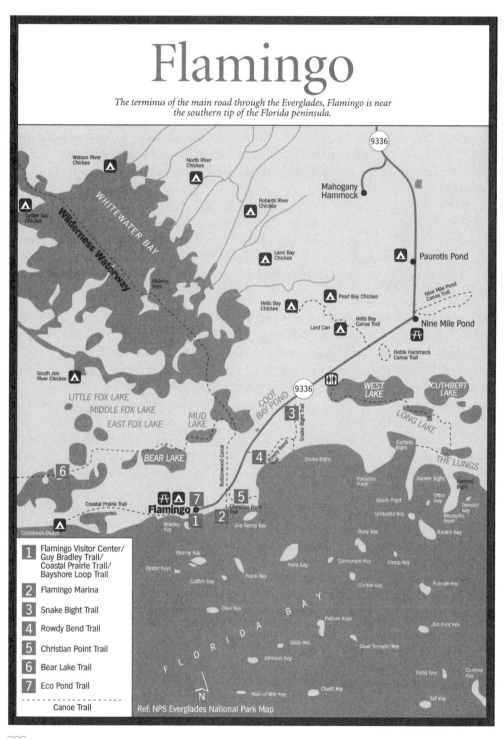

# Flamingo

*The terminus of the main road through the Everglades, Flamingo is near the southern tip of the Florida peninsula.*

**1** Flamingo Visitor Center/ Guy Bradley Trail/ Coastal Prairie Trail/ Bayshore Loop Trail

**2** Flamingo Marina

**3** Snake Bight Trail

**4** Rowdy Bend Trail

**5** Christian Point Trail

**6** Bear Lake Trail

**7** Eco Pond Trail

- - - - Canoe Trail

Ref: NPS Everglades National Park Map

**Activities:** Wildlife viewing, picnicking.

**Facilities:** Picnic tables, restrooms at West Lake.

**Dates:** Open year-round.

**Closest town:** Mahogany Hammock to Flamingo, 20 miles.

**For more information:** Everglades National Park Headquarters, 40001 State Road 9336, Homestead, FL 33034. Phone (305) 242-7700.

# Flamingo

[Fig. 11, Fig. 13] Located at the very southern tip of the Florida peninsula, at the terminus of the main road, Flamingo is the perfect base camp for the entire range of activities available in the park. Wildlife viewing, canoeing, hiking, boating, camping, fishing, bicycling, guided tours, and ranger-led activities all spring from this small community.

From boats to bicycles, if you didn't bring it, you can rent it. Flamingo is also the site of the only food services and overnight lodging in the park.

Much of the activity takes place around the Marina, which serves as a gateway to the water-based part of Everglades National Park. To the south is world-famous Florida Bay, with its hundreds of mysterious keys and its world-class sport fishing, which can be viewed any Saturday morning on at least one of the fishing shows. To the northwest lies Whitewater Bay, one of Florida's largest and most remote bodies of water, and beyond that the mangrove backcountry of hidden inland bays, narrow twisting creeks, and broad tidal rivers awaits the intrepid explorer.

Flamingo is also notorious for its mosquitos and no-see-ums (biting midges). Be prepared with long-sleeved shirts, and always have mosquito repellant (also known as Flamingo perfume) nearby. Aerosol and pump sprays are for sale anywhere anything is for sale in Flamingo, including the gift shop, marina, and even the lobby of the Flamingo Lodge. Bug suits and head nets can be purchased at the marina store.

The town of Flamingo was established in 1893 when its citizenry of plume hunters, renegades, fishermen, and farmers had to choose a name in order to obtain a post office. The 1910 federal census record shows 49 people living in Flamingo and Cape Sable. Most listed their profession as farming, which included growing sugar cane for the making of syrup and moonshine.

In 1915, the Roberts Hotel, located in Flamingo, had four bedrooms for guests and extra mattresses on the floor for the overflow. For dealing with mosquitos every house had an assortment of smudgepots, and a "loser" room, where a palmetto fan was used to "lose" the mosquitos before coming inside.

The only way there was by boat. Supplies were shipped in from Key West, Fort Myers, or Tampa, and cane syrup, fish, and produce were traded in return. Sometime after Royal Palm State Park was created in 1916, the Ingraham Highway reached Flamingo.

It was a rough country that required some ingenuity for survival. Consider the story about the time a proliferation of rats destroyed the cane crop. The townspeople took up a collection and one Gene Roberts, son of the hotel owner, headed for Key West where he offered 10 cents for every cat delivered to the dock.

Forty dollars poorer, and 400 cats richer, he set sail for Flamingo in his small boat. "That 90-mile trip was the worst I ever made," he is said to have stated upon reaching the Flamingo shore. The cats reportedly headed straight for the brush, never to be seen again. But the rat problem did go away.

Flamingo's current 200 residents are employees of the National Park Service and the concessioner. The settlement is composed of housing for the employees, a visitor center, a gift shop, a campground, a lodge, a restaurant, a convenience store, and a marina.

A small museum in the visitor center explains how the various habitats—mangrove forests, coastal prairies, freshwater bays, and saltwater estuaries—intertwine to create the unusual ecosystem found in the Flamingo area. Ranger-led activities available at the visitor center during peak season, from mid-December to early April, include naturalist talks, hikes, canoe trips, and campfire programs.

You might wish to take a moment to stop by the gift shop and see the display of Clyde Butcher photographs of the Everglades. Clyde Butcher is the preeminent Everglades photographer. His stunning black-and-white landscape photos capture the essence of South Florida wildlands.

Also note the plaque at the base of the stairs near the visitor center that once stood on Cape Sable over the grave of Guy Bradley, an Audubon Society warden, who was murdered by plume hunters in 1905. His death led directly to federal legislation banning the killing of wading birds.

According to somewhat conflicting stories, Bradley was shot while trying to apprehend plume hunters on the Oyster Key bird rookery, and his body was discovered somewhere near Flamingo. The large key in Florida Bay just to the west of Flamingo is named Bradley Key in his honor.

Flamingo's location on the shore of Florida Bay, where the Everglades meets the salt water, creates a diversity of wildlife viewing opportunities that can be found nowhere else in the park.

Birds, mammals, and reptiles that are rare elsewhere can be commonly seen in and around this small coastal community. Opportunities exist to see bald eagles, brown pelicans, bottle-nosed dolphins, great white herons, American crocodiles, American alligators, West Indian manatees, loggerhead sea turtles, black skimmers (*Rynchops niger*), roseate spoonbills, marsh rabbits, short-tailed hawks (*Buteo brachyurus*), smooth-billed ani (*Crotophaga ani*), and many more animals.

Rare sightings can occur of flamingos, scarlet ibis, and pink ibis. The very fortunate might catch a glimpse of one of the accidental visitors. A Key West quail dove (*Geotrygon chrysia*), occasional bananaquits (*Coereba flaveola*), and even an African abdin stork (*Ciconia abimii*), which appeared in December of 1998, are among the oddities that have shown up in Flamingo over the years.

The marina is where exploration of much of the park begins. Located on the Buttonwood Canal near the entrance to Florida Bay, it has both a saltwater side and a freshwater side. The freshwater side leads into the Everglades backcountry by way of the Buttonwood Canal and through Whitewater Bay. The saltwater side is the starting point for boat trips into Florida Bay.

The Buttonwood Canal, begun in the 1920s and widened and finished in the 1950s, once connected Florida Bay with Coot Bay and the Everglades backcountry waters. When it finally became obvious that the daily exchange of tides was damaging the delicate brackish-water balance of the inland estuary the Park Service, in 1982, installed a concrete plug in the canal.

There are boat ramps on each side of the plug and a lift for transferring small to medium-sized boats from one side to the other. The marina is open year-round and can accommodate up to 50 boats. Boat-launching ramps are available and there are a limited number of electricity and water hook-ups. The marina store is the only food service available year-round.

Other marina concessions include boat tours of Florida Bay and the backcountry. Concessionaires also rent bicycles, canoes, kayaks, motorized skiffs, and houseboats for fishing and exploring the backcountry. The houseboats, available October to May, sleep up to eight people and come fully equipped.

The various boat tours provide a comfortable way to see the various habitats and generally offer excellent opportunities for wildlife viewing. Tours into the mangrove wilderness of Whitewater Bay and Coot Bay offer a good chance to see manatees, alligators, and American crocodiles, as well as a wide assortment of wading birds.

Other cruises explore the marine feeding and nursery grounds of Florida Bay, providing visitors a chance to see a mix of bird species including herons, egrets, pelicans, cormorants, ibis, ospreys, bald eagles, and black skimmers. It's also possible to encounter dolphins, sea turtles, and sharks.

Most general cruises run one and a half to two hours, and charge a moderate fee. More expensive cruises that stay out longer and carry few people are also available.

Saltwater fishing out of Flamingo can be nothing short of spectacular. Snook, tarpon, spotted seatrout, redfish, bonefish, and permit roam the flats of Florida Bay. In the winter, many of the same species, especially snook and redfish, will journey far into the backcountry where they can be wrestled out of the mangrove roots with a well-placed cast.

Simply put, it takes a boat to go fishing out of Flamingo. It doesn't have to be a big boat, even canoeists can paddle to some fine action in Florida Bay or inland to Whitewater Bay. The only shore-based fishing takes place from the beaches of Cape Sable, and it takes a boat to get there. The marina can arrange full or half-day fishing charters year-round. All charters include fishing licenses and fishing tackle.

If you're spending the night in Flamingo don't pass up a chance to take in the night sky. With the nearest city light source at least 50 miles away, it's worth the effort to drive a few miles up the road, or at least walk to the shore of Florida Bay with your back to the lights of Flamingo and behold a sight not often seen in today's society. Within moments the constellations will take shape—Orion's Belt, the Big Dipper and Little Dippers, the Pleiades, and even the Milky Way are visible.

Tent and RV camping sites are available at the Flamingo campgrounds. There are 300 walk-in and pull-through sites but they can fill up early during the busy winter season. There are centrally located bathrooms, sinks, and cold showers, but no hook-ups.

**Directions:** Flamingo is 38 miles from the main entrance.

**Activities:** Hiking, biking, canoeing, wildlife viewing, camping, boating, fishing, ranger-led activities, boat tours.

**Facilities:** Visitor center museum, restrooms, gift shop, convenience store and fuel, and campground.

**Dates:** The marina is open year-round, many other facilities and concessions are seasonal. Call for details.

**Fees:** Fees are charged for camping, tours, and concessions.

**Closest town:** Homestead is 48 miles to the north.

**For more information:** Everglades National Park Headquarters, 40001 State Road 9336, Homestead, FL 33034. Phone (305) 242-7700. Camping reservations can be made through the National Park Reservation Service. Phone (800) 365-2267 in the U.S., (301) 722-1257 outside the U.S., or (888) 530-9796 with a TDD for the hearing-impaired. For current boat tour times and fees and guided fishing fees write to #1 Flamingo Lodge Highway, Flamingo, FL 33034. Web site www.flamingolodge.com Phone (941) 695-3101 and ask for the activity booth. Fax (941) 695-3921.

## RESTAURANTS AND LODGING IN FLAMINGO

All of the concessions in Flamingo are managed by Amfac Parks & Resorts. For more information, contact Flamingo Lodge Marina & Outpost Resort, #1 Flamingo Lodge Highway, Flamingo, Florida 33034. Web site www.flamingolodge.com Phone (800) 600-3813 or local (941) 695-3101. Fax (941) 695-3921.

### FLAMINGO LODGE RESTAURANT AND ANGLER'S BAR

1 Flamingo Lodge Highway, Flamingo. Overlooking Florida Bay, this restaurant has a unique competitive advantage besides the great view. It's 50 miles to the nearest alternative. Maybe for that reason the high quality of its food and service is always a little surprising, but nonetheless, always reliable.

While dining in the restaurant don't be surprised to see dolphins cavorting in the bay or pelicans diving for their own dinner. The menu features a selection of seafood, steak, chicken, vegetarian dishes, and local specialties like conch fritters. It's decorated with local original art, and open seasonally, November to April. The dress is casual and reservations are not accepted unless it's a group of six or more. The restaurant

# Did You See a Pink Bird?

If you see a pink bird, chances are good it was either a roseate spoonbill, flamingo, pink ibis, or scarlet ibis.

To distinguish the spoonbill from the flamingo in flight, the roseate spoonbill's wing is solid pink, whereas the trailing edge of a flamingo wing is black. While wading, the best way to distinguish the two is by their bill shapes. The roseate has a long, spoonlike bill while the flamingo has a sharply bent heavy bill.

The pink ibis and scarlet ibis are smaller birds with long, downcurved beaks. The pink ibis, introduced into Miami in the 1960s, is a hybrid between the native white ibis and scarlet ibis. Scarlet ibis are a very bright scarlet color and can be distinguished by their long, downcurved beaks. Both the scarlet and the pink ibis have the same structure, size, and black wing tips as the white ibis.

staff will also gladly cook your freshly caught fish just how you like them. *Moderate. Phone (941) 695-3101.*

### BUTTONWOOD PATIO CAFE

1 Flamingo Lodge Highway, Flamingo. This small restaurant features pizzas, sandwiches, and salads and is open year-round, but it provides only limited food service during the winter and summer months. *Inexpensive. Phone (941) 695-3101.*

### FLAMINGO LODGE

1 Flamingo Lodge Highway, Flamingo. This lodge is open year-round. It has 103 air-conditioned rooms plus 24 cottages with kitchen facilities. Although it is more than 40 years old and scheduled for renovation, the facility is clean and well-kept. Many of the rooms have a view of Florida Bay and there is a swimming pool. *Moderate. Phone (941) 695-3101.*

### CAMPING

The Flamingo campgrounds has 64 walk-in tent sites and 234 drive-in sites. There are no RV hook-ups. There is a dumping station and centrally located bathrooms. Camping reservations can be made through the National Park Reservation Service. Phone (800) 365-2267 in the U.S., (301) 722-1257 outside the U.S., or (888) 530-9796 with a TDD for the hearing-impaired.

### FLORIDA BAY

[Fig. 13] The features of Florida Bay epitomize much of the special nature and beauty of South Florida—clear blue waters, dark green mangrove islands, and miles of shallow grass flats alive with a richly diverse marine ecosystem. The bay is famous for both its sport fishing and its rich diversity of wildlife.

Anglers from around the world come for the bay's legendary shallow water flats fishing, which has been made famous on TV fishing shows and in outdoor publica-

# Ouch! What Was That?

If you feel a sting and don't know what caused it, you're probably the victim of a no-see-um. You can expect more where that came from. No-see-ums, also known as sandflies, are actually biting midges that can be extremely bothersome along the saltwater coast, especially at sunrise and sunset.

Five species are believed to inhabit coastal areas *(Culicoides furens, C. mississippiensis, C. hollensis, C. harbosai, and C. melleus)*. Appropriately named, they appear as little more than a tiny black speck on your skin, but there's no mistaking their sharp bite.

No-see-ums can't bite through clothing. Most strong insect repellents will also keep them away. Skin-So-Soft, a bath oil made by Avon, is also known to defeat no-see-ums, but has little effect on saltwater mosquitos. Campers should be aware that only the smallest screening will keep them out of your tent or RV.

tions. If fishing isn't your preference even a brief tour of the bay will bring you face to face with many of the park's more interesting wildlife species.

Loggerhead sea turtles, bottle-nosed dolphins (*Tursiops truncatus*) and West Indian manatees thrive within a few miles of alligator-laden swamps separated by narrow strips of land where saltwater crocodiles still lay their eggs.

Florida's unique mix of bird life is represented by wood storks, blue herons, brown and white pelicans, roseate spoonbills, and numerous others that feed in the bay's waters and nest on its islands. Even the occasional flamingo and scarlet ibis (*Guara rubra*) visit the bay.

The triangular-shaped bay is bordered by the Everglades to the north and the Keys to the east and south. It covers an area of 400,000 to 550,000 acres, depending on where the western boundary with the Gulf of Mexico is measured. Its waters are dotted with 237 mangrove islands.

When healthy, Florida Bay is one of the most productive estuaries in the United States: 140 species of mollusks, 32 species of crustaceans, and 24 species of amphibians and reptiles inhabit its waters, along with tarpon, redfish (*Sciaenops ocellata*), snook, bonefish, and gray snapper that draw so many anglers to its famous backcountry fishing.

All of these species depend in part upon the bay's bountiful growth of turtle grass (*Thalassia testudinum*). The most common seagrass in the bay, turtle grass continues to survive despite problems with the bay's salinity. Other, less-tolerant types of seagrass have died back due to changes in the natural plumbing system of the Everglades.

Pink shrimp (*Penaeus duorarum*) also depend on the bay's seagrasses. Larval shrimp drift into the bay from the Dry Tortugas spawning grounds. Here they settle on seagrass habitat and bare sand bottom. When mature they ride the currents back out to the Dry Tortugas to start the cycle over again.

Florida Bay's current ills are rooted in the same problems affecting Everglades

National Park. Without its normal freshwater input, the bay underwent a gradual transition from pristine estuary to hypersaline saltwater lagoon. By 1992 severe algal blooms and hypersaline waters were flowing out of Florida Bay and through the Keys, damaging the coral reefs. The decline in water quality was halted, at least temporarily, by an increase in freshwater flow resulting from a succession of rainy years in South Florida during the mid- to late-1990s. The long-term results will depend on a successful restoration of the entire Everglades ecosystem.

**Directions:** Florida Bay is located directly off the coast of the southern tip of Florida. It comprises up to 550,000 acres between the mainland peninsula and the upper Florida Keys.

**Activities:** Fishing, boating, canoeing, wildlife observation.

**Closest town:** Flamingo

**For more information:** Florida Bay Research Program at Everglades National Park, South Florida Research Center, Everglades National Park, 40001 State Road 9336, Homestead, Florida 33034-6733. Web site www.nps.gov/ever/eco/fbrp.htm For boat tours and fishing guide information contact Flamingo Marina, #1 Flamingo Lodge Highway, Flamingo, FL 33034. Web site www.flamingolodge.com Phone (941) 695-3101. Fax (941) 695-3921.

## FLAMINGO VISITOR CENTER

[Fig. 11(1), Fig. 13(1)] Wildlife viewing in Flamingo should start at the information booth in the park's visitor center. Talk with the rangers about wildlife known to be in the area. Also ask to see the wildlife observation log (often kept behind the counter) for recent unusual wildlife sightings reported by other visitors. Depending upon the time of year, the second floor breezeway between the information booth and the restaurant provides a terrific view of shorebirds on a mud flat just offshore in Florida Bay. A spotting scope or strong pair of binoculars will be useful in sighting white pelicans, brown pelicans, laughing gulls, royal terns (*Sterna dougallii*), sanderlings, herring gulls, great white herons, and an occasional bald eagle.

**Directions:** Located in the park visitor center in Flamingo.

**Facilities:** Museum, information booth.

**Dates:** Open year-round.

**Closest town:** Flamingo.

**For more information:** Everglades National Park Headquarters, 40001 State Road 9336, Homestead, FL 33034. Phone (305) 242-7700.

**ZEBRA BUTTERFLY**
(Heliconius charitonius)
This species belongs to a family of tropical butterflies. Most predators ignore the delicate zebra butterfly because it has a disagreeable taste.

## FLAMINGO MARINA

[Fig. 13(2)] Another important stop for both tidal information and wildlife viewing is the Flamingo Marina. Flamingo's tides occur twice a day, with highs and lows about six hours apart. Low tide, when the mud flats are exposed, is preferable for most birding or exploring along Florida Bay on foot.

The tides are posted daily above the check-out counter in the marina store. Tide charts are also available in many of the local fishing publications on sale here.

Despite the boat traffic and general hubbub in the marina, a number of wildlife species can be viewed here. For instance, a number of large alligators along with a trio of saltwater crocodiles are known to regularly hang around in the Buttonwood Canal and near the boat ramps. Ask the marina personnel where the crocodiles were last seen.

Brown pelicans can usually be seen begging for a handout from returning anglers. Black skimmers like to take up positions around the freshwater boat ramp. In winter West Indian manatees can often be seen in the freshwater side of the marina.

Natural history boat tours of Florida Bay and the backcountry leave from the marina. You can also hire backcountry and Florida Bay fishing guides or arrange for a custom tour. Bicycles, canoes, kayaks, and small motorized skiffs are also available for rent. Houseboats may be rented through the lodge by calling (941) 695-3101, and reservations are suggested.

The marina store has light groceries year-round. It stocks a wider variety of foods during the summer when other food service is limited.

**Directions:** The marina is located on the Buttonwood Canal in Flamingo, east of the lodge.

**Activities:** Boat tours, canoeing, fishing, bicycling, wildlife viewing.

**Facilities:** Boat slips, marina store.

**Dates:** Open year-round.

**Closest town:** Flamingo.

**For more information:** Flamingo Marina, #1 Flamingo Lodge Highway, Flamingo, FL 33034. Web site www.flamingolodge.com Phone (941) 695-3101. Fax (941) 695-3921.

## FLORIDA BAY SHORELINE

The shoreline of Florida Bay is another good place to look for wildlife. Although partially covered with mangroves, there are long open areas behind the Flamingo Lodge (*see* page 189) and along the walk-in campgrounds. A paved trail runs between the lodge and the campgrounds and offers additional views of the bay. At the water's edge, you can also see the exposed, muddy marl that overlays the oolite limestone in this part of the park.

Sunrise visitors will be rewarded not only with beautiful scenes of orange and red pastels painted upon the sky and on the bay's calm water, but also with a chance to see and hear the wildlife waking up for the day.

From behind the lodge you can often see osprey circling over the bay looking for an unwary fish to dive upon. Shorebirds, such as sanderlings and semipalmated plovers (*Charadrius semipalmatus*), often search out food tidbits in the washed-up debris. Little blue herons and black-crowned night herons will often take up a convenient perch along the shore.

In the water, southern stingrays scurry off at your approach while small bands of roving mullet jump and skitter at imaginary predators. A dolphin might breach for air only a few yards offshore, and that bright reflection of sunlight you see could come from the silver scales of a rolling tarpon.

Overhead, flocks of wading birds can be seen making their way from nighttime rookeries on

# Snakes in the Park

Four secretive and seldom seen poisonous snakes make their home in the Florida Everglades: They are the Eastern diamondback rattlesnake (*Crotalus adamanteus*), Eastern coral snake (*Micurus fulvius fulvius*), Florida cottonmouth water moccasin (*Agkistrodon piscivorus conanti*), and dusky pigmy rattlesnake (*Sisturus milarius barbouri*).

Usually less than 2 feet in length, with alternating black, red, and orange bands, the Eastern coral snake has to chew to inflict a bite. Many coral snake bites occur when children pick up what looks like a pretty bracelet.

Florida cottonmouth water moccasins have a large triangle-shaped flat head and a cottony whiteness inside their jaws. They are dark brown, with yellowish-brown bands, are up to 3 to 4 feet in length, and have a blunt tail. It is usually found near or in water.

Besides the distinctive and chilling rattle that you'll hear if you get too close, the Eastern diamondback rattler has recognizable black diamond patterns outlined in black and yellow. Although averaging about 4 feet in length, the largest Eastern diamondback rattlesnake ever captured was 8 feet 3 inches long.

The dusky pygmy rattlesnake, which seldom reaches lengths of more than 20 inches, is mostly gray on its back with large black splotches running in a line. Although common throughout Florida and abundant in the Everglade marsh and palmetto environments, dusky pygmy rattlesnakes tend to remain well-hidden and are seldom seen.

There are 22 other nonpoisonous snake species in the park, including the Florida banded water snake (*Nerodia fasciata piciata pictivenitris*), the Florida green water snake (*Nerodia cyclopion floridana*), the redbelly water snake (*Nerodia erythrogaster*), the Mississippi green water snake (*Nerodia cyclopion*), the brown water snake, and the endangered Eastern indigo snake (*Drymarchon corais couperi*), the largest snake in America, reaching lengths of 8 feet or more.

mangrove islands to inland feeding grounds. A reverse of the process takes place in the evening.

You also might see the brown, armored, tank-like shell of a horseshoe crab (*Limulus polyphemus*). Ancient relatives of this species were present on our continent some 520 million years ago, although the current genus dates back only about 20 million years. Although called a crab, and once considered a true crustacean, these dark brown arthropods are only distantly related to such crustaceans as true crabs, shrimps, and lobsters. As members of the Merotomata class, they also have many similarities with members of the Arachnida class, which includes spiders, scorpions, and ticks. In the summer they mate and spawn along the shoreline and the beaches of Cape Sable.

Those styrofoam balls that are almost always scattered along the shoreline once served as marker buoys for commercial crab traps. They frequently break free in storms and float up onto the shore.

**Directions:** Park in the Flamingo Lodge parking lot and walk to the bay behind the buildings. Or park at the campgrounds and walk through the tent sites to the bay.

**Activities:** Wildlife viewing.

**For more information:** Everglades National Park Headquarters, 40001 State Road 9336, Homestead, FL 33034. Phone (305) 242-7700.

### ECO POND

[Fig. 13] Between the visitor center and the campgrounds is Eco Pond, which is actually the final stage of the park's wastewater treatment system. The cleaned water re-enters the ecosystem through evaporation and by seeping into the ground.

Various parts of the pond can be viewed from a tower, a short dock, and an unpaved 0.5-mile trail that surrounds the pond. Alligators, birds, bobcats, and marsh rabbits can all be seen from the trail. In spring, roseate spoonbills bring their young to the pond for the feeding opportunities and join with great blue herons, great white herons, white ibis, pied-billed grebes, and American bitterns.

The rushes surrounding the lake often hold kestrels, smooth-billed ani, and tricolored herons. In the coastal prairie behind the pond look for marsh hawks (northern harrier) (*Circus cyaneus*) and red-shouldered hawks. Note the white, twisted buttonwood trees, left over from Hurricane Donna in 1960, that various resident and migrating hawks often use for perches.

The open prairie has been formed and is maintained by passing hurricanes and tropical storms that carry salt water and marl (limey mud) miles inland from Florida Bay. Only low-growing desertlike succulents and cactus are capable of survival in these dry, salty conditions. Look for the multichambered glasswort (*Salicornia birginica*), the sea oxeye daisy, saltwort, also known as pickle weed (*Batis maritima*), and prickly pear cactus (*Opuntia stricta*).

**Directions:** Located between Flamingo Lodge and the campgrounds.

**Activities:** Wildlife viewing.

**Facilities:** Observation decks.
**Dates:** Open year-round.
**Closest town:** Flamingo.

### ☙ CALENDAR OF WILDLIFE AND PLANT VIEWING IN FLAMINGO

Every month provides a different opportunity for wildlife and plant viewing in the Flamingo area. Following is a quick guide to some of the highlights that take place each month.

**January:** Osprey can be seen carrying nesting material along the shores of Florida Bay. Look for manatees in the boat basin in the marina. Also check for black skimmers standing on the Whitewater Bay boat ramp. Mrazek Pond may hold large groups of wading birds. West Lake may hold an assortment of waterfowl, including pintails, blue-winged and green-winged teals, and northern shovelers. Watch for short-tailed hawks circling over the trees.

**February:** Reddish egrets and red-shouldered hawks begin nesting in the treetops. Smooth-billed ani can be seen at Eco Pond. Manatees might be found at the marina on cold mornings. By the end of winter, laughing gulls will be molting into their summer plumage. Cypress trees will begin to sprout new, pastel green needles.

## Hurricanes

When Hurricane Andrew roared across the park in August 1992 with 164 mph winds, Everglades National Park was severely damaged and was temporarily closed. The park's trees were the most dramatically affected. More than 70,000 acres of mangrove forest was flattened, along with a number of mature hardwood hammocks and between 25 and 40 percent of the pines.

Also hit hard were park employees, over half of whom lost their homes. The original landmark visitor center was also destroyed, along with many of the man-made structures such as boardwalks and visitor information displays.

The effect of the storm on the park's wildlife population varied from species to species. All of the 32 radio-collared deer that were part of an ongoing study survived. Also, resident populations of white ibis and egrets seemed unaffected, as were the few remaining Florida panthers that still use the park.

On the other hand, alligators, which were nesting in August, were less fortunate. About 25 percent of that year's newly hatched young were in nests destroyed by the storm. In addition, about 10 percent of the known wading bird rookeries were in the direct path of the storm and some were destroyed.

Big storms are not new to a habitat adapted to a hurricane-prone climate. Interpretive signs near Flamingo have for many years pointed out remnants of great trees blown down by Hurricane Donna in 1960. Though most species recover after storms, the process can sometimes take a decade or longer.

**March:** Look for swallow-tailed kites arriving after their winter vacation in South America, circling over West Lake and above the trees along the main road. Red-winged blackbirds begin departing for their northern nesting grounds. With their nesting season over, large numbers of roseate spoonbills and their young often appear at Eco Pond. Watch along the Snake Bight Trail for bromeliades beginning to bloom.

**April:** Alligator mating season is marked by deep bellowing from the big territorial males. North American wintering birds such as ducks and shorebirds begin to leave for their northern nesting areas. Summer residents such as white-crowned pigeons and gray kingbirds (*Tyrannus dominicensis*) arrive from the tropics along with waves of other migrants, many of which are just passing through. Mosquito populations begin to increase.

**May:** Summer wet season rains begin refilling the sawgrass prairies and ponds. Swamp lilies bloom. Brown pelican and white ibis chicks hatch in Florida Bay rookeries. Loggerhead sea turtles begin egg-laying on isolated beaches. Alligators can sometimes be seen building nests at Eco Pond. White-tailed deer fawns are often seen moving with their mothers. As their nesting season begins, the mangrove cuckoo can be spotted in places like the Snake Bight Trail.

**June:** Butterfly orchids bloom from their aerial perches in the area's buttonwood and mahogany trees. Green anoles *(Anolis carolinensis)* hatch this month. Black-necked stilt (*Himantopus mexicanus*) nesting is at its peak in the freshwater marshes. Common nighthawks (*Chordeiles minor*) can be seen at dusk swooping down on large insects along the roads. In the daytime, barn swallows swarm in large flocks while feeding on dragonflies.

**July:** Young alligators and crocodiles begin to hatch this month. Look closely in area ponds for 6-inch baby alligators. Soft-shelled turtles begin to nest along the road edge. Snook and tarpon move out from the inland mangrove waterways and into the flats of Florida Bay.

**August:** Loggerhead turtles begin hatching and making their way to sea. Red mangrove seeds have already begun germinating in preparation for being dropped in the water.

**September:** White-crowned pigeons, gray kingbirds, and swallow-tailed kites begin to depart for their wintering areas in the tropics. Huge follow-the-leader flocks of white pelicans arrive from northern prairies.

**October:** Numbers of wintering waterfowl, shorebirds, peregrine falcons, and turkey vultures continue to increase. Blue-winged teal and American coots usually show up early in the month in Mrazek Pond.

**November:** Bald eagles begin courtship activities and nest building in the park. Watch from the visitor breezeway for activity on Eagle Key just offshore. On cool mornings look for manatees in the freshwater side of the marina.

**December:** The first bald eagle chicks hatch. Numbers of ducks increase on Florida Bay and area ponds. Scissor-tailed flycatchers arrive in small numbers to spend the remainder of the winter. Great southern white butterflies (*Ascia monuste*) hatch in large numbers. Salt marsh mosquito numbers begin to decline.

## FLAMINGO AREA HIKING TRAILS

The coastal area of the park has numerous and varied hiking trails. Two of the trails, Snake Bight and Rowdy Bend, are open to bicycling and have a good riding surface. It should also be noted that trail conditions can change very quickly in the low-lying lands. Check at the information counter for current conditions of any trail you plan to hike or bicycle.

Off-trail hiking, called slogging in wet areas, is permitted park-wide, but caution is advised. Mucky soil, sharp rocks, sink holes, and impenetrable walls of vegetation can make walking tricky. Although alligators and snakes tend to avoid humans, care is still important. In the Flamingo area, the coastal prairies can be inviting to the off-trail explorer when the mosquito levels are low.

**For more information:** Everglades National Park Headquarters, 40001 State Road 9336, Homestead, FL 33034. Phone (305) 242-7700.

### SNAKE BIGHT

[Fig. 13(3)] This is the most popular trail in the Flamingo area. It passes through a mature tropical hardwood hammock on its way to the bight. "Bight" is a local name for a small cove along the shoreline between two points of land. A boardwalk at the end of the trail extends beyond the mangroves and offers an unobstructed view of the mud flats. This is one of the few areas of the park where flamingos are occasionally spotted. Planning your trip to arrive around low tide will enhance birding opportunities. Also watch for the mangrove cuckoo on the way out and back. The wide, smooth trail is popular with bicyclists. Mosquitos can be plentiful any time of the year.

**Directions:** From Flamingo go north 4 miles on the main road. The trail head is on the right.

**Trail:** 1.6 miles one way.

### ROWDY BEND

[Fig. 13(4)] The Rowdy Bend Trail explores an old overgrown roadbed shaded by buttonwoods and enters open coastal salt prairie. The trail begins at the main park road and joins with the Snake Bight Trail near its end. Bicyclists are permitted on the trail. Mosquitos can be plentiful any time of the years.

**Directions:** From Flamingo go north 3 miles on the main road. The trailhead is on the right.

**Trail:** 2.6 miles one way.

### CHRISTIAN POINT

[Fig. 13(5)] Wander a rustic path that begins among dense buttonwoods full of airplants and ends in open coastal prairie along the shores of Snake Bight. The prairie is good habitat for raptors. Warning: The trail is not well marked where it crosses the prairie and appears to run in many directions at once. It also does not end with a boardwalk, as does the Snake Bight Trail. A thick fringe of mangroves separates the coastal prairie from the bay.

**Directions:** From Flamingo go north 7.5 miles north on the main road. The trailhead is on the right.

**Trail:** 1.8 miles one-way.

### BEAR LAKE

[Fig. 13(6)] This trail journeys through a dense hammock of hardwoods mixed with mangroves to the edge of Bear Lake. It's an excellent trail for viewing woodland birds, and many different tree types. However, the 2-mile Bear Lake Road that parallels the Buttonwood Canal and connects the main road to the trailhead may be closed due to erosion or muddy conditions.

**Directions:** From Flamingo take the main road 0.5 mile to the Buttonwood Canal. Just before crossing the bridge turn left onto Bear Lake Road. Travel north for 1.5 miles to the trailhead.

**Trail:** 1.6 miles one-way.

### ECO POND

[Fig. 13(7)] The Eco Pond Trail circles a freshwater pond and provides visitors an excellent opportunity to enjoy a wide variety of wildlife. It includes a view of a coastal prairie habitat. A viewing platform affords some good bird-watching opportunities, especially at sunrise and sunset.

**Directions:** From Flamingo go 0.5 mile towards the campgrounds. Eco Pond is on the right-hand side of the road.

**Trail:** 0.5 mile loop.

### GUY BRADLEY

[Fig. 13(1)] A paved path, the Guy Bradley Trail is named for the game warden killed in 1905 while protecting wading birds from plume hunters. The scenic trail connects the walk-in campground and amphitheater with the Flamingo Visitor Center. Following the shoreline of Florida Bay, it provides visitors an opportunity to see a variety of birds and butterflies. This trail can have a lot of mosquitos on it. Be sure to have protection any time of the year.

**Directions:** Trail connects the visitor center to the campground's amphitheater along Florida Bay. Park in the Flamingo Visitor Center parking lot, or at the amphitheater in the campgrounds.

**Activities:** Hiking, wildlife viewing.

**Trail:** 1 mile one-way.

### BAYSHORE LOOP

[Fig. 13(1)] The beginning of this trail tunnels through a thick hammock, then opens into the coastal plain. From here it meanders along the shore of Florida Bay. Watch for remnants of a former outpost fishing village. The coastal prairie is where the first residents to this inhospitable land chose to settle.

The trail begins at the Coastal Prairie trailhead at the back of Loop C in the Flamingo campground. Veer left toward the bay at the trail junction. Mosquitos can be very heavy on this trail any time of the year.

**Directions:** At the Flamingo campground tell the park employee at the registration booth that you want to walk the Coastal Trail. Then follow the signs to Loop C and look for a trail marker.

**Trail:** 2-mile loop trail.

### COASTAL PRAIRIE

[Fig. 13(1)] Following an old roadbed, this trail lets you step back a little in time. The road was once used by wild cotton pickers and fishermen. It is shaded by buttonwoods and there are open expanses dotted by succulent coastal plants like saltwort, glasswort, and prickly pear cactus. The trail begins at the rear of Loop C in the Flamingo campground. A backcountry permit is required for overnight camping at the Clubhouse Beach Campsite at the end of the trail.

Warning: Mosquitos can be fierce in the coastal environment. Also this trail has suffered flooding problems the past few years as have the campsites on the bay. Be sure to talk with the rangers at the information booth in Flamingo about current conditions.

**Directions:** At the Flamingo campground tell the park employee you want to walk the Coastal Prairie Trail. Then follow the signs to Loop C and look for a trail marker.

**Trail:** 7.5 miles one-way.

### FLAMINGO AREA CANOE TRAILS

Canoeing opportunities are widespread and varied in the Flamingo area. They can include twisting mangrove creeks, freshwater lakes, broad inland bays, or scenic coastal tours. Many of the inland trails have changed character over the years and some information sources are outdated. Sections of some trails have silted in, and others have been at least partially blocked by fallen trees.

In addition, winds and tides on Florida Bay and Whitewater Bay can significantly affect your trip. Check at the information booth for current conditions, recommended options, and relevant maps.

**For more information:** Everglades National Park Headquarters, 40001 State Road 9336, Homestead, FL 33034. Phone (305) 242-7700.

### NOBLE HAMMOCK

[Fig. 11] This trail winds through a maze of shady mangrove-lined creeks and small ponds. Sharp corners and narrow passageways require both patience and good maneuvering skills. During the dry season (usually in the winter), the trail can be impassable due to low water. To the canoeist's advantage, the waters of this trail can be calm on a windy day. Motors are prohibited.

**Directions:** From Flamingo go north 10 miles on the main road.

*Nine Mile Pond is a great destination for canoeists and largemouth bass fishermen.*

**Activities:** Canoeing.
**Trail:** 2-mile loop.
**Dates:** Open year-round.
**NINE MILE POND**

[Fig. 11] This scenic trail passes through a shallow sawgrass marsh with scattered mangrove islands and small ponds. Watch for alligators, wading birds, osprey, and an occasional bald eagle. The route is marked with numbered white poles. Motorized craft are prohibited.

It's a little known secret, but Nine Mile Pond holds some pretty good largemouth bass fishing. Take a lightweight fishing rod and a couple of plastic worms and have some fun. However, the Florida Fish and Wildlife Conservation Commission has issued a warning against eating any freshwater fish out of Everglades National Park because of high levels of mercury contamination. Scientists are still exploring the source of this contamination.

**Directions:** From Flamingo go north on the main road for 11 miles. The Nine Mile Pond parking lot is on the right.

**Activities:** Canoeing, fishing, wildlife watching.
**Trail:** 5.2-mile loop.
**Dates:** Open year-round.
**HELL'S BAY**

[Fig. 11] As the story goes, old timers called it a place that is "Hell to get into and hell to get out of," thus the name Hell's Bay. This sheltered, canopied canoe trail follows a tortuous, twisting route through the mangroves. You can expect many turns so tight it takes two strokes forward and one stroke back to get around.

The 5.5-mile trail passes a series of three backcountry campsites. Lard Can is at 3 miles, Pearl Bay Chickee is at 3.5 miles, and Hell's Bay Chickee is at the end of the route. Hell's Bay is a picturesque, inland, brackish water bay.

The trail is well marked with more than 160 numbered poles. Motors are prohibited from the trailhead on the main road to the Lard Can campsite. A backcountry permit is required for overnight camping.

**Directions:** From Flamingo go 9 miles north on the Main Road.

**Activities:** Canoeing, camping.

**Trail:** 3.0 miles to Lard Can, 3.5 miles to Pearl Bay Chickee, 5.5 miles to Hell's Bay Chickee.

**Dates:** Open year-round.

### BEAR LAKE CANAL

[Fig. 11] This backcountry trail travels part of the way down along the old Homestead Canal that was dug to carry produce and other staples to and from the Cape Sable region and to help drain the area. If the Bear Lake Road next to the Buttonwood Canal is closed, canoeists will have to travel down the Buttonwood Canal, then handle a 200-yard portage to the Homestead Canal.

The route goes to Bear Lake, and then beyond to Lake Ingraham. A plug in the canal near Lake Ingraham also has to be portaged.

Although it's an attractive canoe route that includes paddling along a tree-covered historic canal, the trail is difficult any time of the year and impassable during the dry season. Trees may block the route, and many sections of the old canal have silted in, leaving little water for paddling. Tides and wind can also be a problem in Lake Ingraham and the East Cape Canal leading out of the lake. You cannot paddle against the tide in the canal.

For obvious reasons, it's very important to plan your trip carefully and to check with the rangers at the visitor center in Flamingo before starting out. Canoeists planning a trip to Cape Sable will probably be better served by taking the outside route along the coast of Florida Bay (*see* Flamingo to Cape Sable page 203.)

**Directions:** Take the main road north from Flamingo to the Buttonwood Canal. Before crossing the canal turn left on Bear Lake Road. If the road is closed, launch at the freshwater boat ramp at the Flamingo Marina and portage 200 yards from the Buttonwood Canal to the Bear Lake Canal.

**Activities:** Canoeing, wildlife watching.

**Trail:** 1.6 miles to Bear Lake and 11.5 miles one-way to Cape Sable from the trailhead on the Homestead Canal.

**Dates:** Open year-round with sufficient water levels. Can be closed between Markers 13 and 17 during low water.

## MUD LAKE LOOP

[Fig. 11] This trail passes through a variety of habitats and connects the Buttonwood Canal, Coot Bay, Mud Lake, and the Bear Lake Canoe Trail. Birding is often good in Mud Lake. If you see coots in Coot Bay Pond, you're witnessing a recovery of the ecosystem that's been under way since the Buttonwood Canal was plugging in 1982. Coots are returning to the lake named for their previous numbers after a 30-year absence—clear evidence that inland bay salinities have been returning to normal.

Launch at Coot Bay Pond on the main road. The trail includes a 200-yard portage from the Bear Lake trailhead to the Buttonwood Canal. Motors are prohibited on Mud Lake, Bear Lake, and the Bear Lake Canal.

**Directions:** From Flamingo go 3.5 miles north on the main road to Coot Bay Pond.

**Activities:** Canoeing, wildlife viewing.

**Trail:** 6.8-mile loop.

**Dates:** Open year-round.

## WEST LAKE

[Fig. 11] There is a lot of open water on this canoe trail that leads through a series of large lakes connected by narrow mangrove-lined natural channels. The route passes though excellent alligator and crocodile habitat. In the winter, West Lake often contains large numbers of migrating waterfowl along with large rafts of American coots.

West Lake is closed to vessels with motors greater than 5.5 horsepower. Motors are prohibited from the east end of West Lake to Garfield Bight on the coast. This trail is not recommended on windy days due to the dangerous chop that can build up on exposed waters.

The West Lake Trail ends at the Alligator Creek backcountry campsite. The campsite can also be reached out of Flamingo by following the coast then turning into Garfield Bight. A backcountry permit is required for camping.

**Directions:** From Flamingo go 7 miles north on the main road. The West Lake boat ramp is at the end of a short access road to the right.

**Activities:** Canoeing, fishing, wildlife viewing, camping.

**Trail:** 7.7 miles one-way.

**Dates:** Open year-round.

## BACKCOUNTRY BOATING AND CAMPING

One of the best ways to connect with the true wilderness of Everglades National Park is to take an overnight or longer boat, kayak, or canoe trip to one of the backcountry campsites. Camping trips to some of the more interesting and unique areas in the park can be staged out of Flamingo.

The Everglades backcountry includes the great mangrove forest along the southwestern tip of Florida, the wide inland bays and waterways extending to the edges of the sawgrass, the beaches of Cape Sable, and the various small islands dotting the coast near the northwestern part of the park.

Forty-six designated campsites are located on beaches, ancient Indian mounds, and chickees, which are open, elevated, 10-by-12-foot wooden platforms constructed for camping in the mangrove estuary. Each chickee has a chemical toilet and a shelter with a roof. The number of persons on each platform is limited, so reservations are needed. Beach sites don't have toilets or shelters; however, some ground sites have toilets.

Flamingo is also the southern terminus of the 99-mile-long Wilderness Waterway, a marked powerboat and paddle trail that traverses the backcountry of Everglades National Park beginning at the Gulf Coast Ranger Station and Visitor Center in Everglades City on the southwestern Florida coast.

The Wilderness Waterway trip, which takes at least one day by powerboat and eight days by canoe, should not be attempted without careful planning, and a full understanding of how to use navigation charts and conditions expected in the Everglades backcountry.

Regardless of the length of trip you plan, ask for a backcountry trip planner and purchase navigation charts from the Flamingo Marina. You can also order charts from the Florida National Parks and Monuments Association, 10 Parachute Key #51, Homestead, FL 33034-6735, (305) 247-1216, www.nps.gov/ever/fnpma.htm The planner contains safety information such as how to file a float plan, recommended navigation charts, and descriptions of the various sites.

A backcountry permit is required to use any of the backcountry campsites. A fee is charged and permits are available only 24 hours in advance from the ranger station in Flamingo.

### FLAMINGO TO CAPE SABLE

Cape Sable is the name given to the southwestern tip of the Florida peninsula. For the purposes of campers, boaters, and anglers, the name refers to the three sandy capes along the coast and the 15 miles of deserted white beach that connects them. The cape is separated from the rest of the park by Whitewater Bay, Lake Ingraham, and the East Cape Canal.

Each of the three capes is a designated backcountry campsite. East Cape is 10 miles southwest of Flamingo and is the southernmost point in the continental United States. Five miles beyond, around the tip of Florida to the northwest, is Middle Cape, arguably one of the finest campsites in the park. And 5 miles beyond that is Northwest Cape, a less popular but no less attractive campsite.

The 5-mile stretch of beach between East Cape and Middle Cape is one of the most scenic spots in all of Florida. Pure white beaches separate the dark green vegetation from the deep blue water. Yucca plants (*Yucca aloifolia*), coconut palms (*Cocos nucifera*), and gumbo-limbo trees give the thick tangle of vegetation above the beach a true tropical flavor. More lightly colored sea purslane *(Sesuvium portulacastrum)* and sea oats (*Uniola paniculata*) anchor the soft ground at the top of the beach.

The Cape Sable beaches are bright white because they're composed more from seashells than sand. A handful of the beach sand reveals tiny shells of all sizes and colors mixed in with the powdery residue of millions and millions of crushed seashells.

Exploring inland past the fringe of thick vegetation above the beach reveals a wide overwashed coastal prairie similar to the prairies found west of Flamingo. Thick patches of Spanish bayonets *(Yucca aloifolia)* and prickly pear cactus *(Opuntia vulgaris)* can make walking difficult in some places. Red mangroves surround a couple small inland lakes.

Since the 1600s, Middle Cape has been the site of a small Spanish fort, a cattle ranch, and a coconut plantation. Because of its isolation, it's also been used over the years as an exit point for fleeing Confederate dignitaries after the Civil War, and an entrance point for illegal aliens.

Today, the only signs of man's intrusion are a few coconut palms growing in a row, a couple of nearly overgrown building foundations, and the remains of a cattle dock. Since Cape Sable became a part of Everglades National Park in 1947, the occasional hurricane has swept away most of the other traces of man's earlier presence and helped return the land to its natural state.

Only empty shells are allowed to be collected along the cape's beaches. Live mollusks you're likely to see such as waved whelks *(Buccinum undatum)* and sand dollars *(Mellita quinquiesperforata)* cannot be removed from park waters. Common marine animals often seen at the water's edge are horseshoe crabs, common sea star (*Asterias forbesi*), roughback batfish *(Ogcocephalus parrus)*, and stingrays.

Bird-watchers will enjoy close encounters with great blue herons, willets, double-crested cormorants, royal terns, laughing gulls, semipalmated plovers, and ruddy turnstones (*Arenaria interpres*). During the daytime, brown pelicans dive into schools of baitfish just off the beach, while bottle-nosed dolphin attack from below. Flocks of sanderlings can often be seen flitting back and forth just above the beach, changing color with every turn, first showing their dark backs then their light bellies.

At sunset, black skimmers fly low and fast just inches off the beach, trailing their extended lower mandibles in the water ready to snap their beaks closed on any small fish that fails to see them coming. The cape is also a regular stopping place for migrating peregrine falcons, and there's a rare chance you might spot a Cape Sable seaside sparrow. Magnificent frigatebirds can often be spotted riding the rising thermals high overhead.

The best fishing from the beach takes place at Middle Cape because of deeper water near shore and the currents set up by the changing tide. As the tide rises each day, currents begin flowing around the point and over a sandbar that extends into the gulf with ever increasing force. A broad assortment of predators, including seatrout, snook, redfish, and tarpon, are drawn to the fast-moving water to feed.

Nighttime activities can include shark fishing for hard-fighting blacktip *(Carcharhinus llimbatus)* and spinner sharks *(Carcharhinus brevipinna)*, or crabbing for tasty blue crabs *(Callinectes sapidus)* destined for a pot of boiling water.

Camping is allowed at all three of the capes. Boaters will prefer Middle Cape, which has the deepest water nearshore. Canoe and kayakers may find the 10 miles to East Cape far enough. The shape of Middle Cape usually provides a calm harbor on one side or the other during windy conditions.

A backcountry permit must be obtained at the Flamingo Visitor Center no more than 24 hours in advance. All supplies must be carried in and out, including water.

Although the weather is generally mild in the winter, cold fronts can occasionally move through South Florida, quickly dropping the temperature and creating long periods of rainy and windy weather. A second anchor, extra rope, long tent stakes for holding in the soft sand, and plenty of warm clothing are important to pack for a winter camping trip, even if it's 85 degrees Fahrenheit on the day you start out.

In summer, towering thunderstorms can sweep inland from Florida Bay, dropping 1 or 2 inches of rain in less than an hour. Also during warm months saltwater mosquitos and aptly named no-see-ums, which are small biting flies almost impossible to see, can be tortuous. A large supply of insect repellant, and a tent with no-see-um-proof screening is a must almost any time of the year.

The cape can be reached by boat or canoe out of Flamingo. Coast Guard Nautical Chart 11433 will be useful. Boaters should follow the marked channel out of Flamingo and travel west to East Cape. Paddlers can follow the coastline but should be aware of expected tides and wind direction before starting out. As a general rule, don't attempt to paddle against winds over 10 mph, or against the tide for any length of time. In addition, low water between Bradley Key—just west of Flamingo—and the mainland can force you to paddle well offshore to get around the large island.

While in Florida Bay watch for osprey, bottle-nosed dolphin and four species of sea turtles—loggerhead, green, Kemp's ridley, and hawksbill.

An inside canoe route that follows the Bear Lake Canoe Trail and the old Homestead Canal is shown on park maps and described in some park literature, but it is very difficult to traverse and impossible in some seasons. If you're determined to try the inside route, check with the rangers at the information booth in Flamingo for current conditions and allow for additional travel time.

**Directions:** Launch from the saltwater boat ramp at the Flamingo Marina and travel 10 miles west through Florida Bay. Camp at East Cape or Middle Cape.

**Activities:** Canoeing, hiking, shelling, fishing, crabbing, wildlife watching.

**Facilities:** None.

**Dates:** Open year-round.

**Fees:** A fee is charged for backcountry permits.

**Closest town:** Flamingo.

**For more information:** Everglades National Park Headquarters, 40001 State Road 9336, Homestead, FL 33034. Phone (305) 242-7700.

## FLAMINGO TO LAKE INGRAHAM

Lake Ingraham is located just inside the extreme southwestern tip of Florida. Named for a turn-of-the-century vice president of the Florida East Coast Railway, it's a shallow, inland, saltwater lake connected by short canals to the Gulf of Mexico at the north end and Florida Bay at the south end. It can be reached only by boat or canoe out of Flamingo.

The East Cape Canal entrance to the lake is located about 9 miles east of Flamingo. A second entrance, the Middle Cape Canal, connects the lake to the sea just above Middle Cape.

Surrounded by a marshy shoreline that's covered with a mixture of red and black mangroves, the lake itself is 4.5 miles long and varies in width from about 800 to 1,500 yards. A shallow channel is marked down the middle of the lake.

It's the incredible bird life that makes a trip to Lake Ingraham worth the effort. Thousands of wading and diving birds feed and rest on the miles and miles of mud flats in the lake. At low tide the birds spread out over the exposed mud flats. As the tide rises, the brown and white pelicans, sea gulls, black skimmers, willets, roseate spoonbills, great blue herons, double-crested cormorants, and many others gather tightly on the exposed bars to wait for the next tidal change. The lake is an excellent place to see a rare great white heron.

The canals connecting Lake Ingraham to the sea were dug as part of a failed plan to drain Cape Sable and the lands to the north for development purposes. Exposure to the tides immediately began to change the salinity of the lake. The tides also brought erosion and deposits in the form of mud banks, gravel bars, and channels. The East Cape and Middle Cape canals themselves are about three times their original width due to erosion.

Before the canals were opened, the water was fresh enough for turn-of-the century steam schooners to use in their boilers. The only way into the lake at that time was through the narrow and twisting Little Sable Creek, which runs from the north end of the lake behind Northwest Cape to the Gulf of Mexico.

An early pioneer and author named Lawrence Will wrote about his experiences in the 1920s while working on the floating dredge that dug the canals to the lake. In a book about his experiences, *A Dredgeman of Cape Sable*, he refers to Lake Ingraham as the "Lake of Grief" because of the trying times the dredge crew had while attempting to cut a channel through the lake's soft mud.

Attempts at development failed long before the area became a part of the national park, but the canals changed the lake forever. That same organic ooze, however, that caused so many difficulties for the dredge crew, also provides a home to many organisms that in turn have an important role in the food web that draws fish and birds to the lake.

Anglers will find the lake very fishing friendly. Redfish, drum, seatrout, tarpon, and sheepshead *(Archosargus probatocephalus)* swim in these waters year-round. Both Middle Cape Canal and East Cape Canal are good fishing spots because they have the deepest water around.

If you watch the tides and use a little common sense, there's no reason not to discover Lake Ingraham and all it has to offer. Most small motorized boats can get around in the lake at high tide. Low tide is reserved for canoes or boats with very shallow draft.

Canoeists will not be able to paddle against the tidal current in either of the canals. Also, the slurry of mud and water is deep in places on the lake's bottom, so never assume you can step out into shallow water and actually find the bottom. Probe around a little with a paddle first.

Canoeists wishing to explore the lake should plan to stay at least one night at Cape Sable. Most motorized craft can reach the lake in 30 minutes to an hour.

**Directions:** Launch from the saltwater boat ramp at the Flamingo Marina. Travel west in Florida Bay to the East Cape Canal to Lake Ingraham.

**Activities:** Canoeing, fishing, crabbing, wildlife viewing.

**Facilities:** None.

**Dates:** Open year-round.

**Fees:** A fee is charged for backcountry camping permits.

**Closest town:** Flamingo.

**For more information:** Everglades National Park Headquarters, 40001 State Road 9336, Homestead, FL 33034. Phone (305) 242-7700.

### FLAMINGO TO CANEPATCH

An excellent choice for an extended adventure into the backcountry is a trip to Canepatch. This remote campsite deep in the Everglades backcountry is touched by many of the habitats that make the park special. It's a 30-mile trip from Flamingo through an unmarked mangrove forest. For canoeists there are a number of other campsites along the way for stopping over.

The Canepatch site is located on one of the many Calusa Indian shell mounds that have dotted the Everglades backcountry for thousands of years. The site was later inhabited by Seminole Indians, until as late as 1928. The campsite was named for the remnant growths of sugar cane left over from a Seminole farming operation. Banana and lime trees still growing on the mound date to that same operation.

The route begins on the freshwater side of the Buttonwood Canal plug and follows the marked channel of the Wilderness Waterway to the Little Shark River, and on to the Shark River. From there the route leaves the Wilderness Waterway behind and turns to the northeast through Tarpon Bay and towards the heart of the Everglades. Finally, it travels a trip down the narrow, winding Avocado Creek to the Canepatch site. Use Coast Guard Nautical Chart 11433 to navigate through the backcountry.

The mangrove forest along the Shark River is one of the largest and most developed mangrove forests in the world. Yet if you look back into the trees you can sometimes pick out the large stumps of long-dead mangroves more than 2 feet in diameter that once reached heights of 100 feet. These giants were destroyed by Hurricane Donna in 1960, but destruction and recovery are part of the natural process of the Everglades, and the younger trees are well on their way to reaching the magnificence of their predecessors.

The area east of Canepatch is characterized by a number of narrow, mangrove-lined freshwater branches (wide creeks) carrying water from the Shark Valley to the Shark River and on to the gulf. This marks the end of the journey for much of the water flowing through the Everglades ecosystem.

If you journey up the largest of these, Rookery Branch, you'll begin to see a change in the vegetation. Red mangrove remains the predominant species for awhile, but there are also a few small willows, some patches of grass and bulrush, and even an occasional stunted cypress. If you keep going for about 4 miles, the mangroves abruptly stop and you soon find yourself looking out over the western edge of the great river of grass.

Although named for a large rookery that no longer exists, Rookery Branch still draws a lot of birds. Wood storks, white-crowned pigeons, osprey, kingfishers, great blue herons, white ibis and swallow-tailed kites can regularly be seen there.

Fishing is terrific in the waters around Canepatch, in part because of the large number of both freshwater and saltwater species that can be caught nearby. Largemouth bass are plentiful in Rookery Branch and are joined in the winter by snook, redfish, tarpon, gray snapper, and sharks. The saltwater species will make better fare if your interest lies in fried fish for dinner. The Florida Fish and Wildlife Conservation Commission has issued a consumption advisory against eating freshwater fish caught in Everglades National Park because of mercury contamination.

Just for fun one night you may want to try shining a light across the water from the dock at Canepatch to see how many sets of glowing alligator eyes you can count. Their eyes looked like eerie little flames and the farther apart the flames, the bigger the gator.

**Directions:** Depart from the freshwater side of the Flamingo Marina and follow a planned route through Whitewater Bay, Little Shark River, Shark River, Tarpon Bay, and Avocado Creek.

**Activities:** Boating, camping, fishing, wildlife viewing.

**Facilities:** Dock, chemical toilet, picnic tables.

**Dates:** Open year-round.

**Fees:** A fee is charged for a backcountry camping permit.

**Closest town:** Flamingo is 30 miles to the south.

**For more information:** Everglades National Park Headquarters, 40001 State Road 9336, Homestead, FL 33034. Phone (305) 242-7700.

## BUTTONWOOD CANAL TO COOT BAY AND MUD LAKE

Although you may be passed on occasion by private boats and large tour boats, a trip down the Buttonwood Canal into Coot Bay presents plenty of wildlife viewing opportunities and a chance to witness a situation where man has learned to correct his mistakes.

From the freshwater ramp in Flamingo, boaters and canoeists travel north along the Buttonwood Canal. Watch along the banks for large alligators and one of the few saltwater crocodiles that have taken up residence in the canal. Except for a section of the east bank, both sides of the canal are covered with an intertwining mass of red and black mangrove trees.

Red mangroves are the ones with prop roots like so many legs hanging down into the water. The Seminoles called them the trees that walk. Black mangroves are easy to tell by the pneumatophores (breathing roots) that stick up from the mud all around the tree. Buttonwoods, another type of mangrove, usually are found on the higher ground behind the other two.

Look carefully among the prop roots of the red mangroves for little blue herons, tricolored herons, and yellow-crowned night herons. Watch for osprey perched on top of the highest trees.

Three miles from Flamingo the canal enters Coot Bay. In winter look for migrating waterfowl here.

Following the shoreline of Coot Bay around to the left you'll come to Mud Creek, a narrow, canopied stream connecting to Mud Lake. These waters are also worth fishing. Live shrimp or artificial lures will attract seatrout, redfish, snook, and mangrove snapper. Local anglers concentrate their efforts near either end of Mud Creek where it opens up into the lakes. Another good fishing spot is Tarpon Creek, which connects Coot Bay to Whitewater Bay.

West Indian manatees are often sighted in the Buttonwood Canal and in Tarpon Creek. Their presence is often revealed by concentric upwellings on the surface caused by the swimming motion of the manatees' broad tail. Sometimes you can hear them breach the surface for an occasional breath of air.

Part of the Buttonwood Canal connecting Coot Bay and the inland waters with Florida Bay was dug in 1922, as a spur of the Homestead Canal. In the 1950s, the National Park Service widened the canal from 35 to 50 feet, and extended it north another 0.8 mile into Coot Bay in order to "provide a safe and convenient boating route from Florida Bay to the backwaters of Everglades National Park."

What may have seemed like a good idea for the convenience of boat traffic turned out to be a terrible blow to the natural system. For thousands of years fresh water had flowed from the river of grass into the eastern side of Whitewater Bay and on into Coot Bay. The fresh water played an important role as a nursery grounds for many species of saltwater game fish, crustaceans, and waterfowl. In fact, Coot Bay was named for the thousands of coots that once fed upon the freshwater grasses that grew there.

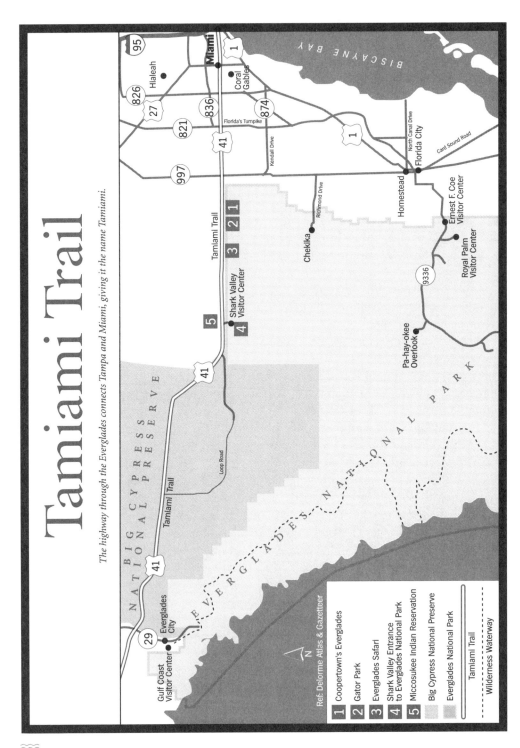

# Tamiami Trail

*The highway through the Everglades connects Tampa and Miami, giving it the name Tamiami.*

Although spawned in the Gulf of Mexico, the eggs or larvae of various saltwater species, including pink shrimp, would float by way of the Shark River into the inland bays, where they could grow up safe from attack by large predatory fish less able to tolerate the brackish water. As the fish and shrimp grew larger they moved toward the higher salinities, eventually reaching the same gulf waters they were spawned in.

All that ended, however, when the inland bays were exposed to the tidal forces of Florida Bay. The natural water flow patterns and salinity rates were drastically altered. Fresh water still poured in from the Everglades, but it was immediately swept through the Buttonwood Canal on the first outgoing tide and replaced with saltier water from Florida Bay on the next incoming tide.

Within a few years all signs of freshwater vegetation were gone. Even the sawgrass at the northeastern edge of Whitewater Bay began to retreat. Game fish populations of snook, seatrout, redfish, and tarpon dropped throughout the inland waters. For decades not a single coot was ever seen on Coot Bay.

In 1968, the Buttonwood Canal Restoration Project was initiated and a decision was made to correct the damage by installing a concrete dam next to the marina. On August 2, 1982, 24 years after it was opened, the Buttonwood Canal was closed and the tidal flow of saltwater was finally stopped.

Within a couple years fishing had improved throughout the inland bays. Snook, seatrout, and redfish were again being caught in Coot Bay in numbers not previously recorded. More recently, coots have returned to Coot Bay after a long absence.

**Directions:** Depart from the freshwater ramp at the Flamingo Marina. Follow the Buttonwood Canal to Coot Bay.

**Activities:** Boating, fishing, wildlife viewing.

**Facilities:** None.

**Dates:** Open year-round.

**Closest town:** Flamingo.

For more information. Everglades National Park Headquarters, 40001 State Road 9336, Homestead, FL 33034. Phone (305) 242-7700.

# Arthur R. Marshall Loxahatchee National Wildlife Refuge

[Fig. 3(2)] If bird-watching is an important part of your visit to South Florida, you may want to plan a side trip to the Loxahatchee National Wildlife Refuge. A preserved portion of the historical northern Everglades, combined with active management of a series of man-made ponds, makes it the perfect site to add a few species to your checklist.

Located west of Boynton Beach, about 17 miles southwest of West Palm Beach, the refuge was established in 1951, and encompasses one of the conservation areas that were established to help control water flow through the Everglades and throughout Florida. The refuge includes about 145,000 acres of Everglades habitat, including tree islands, sawgrass, wet prairies, and sloughs.

When you arrive, check at the visitor center for recent sightings and pick up a bird list. More than 250 sightings have been compiled by refuge personnel and local birding experts. Many of the same common species of birds found in Everglades National Park can be seen in the refuge, including great blue herons, anhingas, white ibis, little blue herons, tricolored herons, great egrets, cattle egrets, snowy egrets, and black-crowned night herons.

In the winter, the refuge is home to thousands of migrating waterfowl, which share the area with resident egrets, herons, and ibis. Many of the species regularly come to a series of water impoundments designed to provide native habitats and foods to both migrating and resident birds. Water levels are controlled in the 10 separate impoundments to encourage nesting and feeding of different species. The impoundments are surrounded by dikes that are easy to stroll along while watching for wildlife.

This is one of the areas where the Everglades snail kite is occasionally spotted, although sightings are not very common. Also while walking along the dikes watch for cottonmouth moccasins lying at the water's edge. Mammals you might see include rabbits, otters, and white-tailed deer.

The Cypress Swamp Boardwalk is a 0.4-mile, level, and rail-less boardwalk through a small cypress head. The beautiful, thick vegetation crowded together beneath the cypress canopy is favored habitat for pileated and red-bellied woodpeckers, yellow-billed cuckoos, screech owls, great-horned owls, and a variety of songbirds. During spring and fall migrations, the cypress swamp is a stopover for traveling vireos and warblers.

The swamp floor is covered with a mixture of ferns and a scattering of cypress knees. Cypress knees either help the trees stand up in the wet soil, or help the trees breathe, or both. Among the ferns growing on the forest floor are leather fern, strap fern, and swamp fern. Epiphytes like wild pine and Spanish moss grow in the tree branches overhead.

A 5.5-mile Everglades Canoe Trail loops through a small portion of the refuge and gives you a chance to visit the Everglades habitats up close. Sloughs have water deeper than the surrounding habitats and support plants like spatterdock and water lilies. Wet prairies have short, emergent plants and shallow water levels. Sawgrass grows in solid stands, scattered around with other plants. Tree islands are formed where small plants were able to get a foothold in the exposed peat bottom. They were followed by larger shrubs and trees, which form canopies high overhead. The islands often have a thick border of wax myrtle, common buttonbush (*Cephalanthus occidentalis*), and cocoplum.

The refuge is surrounded by a large canal. A stroll along the canal bank is a good way to see wildlife. During times of low water, or on cool sunny days, you can see some very big alligators. Give them a wide berth.

There are no picnic or camping facilities in the refuge. State of Florida fresh water fishing regulations and license requirements apply to fishing in the refuge (*see* Appendix E, page 297).

**Directions:** Located on US 441 between SR 804 (Boynton Boulevard) and SR 806 (Atlantic Avenue in Delray Beach).

**Activities:** Wildlife viewing, canoeing, boating, fishing.

**Facilities:** Visitor center, boat ramp, boardwalk, observation tower.

**Dates:** Open year-round.

**Fees:** A fee is charged for entering the refuge.

**Closest town:** Boynton Beach is 6 miles to the east.

**For more information:** Arthur R. Marshall Loxahatchee NWR, 10216 Lee Road, Boynton Beach, FL 33437-4796. Web site www.fws.gov/~r4eao/nwrlxh.html Phone (561) 734-8303.

## SAWGRASS RECREATION PARK

[Fig. 3(3)] Between Loxahatchee National Wildlife Refuge and Everglades National Park, Sawgrass Recreation Park west of Ft. Lauderdale provides another chance to visit the Everglades. If you don't have a chance to try the airboat rides along Tamiami Trail, this park can be another option.

Sawgrass Recreation Park is located on the edge of one of the Everglades conservation areas. The private operation runs airboat tours into the Everglades habitat where you'll get a close-up view of an alligator in the wild. On a typical ride you might also see boat-tailed grackles, coots, ospreys, great egrets, great blue herons, and common moorhens.

The airboat driver will stop so you can touch a piece of sawgrass. You'll notice how the teeth are curved in one direction. Rubbing the blades in one direction, from the top to bottom, causes a sharp cut, in the other direction, bottom to top, nothing happens.

A reptile exhibit has alligator pens with a 13-foot monster, a box turtle, a saltwater crocodile, and a variety of snakes.

There's also a captive Florida panther on the grounds two to three days a week. An eighteenth century native Seminole Indian village tells the story of the Seminole Indians. A craft stand sells hand-made items.

There are tour guides at each of the attractions. They give short talks and answer questions. Fishing is also allowed in the conservation areas, which are open to the public. State fishing regulations apply (*see* page 297).

**Directions:** Take I-75 to US 27. Travel north 2 miles to the recreation park.

**Activities:** Airboat rides, wildlife viewing, fishing.

**Facilities:** Wildlife exhibits, Indian village, gift shop.

**Dates:** Open year-round.

**Fees:** There is an entrance fee, which includes the airboat ride, Indian village, and wildlife exhibits.

**Closest town:** Fort Lauderdale is 18 miles to the east.

**For more information:** Sawgrass Recreation Park, 5400 North Highway 27, Fort Lauderdale, FL 33329. Phone (954) 389-0202. Web site www.evergladestours.com

# Tamiami Trail—Miami to the Western Everglades

[Fig. 14] The Tamiami Trail (US 41) connecting Tampa to Miami (Tam-Miami) was the first road built across the Everglades. Its completion in 1928 was an example of man's determination to perform a questionable and difficult engineering feat despite the possible consequences to the environment. Built upon an elevated base of limestone rock blasted from a parallel-running canal, the Tamiami Trail became the first major impediment to the historic sheet-flow of water across the river of grass.

Construction began in 1915, but with only the eastern portion in Dade County completed, it was abandoned in 1918. In 1923, a political deal was struck in the manner in which many deals were crafted to open the Florida wilderness. The Florida legislature agreed to create Collier County on the southwestern coast of Florida in return for a promise from Barron G. Collier, who owned three-quarters of the land in the new county, that he would finally complete construction of the highway.

The renewed effort was aided by a publicity stunt that same year in which 10 Model T Fords were driven, dragged, and pushed across the Everglades to prove it could be done. All that was needed was a road.

When Collier's endeavor bogged down, the state finally took over and completed the road. The opening of Tamiami Trail meant that the sheet flow of water through the Everglades was squeezed into culverts beneath the road—when it wasn't flowing over the top.

By the early 1960s, a system of canals and reservoirs throughout South Florida had

## Things To Know While Driving the Tamiami Trail

These are tips from the National Park Service:

—Use headlights when driving the trail. Parking along the highway is hazardous. Pull completely off the road. Pass with caution.

—Fill your gas tank before embarking. Gas is not available between Everglades City and the Miccosukee Indian Reservation.

—Wildlife (including endangered Florida panthers) cross the Tamiami Trail. Observe speed limits for their well being, and the safety of you and your passengers.

—Alligators and other wildlife are protected. Do not disturb or feed them.

gained control of almost all overland flow of the water outside of Everglades National Park. And in 1962, flood gates along the Tamiami Trail were closed, and the natural flow of water through the Everglades was changed forever.

You can see some of the huge flood gates on the north side of the road. Within the next few years they will become part of an even grander attempt to rebuild the plumbing of the South Florida water system. Although the park is now guaranteed the delivery of specified amounts of water during specified seasons, many conservationists argue that the delivery schedule still fails to follow a natural regimen. That same voice is also calling for the trail to be redesigned to again allow free-flowing water movement to the south.

As traffic has increased along the highway, the western portion of the road has also become a constant danger to wildlife such as otters, raccoons, bobcats, and the endangered Florida panther, which roam large areas of the Everglades when hunting and seeking mates. You'll note a 45 mph nighttime speed limit to help protect the animals.

## Sapodilla

In case you were wondering, those large trees in the parking lot at the Shark Valley Visitor Center and the Ernest Coe Visitor Center are sapodilla trees. Native to tropical America, it is a tree with multiple uses. The hard, red wood is economically valuable as lumber. Its sap is the source of chicle, used to make chewing gum. It is a slow-growing, long-lived tree that is used for landscaping throughout extreme South Florida. In the tropics it can grow to 100 feet.

An ornamental evergreen, the sapodilla bears small ball-like flowers on slender stalks at leaf bases. The nearly round fruit is hard and astringent when immature, turning soft, juicy, and sweet with the consistency of a pear. The skin is reddish brown with a sandpaper texture. Sapodilla fruit is best eaten fresh from the tree, chilled and spooned out of the thin skin, or added to salads or desserts.

Nevertheless, the trail's existence today furnishes the traveler with a scenic overview of Everglades habitats stretching from Miami to the Gulf of Mexico. The eastern half of the trail runs parallel to the northern border of Everglades National Park, and across the sawgrass prairie of the Shark River Slough. Beyond the slough to the west, the Tamiami Trail enters the western Everglades and passes through the Big Cypress National Preserve. The scenic backdrop changes from sawgrass prairie to cypress heads and dark swamps. Past Big Cypress, as the Trail begins to curve north toward Naples, it enters the saltwater mangrove estuaries of Southwestern Florida.

As you drive west from Miami and leave the urban sprawl behind, the road begins to cross the Shark River Slough, the heart of the river of grass. The borrow canal on the north side of the highway, just like any other area in the Everglades that holds water year-round, is regularly attended by a large selection of the area's wildlife.

Watch the clumps of cypress trees along the far edge of the canal for great blue herons, great egrets, snowy egrets, anhingas, and osprey. At the water's edge look for green-backed herons, little blue herons, and sora rails. Swimming around the wide lily pads of the spatterdock plants you'll see American coots, common morehens, and purple gallinules. Alligators and soft-shelled turtles lurk in the waters below.

You may also notice the white papery bark and small dark green leaves of melaleuca (*Melaleuca quinquenervia*) trees. If you drove down from the north along the Florida turnpike, you probably saw thick, impenetrable stands of these trees in the area west of Miami. The native Australian melaleuca were intentionally introduced by land developers in hopes the plant's water-loving roots would help to dry up the Everglades. Seeds were actually scattered by airplane over parts of the Everglades. The absurd plan failed, but the melaleuca found a home with no competition. The prolific trees quickly spread throughout South Florida, displacing native habitats.

Today the resilient trees are the target of widespread eradication programs in many parts of the Everglades and Big Cypress National Preserve. The effort is being pursued by teams of determined volunteers from local sportsman/conservation organizations along with scientists from the National Park Service, who descend on one area at a time pulling up or girdling and poisoning every single tree they can find. Even one overlooked melaleuca can disperse thousands of seeds and quickly repopulate an area.

Another invasive plant you may notice along the trail because of its red berries and dark green foliage is the Brazilian pepper. One large clump can be seen just to the west of Gator Park on the south side of the road (about 6 miles from SR 997). Firmly entrenched in South Florida, the pepper is quick to take over disturbed land along canal banks or abandoned farms. Its bright red berries are eaten and transplanted by many songbird species, including large flocks of robins that pass through on their annual migrations.

**Directions:** From the Coe Visitor Center in Everglades National Park take SR 9336 for 10 miles to Homestead. Turn left (north) onto SR 997 (Krome Avenue) for 20.5 miles to US 41, which is the Tamiami Trail. From the Florida turnpike, exit at US 41 and go west. In Miami, SW 8 Street turns into US 41 west of town. From Naples take US 41 south and west across the Everglades.

**Activities:** Wildlife watching, airboat and swampbuggy rides, scenic driving.

**Facilities:** Museums, restaurants, tram rides.

**Dates:** Some private concessions are seasonal.

**Fees:** Fees are charged at concessions along the Tamiami Trail.

**Closest town:** Tamiami Trail begins in Miami.

**For more information:** Everglades National Park Headquarters, 40001 State Road 9336, Homestead, FL 33034. Phone (305) 242-7700. Ask for information on driving the Tamiami Trail.

## ALLIGATORS, AIRBOATS, AND SWAMP BUGGIES

A number of commercial operations along the Tamiami Trail between SR 997 and the Big Cypress National Preserve offer airboat and swamp buggy rides along with wildlife exhibits and shows. Many also maintain an alligator farm, and for a small fee you can see hundreds of huge gators sunning or lying half submerged in the stagnant water.

Many of the concessions also have gift shops and restaurants specializing in gator tail, frog legs, and catfish. At some stops you can even pick up a couple pounds of alligator meat or frog legs.

Airboat rides usually consist of a excursion into the sawgrass, a look at a tree hammock or cypress head, and an even closer look at wading birds and an alligator or two in the wild. There's also the inevitable fancy maneuvering and wide-sliding turns these craft are known for. Most rides are moderately priced and generally worth the experience.

Airboats, and to a lesser extent, swamp buggies are a traditional part of the Everglades experience. Developed shortly after World War II as a means to access the swamp, airboats are an admittedly loud boat powered by a big high-revving engine that drives an airplane propeller. The prop is mounted in a cage behind the driver who sits up high directly in front of the engine. Swamp buggies, high-framed wheeled-vehicles that can operate in deep mud and water, were developed to provide a way for people to get into and out of the Everglades with some degree of comfort. Another vehicle, used only in some parts of the eastern Everglades and called a half-track, uses a drive track similar to that on an army tank to move along on top of the muck and grass.

Private use of all of these vehicles is prohibited within Everglades National Park, and regulated in public lands outside of the park.

### COOPERTOWN'S EVERGLADES

[Fig. 14(1)] The small settlement of Coopertown, with a population of eight, has offered airboat tours since 1945. The tour covers about eight miles. This is the original airboat tour business on the Tamiami Trail and has been rated "Florida's best" by the *Miami Herald* newspaper.

**Directions:** Travel 5 miles west of SR 997 on Tamiami Trail (US 41).

**Activities:** Airboat tours, alligator exhibit, Indian village.

**Facilities:** Restaurant, gift shop, arts and crafts.

**Dates:** Open year-round.

**Fees:** A fee is charged for the airboat rides.

**Closest town:** Miami is 5 miles to the east on the Tamiami Trail (US 41).

**For more information:** Coopertown's Everglades, PO Box 440727, Miami, FL 33144. Phone (305) 226-6048.

### GATOR PARK

[Fig. 14(2)] A friendly staff operates "the longest airboat ride in the Everglades." Gator Park has wildlife shows and offers chances to hold a small alligator and other wildlife for photo opportunities. The show includes rehabilitated animals that have been injured and can no longer be released into the wild. A picnic area is also available. Note the "fully dressed" alligator sitting in the rocking chair on the front porch.

**Directions:** Travel 6 miles west of SR 997 on Tamiami Trail (US 41).

**Activities:** Airboat tours, wildlife exhibits, wildlife show.

**Facilities:** Restaurant, gift shop, RV Park with full hook-ups.

**Dates:** Open year-round.

**Fees:** A fee is charged for airboat rides and wildlife shows.

**Closest town:** Miami is 6 miles to the east on US 41.

**For more information:** Gator Park, 24050 SW 8 Street, Miami, FL 33187. Phone (305) 559-2255.

### EVERGLADES SAFARI

[Fig. 14(3)] This multifaceted operation has a fleet of large airboats on which large groups take 40-minute rides into the Everglades. It also holds wildlife nature shows, alligator wrestling demonstrations, tours of an alligator farm, and walks on a nature trail through a hardwood hammock. The large gift shop has a complete collection of handmade Indian jewelry, Indian dolls, and other craft items.

**Directions:** Travel 9 miles west of SR 997 on the Tamiami Trail (US 41).

**Activities:** Airboat rides, nature trail, alligator wrestling,

**Facilities:** Alligator farm, restaurant, gift shop, observation platform, museum exhibits.

**Dates:** Open year-round.

**Fees:** A fee is charged for airboat rides and wildlife shows.

**Closest town:** Miami is 9 miles to the east on the Tamiami Trail (US 41).

**For more information:** Everglades Safari, PO Box 535, Naples, FL 34106. Phone (305) 226-6923.

### SHARK VALLEY ENTRANCE TO EVERGLADES NATIONAL PARK

[Fig. 14(4)] The Shark Valley entrance to Everglades National Park is 18 miles west of SR 997. One of the most highly visited sites in the park, it features a 15-mile, paved loop trail into the river of grass and some of the best wildlife concentrations in the park. No motorized vehicles are allowed on the trail except open-air trams operated by a park concessionaire.

If you only have a couple hours to spend in the park, this is the place to go. The tram ride furnishes a solid overview of the Everglades. A park naturalist narrates the trip, stopping to point out alligators, deer, and wading birds like great blue herons, wood storks, and white ibis. Shark Valley is also the best place in the park for spotting an endangered snail kite.

Of course there is no valley at Shark Valley, at least not in the traditional sense. The Shark River Slough is the part of the Everglades known as the river of grass. It is a great, wide drainage basin that carries water, however slowly, southwest to the Shark River and on to the Gulf of Mexico.

When the system worked naturally, water in the slough came from rain falling as far north as Orlando. Working its way south, the water entered Lake Okeechobee. Then, as the lake rose it spilled over the lower rim, filling the river of grass. Falling only 20 feet in elevation from the lake to the coast, the water would take months to reach the tide.

Today, dikes and pumping stations north of Everglades National Park decide where the water will go and how much will be allowed to flow into the park. Only then, after the water has been allowed to pass the Tamiami Trail, the natural system takes over again.

Nowhere is this more evident than when standing atop the 50-foot observation tower. Although you can't see it, you can know, when looking southwest, that the next 50 miles of this wilderness belong to the plants and animals. Not one man-made structure stands between the tower and the southwestern coast.

The tram ride takes about two hours, and stops midway at the observation tower. A ramp leads to the top. The tower provides a panoramic view of the river of grass. This is one of the best spots to get a true feel for the vastness, the "ever" part of the Everglades. A borrow pond behind the tower usually attracts a number of large alligators and wading birds. An even better way to experience the Everglades is to bicycle the loop road. Bicycles are available for rent from the concessionaire. You'll see more wildlife traveling at your own pace. You'll also be able to stop more often, and for as long as you want, provided you get back before the parking lot closes at 6 p.m. Be sure to carry water, and a rainsuit in the warmer months for the afternoon thunderstorms.

The canal and bank along the west side of the trail offer a close-up view of the wildlife. Watch for marsh rabbits, green-backed herons, anhingas, water snakes, sora rails, and maybe the colorful southeastern lubber grasshopper (*Romalea guttata*). That deep grunting you hear is most likely a pig frog.

Never feed or approach the alligators. An unfortunate accident occurred here a few years ago when a child on a bicycle fell into a canal and was injured by a large alligator. Also watch out for fire ant nests that look like a pile of sand by the trail.

If you're looking for something to do while waiting for a tram, the Bobcat Hammock Boardwalk is a 0.3-mile loop that starts behind the visitor center. It passes through a mature growth of 8-foot-tall sawgrass, and then wanders beneath the canopy of a beautiful little bayhead with thick clumps of leather fern, cocoplum, red bay, wax myrtle, willows, and dahoon holly (*Ilex cassine).* The bayhead is only a few inches higher than the surrounding land, so these are all trees and plants that can stand in water part of the year.

The trams run all day, departing every hour in season and less often in the offseason, with reservations taken during the season (December through April) for the early and late trips. Reservations can be made up to a month in advance. Trips during the middle of the day operate on a first-come first-served basis, 30 minutes before tram departure time. For information on tram tours and bicycle rentals call (305) 221-8455.

**Directions:** Travel 18 miles west of SR 997 on the Tamiami Trail (US 41).

**Activities:** Hiking, bicycling, tram tours, wildlife viewing.

**Facilities:** Visitor center, restrooms, nature trails.

**Dates:** Open year-round.

**Fees:** An entrance fee and a tram ride fee are charged.

**Closest town:** Miami is 18 miles to the east on the Tamiami Trail (US 41)

**For more information:** Everglades National Park Headquarters, 40001 State Road 9336, Homestead, FL 33034. Phone (305) 242-7700.

### MICCOSUKEE RESTAURANT AND INFORMATION CENTER

[Fig. 14(5)] Across the road from the entrance to the Shark Valley, and just west of the border of the Miccosukee Indian Reservation, this nicely decorated Miccosukee restaurant offers a chance to taste traditional Indian fare. Amid a display of murals depicting Indian life you can sample frog legs, fried catfish, and alligator bites. Indian fry bread and fried pumpkin bread are also popular treats. In cool weather you can eat on the patio and watch for alligators in the canal or see snail kites flying over the Everglades. The food is inexpensive.

The information center connected to the restaurant has a few displays of Indian artifacts along with a selection of information on area attractions. An airboat concessionaire will take you on a 30-minute ride out and back to a small Indian camp where you can observe traditional crafts such as cooking and sewing.

**Directions:** Travel 18-miles west on Tamiami Trail from SR 997.

**Activities:** Airboat rides.

**Facilities:** Restaurant, information center.

**Dates:** Open year-round

**Fees:** There is a charge for airboat rides.

**Closest town:** Miami is 18 miles to the east on the Tamiami Trail (US 41).

**For more information:** Miccosukee Indian Village and Airboat Rides, PO Box 44021, Miami, FL 33144. Phone (305) 223-8380.

### MICCOSUKEE INDIAN VILLAGE AND AIRBOAT RIDES

[Fig. 14(5)] If you've ever see an old Florida tourist brochure, it probably featured a photo of alligator wrestling from the Miccosukee Indian Village on the Tamiami Trail. A long-time tourist attraction, it's become a part of the fabric of Florida.

About 18.5 miles west of SR 997 on the Tamiami Trail, the village features a number of aspects of Indian life. A tantalizing gift shop stocked with Indian crafts including patchwork jackets, skirts, blouses, and beadwork precedes entrance into the main grounds. Inside you'll find a Miccosukee Indian village, arts and crafts demonstrators, guided tours, a museum, live alligators, and of course alligator shows. Craft-making on display varies from season to season but includes wood carving, beadwork, jewelry making, doll making, and basket weaving.

Take a moment to stop by the pit holding Tiny, a 14-foot alligator, one of the largest in captivity. You won't see Tiny in the wrestling show.

Alligator wrestling was not invented to pull in tourist dollars. Instead the ability to capture and control a live alligator is one of the skills the Indians had to learn when they were initially forced into this inhospitable land.

One of the main staples for food and other items, such as shoes and battle shields, was the alligator. However, since alligator meat spoils quickly, a way had to be devised to capture the animals alive and hold them until they were needed. When early European settlers saw Indians capturing an alligator, they apparently thought it looked like a man wrestling an alligator, and the term stuck.

The wrestling arena at the Miccosukee Village is a circular sandy area with a narrow moat running around the inside with half a dozen 8-foot alligators inside. The wrestler gets in with the alligators, eventually picks one out, and grabbing its tail, drags it onto the sand. The alligator immediately heads back for the water. Five or six times in a row, the alligator pulls the man towards the water, and the man pulls the alligator back into the arena.

When the tug of war is finally over, the wrestler moves around with a long stick and taps the creature on the nose a couple times so it will open its mouth wide and hiss. That's when the crowd takes a couple steps back.

After a few minutes, the man grabs the alligator by its long snout, holding it closed while the animal thrashes back and forth for a few seconds. Although alligators have 3,000 pounds per inch of crushing pressure, the muscles that open their mouths are much weaker. Positioning himself on the alligator's back, the wrestler first opens the alligators mouth so everyone can see the 80 sharp teeth. He then wedges the alligator's jaws under his own chin and holds the animal tightly with no hands. In the wild this is when an Indian would use his hands to tie the powerful jaws closed.

A museum on the property tells the story of the Miccosukee tribe. A branch of the Creek tribe of Alabama and Georgia that spoke the Hitchiti language, the Miccosukees migrated into Florida in the early 1700s. They were followed later by the Seminoles, who spoke the Muskogee language.

Both groups first migrated south into the Florida panhandle ahead of European settlers, then later into South Florida to avoid the Indian Removal Act of 1830. Despite United States military action and three Seminole wars in the 1800s, the tribes dwindled in number, but never surrendered. Their knowledge of survival in the treacherous land contributed to the success of their resistance.

Today the Miccosukee who choose to live on reservation land live mostly along the Tamiami Trail. Many Seminoles live on the Big Cypress Seminole Reservation and on five other reservations in South Florida. Both tribes have their own law, police, and judges.

**Directions:** Travel 18.3 miles west on Tamiami Trail from SR 997.

**Activities:** Alligator wrestling, airboat rides.

**Facilities:** Museum, Indian village, wildlife exhibits, gift shop.

**Dates:** Open year-round.

**Fees:** A fee is charged to enter the facility and for the airboat rides.

**Closest town:** Miami is 18 miles to the east.

**For more information:** Miccosukee Indian Village and Airboat Rides, PO Box 44021, Miami, FL 33144. Phone (305) 223-8380.

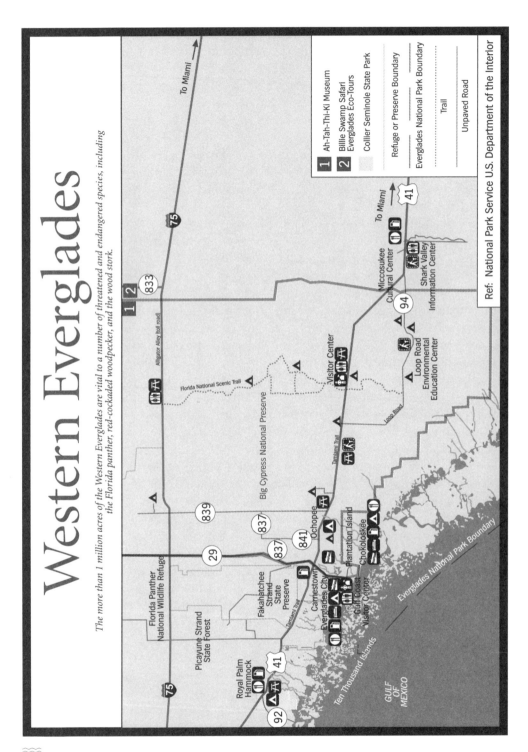

Western Everglades

*The more than 1 million acres of the Western Everglades are vital to a number of threatened and endangered species, including the Florida panther, red-cockaded woodpecker, and the wood stork.*

1 Ah-Tah-Thi-Ki Museum
2 Billie Swamp Safari
Everglades Eco-Tours
Collier Seminole State Park

Refuge or Preserve Boundary
Everglades National Park Boundary
Trail
Unpaved Road

Ref: National Park Service U.S. Department of the Interior

To Miami

75

833

1 2

Florida National Scenic Trail

Alligator Alley (toll road)

Big Cypress National Preserve

Florida Panther
National Wildlife Refuge

Picayune Strand
State Forest

Fakahatchee
Strand
State
Preserve

839

837

837

841

29

Ochopee

Carnestown

Everglades City

Gulf Coast
Visitor Center

Tamiami Trail

Plantation Island

Chokoloskee

Ten Thousand Islands

GULF
OF
MEXICO

Royal Palm
Hammock

41

75

92

Everglades National Park Boundary

Visitor Center

Tamiami Trail

Loop Road
Environmental
Education Center

Loop Road

94

Miccosukee
Cultural Center

To Miami

41

Shark Valley
Information Center

222

# Western Everglades: Big Cypress to Ten Thousand Islands

T he area known as the Western Everglades includes Florida's "other" great watershed. [Fig. 15] Spanning an area roughly from the Okaloacoochee Slough headwaters near Immokalee to the coastal estuaries of southwestern Florida, the Western Everglades encompasses more than 1,000,000 acres of extensive wet prairies, pine islands, cypress strands, backcountry waterways, and mangrove forests.

Much like the eastern side of the Everglades, the general geologic structure of the Western Everglades is of a large, barely sloping watershed where seasonal rainfall travels through a system of sloughs and across wetland prairies until it finally reaches the tidal mangrove estuary. The seasonal wet and dry patterns define and maintain the varied habitats.

The extraordinary biological richness and diversity of these habitats is vital to a

[ *Above:* Big Cypress Swamp covers 2,400 square miles within the Florida Everglades ]

# Big Cypress National Preserve

*The first national preserve ever created, Big Cypress protects 729,000 acres.*

| | |
|---|---|
| **1** | Clyde Butcher Big Cypress Gallery |
| **2** | Big Cypress Bend Boardwalk |
| **3** | Turner River Canoe Trail |
| **4** | Halfway Creek Canoe Trail |
| **5** | Watson Place |
| **6** | Wilderness Waterway Canoe Trail |
| **7** | Florida Panther NWR |
| **8** | Fakahatchee Strand State Preserve |

Ref: NPS Big Cypress National Preserve

number of threatened and endangered species, including the Florida panther, red-cockaded woodpecker, wood stork, and West Indian manatee. The region contains a mosaic of relatively new public land holdings, the Big Cypress National Preserve, the Fakahatchee Strand State Preserve, the Picayune Strand State Forest, the Panther National Wildlife Refuge, and the famous Ten Thousand Islands region of Everglades National Park. There is also a 69,900-acre Seminole Indian Reservation and a 76,800-acre Miccosukee Indian Reservation in part of the swamp.

Because of the widespread attention being paid to the problems affecting the imperiled river of grass in the Eastern Everglades, the Western Everglades has earned the nickname "Forgotten Everglades" from some conservationists. Nevertheless, development along the southwestern Florida coast, one of the fastest growing areas in the country, is having an impact on the remaining natural lands in the Western Everglades. Water quality has declined in estuarine areas, along with changes in the timing and flow of freshwater.

Fortunately, major conservation organizations have recognized that the time to act is long before environmental problems reach a critical stage like they have elsewhere in the Everglades. The National Wildlife Federation and the Florida Wildlife Federation (FWF), have opened a joint office in Naples and are now working to enhance public and government awareness of the importance of protecting the Western Everglades. (For more information on the natural and human history of the Everglades, see the introduction to the Florida Everglades: Everglades National Park to Shark Valley, page 153.)

**For more information:** National Wildlife Federation, Everglades Project, 5051 Castello Drive, Suite 240, Naples, FL 34103. Phone (941) 643-4111. E-mail thoemke@nwf.org.

# Big Cypress Swamp

[Fig. 15, Fig. 16] It's easy to tell when the Tamiami Trail passes into the confines of the Big Cypress Swamp. Cypress trees simply take over the landscape. For 35 miles the road passes through one cypress head after another, exposing cutaway views of these wildlife sanctuaries to the passing motorist.

Anhingas and herons perch on branches over open water sloughs. Alligators and turtles can even be seen from passing automobiles. In some cypress heads, thick growths of Spanish moss hang from every branch. A true airplant, like the other epiphytes adorning the trees, Spanish moss takes nothing from its host plant; it is only a place to hang. Early settlers found Spanish moss made a decent mattress stuffing.

As tempting as it is to pull over at every scenic spot, the Tamiami Trail is a dangerous highway, and roadside sightseeing should be reserved to many of the off-road drives available in the Big Cypress Swamp.

Covering more than 2,400 square miles of South Florida, the name Big Cypress refers to the vastness of the area, not the size of trees found there. Much like in the river of grass, almost 60 inches of wet-season rains fall from May to October, filling the sloughs and flooding the surface of Big Cypress. Following the minute slope of 2 inches per mile, the 1-foot-deep water flows slowly towards the coastal estuaries of Everglades National Park. The slow drainage extends the period of time water stays on the land.

The main drainage ways in Big Cypress are the big sloughs that hold the deepest water. With names like Fakahatchee and Gator Hook, these densely forested strands once held giant cypress trees that were cut during the 1930s and 1940s to build stadium seats and pickle barrels.

The dark, humid environment of the bigger and deeper sloughs is perfect for the growth of rare orchids, like the ghost orchid (*Polyradicion lindleyii*). The frog-shaped flower of the ghost orchid is pollinated by the giant sphinx moth (*Cocytius antaeus medor*). The larvae of the giant sphinx moth in turn feed exclusively on the leaves of pond apple trees. And so it goes.

About one-third of Big Cypress is covered with cypress. In places where the limestone has eroded and deeper soils have collected, the cypress heads become high, dome-shaped clusters. Were the soil is thinner, the cypress don't grow as thick or as tall.

There are two species of cypress in the swamp, baldcypress (*Taxodium distichum*) and pond cypress (*Taxodium ascendens*). The baldcypress has a straight trunk with brown bark. The needles are a feathery light green and lie flat on the plane of the branches. Under optimum growing conditions the trees may reach heights of 125 feet.

Pond cypresses have needles that point upward and are more closely angled to the twigs. The trees are shorter and grow better in soils with fewer nutrients and less water. Dwarf cypresses, which are a majority of the cypresses in the swamp, are a stunted form of the pond cypress. Although as old as regular pond cypresses, they are severely stunted because they grow in shallow, low-nutrient soils. Dwarf cypresses can be seen scattered around on the wet grass prairies.

Although related to pines, cypress trees are deciduous. In Big Cypress they lose their needles in November, regaining them in February and March.

The swamp also includes wide expanses of slash pine forest, mixed hardwood hammocks, wet prairies, dry prairies, marshes, and estuarine mangrove forests. It only takes an elevation change of a few inches to change the dominant species and habitat type. Baldcypress trees grow largest in low areas that stay wet all year, while slightly higher terrain that dries out in the winter supports open expanses of prairie grasses and dwarf pond cypress. On even slightly higher land, cabbage palm forests and pinelands dominate the landscape.

Only in a few places can you see old, mature cypresses, many more than 500 years old. The Big Cypress Bend boardwalk in the Fakahatchee Strand and a section of the Turner River Loop Road pass through some of the biggest cypress trees left in the area.

The Big Cypress Swamp has also seen plenty of attempts at real estate development over the years. Lots that are underwater half the year were sold sight unseen. Oil exploration proved successful and some drilling and pumping still takes place in Big Cypress under careful management, as does some cattle grazing.

In the dry season, after most of the water has drained off the land, the wildlife gathers at the remaining pools. White-tailed deer, wild turkey (*Meleagris gallopano*), bears, wild hogs, Everglades mink (*Mustela vison*), and otters have to move closer together. Gars, largemouth bass, bream, bluegill, and snapping turtles gather beneath herons and ibis perched in the trees above.

Even the water is alive with a world of miniature aquatic creatures. Copepods, waterfleas, grass shrimp, and mosquito larvae are part of a busy food web that will eventually feed larger fish and birds. Here mosquito larvae is eaten by the gambusia minnow, which is eaten by various sunfish, which are eaten by great blue herons, anhingas, and snapping turtles.

Other parts of the web are more restrictive, such as the endangered snail kite, which feeds its chicks only the meat of the freshwater apple snail. The formula is simple: no water, no snails; no snails, no snail kites.

## BROMELIAD
(Tillandsia)

Members of the Bromeliad family are epiphytes: they attach to trees for support but take no direct nourishment from their hosts. They live on nutrients leached by rain and dust particles trapped by the silvery scales covering their branches.

The Big Cypress Swamp also houses the southernmost colony of red-cockaded woodpeckers. These cavity-nesters require mature pine trees in which to drill their homes.

Rare Florida panthers are also known to roam Big Cypress, but are seldom seen. Bobcats are much more common and are more commonly seen. Even black bears are far more common than panthers, but seeing one in the daytime is unusual.

The evening bat (*Nycticeius hymeralis*) has also been spotted in Big Cypress. Look for it in flight around sunset. Several species of venomous snakes, including the Eastern diamondback rattlesnake, dusky pigmy rattlesnake, cottonmouth moccasin and coral snake, reside in the preserve, along with numerous other less dangerous species. Watch where you walk, where you sit, and where you put your hands.

### BIG CYPRESS NATIONAL PRESERVE

[Fig. 15, Fig. 16] The Big Cypress National Preserve protects a large part of the Big Cypress Swamp, the heart of the Western Everglades system. Roughly half the size of Everglades National Park, the Big Cypress National Preserve was created in 1974 when the U.S. Congress purchased 570,000 acres. It was the first national preserve ever created. Expanded in 1988, today 729,000 acres are protected.

A national preserve is different from a national park in that traditional recreational vehicles, such as swamp buggies, and traditional uses, such as hunting, grazing, and oil drilling, have been allowed to continue, although under strict management from the National Park Service. Collection of plants and animals is prohibited under federal law.

Fishing is allowed throughout the Big Cypress Preserve under the auspices of the Florida Fish and Wildlife Conservation Commission. You must have a fishing license for any freshwater fishing. See Appendix E for more information on fishing licenses in Florida.

There are some limited hiking opportunities available in the preserve, but the main attractions for visitors are the loop roads that provide easy access to some of the more remote, and more beautiful, parts of the swamp. Privately owned, off-road vehicles can also be used by permit only to access certain areas of the preserve. Bicycles and horses are allowed in designated areas.

Bicycling is allowed on a series of limerock trails within the preserve. The same trails are also used by off-road vehicles and hikers.

The subtropical climate means mild winters and hot, wet summers. Wear lightweight clothing in hot weather. Long-sleeved shirts, pants, sturdy shoes, and bug repellent are recommended for hiking. The busiest visitor season is from Christmas through Easter. Two highways cross the preserve, Interstate 75 and US 41, while SR 29 runs parallel to the western border. Almost all entrances to the preserve, including the visitor center, are along US 41. The Big Cypress Visitor Center offers an excellent 15-minute movie about the preserve, a wildlife exhibit, and book sales. During the winter season the preserve schedules ranger-led wet walks, canoe trips, bicycle tours, and campfire programs at the campgrounds.

There are six primitive campgrounds scattered around the preserve; all allow tent camping and most accommodate motor homes. A dump station is available for a small fee. Several small motels and private campgrounds can be found around the Everglades City area.

*The waters of Big Cypress are alive with copopods, waterfleas, grass shrimp, and mosquito larvae, which will eventually feed larger fish and birds such as great blue herons and anhingas.*

**Directions:** From SR 997 in Miami travel west 22 miles along US 41 to reach the edge of Big Cypress National Preserve. From Naples travel 28 miles south, then east on US 41 to reach the western end of the Big Cypress National Preserve.

**Activities:** Hiking, bicycling, horseback riding, camping, canoeing, auto touring, photography, picnicking, birding, and wildlife viewing.

**Facilities:** Visitor center, campgrounds.

**Dates:** Open year-round.

**Fees:** There is no entrance fee. There is a fee for obtaining an off-road permit and for camping and using the dumping station.

**Closest town:** Everglades City is 4 miles south of US 41 on SR 29. Naples is 28 miles west of SR 29 on US 41.

**For more information:** Big Cypress National Preserve, HCR61, Box 110, Ochopee, FL 33943. Web site www.nps.gov/bicy. Phone (941) 695-4111.

**FLORIDA NATIONAL SCENIC TRAIL**

[Fig. 15, Fig. 16] A 31-mile section of the Florida National Scenic Trail crosses the refuge from the Loop Road on the south to a limited access site on Interstate 75. It crosses US 41 at the visitor center.

The Florida Trail passes through a cross section of the preserve's habitat types.

Hikers should be prepared for wet areas any time of the year, and for ankle-deep to waist-deep water in the rainy season. There are two primitive campsites along the trail in the preserve, but no potable water. The first campsite is 6.9 miles from the visitor center. The second campsite is 16.7 miles from the visitor center.

Many backpackers take a two-, three-, or four-day, out-and-back hike from the visitor center. Two side loops in the trail make it possible to travel mostly different ground on the way out and the way back.

Another 8.3 mile trail section extends south from the visitor center to the south side of the Loop Road. No potable water or campsites are along this trail section, but both ends can be reached by car which allows for a one-way hike.

**Directions:** Trails north and south begin at the Big Cypress National Preserve Visitor Center.

**Trail:** 31-miles in various combinations.

### LOOP ROAD AUTO TRAIL

[Fig. 15, Fig. 16] One of the most enjoyable and popular activities in the Big Cypress National Preserve is a slow drive down one of the many back roads open for auto touring. Most are graded dirt roads originally built for timber harvesting and later used by plant harvesters, hunters, and early residents.

Although all of the roads are passable year-round, it's a good idea to stop by the visitor center for information on current conditions. There are no services on any of the roads.

The most popular, Loop Road (CR 94), is a 26-mile single-lane road with an unimproved surface. It can take two to three hours to travel the entire length of the road, which can be driven from either direction. Watch out for potholes, of which there are many. During the wet season, sections of the Loop Road can suffer from shallow flooding.

The road connects to the Tamiami Trail at two points 19 miles apart: at the Tamiami Trail Ranger Station at the eastern edge of the preserve and at Monroe Station, 4 miles to the west of the visitor center. The first 9 miles of the road from the east is paved and leads to the Loop Road Education Center. The Tree Snail Hammock Nature Trail is a short, self-guided trail located across from the education center. The trail winds through a hardwood hammock and explains local plants and animals.

The Loop Road passes straight through the heart of a series of splendid cypress heads, and past wide expanses of dry prairies, wet prairies, and dwarf cypress forests. Watch for white-tailed deer and turkey on the prairies in early morning and late evening. Along some sections cocoplums and sabal palms (*Sabal palmetto*) line the road.

In the cypress heads, stop at some of the hundreds of small open pools along the road. In the clear water you'll see gar and largemouth bass, maybe an otter or an alligator, and always a few birds perched or standing nearby. Cypress stand tall and solemn around the pool, their fairy land branches resplendent with epiphytes and tree orchids while their bases are decorated with dark green ferns. The small yellow-ish-green, white, and pink blossoms of the Florida butterfly orchid are common in many of these cypress heads.

During the dry season you may encounter alligators that have migrated to the remaining ponds near the road lying on the road. Resist the urge to get out of the car for a closer look. Alligators can travel very fast on land. They'll move out of the way as your vehicle draws closer.

**Directions:** The eastern entrance to the Loop Road (CR 94) at the Tamiami Ranger Station is 15 miles east of the Big Cypress National Preserve Oasis Visitor Center. The western entrance is 4 miles west of the visitor center.

**Trail:** 26 miles. Approximately 9 miles is paved and the remainder is unimproved road with potholes and occasional flooding.

### TURNER RIVER ROAD AND BIRDON ROAD LOOP

[Fig. 15, Fig. 16] The Turner River Road (CR 839) and Birdon Road (CR 841) form a popular, 17-mile loop-drive through open grass prairie dotted with slash pine and baldcypress. This maintained dirt and gravel road is ideal for viewing wildflowers in the prairies and along canals. The roads are wide, fairly smooth, and mostly free of potholes, but they can be very dusty during dry times.

The canal along the first part of the Turner River Road is great for bird-watching. Coots, Florida gallinules, glossy ibis, pied-billed grebes, anhingas, and great blue herons are commonly seen. The large black bird with the shiny coat and the long tail sitting in the bull rushes is a boat-tailed grackle (*Quiscalus major*).

Notice the mature baldcypresses along the east side of the CR 839. Some of the few remaining cypress trees that escaped the timber boom of the 1930s and 40s can be seen along the Turner River Road.

Two hiking trails can be found along CR 839 that follow roads which originally led to oil drilling pads. Closed to regular traffic, they are now multiple-use recreation trails. The Concho Billy Trail (2.5 miles one-way) is used by hikers, mountain bikers, and off-road vehicle riders. The Fire Prairie Trail (also 2.5 miles one-way) is a biking and hiking trail.

You might see a swamp buggy along this road. If you're in a car, the top of the buggy's wheels will be at eye level, with the engine and seating compartment many feet higher. These elevated vehicles, designed to run in relatively deep water, were developed to provide access to remote areas of Big Cypress.

Seven miles down Turner River Road the route turns left onto Wagon Wheel Road (CR 837), which crosses a wide wetland prairie. Watch along this section for glossy ibis, belted kingfisher, and northern rough-winged swallows (*Stelgidopteryx serripennis*) diving for insects over the grasses in the evening. The swallows are common in South Florida from fall through spring. In the summer this is a good place to watch the great flat-bottomed thunder storms forming every afternoon over Big Cypress.

At the next intersection Wagon Wheel Road continues to SR 29, and Birdon Road

(CR 841) continues back to the Tamiami Trail.

**Directions:** Turner River Road turns north off the Tamiami Trail (US 41) 14 miles west of the visitor center and 7 miles east of SR 29. Birdon Road turns north off the Tamiami Trail (US 41) 18 miles west of the visitor center and 3.5 miles east of SR 29.

**Trail:** 17-mile loop road.

### CLYDE BUTCHER BIG CYPRESS GALLERY

[Fig. 16(1)] Appropriately situated in the middle of a cypress strand, Clyde Butcher's Big Cypress Gallery is located just 0.5 mile east of the Big Cypress Preserve visitor center on the Tamiami Trail.

The preeminent Everglades photographer, Clyde Butcher uses black and white photography and wide format cameras to capture the elaborate detail and textures that distinguish the intricacies of the untouched Everglades landscape. Featured in numerous documentaries and articles, Butcher is known for his incredible patience. He sometimes spends hours or days standing in waist-deep water waiting for just the right light or cloud formation before taking even one photo.

A large selection of his breathtaking photographs can be seen and purchased at the gallery. There's also a very enjoyable nature walk behind the gallery on one of the prettiest little trails you'll find in Big Cypress. It offers an up-close view of a variety of ferns and orchids growing on the cypress trees. Butcher often holds photographic workshops on the lands surrounding the gallery.

**Directions:** The Big Cypress Gallery is located 0.5 mile east of the Big Cypress National Preserve Oasis Visitor Center on the south side of the road.

**Facilities:** Photo art gallery, nature trail.

**Dates:** Open daily, year-round.

**Fees:** None.

**Closest town:** Everglades City is 21.5 miles to the west on US 41, then 4 miles south on SR 29.

**For more information:** Big Cypress Gallery, 52388 Tamiami Trail, HC61-Box 16, Ochopee, FL 34141. Phone (941) 695-2428. Web site www.clydebutcher.com.

### FAKAHATCHEE STRAND STATE PRESERVE

[Fig. 15, Fig. 16] Bordering the western side of the Big Cypress National Preserve, the 74,000-acre Fakahatchee Strand contains some of the most unusual natural features in Florida. The word "strand" refers to linear swamp forests that develop along large sloughs in the Big Cypress Swamp. The sloughs are created by water flowing over and beneath the landscape, slowly dissolving the limestone base. The sloughs then accumulate deep layers of organic soil, which support the healthy cypress forest.

The Fakahatchee Strand, which is about 20 miles long and 3 to 5 miles wide, is the major drainage slough of southwestern Big Cypress Swamp. It contains the largest stand of native royal palms and largest concentration and variety of orchids in North America, as well as other plants that are extremely rare. Its unique forest of cypress trees and royal palms may be the only one in the world.

According to a 1997 paper, "Adaptations in Fakahatchee," by D.F. Austin, Ph.D., director of environmental sciences at Florida Atlantic University, rare orchids found in the strand include the tiny orchid (*Lepanthopsis melanantha*), hidden orchid (*Maxillaria crassifolia*), and ghost orchid. Rare bromeliads found in the strand include the fuzzy-wuzzy air plant (*Tillandsia pruinosa*,) which grows on pond apple trees, the nodding catopsis (*Catopsis nutans*), and the powdery catopsis (*Catopsis berteroniana*).

Although the strand has seen its share of logging activity and some attempts to drain the wetlands, many of the natural features are still present. One reference cites a documented 484 plant species within the preserve. Nearly 70 percent of the tree species are of tropical origin, as are 86 percent of the ferns and 88 percent of the orchids. The preserve also contains many of the same wildlife species encountered in the Big Cypress National Preserve. The Florida panther, wood stork, Florida black bear, mangrove fox squirrel (*Sciurus niger*), and the Everglades mink have all been documented within the strand preserve area.

## BARRED OWL
(Strix varia)
This owl has a far-carrying, rhythmic hoot, which may be heard day and night, that sounds like "Who cooks for you? Who cooks for you?" It also gives a hair-raising, catlike scream.

Except for the W. J. Janes Scenic Drive, access to the strand is limited by its dense, junglelike vegetation. Facilities and activities in the preserve are also slim. Rangers lead swamp walks through the cypress forest and the pond apple sloughs to view rare plants. Walks take place November through February. Reservations are required and long pants, secure footwear, food, water, and insect repellent are recommended. For reservations call (941) 695-4593.

**Directions:** Drive north on SR 29 from US 41 for 2.3 miles to the village of Copeland. Turn west (left) onto W. J. Janes Scenic Drive and go 3 miles to the ranger station. Big Cypress Bend Boardwalk is located 7 miles west of SR 29 on US 41.

**Activities:** Hiking, auto touring, wildlife viewing.

**Facilities:** Interpretive boardwalk.

**Dates:** Open daily year-round.

**Fees:** None.

**Closest town:** Everglades City is 4 miles south on SR 29 from the intersection with US 41. Naples is 28 miles to the west on US 41.

**For more information:** Fakahatchee Strand State Preserve, PO Box 548, Copeland, FL 33926. Phone (941) 695-4593.

## BIG CYPRESS BEND BOARDWALK

[Fig. 16(2)] A 2,000-foot-long boardwalk at Big Cypress Bend meanders through one of the more magnificent stands of remaining of old growth cypress, enabling the visitor to experience the beauty of this unusual swamp before man intruded (but without getting your feet wet).

The boardwalk is a good place to spot pileated woodpeckers, blue-gray gnatcatchers (*Polioptila caerulea*), and a pair of nesting bald eagles from mid-December through early May.

**Directions:** Big Cypress Bend is on US 41, 7 miles west of SR 29.

**Trail:** 2,000 yards.

## W. J. JANES SCENIC ROAD

[Fig. 16] The 12.5-mile-long W. J. Janes Scenic Road is certainly appropriately named. Left over from an attempt to develop the region, it's a smooth, dirt and gravel track that runs from one end of Fakahatchee Strand State Preserve to the other. The spectacular scenic drive passes right through the remarkable strand.

In some places, walls of cypress trees and sabal palms grow so high, and so close, the road becomes a tunnel beneath a vast canopy blocking out the sun. In other places thick carpets of ferns and cocoplum trees line the road. At one point the road actually passes through a royal palm-cypress forest. Groves of the stately palms, rising over 100 feet, appear on each side of the road.

About 6 miles from Copeland, the road widens into a small parking area. On the east side of the road an old logging road has been turned into a hiking trail that runs 2.5 miles into the strand. The trails is slightly elevated above the surrounding wetland. Janes Road is a good place to look for raptors like red-tailed hawks that watch the road for any prey that tries to sneak across. In the late evening it becomes a hunting ground for barred owls (*Strix varia*). It's also not that unusual to catch a glimpse of a bobcat dashing across the road. Although there are also Florida panthers in the strand, the chances of seeing one are probably about the same as winning the Florida lottery.

The scenic drive ends at a canal on the border of the Picayune Strand State Forest. Beyond here lie the remnants of a failed attempt to create a giant development in this part of the swamp. Hundreds of crisscrossing, unused, and deteriorating roads that once represented the dreams of many people are now scheduled to be removed and the land will one day be restored to its original beauty.

Although the road continues into the abandoned subdivision, the Park Service recommends you obtain a local map before continuing. Many roads may be unfavorable for travel. The best option is to enjoy the drive back down to Tamiami Trail.

**Directions:** Drive north on SR 29 for 2.3 miles to the village of Copeland, and then turn west (left) onto W. J. Janes Scenic Road, the access route through the state preserve. The preserve office and ranger station are 3 miles along this road.

**Activities:** Auto touring, wildlife viewing.

**Trail:** 12.5 miles one-way.

### FLORIDA PANTHER NATIONAL WILDLIFE REFUGE

[Fig. 15] The Florida Panther National Wildlife Refuge north of the Fakahatchee Strand protects another piece of the Big Cypress Swamp. The 29,410-acre refuge is closed to all public access and use. The entrance is located on SR 29.

The U.S. Fish and Wildlife Service pursues management activities on the land including extensive prescribed burning and exotic plant control. Limited hydrologic restoration is also being undertaken. Wildlife population monitoring is a primary management task as is conducting research on habitat enhancement for Florida panthers.

Endangered or threatened species in the refuge include the Florida panther, Florida black bear, Big Cypress fox squirrel (*Sciurus niger*), river otter, American kestrel, wood stork, snail kite, bald eagle, Florida grasshopper sparrow (*Ammodramus savannarum*), American alligator, Eastern indigo snake, and striped mud turtle (*Kinosternon baurii*).

Other wildlife species residing in the refuge are bobcat, white-tailed deer, hogs, raccoons (*Procyon lotor*), Eastern cottontail rabbits (*Sylvilagus floridanus*), nine-banded armadillos (*Dasypus novemcinctus*), largemouth bass, bluegills, Florida gar, and 115 species of migratory and

*Florida panthers can leap 20 feet.*

nonmigratory birds including little blue heron, limpkin (*Aramus guarauna*), northern harrier, Arctic peregrine falcon, reddish egret, roseate spoonbill, sandhill crane (*Grus canadensis*), swallow-tailed kite, snowy egret, tricolored heron, and white ibis.

The refuge office, located in the Naples Comfort Inn, includes an entry area that houses several displays. These include a swamp scene with a mounted cougar, characteristic plants and animals, and a short taped message on the biology of the panther. Also included within the room are photographs explaining refuge management techniques and maps of nearby environmental areas.

**Directions:** The refuge entrance is on SR 29 north of Interstate 75.

**Activities:** Panther National Wildlife Refuge is closed to public use.

**For more information:** Ten Thousand Island NWR, 3860 Tollgate Boulevard, Suite 300, Naples, FL 33942. Phone (941) 353-8442.

### PICAYUNE STRAND STATE FOREST

[Fig. 10, Fig. 15] The 73,335-acre Picayune Strand State Forest, located west of the Fakahatchee Strand State Preserve, is a key component in the effort to protect and restore the Western Everglades. Portions of the area, however, are still in the process of coming under public ownership.

Once the proposed site of the largest subdivision in the world totaling 173 square miles, the land is being purchased in preparation for habitat and hydrological restoration. Eventually more than 290 miles of roads will be removed and 50 miles of canals will be filled in.

There are currently no visitor facilities or general public access to the newly purchased land.

**For more information:** Fakahatchee Strand State Preserve, PO Box 548, Copeland, FL 33926. Phone (941) 695-4593.

### SEMINOLE INDIAN RESERVATION

[Fig. 15] Visiting the Seminole Indian Reservation, which encompasses 69,900 acres of the Big Cypress Swamp, is both a delightful and educational experience. The Seminole tribe has created two quite different facilities, the Ah-Tah-Thi-Ki Museum and the Billie Swamp Safari. Both sites can be visited on the same day and together will provide a more than complete understanding of the Seminole tribe and its place in Florida history.

Snake Road (CR 833), which runs north from Exit 14 on Alligator Alley (I-75) across a corner of the Miccosukee Reservation and into the Seminole Reservation, is a 17-mile scenic experience by itself, passing through golden waves of sawgrass habitat and then into the swamps and cypress heads of the Big Cypress Swamp. There's a rest area at Exit 14 with fuel and food. It's one of the few facilities you'll see along Alligator Alley.

In the canal along the Interstate and the smaller canal along Snake Road, watch for alligators, anhingas, great egrets, great blue herons, American coots, boat-tailed grackles, turkey vultures, snowy egrets, wood storks, tricolored herons, black-crowned night herons, belted kingfishers, limpkins (*Aramus guarauna*), and moorhens. The lily pads in the canals belong to spatterdock plants, which anchor on the bottom. The dark green floating plants with the purple flowers are water hyacinths (*Eichhornia crassipes*).

Along Alligator Alley you'll also pass some of the large water control structures and pumping stations that control the water flowing through the Everglades.

Both the Seminoles and Miccosukees were once members of the Creek Nation that spoke different languages. In the late 1700s and early 1800s, the tribes migrated into northern and central Florida ahead of European settlement. After the U.S. took control of Florida in 1821, competition for land increased. Three separate wars were consequently fought (in 1816–1818, 1835–1842, and 1856–1858) to remove the Indians from Florida. The U.S. used its best troops and spent more than $40 million to remove 3,000 Indians and kill 1,500 more.

Somewhere between 200 and 300 Indians hid themselves in the swamp and hammocks of the Everglades and Big Cypress, refusing to surrender or be conquered. Today 3,000 descendants of those courageous people live in the Florida Everglades. A trip to the Seminole Reservation is a chance to hear their story. It's a good one.

**Directions:** The reservation is between Naples and Fort Lauderdale off I-75. Travel north from Exit 14 on SR 833 for 17 miles.

**Activities:** Tours.

**Facilities:** Museum, wildlife and nature park.

**Dates:** Open year-round.

**Closest town:** Fort Lauderdale is 45 miles east on I-75. Naples is 55 miles west on I-75.

**For more information:** Ah-Tah-Thi-Ki Museum, Seminole Tribe of Florida, HC-61, Box 21-A, Clewiston, FL 33440. Phone (941) 902-1113. Web site www.seminoletribe.com.

### THE AH-TAH-THI-KI MUSEUM

[Fig. 15(1)] This splendid facility, which opened in 1997, provides a remarkably uplifting educational experience. A creative and very entertaining 18-minute film shown on five screens introduces you to the Seminole people, their history, their present, and their future. More than 5,000 square feet of exhibits feature lifelike displays of how the Seminoles lived in the 1800s—how they hunted, cooked, played, and survived both the harsh land and the harsher U.S. government. Many artifacts on display are on loan from the Smithsonian Institute.

The museum is located next to a beautiful cypress forest with a 1-mile long boardwalk through it. Along the walk more than 40 plants are identified, with their common names, Indian names, and uses as carving materials, foods, and natural medicines by various tribes. For instance, Spanish moss was used as a sponge and to make tea for treating swelling from rheumatism and high blood pressure. Resurrection fern was boiled and then used for drinking and as a steam bath to treat depression. Pop ash (*Fraxinus caroliniana*), a small tree, was used for fuel and the making of bows, arrows, and spoons. The bark was boiled and used as an ingredient in medicine for treatment of the eyes and liver and stomach ailments.

The boardwalk ends at a mock-up of a Seminole village where you can witness traditional craftspeople making dolls, cooking, and wood carving. There's also a gift shop with Native American arts and crafts, clothing, and books for sale.

**Directions:** The Ah-Tah-Thi-Ki Museum on the Big Cypress Reservation is off I-75 between Fort Lauderdale and Naples. At Exit 14 travel north 17 miles on CR 833.

**Facilities:** Museum, boardwalk, Indian village.

**Dates:** Open Tuesday through Sunday. Closed on major holidays, including Native American Day.

**Fees:** An entrance fee is charged.

**Closest town:** Naples is 55 miles west on I-75. Fort Lauderdale is 45 miles east on I-75.

**For more information:** Ah-Tah-Thi-Ki Museum, Seminole Tribe of Florida, HC-61, Box 21-A, Clewiston, FL 33440. Phone (941) 902-1113. Web site www.seminoletribe.com/museum.

### BILLIE SWAMP SAFARI EVERGLADES ECO-TOURS

[Fig. 15(2)] The Billie Swamp Safari is an entirely different experience from the museum, but is no less entertaining with swamp buggy and airboat rides and a number of animal attractions.

The most impressive and informative activity is a swamp buggy eco-tour through 2,000 acres of the Big Cypress Swamp. From an elevated vehicle you'll penetrate the thick cypress heads and slog past such native and non-native wildlife as white-tailed deer, wild hogs, Axis deer (*Axis axis*), ostrich (*Struthio camelus*), American bison (*Bison bison*), and water buffalo (*Bubalus bubalis*).

The driver also takes the time to point out various plants and describe their uses. There's even an opportunity to taste one and rub another on your arm for mosquito protection. And there's a stop to visit with the "largest alligator in captivity," a 13-foot 8-inch monster known as Superman.

The airboat tour is more or less a weaving ride along a narrow canal that includes a stop to use dog food to tease large alligators to come close to the boat. If you only have time for one activity, choose the swamp buggy ride.

You can also see exhibits of crocodiles, alligators, and other reptiles including a number of native snakes. There are also regular reptile and amphibian shows in the herpetarium.

The Swamp Water Café features a variety of traditional Seminole foods including catfish, frog legs, gator-tail nuggets, venison burgers, and traditional Seminole fry bread. The food is very good and the decorations are interesting—oil paintings depicting Indian scenes, animal head mounts, skulls, and spears. Food is inexpensive.

You can stay overnight in the Seminole Camping Village in native-style screened chickees, which are fairly spartan. The small, clean, elevated cabins have beds for sleeping, mosquito netting, and little else. Similar to a campground, there are public bathrooms and showers. Reservations are recommended.

There's also a large and interesting gift shop that carries authentic crafts such as wood carvings and clothing, and not so authentic items such as rubber alligators and T-shirts.

## Bird Adaptations for Feeding

Many of the bird species that inhabit the Ten Thousand Island area have their own unique adaptation that helps them acquire sustenance from the local habitat. These adaptations enable various species to share the same environment without competing directly with each other.

Bald eagles have broad wings for soaring and flying long distances, and sharp eyes to see their prey from great heights.

Osprey hunt by diving feet first in the water and grabbing their prey with their sharp talons.

White ibis and wood storks feed by feel, probing the soft bottom with their beaks.

Great egrets wade through the shallows using their large beaks to catch frogs, fish, and crabs.

Black skimmers fly just above the surface catching small fish by actually skimming their large lower beaks through the water.

Brown pelicans plunge head first into schools of fish, stunning them and then scooping them up.

**Directions:** The Billie Swamp Safari on the Big Cypress Reservation is off I-75 between Naples and Fort Lauderdale. At Exit 14 travel 17 miles north on CR 833. Turn left on West Boundary Road and go 3.5 miles.

**Activities:** Swamp buggy and airboat rides, herpetarium and wildlife shows.

**Facilities:** Camping village, restaurant, gift shop.

**Dates:** Open year-round.

**Fees:** A fee is charged for airboat and swamp buggy rides and for camping.

**Closest town:** Naples is 55 miles west on I-75. Fort Lauderdale is 45 miles east on I-75.

**For more information:** Billie Swamp Safari, Seminole Tribe of Florida, HC-61, Box 21-A, Clewiston, FL 33440. Phone (800) 949-6101. Web site www.seminoletribe.com/safari.

# Ten Thousand Islands

[Fig. 15, Fig. 16] Florida's world-famous Ten Thousands Islands region is the final destination for the vast amounts of water flowing out of the Big Cypress Swamp. A myriad of mangrove islands, channels, bays, oyster bars, and creeks, the Ten Thousand Islands cover nearly 200,000 acres of coastline from Cape Romano off the coast of Marco Island, to just north of Cape Sable on the southwestern tip of Florida.

Most of the access to the region is through Everglades City and Chokoloskee, two very small and charming southern coastal towns that are beginning to bulge a little with the growth of tourism but are still holding onto a respectable part of their history. The towns' location at the very end of the highway (SR 29) and on the edge of the Ten Thousand Islands and the Everglades backcountry has defined both their history and their current popularity.

A majority of the Ten Thousand Islands region (actually the islands number in the hundreds) is protected within Everglades National Park. The recent establishment of the 20,000-acre Ten Thousand Island National Wildlife Refuge provides management for most of the remainder of the region.

It's a place worthy of protection—a land where all the right ingredients come together to create a life-nourishing brew. Shallow coastal waters, abundant fresh water to mix with the salt water, nutrients from soil and decaying plants, and sunlight, have given rise to one of the most extensive and productive mangrove estuaries in the world.

Globally, mangrove habitats are as critical and perhaps as threatened as the world's rain forests. Everglades National Park protects 90 percent of all the mangroves in Florida.

The whole life-propelling system actually begins with the mangrove trees, the solar panels of the estuary. Powered by the sun, they capture and store energy. As the trees grow, older leaves turn yellow and drop into the water, sending energy into the system. The leaves are colonized by algae and fungi and then either decay or are eaten by small crabs, snails, and fish—initiating the tropical food chain. More than 3 tons of leaves can fall from a single acre of mangroves every year.

Many of the mangrove islands contain impressive shell mounds that were created by earlier inhabitants, the Calusa Indians. There are a very few instances of Native American tribes in North America able to depend almost entirely on fishing and gathering shellfish, and most of those were in the Pacific Northwest. But from as early as 1450 B.C. until the 1700s, the Southwest Florida Calusa Indians did just that and in the process developed an advanced maritime culture and social system.

The mounds were created from oyster and whelk shells, some discarded after eating, others hauled in specifically for building purposes. In some cases the builders created dry ground where none existed. In others the Indians piled shells on existing islands. More than 100 shell mounds in varying sizes, from small refuse heaps to large islands, exist from Tampa through the Ten Thousand Islands. Chokoloskee Island is one such mound.

The Calusa made tools, weapons, and everyday household items out of shells, wood, bone, antler, and shark teeth. Masks, bowls, platters, canoes, and canoe paddles were carved out of wood. Axes, hammers, drills, dippers, and spoons were made from shells. Antler was used for knife handles and necklace beads. Shark teeth and barracuda jaws were used for knife and saw blades.

With European contact in the 1500s, however, came European diseases against which the Calusa had no resistance. By 1763, when the English gained control of Florida from the Spanish, the Calusa population had been reduced from an estimated 20,000 to several hundred, who were reported to have migrated to Cuba.

Small groups of Seminole Indians inhabited and farmed some of the shell mounds during the nineteenth century between government efforts to force their removal to the West. A military fort established on Chokoloskee Island in 1855 served as a base of operations for military forays into the mangrove country. Soldiers destroyed Indian homes and crops at every opportunity.

In 1857, a campaign of 75 men originated in Chokoloskee and proceeded up the Turner River. After three days of searching, the men discovered and destroyed a large Indian settlement and its crops. The Indians attacked, killed the captain in charge, and effectively ended the incursion.

Nevertheless, it was the last battle fought between the U.S. government and Native Americans in Florida. Another 164 Indians from South Florida were moved to Oklahoma to join the thousands of others from the Southeast that survived the forced migration. The remaining Seminoles were finally left alone.

Within a few years, the first settlers arrived in the Everglades City-Chokoloskee area. Trading posts were established serving both settlers and Indians, and white man's civilization slowly took over.

Today the Ten Thousand Islands serve as a place of recreation and exploration for outdoor-minded visitors from the world over. Some of the foremost shallow-water sport fishing opportunities in the world exist in the tidal channels, rivers, and creeks running between and around the islands. Fishing guides, fishing advice, fishing charts, and fishing tackle can be found in Everglades City and Chokoloskee.

Bird-watching is superb year-round, reaching a peak when migrants join the resident species in the winter. The best birding opportunities will come from a trip on the water, either with a commercial boat tour operation, with an eco-tourism company, or by renting a boat or canoe and striking out on your own.

If you just want to take a boat ride (and you haven't seen the Ten Thousand Islands until you do), there are dozens of options. Airboat tours are offered on the Tamiami Trail and in Everglades City. Tour boats also run out of a number of locations in Everglades City. Power boats, canoes, and kayaks can be rented in Everglades City and Chokoloskee.

You can also visit an alligator farm or a circa 1910 trading post, take a swamp buggy ride, or fly over the backcountry in a small airplane. Wildlife lovers will discover a world where nature still reigns, where brown pelicans, manatees, alligators, and bald eagles call each other neighbors. And where man is just a guest.

**Directions:** Everglades City is 4 miles south of US 41 on SR 29. Chokoloskee is 7 miles south of US 41 on SR 29.

**Activities:** Fishing, wildlife viewing, canoeing, boat tours.

**Facilities:** Lodging, restaurants, boat tour operations, eco-tour operations, boat rental operations.

**Dates:** Many facilities are seasonal. Winter is the busiest time of the year.

**For more information:** Everglades Area Chamber of Commerce at the corner of US 41 and SR 29, PO Box 130, Everglades City, FL 34139. Phone (941) 695-3941. Web site chamber@florida-everglades.com.

### FISHING IN THE TEN THOUSAND ISLANDS

Fishing in the Ten Thousand Islands is nothing new. The bounty of fish and wildlife found here has been feeding mankind for thousands of years. In fact, one of the most remarkable finds of ancient fishing equipment took place in the late 1800s during an excavation on Marco Island under the direction of a Smithsonian archeologist by the name of Frank Hamilton Cushing.

Digging into a mound dating back to 650 A.D., the Cushing expedition found advanced fishing tackle including composite fish hooks that were constructed out of items found in the environment. The hook shanks were made of small forked branches of a tree. Barbed points carved from deer bone were attached to the shorter fork with sinew and black rubber-gum cement made from the sap of a tree. Some hooks even had remnants of fishing lines, which were woven from palm or palmetto fiber, attached to them.

Even more interesting is the mention of what might have been artificial fishing spoons made from "the pearly nacre of the pinna shell." Also found on the site were plug-shaped floats made from gumbo-limbo wood, sinkers made from thick columellae of conch and whelk shells (the columellae is the tightly spiraled center of a large shell), and "reels or spools" made from clamshells for holding fishing line.

We also know that early Florida anglers ate more than 40 species of fish. Seatrout and redfish were among the most common remains in South Florida sites. The anglers also took plenty of sheepshead, catfish, jacks, black drum, snook, mullet, snapper, grouper, and as many as ten species of shark.

Regardless of their method of taking or the target of their prey, they were fishermen in the true sense of the word. They understood the movement of fish, the tides, the currents, and the seasonal migrations. They had to know these things. A tribe couldn't spend too much time not catching fish.

What we have no way of knowing is if they ever pursued fish for entertainment or if it was always just a job. Surely the thrill of the hunt was as great as or greater than it is today.

The anglers that come to the Ten Thousand Islands today are seeking something else. An escape from everyday life, a respite, a chance to reconnect with nature, for at least a brief time. The majority of the fishing in the Ten Thousand Islands is light-tackle, inshore action for snook, redfish, seatrout, tarpon, and snapper. Most guides operate shallow-running flats boats with casting platforms on the front and poling platforms on the back. Fishing guides are plentiful in Everglades City and Chokoloskee. They can be hired for half-day, or full-day trips.

The most popular prey is the snook, a wily, warm-water fish known both for the fight it puts up and its taste on the dinner table. They can reach weights of 40 pounds or more but most snook caught are in the 5 to 10 pound range.

As the story is told around Everglades City, the snook fishing craze was started by a local fishing guide who was experimenting in the kitchen, not on the water. Prior to the early 1950s, snook were always thought to be inedible, tasting like soap when cooked, and in fact were called soap fish. That was until a fishing guide decided to defy local culinary tradition and removed the skin on a snook filet before it hit the frying pan. The snook proved to be delicious: the soapy taste was gone with the skin.

These days dinner is the secondary reason for most sport fishing trips. The days of high harvests have been replaced with low bag limits and a conservation-oriented "catch-and-release" attitude that has become popular as a way to ensure good fishing the next time.

For Florida fishing license information check with your guide and see Appendix E.

SALT MEADOW CORDGRASS
(Spartina patens)
This marsh species has a narrow leaf
blade and flowers in summer.

# Everglades City/Chokoloskee

*Everglades City is a center for eco-tourism, offering boat tours, canoe outfitters, and fishing guides.*

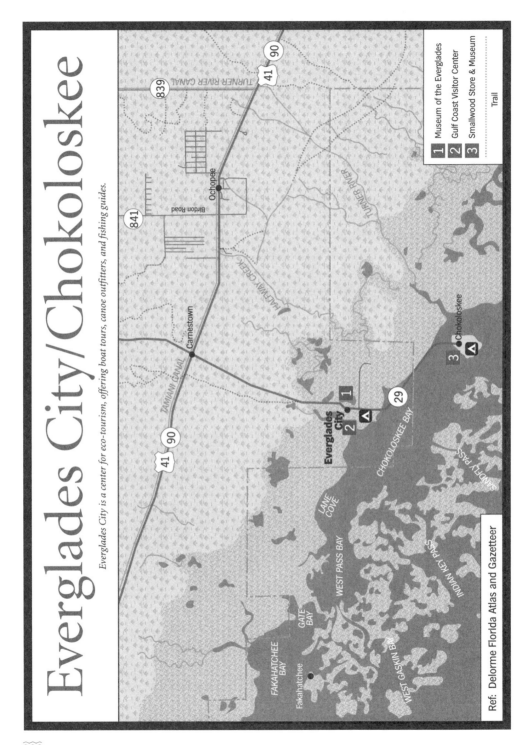

1 Museum of the Everglades
2 Gulf Coast Visitor Center
3 Smallwood Store & Museum

⋯⋯ Trail

Ref: Delorme Florida Atlas and Gazetteer

# Everglades City

[Fig. 15, Fig. 16, Fig. 17] With a population of a little more than 500, Everglades City would hardly seem to earn the title "city." Except in the winter, when Everglades City swells with thousands of visitors who come to connect somehow with the Ten Thousand Islands.

The first settlers arrived in the wilderness that would someday become Everglades City just before the Civil War. By the turn of the century, they had carved out a small fishing and farming community on the banks of what today is known as the Barron River. William Smith Allen was the first to pioneer and develop the land in 1870. He built a home on the site of the present day Rod and Gun Club.

Early pioneers earned a living farming and commercial fishing. The fertile soil and year-round growing season made it possible to grow vegetables for home use and for the winter markets up north. Tomatoes, cucumbers, eggplants, peppers, cabbages, pineapple, avocados, bananas, and sugar cane grew well in the warm climate. Early commercial fishing operations caught mostly mullet, which was salted and packed into barrels for shipment to Key West and other markets.

In 1892 George W. Storter Jr. opened the first general store and trading post and operated it for 30 years. Commerce increased as boats ran from Tampa to Key West and all stops in between. Indians traded and sold furs, beeswax, craft items, and alligator hides; in return they bought coffee, hand-cranked sewing machines, cloth, colored beads, and ammunition.

In 1922, the Storter holdings were sold to Barron G. Collier, a wealthy business-man who made his money in the advertising trade in New York City. Collier eventually purchased more than a million acres in southwestern Florida which he hoped to drain and develop.

In 1923, Collier's promise to the Florida legislature to complete the Tamiami Trail was accepted in return for the creation of Collier County in which Barron Collier owned 90 percent of the land. At the time there wasn't a single mile of paved road in the county.

The Tamiami Trail had been completed to the eastern edge of the Big Cypress Swamp years earlier, but the western half had been abandoned. Collier started the job as promised, but progress was slow. Drilling and blasting the hard limestone into road-building rubble proved to be difficult and time-consuming. The workers were only able to complete about 80 feet of road per day.

When Collier's operation lost momentum, the state took over and finished the job. The last 35 miles came in at a cost of $25,000 per mile.

Completion of the Tamiami Trail improved transportation between Tampa and Miami and helped develop cattle ranching and farming in Collier County. Although the trail passed 4 miles to the north, Everglades City remained a small town at the end of the highway.

*The Brazilian pepper tree has dark green leaflets and a bright red fruit.*

In the early 1900s, the first sportsmen began coming to the area for the bountiful fishing and hunting. As the number of sportsmen continued to grow over the decades, others began coming for different interests—bird-watching, boating, and camping.

Today Everglades City is a center for eco-tourism businesses aimed mostly at getting the visitor onto the water. Boat tours, airboat rides, canoe outfitters, and fishing guides abound. You can also choose to look a little deeper and add a dab of history to your outdoor adventures.

**Directions:** Everglades City is 4 miles south of US 41 on SR 29.

**Activities:** Fishing, boating, wildlife viewing, nature exploring.

**Facilities:** Restaurants, lodging, eco-tour guides, campgrounds.

**Dates:** Activity is seasonal. June, July, and August are the slowest months.

**Closest town:** Naples is 32 miles to the north.

**For more information:** Everglades Area Chamber of Commerce at the corner of US 41 and SR 29, PO Box 130, Everglades City, FL 34139. Phone (941) 695-3941. Web site chamber@florida-everglades.com.

## MUSEUM OF THE EVERGLADES

[Fig. 17(1)] The Museum of the Everglades is located in a commercial laundry building that was originally opened for business in 1927 as part of Barron Collier's planned community and company town.

The museum, which opened in the spring of 1998, displays artifacts and photographs in a historical context that details 2,000 years of human habitation in southwestern Florida. Volunteer members of the historical society are on hand to provide assistance and answer questions. Even a short visit will provide a historical overview of the town and surrounding area. The museum also holds lectures and tours. Plus, you can pick up a self-guided walking tour guide of Everglades City that leads you to 10 historical sites and buildings.

**Directions:** The Museum of the Everglades is located on the town circle at 105 West Broadway in Everglades City (next to Susie's Station Restaurant).

**Activities:** Historical exhibits, lectures, gift shop, walking tours.

**Dates:** Open year-round, Tuesday through Saturday except national and county holidays.

**Fees:** A small donation is requested.

**For more information:** Museum of the Everglades, 105 West Broadway, Everglades City, FL 34139. Phone (941) 695-0008. Web site www.colliermuseum.com.

### FISHING GUIDES IN EVERGLADES CITY

Fishing guides are plentiful in Everglades City. Most specialize in live bait and plug casting for snook, tarpon, redfish, cobia, and seatrout in shallow water. While most specialize in conventional tackle, others can cater to fly-fishermen.

**For more information:** For a list of fishing guides contact the Everglades Area Chamber of Commerce, PO Box 130, Everglades, FL 34139. Phone (941) 695-3941. Web site chamber@florida-everglades.com. The Coastal Conservation Association Florida maintains a list of guides on its web site. Click on Southwest Region Guides. It can be contacted at CCA Florida, 904 East Park Avenue, Tallahassee, FL 32301. Phone (850) 224-3474. Web site www.cca-florida.com.

### BOAT AND AIRBOAT TOURS

Most of the boat tours offer standard or tailored cruises of various lengths through the Ten Thousand Islands. The Gulf Coast Visitor Center of Everglades National Park also offers boat tours. Airboat rides generally explore the narrow, winding mangrove creeks of the Everglades backcountry.

Canoe and kayak outfitters rent equipment and lead multiday trips into the backcountry. Discount coupons for many of the attractions in Everglades City can be picked up at the Everglades Area Chamber of Commerce at the corner of SR 29 and US 41.

#### WOOTEN'S AIRBOAT TOURS, SWAMP BUGGY RIDES AND ANIMAL SANCTUARY

This is one of the most famous operations in the Everglades. The airboat rides cross a sawgrass prairie as well as explore the mangrove backcountry. Swamp buggy tours explore cypress swamps. There are also wildlife shows and exhibits featuring alligators, panthers, deer, bobcats, and otters.

**Directions:** Located on Tamiami Trail just east of SR 29.

**Activities:** Swamp buggy and airboat tours, wildlife shows.

**Facilities:** Gift shop, wildlife exhibits.

**Dates:** Open daily.

**Fees:** A fee is charged for all activities.

**For more information:** Wooten's Airboat Tours, PO Box 121, Ochopee, FL 33943. Phone (800) 282-2781.

### CAPTAIN DOUG'S FLORIDA BOAT TOURS

This is the largest and oldest airboat touring operation in Everglades City. Tours survey the mangrove forest backcountry and include a brief visit to a sawgrass wetland. Included is an alligator show and a visit to an Indian village. Especially enjoyable are small airboat rides for less than six people. Although more expensive, they offer a more intimate experience in an authentic Everglades airboat. Open seven days a week.

**Directions:** Located at the Captain's Table Resort, one mile past the Everglades City bridge.

**Activities:** Airboat tours.

**Facilities:** Gift shop.

**Dates:** Open daily.

**Fees:** A fee is charged for boat tours.

**For more information:** Captain Doug's Florida Boat Tours, 102 Broadway, Everglades City, FL 34139. Phone (800) 282-9194.

### BARRON RIVER CHARTER

Captain Sophia Stiffler pilots a 22-foot deck (pontoon) boat and operates tours of the Ten Thousand Islands toward the Gulf of Mexico. The boat holds up to six people and is a good choice for families wanting to design their own trip. Trips can include shelling, fishing, exploring, and bird-watching. The deck boat is also a good photography platform.

**Directions:** Located at Dock 164-167 at the Barron River Marina.

**Activities:** Customized boat tours.

**Dates:** Open year-round.

**Fees:** A fee is charged for boat tours.

**For more information:** Phone (941) 695-1000.

### EVERGLADES RENTALS & ECO ADVENTURES

For those wishing to strike out on their own, this outfit rents all the equipment you'll need. It also leads multiday paddle trips into the Everglades backcountry or the Gulf of Mexico side of the Ten Thousand Islands. Half-day and full-day trips also available.

**Directions:** Office is at the Ivey House—107 Camellia Street, Everglades City.

**Activities:** Canoe, kayak, bicycle, kayak and camping equipment rentals; eco-tours.

**Dates:** Open seasonally.

**Fees:** A fee is charged for rentals and guided tours.

**For more information:** Everglades Rentals and Eco Tours, 107 Camelia Street, Everglades City, FL 34139. Phone (941) 695-4666.

### EVERGLADES NATIONAL PARK BOAT TOUR

A two-hour boat tour operates daily out of the Gulf Coast Visitor Center [Fig. 17(2)]. The cruise follows a loop route through the heart of the Ten Thousand Islands. A naturalist relates the natural history of the area and helps identify wildlife.

Manatees are spotted 80 percent of the time. Bottle-nosed dolphin, osprey, and bald eagles are commonly seen. Open year-round including holidays.

**Directions:** Located on the causeway between Everglades City and Chokoloskee Island.

**Activities:** Boat tours.

**Facilities:** Information counter, natural history museum, bookstore.

**Dates:** Open year-round.

**Fees:** A fee is charged for boat tours.

**For more information:** Everglades National Park, PO Box 119, Everglades City, FL 33929. Phone (800) 445-7724.

## DINING IN EVERGLADES CITY

Dining can be a real treat in Everglades City, with a different place to try every day. There are no fast food chains or all-night breakfast grills. Many restaurants occupy historic old buildings. In general, the restaurants serve a wide selection of local seafood and traditional favorites. Many restaurants will also be happy to prepare your catch in any way you choose.

### OYSTER HOUSE

PO Box 367, Everglades City, FL 34139. The Oyster House on the causeway between Everglades City and Chokoloskee is a restaurant that could only be found in a land where the swamp meets the Gulf of Mexico. The museum-like setting features a huge stuffed black bear, models of sailing vessels, trophy mounts of largemouth bass, swordfish, and sawfish, carved wooden alligators, murals of coastal life, totem poles, and a stuffed opossum. Maybe the best hybrid of the two worlds is a cypress clock adorned with oyster shells.

Food also comes both from the swamp and the gulf. You can have gator tail or grouper, frog legs or lobster, bay scallops, catfish, or shrimp any way you want it. The most fun is to mix a fried or broiled platter of delicacies from both worlds, but whatever you choose, don't pass up at least a sampling of the gator tail, lightly fried southern style in bite-sized pieces. A 75-foot tower on the property offers a terrific panoramic view of the mangrove forest and the nearby small towns. And the walk up is a good way to work off a little of your meal. Casual dining. *Inexpensive. Phone (941) 695-2073.*

### OAR HOUSE RESTAURANT

305 North Collier Avenue, Everglades City, FL 34139. The Oar House Restaurant is located on SR 29, just as it enters Everglades City. In a coastal setting the restaurant serves local favorites such as turtle cooter (fried freshwater turtle), gator tail, frog legs, and the usual steak and hamburger fare. With a full-service breakfast served everyday, it's a favorite for local fishing guides and their clients. Full cocktail lounge. Dress is casual. *Inexpensive. Phone (941) 695-3535.*

### SUSIE'S STATION RESTAURANT

Susie's Station Restaurant is located next to the Museum of the Everglades on the city circle. Even if you're not hungry, stop in for a quick look around at this converted 1920s gas station and general store. There's a 1920 Oldsmobile sitting inside and an interesting collection of turn-of-the-century store items from a time when chain was 2 cents a foot, and dry goods were 15 cents a yard. Food is basic lunchtime sandwich fare. Try the Key lime pie. *Inexpensive. Phone (941) 695-2002.*

### EVERGLADES SEAFOOD DEPOT RESTAURANT

102 Collier Avenue, Everglades City, FL 34139. Located in the original Everglades Train Depot, which first opened in 1928. This restaurant gives diners a pleasant view of mangrove-shrouded Lake Placid. Don't be surprised to see an alligator cruise by during dinner. There is a nice covered dining area next to the water for times when the weather cooperates.

It serves a full seafood fare of local favorites in a casual atmosphere. Stone crabs are hugely popular when in season from October 15 to May 15. It also specializes in large deep-water lobster. Most meals are inexpensively priced; lobster and stone crabs are slightly more expensive than other meals. *Inexpensive. Phone (941) 695-0075.*

### BLUE CRAB CAFÉ

PO Box 383, Everglades City, FL 34139. Located on the Tamiami Trail (US 41), just east of SR 29, the Blue Crab Café brings a little Maryland crab cuisine to the Everglades. Owned and operated by Tony Hickman and Joan Griffin, it specializes in a variety of blue crab dishes made fresh every day. Tony even steams the crabs right on the front porch. The Maryland crab cake on a Kiser bun is a local favorite.

Other choices include oysters, shrimp, stone crabs, conch fritters, frog legs, gator nuggets, and Indian fry bread. The surf and turf and snow crab are reasonably priced with large helpings. Casual dining. *Inexpensive. Phone (941) 695-2682.*

### LODGING IN EVERGLADES CITY

Everglades City has a limited variety of accommodations, including about a half dozen motels, lodges, resorts, and inns, and about as many RV parks. Other accommodations are available on Marco Island 26 miles north on US 41. A full list of lodging options can be obtained by contacting the Everglades Area Chamber of Commerce, Inc., PO Box 130, Everglades City, FL 34139. Phone (941) 695-3941.

### THE ROD AND GUN CLUB

200 Broadway, Everglades City, FL 34139. Located on the banks of the Barron River just off the city circle, this is the most famous lodging in Everglades City. Built in 1850, on the site of the first homestead in Everglades City, it's a beautiful southern mansion turned into a lodge. A magnificent, all wood, heavily varnished lobby harks back to an earlier time when sportsmen gathered in the evening to discuss the day's hunting or fishing trip. Over the years it's been visited by a long list of presidents and movie stars. It also includes a waterfront restaurant, dock space, and fishing guides. Checks or cash only. *Moderate to expensive. Phone (941) 695-2101.*

**ON THE BANKS OF THE EVERGLADES BED & BREAKFAST INN**

201 West Broadway, Everglades City, FL 34139. Located right next door to the Rod and Gun Club, On the Banks of the Everglades is a bed and breakfast established in the Bank of the Everglades, the first bank to serve Collier County in the 1920s. The refurbished building has 12 rooms but has retained some of its banking character, including bags of "money" laying around in the lobby and hallways. Breakfast is served in the Walk-in Vault. *Moderate to expensive. Phone (888) 431-1977. Web site www.banksoftheeverglades.com.*

**THE IVEY HOUSE BED AND BREAKFAST**

107 Camellia Street, Everglades City, FL 34139. This historic building was first built as a recreation hall for workers on the Tamiami Trail. In 1925 it was moved to its present site, and in 1928 it was converted into a boarding house. It offers an Everglades library, complimentary bicycles, canoe and kayak rentals, and deck boat adventures. The Ivey House is affiliated with a canoe and kayak outfitter that can customize any Everglades adventure you might have in mind. *Moderate. Phone (941) 695-3299.*

**BARRON RIVER RESORT, MOTEL AND RV PARK**

PO Box 116, Everglades City, FL 34139. Located directly on the Barron River at the Everglades City bridge, this motel and RV park offers easy access to the Ten Thousand Islands and the Gulf of Mexico. The resort includes waterfront efficiencies, one- and two-bedroom apartments, and an RV park with full hook-ups, cable TV, and telephone. Some sites are waterfront. It also has a full-service marina, bait and tackle store, and boat rentals. *Moderate. Phone (941) 695-3591.*

# Chokoloskee Island

[Fig. 17] A 3-mile-long, low-lying causeway connects Everglades City with Chokoloskee Island. The causeway was built in 1955, but the island has a much longer history of human habitation. Beyond Chokoloskee to the south is a vast mangrove forest protected by Everglades National Park.

A quiet island of roughly 150 acres and a couple hundred residents, Chokoloskee is actually a large shell mound, owing its 20-foot elevation, the highest point of land around, to the work of the Calusa Indians. During the hurricane of 1910, residents on the island who survived by moving to the only piece of land remaining above water gained a true understanding of why the Indians built their mounds so high. They too knew about hurricanes and storm surges.

The island is situated at the lower end of the large, shallow Chokoloskee Bay, which lies between the mainland and the Ten Thousand Islands. The 10-mile-long, 2-mile-wide bay doesn't have a place in it with a depth of more than 5 feet. Sometimes

# The Story of Ed Watson

The following version of how Edgar Watson came to a violent end is based on the publications *Man in the Everglades*, by Charlton W. Tebeau, and *The Everglades: River of Grass* by Marjory Stoneman Douglas. Tebeau's version was in part related by C. S. "Ted" Smallwood. Watson's life is also chronicled in noted novelist and naturalist Peter Matthiessen's Everglades trilogy, *Killing Mister Watson, Lost Man's River*, and *Bone by Bone*. Ed Watson was a red-haired, blue-eyed Scotsman who purchased a 40-acre, shell-mound island, 17 miles south of Chokoloskee and began farming this claim in 1892. He grew winter vegetables for the Key West-New York produce market, and sugarcane, which he processed into syrup. By 1910 he had organized the most successful farming operation in the Everglades.

Watson's notoriety isn't a result of his success as a farmer, however, but comes from a life of violent acts that he either committed or, at least was accused of committing. Originally from central Florida, he headed to the Midwest after shooting a farm hand on his family's farm. Somewhere in Arkansas or Texas he hooked up with the Belle Starr gang. At some point things went bad and he is suspected of killing the famous lady outlaw. That was apparently followed by an episode in Oregon a few years later where he killed a man in a dispute and fled to Florida.

Next came another killing in Arcadia, Florida, a throat cutting in Key West, and suspicion of at least four other murders. Things came to a head in the summer of 1910 when a series of murders occurred at the Watson Farm. Although Watson laid the blame on another man, suspicions were strong. Some versions say Watson was long in the practice of hiring drifters who had wandered to this remote land to work on his farm. Then when it came time to pay their wages, he killed them instead.

The hurricane of 1910 interfered with an official investigation of the murders. A few days later, when Watson pulled his boat up to the docks at Ted Smallwood's Store he was confronted by an armed group of citizens. When asked to put down his gun, he refused and either shot or attempted to shoot into the crowd. (Some versions say he fired his shotgun but the shells were wet from the hurricane and they didn't fire.)

In any event, the townspeople fired back, and Watson fell dead.

billed as the Snook Capital of the World, Chokoloskee serves as a convenient entrance to the Everglades backcountry for modern day explorers and serious anglers.

Fishing patterns are the same as Everglades City's. Snook, tarpon, redfish, and seatrout are popular and plentiful. Fishing guides are available that will take you to the seldom explored parts of the backcountry. Most guides can accommodate, and in fact welcome, fly-fishing enthusiasts.

Like any pioneer town on the edge of a wilderness, Chokoloskee Island has seen its share of characters—including Totch Brown. A native of Chokoloskee, Totch became a legend for his success as an alligator poacher, smuggler, and story teller, and for his honesty in describing his past. His tales, which are available in his and Peter Matthiessen's book, *Totch: A Life in the Everglades* and on video, *Tales of the Everglades: Totch Brown's Life in the 10,000 Islands*, add a fabric of realism to the twentieth century history of the island. Both are available at the Smallwood Store and Outdoor Resorts.

Another far less scrutable character who has almost grown to mythical proportions is the notorious Ed Watson, a hot-tempered, quick-to-violence pioneer, who ran a farming and produce shipping operation from an island on the Chatham River south of Chokoloskee. In 1910 Watson, who was suspected of multiple murders, was killed by the townspeople of Chokoloskee. It's a story that's been told and retold in magazines and books, and most recently in a historical-fiction format in Peter Matthiessen's novel *The Killing of Mr. Watson*.

Chokoloskee today is a quiet town of commercial fishermen, fishing guides, and a slowly increasing number of seasonal residents. A pair of well-run resort operations blend in with the small community.

But you can still touch the island's history. You can visit the Smallwood Store and see the dock where Watson was shot, or journey into the Everglades backcountry to see where he lived. You can hear the tales of Totch Brown and stop to visit with his nephew, Kenny Brown, at Outdoor Resorts at the base of the causeway. Like Ted Smallwood and Totch Brown, Kenny Brown embodies a living knowledge of the island's short, but vibrant history.

**Directions:** Chokoloskee Island is 7 miles south of US 41 on SR 29.

**Activities:** Fishing, boating, backcountry camping.

**Facilities:** Lodging, campgrounds.

**Dates:** Activity is seasonal. June, July, and August are the slowest months.

**Closest town:** Everglades City is 3 miles north.

**For more information:** Everglades Area Chamber of Commerce at the corner of US 41 and SR 29, PO Box 130, Everglades City, FL 34139. Phone (941) 695-3941. Web site chamber@florida-everglades.com.

## SMALLWOOD STORE AND MUSEUM

[Fig. 17(3)] The most historic building on Chokoloskee Island is the Ted Smallwood Store. It was built in 1906 by Charles Sherod "Ted" Smallwood, one of the early pioneers in Collier County. The building served as store, post office, and Indian trading post. Smallwood remained the area's postmaster until his retirement in 1941, and in the meantime became a part of the history of the island.

The store has been maintained, and in some cases restored to its early days. Walking inside is like walking into an old picture. An array of antiques from the early part of the century surrounds a life-sized mannequin of Ted Smallwood, sitting in a rocker just like he did 60 years ago. The store sits on pilings, and if you look out the back window you'll see the spot where Ed Watson was killed in 1910. Some of Smallwood's reminiscences can be read in the book *The Story of the Chokoloskee Bay Country* by Charlton W. Tebeau. The store was placed on the National Register of Historic Places in 1974, and restoration of the store as a museum was started in 1990 by the nonprofit Ted Smallwood Store, Inc.

**Directions:** Chokoloskee Island is 7 miles south of US 41 on SR 29. Turn right on Mamie Street just after coming onto the island.

**Facilities:** Historic museum, exhibits.

**Dates:** Days and hours are seasonal.

**Closest town:** Everglades City is 3 miles north.

**For more information:** Historic Smallwood Store, PO Box 367, Chokoloskee, FL 33925. Phone (941) 695-2989.

### LODGING ON CHOKOLOSKEE

Most of Chokoloskee Island is covered by private residences. Public lodging and camping is limited.

### CHOKOLOSKEE ISLAND PARK AND MARINA

PO Box 430, Chokoloskee, FL 34138. This is a camper and trailer resort with good access to the Gulf of Mexico side of the Ten Thousand Islands. Tent campers are welcome and overnight accommodations are available. Fishing guides are available. The marina has a boat ramp, dockage, and boat and motor rentals. Open year-round. *Inexpensive to moderate. Phone (941) 695-2414.*

### OUTDOOR RESORTS—CHOKOLOSKEE ISLAND RV RESORT AND MARINA

PO Box 39, Chokoloskee, FL 34138. This resort is a hub for sport fishing on the island. It has a large RV park with waterfront sites. There are overnight accommodations and condos that can be rented by the week. You can rent boats, canoes, kayaks, or hire a fishing guide. Fly-fishing lessons are even available. Talk with Kenny Brown about where the best fishing is, or about a canoe trip or fishing guide he might recommend. *Inexpensive to moderate. Phone (941) 695-2881.*

*Great blue herons feed on fish, frogs, snakes, mice, and birds.*

# Everglades National Park Western Entrance

[Fig. 15, Fig. 17] Access to the western side of Everglades National Park is strictly by water. The Gulf Coast Visitor Center located between Everglades City and Chokoloskee provides information on ways to safely enjoy and experience the Ten Thousand Islands and the mangrove wilderness of the Everglades National Park backcountry. In addition to an information booth, interpretative displays and a short video detail the way in which the natural system operates.

Two-hour boat tours of a portion of the Ten Thousand Islands operate daily out of the visitor center. An on-board naturalist will explain the natural history of the area, including the role of the mangrove, and will point out the wildlife that comes into view. It's common to see a wide variety of the area's birds, including roseate spoonbills, white and brown pelicans, osprey, laughing gulls, and royal terns. Manatees are sighted on about 80 percent of the trips. If you want a close look at black skimmers, they can usually be seen standing in large numbers on the dock at the visitor center between their morning and evening feeding times.

Forty-six primitive campsites are available throughout the backcountry for boaters and paddlers wishing to extend their stay in the wilderness. Sites include ancient shell mounds, old home sites, beaches, and chickees, which are open, 10- by 12-foot elevated platforms constructed for camping in the mangrove estuary. Each chickee has a chemical toilet and a shelter with a roof. A free-standing tent is best suited for use on the chickees because stakes and nails are not permitted. Permits, charts, and backcountry planners are required and will only be issued 24 hours in advance.

Canoes can be rented at the visitor center and in Chokoloskee and Everglades City. Kayaks and power boats can be rented in Chokoloskee and Everglades City.

**Directions:** Everglades National Park Gulf Coast Visitor Center is located on the causeway between Everglades City and Chokoloskee Island.

**Activities:** Boating, canoeing, wildlife watching.

**Facilities:** Boat tours, canoe rentals, interpretive displays, small gift and bookstore, and information booth with daily tides posted.

**Closest town:** Everglades City is 3 miles to the north.

**For more information:** Everglades National Park Headquarters, PO Box 279, Homestead, FL 33030. Phone (305) 242-7700. For information on canoe rentals and boat tours, Everglades National Park Boat Tours, PO Box 119, Everglades City, FL 33929. Phone (941) 695-2591.

## CANOE TRAILS IN EVERGLADES NATIONAL PARK

Two canoe trails that end near the visitor center offer easy, half-day or full-day trips to experience a part of the mangrove backcountry and the Ten Thousand

Islands. On any canoe outing it's important to wear a long-sleeved shirt, and carry insect repellent, water, and a map.

Before starting out always check the conditions report at the visitor center for the chances of rain, tide times, and wind forecasts. Windy conditions in the wide bays have swamped many canoes. A falling tide flows away from the mainland and a rising tide flows inland. In the summer, afternoon thunderstorms can pop up without warning and bring strong, sudden winds. NOAA Chart 11430—Lostman's River to Wiggins Pass—covers the local waters.

Canoe outfitters in Everglades City will arrange for pick-ups and drop-offs.

**For more information:** Everglades National Park Headquarters, PO Box 279, Homestead, FL 33030. Phone (305) 242-7700. For information on canoe rentals contact Everglades National Park Boat Tours, PO Box 119, Everglades City, FL 33929. Phone (941) 695-2591.

### TURNER RIVER CANOE TRAIL

[Fig. 16(3)] This 8-mile trail begins at a launch site on US 41, 0.5 mile west of the H. P. Williams Roadside Park, and ends in Chokoloskee Bay at either Chokoloskee Island or the Everglades National Park Gulf Coast Visitor Center. It passes through a grassy prairie, past cypress trees, and into the mangrove forest. The Turner River enters Chokoloskee Bay opposite Chokoloskee Island. Arranging to end your trip at the National Park Service ramp next to Outdoor Resorts on Chokoloskee Bay will save you paddling 3 miles of open water to the visitor center in Everglades City.

**Directions:** The beginning of the canoe trail is at a canoe launch located 0.5 mile west of H.P. Williams Roadside Park. H.P. Williams Roadside Park is 7 miles east of SR 29 at the intersection of US 41 and Turner River Road (CR 839).

**Trail:** 8 miles one-way. The trail takes 5 to 6 hours to canoe depending on tides and wind.

### HALFWAY CREEK CANOE TRAIL

[Fig. 16(4)] This 6-mile trip launches on Seagrape Drive, which turns off of US 41. Paddlers follow the creek through mangrove-lined channels then south past Plantation Island to Chokoloskee or the Gulf Coast Visitor Center. Take-out points are along the causeway between Everglades City and Chokoloskee Island or at the visitor center in Everglades City.

**Directions:** The Halfway Creek Canoe Trail begins at a boat launch located 0.7 mile down Seagrape Drive. From US 41, Seagrape Drive is 2.2 miles east of SR 29.

**Trail:** 6 miles one-way. The trail takes 5 to 6 hours to canoe depending on tides and wind.

### WILDERNESS WATERWAY

[Fig. 16(6)] The Wilderness Waterway is a 99-mile-long marked powerboat and paddle trail that traverses the backcountry of Everglades National Park between Everglades City and Flamingo. The trip, which takes at least one day by powerboat and eight days by canoe, should not be attempted without careful planning and a full understanding of how to use navigation charts and the conditions expected in the Everglades backcountry. Shorter loop trips can be made from either end of the route.

Regardless of the length of trip you plan, ask for a backcountry trip planner and purchase navigation charts from area bait and marine supply stores. You can also order charts from the Florida National Parks and Monuments Association, 10 Parachute Key #51, Homestead, FL 33034-6735, (305) 247-1216, www.nps.gov/ever/fnpma.htm. The planner contains safety information such as how to file a float plan, recommended navigation charts, descriptions of the various sites, necessary equipment, and park regulations. The chart is a standard navigation chart for these waters, but the various campsites and the Wilderness Waterway are marked. The entire trip requires NOAA Chart 11433 Whitewater Bay, NOAA Chart 11432 Shark River to Lostman's River, and NOAA Chart 11430 Lostman's River to Wiggins Pass.

Mangrove waterways have a tendency to look very much alike. It's easy to get lost if you haven't taken the proper precautions. Review your route with rangers before starting out. Take binoculars so you can see distant channel markers, and carry a compass. In the summer be prepared for thunderstorms and high numbers of insects.

Boats more than 18 feet (5.5 meters) long or with high cabins or windshields should not attempt the trip because of narrow channels and overhanging vegetation.

A backcountry permit is required to use any of the backcountry campsites. A fee is charged and permits are available only 24 hours in advance from the Gulf Coast Visitor Center in Everglades City or the Flamingo Visitor Center in Flamingo. During winter, windy cold fronts can slow your progress and campsites fill up fast.

The mangrove wilderness has a remarkable amount of human history for such an out-of-the-way place. Campsites are on chickees, isolated beaches, Indian shell mounds, and old homesites. Almost every spot has a bit of history attached to it. An invaluable resource as a guide and a source of history attached to many of the campsites is *A Guide to the Wilderness Waterway of the Everglades National Park* by William G. Truesdell. Additional charts, written guides, and historical background books may be purchased at visitor centers or ordered from the Florida National Parks and Monuments Association, 10 Parachute Key, Suite 51, Homestead, FL 33034-6735. Phone (305) 247-1216.

### WATSON PLACE

[Fig. 16(5)] Located 17 miles south of Chokoloskee Island on the Chatham River is a campsite called the Watson Place. It sits on the site where the notorious Ed Watson had his home and operated his farm prior to his demise in 1910 at the hands of the people of Chokoloskee (*see page 252*).

The site can be reached by power boat in little more than an hour and by experienced canoeists in a full day. The Watson Place is a good destination for a partial trip down the Wilderness Waterway and into the backcountry.

Begin your trip in either Everglades City or Chokoloskee Island and follow the

Wilderness Waterway south. The route goes up the Lopez River, then along Crooked Creek. The Lopez River is named for a Spanish family that homesteaded along the river in the late 1800s and lived here for two generations.

From here the Wilderness Waterway crosses Sunday Bay, the first of a series of shallow inland bays along the Wilderness Waterway. Then travel on through Oyster Bay, and into Huston Bay as far as Marker 105. The bays can become very choppy under windy conditions. Paddling across them can sometimes be a challenge. Be sure to have the next channel marker in sight before leaving the last one completely behind.

At marker 105 the route to Watson's Place turns southwest away from the Wilderness Waterway and down a branch of the Chatham River that connects to the main river channel. A small dock and chemical toilet mark the site of the Watson Place, as does a huge royal poinciana tree (*Delonix regia*) that blooms bright pink in the spring. The same tree is plainly visible in a 75-year-old photo of the Watson farm.

Like much of the dry land in the park's backwaters, the Watson Place campsite is mostly a shell mound left by the Calusa Indians. These early Floridians were fishing and gathering shellfish from the Chatham nearly 2,000 years ago. Although gone by the eighteenth century, they left behind this 40-acre shell mound as evidence of their long habitation.

Sometime after the Calusa were gone, Seminole Indians were the first to make use of the high ground for cultivation. Seminole crops of potatoes and sugarcane were last reported at the site in 1856, during the Third Seminole War.

In 1892 Ed Watson purchased the site and ran a profitable vegetable farming and syrup making operation for 18 years.

The campsite is located near where Watson's two-story farmhouse once stood and where he made syrup. All that remains today are two large cisterns, a few rusty pieces of machinery, and some out-of-place vegetation.

In the summer, swallow-tailed kites can sometimes be seen tilting back and forth in the air just above the mangrove treetops. West Indian manatees also frequent these tannin-stained waters, but the animals can only be seen when they rise to take a breath.

The mangroves in this part of the park are very well developed, standing 50 or 60 feet above the water. It's common to see osprey or even a flock of white ibis perched in the high branches. At night you may hear the screaming of raccoons fighting somewhere deep in the forest.

When camping at Watson's or at any of the backcountry sites take extraordinary precautions against raccoons. They'll look through your boat and through everything you might leave outside. They can open any cooler, bait bucket, or live well; and they will.

The Chatham River winds about five miles through the mangrove forest. A tidal river, it carries freshwater runoff from the Everglades to the Gulf of Mexico, and carries salt water inland to the highly productive brackish-water mixing zones.

About 1 mile upstream from Watson's, the river branches into a number of smaller streams that connect to different inland bays. Downstream from Watson's, the Chatham remains much the same for about a mile. Then it begins widening gradually and becomes shallower. Oyster bars dominate the last mile of the river.

The river usually holds a good population of seatrout and snook, especially in the winter. Try drifting a live shrimp, or use any type of plastic grub sold at the local tackle store in Chokoloskee. Casting plugs next to the mangroves is an explosive way to fish if you happen upon a big snook or tarpon. Topwater plugs that run shallow or on the surface and have a lot of action, like a broken-back Rapala or Zara Spook, attract a whole range of backcountry sport fish.

Bottle-nosed dolphins can often be seen in these waters, and if you're in a power boat, don't be surprised to see one come over and play in the bow wave if you go slow enough.

The mouth of the Chatham is probably the most popular place to fish on the river, although it can be difficult to navigate because of an abundance of oyster bars. During high tide, both redfish and snook feed over these oyster bars. Plastic jigs are a good choice for redfish but can be difficult to use in shallow water. A silver or gold spoon is an excellent substitute. They should be fished slow, barely fast enough to make them wobble and stay off the bottom.

**Directions:** Travel from Chokoloskee Island or Everglades City to Watson's Place along a planned route.

**Trail:** 34-mile round trip. The trail takes 1 hour by power boat, or a full day for experienced canoeists.

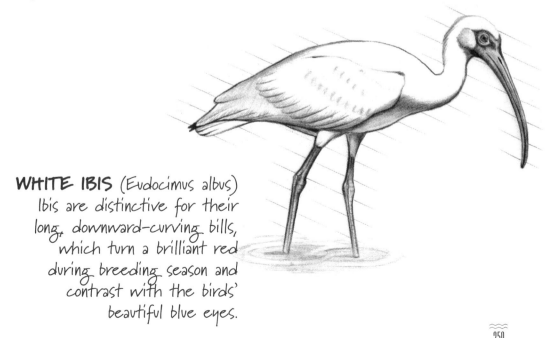

**WHITE IBIS** (*Eudocimus albus*) Ibis are distinctive for their long, downward-curving bills, which turn a brilliant red during breeding season and contrast with the birds' beautiful blue eyes.

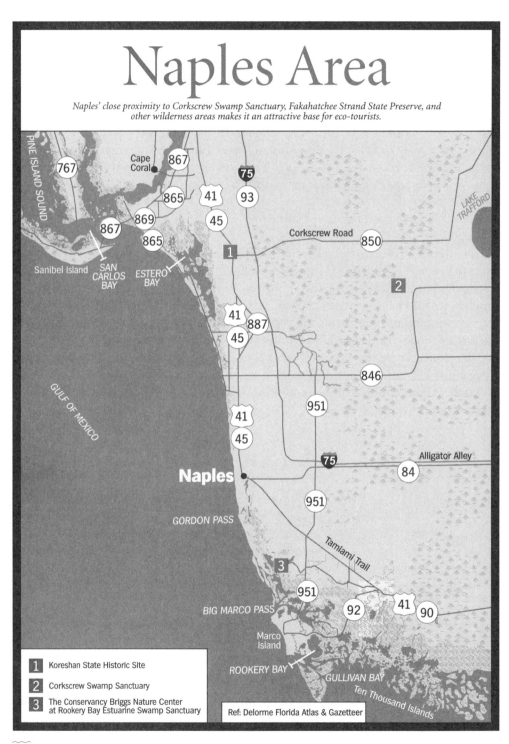

# Naples Area

*Naples' close proximity to Corkscrew Swamp Sanctuary, Fakahatchee Strand State Preserve, and other wilderness areas makes it an attractive base for eco-tourists.*

PINE ISLAND SOUND

767

Cape Coral

867

75

865   41   93

869

45

867

865

Sanibel Island   SAN CARLOS BAY   ESTERO BAY

Corkscrew Road   850

LAKE TRAFFORD

1

2

41   887

45

GULF OF MEXICO

846

951

41

45

75

Alligator Alley

84

Naples

951

GORDON PASS

Tamiami Trail

3

951

BIG MARCO PASS

92   41   90

Marco Island

ROOKERY BAY

GULLIVAN BAY

Ten Thousand Islands

1   Koreshan State Historic Site

2   Corkscrew Swamp Sanctuary

3   The Conservancy Briggs Nature Center at Rookery Bay Estuarine Swamp Sanctuary

Ref: Delorme Florida Atlas & Gazetteer

# Naples

Naples speaks in subdued pastel tones of the good life comfortable wealth makes possible. [Fig. 18, Fig. 19] Whether or not the southwest Gulf Coast city of 25,000 really does have more millionaires per capita than any other Florida city is a matter for the chambers of commerce here and in Palm Beach to decide. Likewise, the claim of "Golf Capitol of the World" might be a point for discussion between Naples and Myrtle Beach, South Carolina. But petty numbers notwithstanding, Naples carries itself with an unmistakable air of class and style few places can rival.

Many of the most celebrated icons of New York, Beverly Hills, and European haute couture, gifts, and art are represented in the Fifth Avenue-Third Street Corridor. Tiffany, Dior, Chanel, Gucci, etc. are elbow-to-elegant-elbow in a downtown district called Historic Old Naples. "Old" is relatively speaking: The salmon, terra cotta, and lemon-hued buildings look as though Disney put them up last week, but

[ *Above:* Naples, a beautiful city along the Gulf of Mexico, is popular with golfers, shoppers, and natural history buffs. ]

# City of Naples

*Millions of winter tourists flock to this city of 200,000 every year.*

**GULF OF MEXICO**

**Naples**

N

Carl Johnson State Park

Bonita Bay Boulevard
Ludbury Boulevard
W. Terry St.
Bonita Springs

**41** ALT

**75**

Bonita Beach Road
Exit 18

**1** Bonita Beach
Wiggins Pass Rd.
Sun Century
111th Ave.
Immokalee Rd.
Exit 17
**846**

Vanderbilt Beach County Park
Vanderbilt Beach Road
**41**
Vanderbilt Extension
J&C Blvd.
Taylor

Delnor-Wiggins Pass State Recreation Area
Seagate Dr.
**2** Neopolitan Way
Pine Ridge Rd.
Exit 16
**896**

Gulfshore
Goodlette-Frank Rd.
Park Shore Dr.
Harbor Dr.
Mooringline Dr.
Santa Barbara Blvd.
**886**

Coastland Mall
Golden Gate Pkwy.

Banyan Blvd.
**951**

Lowdermilk Park
Crayton
7th Ave. North
**3**
Naples Airport
Airport-Pulling Rd.
Mercantile
Industrial
Alligator Alley

Central
3rd Ave. S.
5th Ave. S.
Radio Rd.
Exit 15
Ft. Lauderdale

Olde Naples
Gulfshore Blvd.
6th Ave. S.
8th Ave. S.
Commercial
Davis Blvd.

3rd St. S.
10th Ave. S.
Broad Ave. S.
12th Ave. S.
13th Ave. S.
14th Ave. S.
8th St. N.
10th St. N.
10th st. S.
Old Naples Seaport
Linwood
County Barn Rd.
Charlemagne
Mariette

Naples Beach & Pier
Olde Naples Port Royal
Gordon Dr.
City Docks
Bayshore
Fern St.
Thomasson dr.
Rattlesnake Hammock Rd.

Bay St.
**41**

NAPLES BAY

Tamiami Trail

Isle of Capri Rd.

Key Island
Isle of Capri
**952**
Mainsail Dr.
Collier Seminole State Park

Capri Blvd.
Marco Island Airport
**951**
**92**
**29**

Kendall
Hernando
Tigertail
MARCO RIVER
Bald Eagle Dr.
N. Barfield Dr.
S. Barfield Dr.
Goodland Dr.

Tigertail Beach
N. Collier
San Marco Dr.
South Collier Blvd.
Heathwood

Marco Island
Winterberry Dr.
Goodland
Everglades City
Ten Thousand Islands

Public Boat Ramps Park
Chokoloskee

**1** Barefoot Beach Preserve

**2** Clam Pass Beach County Park

**3** The Conservancy Naples Nature Center

there are some bona fide old-timers, a least by South Florida standards.

The Mercantile Building, the city's oldest surviving landmark, went up in 1919 as the town's first grocery store. The Old Naples Building, circa 1920, was the first drug store, bus depot, town hall, and post office.

Like many Florida coastal towns, Naples came about in the late 1800s as nothing more fashionable than a haphazard fishing hamlet hugging the mangrove swamps and turquoise waters of the Gulf of Mexico. Accessible only by boat, the natives drowsed contentedly in their isolated paradise of beaches and sand dunes, palmettos, baldcypress, and mangroves. The few adventurous tourists, mostly big-game fishermen, stepped off their yachts at the municipal pier and rarely ventured much farther inland.

The scene began to change in 1926, when Barron G. Collier extended his railroad south from Fort Myers and Tampa to Naples and the new county that was named in his honor. Another leap forward occurred after World War II, when affluent Northerners discovered Naples and began building lavish estates that fronted palm-lined boulevards and backed onto waterways perfect for parking their yachts.

In the 1950 U.S. census, Naples counted only about 5,000 residents. Since then, the Florida land boom has barreled in like a typhoon and turned the once-quiet haven upside down. Collier County is today one of the fastest growing counties in the U.S. More than 200,000 now call it home and more are arriving every day. Millions of tourists swell the population every winter, and like other burgeoning areas of South Florida, new subdivisions, shopping centers, resort hotels, and golf courses are putting intense pressure on swamps and other wilderness areas.

Twenty miles to the south, the well-groomed Marco Island was not overlooked by the influx of monied individuals. Still only 48 percent developed, the island displays a combination of multimillion dollar homes and condominiums, four-star resort hotel complexes, and all the shopping and dining opportunities that attend such places.

# Naples Area Attractions

At a cursory glance, this creature comfort capital of posh resorts, extravagant stores, splendid dining, and sparkling white beaches would seem incongruous with the Everglades and other wilderness areas nearby, but it's exactly those very amenities that make it an attractive base for venturing into the wilds. Corkscrew Swamp Sanctuary, Fakahatchee Strand State Preserve, Collier-Seminole State Park, and Briggs Nature Center are all just a short drive from five-star hotels.

Everglades National Park's westernmost visitor center is less that an hour away in Everglades City. From there, day-trippers can explore the Ten Thousand Islands and the Everglades backcounty, or continue down the Tamiami Trail (US 41) to the Big Cypress National Preserve, Miccosukee Indian Cultural Center, and Shark Valley Observation Tower, and return to Naples in time for a walk on the beach before dinner.

### ▓ BEACHES

Tens of thousands of visitors trek annually to the Naples area with the sole purpose in mind of shedding their stress on more than 40 miles of Gulf of Mexico beaches. Two of the city's six public beaches are listed on the national survey of "Best American Public Beaches" by University of Maryland researcher Stephen Leatherman, a.k.a. "Dr. Beach."

### ▓ DELNOR-WIGGINS PASS STATE RECREATION AREA

[Fig. 19] Residents and visitors who flock to this 166-acre narrow barrier island, separated from the mainland by mangrove swamps and tidal creeks, understand why it's perennially among Leatherman's top 10 best beaches. Amenities include wide, clean stretches of sand, lifeguard stations, an observation tower, shaded picnic tables, barbecue grills, a pavilion, bathhouses with restrooms, changing areas, and showers.

The beach is an excellent place for shelling. Most facilities are wheelchair accessible. Fishermen can angle in the surf at Wiggins Pass on the park's north end. Pompano fishing during the cooler months has become popular in recent years as the species has rebounded. The bait of choice is sand fleas that you dig yourself at the beach or purchase from a bait store.

Bring your binoculars and you'll have a chance at seeing West Indian manatees, dolphins, ospreys, and egrets, herons, and other wading birds.

On Wednesday mornings from the first of December to the end of April, interpretive programs conducted by park rangers focus on endangered sea turtles and their nesting habits, native plants, marine mammals, beach habitats, shorebirds, and other environmental topics. Reservations are required for all programs.

**Directions:** 11100 Gulfshore Drive North, off Blue Bill. Off I-75, Exit 17 West.

**Activities:** Swimming, windsurfing, fishing, picnics, interpretive programs.

**Facilities:** Bathhouses with restrooms, changing areas, showers, barbecue grills, concession, observation tower, picnic tables, pavilion.

**Dates:** Open daily 8 a.m. to sunset.

**Fees:** There are admission charges per car and for walk-ins and bikers. No charge for those age 5 and under.

**For more information:** Delnor-Wiggins Pass State Recreation Area, 11100 Gulf Shore Drive, Naples, FL 33963. Phone (941) 597-6196.

### ▓ CLAM PASS BEACH COUNTY PARK

[Fig. 19(2)] Also among Leatherman's "best beaches," Clam Pass is accessed by a 10-foot-wide, 0.75 mile boardwalk through a mangrove swamp and by continuous free tram rides provided for all visitors. The Registry Resort operates the water sports equipment rental and snack bar concessions on the beach. The wide, clean beach has good surf and long stretches for walking and sunbathing. Canoe trips in the tidal creeks are a good opportunity to observe birds and other wildlife that live in the mangroves.

**Directions:** Off Seagate Drive, behind the Registry Resort.

**Activities:** Swimming, beach walking, windsurfing, canoeing, and fishing.

**Facilities:** Bathhouse with restrooms and showers, snack bars and water sports equipment and beach chair rentals.

**Dates:** Open daily sunrise to sunset.

**Fees:** None.

**For more information:** Collier County Parks and Recreation, 3300 Santa Barbara Boulevard, Naples, 34116. Phone (941) 353-0404.

### BAREFOOT BEACH PRESERVE

[Fig. 19(1)] The 342-acre preserve, on a barrier island in the Gulf of Mexico, has immaculate beaches, excellent surf, and an aquatic garden with lush vegetation and wildlife, including loggerhead sea turtles.

**Directions:** Access is from Bonito Beach Road (SR 865).

**Activities:** Swimming, other outdoor recreation.

**Facilities:** Beach, restrooms, and a picnic area.

**Dates:** Open daily sunrise to sunset.

**Fees:** None.

**For more information:** Collier County Parks and Recreation, 3300 Santa Barbara Boulevard, Naples, 34116. Phone (941) 353-0404.

### LOWDERMILK PARK

[Fig. 19] The fully developed municipal park has 1,000 feet of Gulf beach. It's a typical Florida city beach with all the amenities that can draw a big crowd of beach-goers pursuing a variety of activities from volleyball, to soaking up the rays, to just watching the crowd go by. It has convenient metered parking right next to the bear. Duck ponds and sand chairs for wheelchair-bound beach-goers are special features that are available.

**Directions:** Near downtown Naples at the corner of Gulf Shore and Banyan Boulevards.

**Activities:** Swimming, beach walking, volleyball, picnicking.

**Facilities:** Restrooms with showers, picnic areas, concession stand, pavilions, playground, volleyball courts.

**Dates:** Open daily sunrise to sunset.

**Fees:** There is no admission charge. On-street metered parking.

**For more information:** Phone (941) 434-4698.

### NAPLES MUNICIPAL BEACH AND FISHING PIER

[Fig. 19] This beach is a popular in-town place for swimming, sunbathing, walking, and jogging. The 1,000-foot-long pier, originally built in 1887, is a cherished landmark that attracts lots of different kinds of people.

# The Stingray Shuffle

Before venturing into the warm waters of the Gulf of Mexico, swimmers are frequently greeted by signs urging them to "Do the stingray shuffle." These words of advice are intended to enable beachgoers to enjoy their outing, and avoid the painful, sometimes serious, injuries that can result from stepping inadvertently on bluntnose stingrays.

The sand-colored bluntnose rays, averaging about 6 inches across their body, are normally not aggressive. They bury themselves in shallow waters near the shore as protection, and attack only when threatened by a large predator, such as a human foot coming down on top of them.

By shuffling their feet, bathers usually startle the rays and send them into deeper waters. Young rays are considered the most dangerous, because they haven't learned to recognize humans and take evasive action. Mature rays usually stay out of harm's way in deeper offshore waters.

The ray's stinger is on the spine of its tail, near the base of its body. It's made of dentin, a hard, bony substance similar to teeth, and is covered in skin. The toxin the stinger secretes tightens the small veins around the wound. The sting paralyzes small fish that rays feed on. It can stop the heart of a small dog. It is potentially fatal to people with heart or respiratory problems.

Serious, and not-so-serious anglers come at all hours to fish for a variety of the area's gamefish. Seasonal varieties include Spanish mackerel, whiting, pompano, redfish, and even snook. Check with the folks at the concession stand (you'll have to buy bait anyway) about what's hot and what's not.

Others come to stroll the wooden decks and watch the water and flocks of brown pelicans that gather around the pier pilings and battle for discarded fish parts. There's always something going on. Pelicans battle for discarded fish, schools of baitfish swirl around the pilings, and of course every bent rod answers the question "What's biting?"

**Directions:** Gulf Shore Boulevard and 12th Avenue South, near downtown.

**Activities:** Fishing, swimming, walking, jogging.

**Facilities:** Bait shops, fish-cleaning tables, covered shelter at the end of the pier, snack bar, restrooms. Parking in nearby lots and at street meters. Handicapped parking is available at the pier's 12th Avenue entrance.

**Dates:** Open daily 24 hours; concessions open from early morning to early evening.

**Fees:** None.

**For more information:** Phone (941) 434-4696.

## ▨ VANDERBILT BEACH COUNTY PARK

[Fig. 19] This strip of Gulf of Mexico beach between Clam Pass County Park and Delnor-Wiggins Pass State Recreation Area is a favorite destination for Naples area families. There is plenty of walking and stretching room, and a clear, gentle surf. A tropical hammock in the park offers opportunities to observe birds, small animals, and native vegetation. Shelling is good in early morning before too many people have passed.

**Directions:** Located on the west end of Vanderbilt Drive.

**Activities:** Swimming, sunning, beach games, bird and wildlife observation.

**Facilities:** Parking, bike racks, restrooms and showers, wheelchair accessibility. Restaurants are nearby.

**Dates:** Open sunrise to sunset.

**Fees:** There is a parking fee.

**For more information:** Collier County Parks and Recreation, 3300 Santa Barbara Boulevard, Naples, 34116. Phone (941) 353-0404.

# The Conservancy Naples Nature Center

[Fig. 19(3)] The Conservancy of Southwest Florida's Naples Nature Center combines a museum of natural history with a wildlife rehabilitation center. Located in a wooded enclave, off a busy urban boulevard, the Museum of Natural History has "do-touch" tanks where visitors can touch a snake, bird and butterfly eggs, bird skeletons, and a gopher tortoise, and even count an alligator's teeth.

Since 1974, the Wildlife Rehabilitation Center has treated more than 1,700 injured wild birds and animals, including over 100 species of birds, mammals, and reptiles. About 60 percent have fully recuperated and been returned to the wild. Visitors can watch the recuperating patients through the O.W.L.S. online video monitoring system. Bald eagles, red-shouldered hawks, pelicans, raccoons, turtles, and others with catastrophic injuries have a permanent home.

Naturalists lead nature walks and boat tours through the mangrove forest adjacent to the center. Visitors can explore on their own in rental canoes and kayaks. In summer, teenagers may participate in sailing and canoeing lessons. The Nature Store gift shop has a comprehensive book selection, covering every species of Florida plants, birds, fish, and other animals.

**Directions:** 14th Avenue North, off Goodlette-Frank Road.

**Activities:** Nature education, nature trail walks, and mangrove boat tours. Canoe and kayak rentals, sailing classes.

**Facilities:** Museum, gift shop, restrooms, picnic tables, and wildlife rehabilitation center.

**Dates:** Open Monday through Saturday year-round; Sunday, January to March.

**Fees:** There are charges for admission and tours. No admission charge for conservancy members.

**For more information:** The Conservancy of Southwest Florida, 1450 Merrihue Drive, Naples, FL 34102. Phone (941) 262-0304.

# The Conservancy Briggs Nature Center at Rookery Bay Estuarine Research Reserve

[Fig. 18(3)] A visit to The Conservancy Briggs Nature Center means a chance to learn about and explore many of the distinct native habitats and wildlife found in Southwest Florida from the comfort of an elevated boardwalk. An interpretive center and a butterfly garden add to the educational opportunities.

Over the past several decades coastal development has destroyed many of South Florida's vital estuaries, where fresh water from the land meets and mingles with ocean salt water. Only in recent years have substantial efforts been made to preserve these irreplaceable resources. A campaign to save Rookery Bay, 10 miles southeast of Naples, began in 1966 when a small group of concerned individuals grew alarmed at the area's proposed development. Two years later, the citizens group incorporated as the Collier County Conservancy became The Conservancy of Southwest Florida.

In 1978, the conservancy's dedicated efforts paid off. Rookery Bay was designated a National Estuarine Research Reserve, under management of the Florida Department of Environmental Protection. The Briggs Memorial Nature Center, which opened to the public in 1982, serves as the reserve's interpretive center.

An elevated 0.5-mile boardwalk takes visitors through the 12,700-acre reserve's six environmental communities: oak scrub, pine flatwoods, wet hammock, fringe marsh, brackish pond, and mangrove fringe. Before you set off, walk through the interpretive center's Butterfly Garden and see how many of the native plants and 27 species of butterflies you can identify. The boardwalk is circular and goes through four of the communities twice, although information at each numbered station is different. During the November to March winter season, staffers are on the boardwalk to answer questions and point out things of special and unusual interest.

The oak scrub community grows upon ancient dunes, sand bars, and beaches formed tens of thousands of years ago when sea levels were much higher. Named for the scrubby, stunted nature of its vegetation, the oak scrub's dominant trees and shrubs are Chapman's oak (*Quercus chapmanii*), myrtle oak (*Quercus myrrtifolia*), and sand live oak (*Quercus geminata*).

The sandy soil is devoid of many nutrients and fails to trap and hold moisture. Plants and animals that live in this environment have adapted to the heat, drought, and fires. The oaks spread their roots laterally through the soil to absorb water more easily. Their thick waxy leaves are also designed to retain moisture.

The Florida wild rosemary *(Ceraitola ericoides)* is a member of the crowberry family not related to the herb rosemary used in cooking. Like other scrub oak plants, Florida wild rosemary's growth habits are similar to those of plants from Mediterranean climates. Small, hard, shiny, and waxy leaves prevent excessive desiccation, drying out that could be harmful or fatal to the plant.

Saw palmetto *(Serenoa repens)* looks at first like a bush, but it's actually a tree, growing up to 6 or 7 feet high, with its trunk deeply rooted underground. Anyone who has ever been jabbed or sawed by the palmetto's prickly edged leaf clusters knows where the plant gets its name. Like slash pine, it is remarkably fire resistant. As quickly as the flames are doused, new green shoots generate from the trunk's undamaged parts.

A large variety of lichens grow on the scrub community's trees and on the ground. Walking through the oak scrub, your feet crunch on grayish popcorn lichen. Lichens are made up of algae and fungi that live together in a mutually beneficial relationship called symbiosis. Fungi wrap around the algae and absorb water, minerals, and organic matter from tree bark, rocks, and soil. Algae in turn produce carbohydrates through photosynthesis.

The threatened Florida scrub jay *(Aphelocoma couerulescens)* is one of the most celebrated residents of the community. A member of the crow and jay family, and related to a species of California scrub jay, the turquoise and white scrub jay gained notoriety in the 1970s as the first known animal species to practice "helper at the nest" behavior, which scientists have since discovered in other bird and animal species. Birds that don't mate during their first season as adults remain at the nest and help their parents raise their siblings. This gives the young a better opportunity for survival and provides the helpers with on-the-job experience. Due to limited habitat, some of the young stay with their families for several years. Unlike common blue jays, scrub jays are nonaggressive and frequently perch in nearby trees as if posing for pictures. They will also show up for handouts at the reserve's picnic tables.

The pine flatwoods community is dominated by slash pines that attain their height of 100 feet or more because the elevation of their habitat is slightly decreased and the sandy soil contains more nutrients than soil in the oak scrub community. The open environment makes it an attractive habitat for over 100 animal species, including owls, warblers, woodpeckers, green anole, Cuban anole, Southeast five-lined skink, gopher frogs *(Rana capito aesopus)*, Florida mouse *(Podomys floridanus)*, and Eastern indigo snake.

Fast as proverbial greased lightning, green anoles *(Anolis carolinensis)* use their speed to evade a host of potential predators. Like chameleons, they can change colors in a matter of seconds. Skinks have detachable tails. If a predator bites it off, the skink quickly grows a new one. The threatened blue-black indigo snake is North America's largest nonvenomous reptile, growing to a length of 8 feet. Its reddish or blackish jaw and larger size differentiate it from the similar black racer (*Caluber constrictor*), which grows to about 4 feet. Both species immobilize small animals with their powerful jaws. Destruction of gopher tortoise burrows, which the snakes and other animals use as dens and fireproof shelters, is a major reason for the indigo's decline.

The wet hammock community is an environment rich with lush vegetation. A lower elevation makes it the recipient of water runoff from surrounding lands. As a result, the soil contains more organic materials than that in the oak scrub and pine flatwoods. These conditions foster the growth of a dense, intertwined thicket containing plants such as wax myrtle, dahoon holly (*Ilex cassine*), red bay (*Persea borbonia*), leather fern (*Acrosichum danaeifolium*), swamp fern (*Blechnum serrulatum*), and poison ivy (*Toxicodendron radicans*).

Cabbage palm, also known as sabal palm, which is the Florida state tree, thrives in the wet hammock's drier areas. Some cabbage palms have smooth trunks, and others are girdled by old leaf stems called "boots" or "jacks" because they look so much liked an inverted bootjack. The jacks trap debris and moisture, enabling algae and fungi to grow. They, in turn, provide a hospitable environment for serpent figs, a type of epiphyte. The cabbage palm's edible center—its heart—is a gourmet delicacy that tastes mildly like cabbage. When the heart is removed, the tree dies.

Many of these plants have proven beneficial to animals and humans. Indians and early white settlers made tea from wax myrtle bark as a remedy for dysentery, ulcers, gastritis, and other stomach ailments. Birds feed on the wax myrtle's small, green, wax-coated berries, and humans use the berries to make fragrant candles. Birds also feed on the bright red berries of the dahoon holly and poison ivy.

Also commonly found in the hammocks, the leather fern is the largest American fern species. Its tough, leathery leaves can be more than 14 feet long, and they have adapted to tolerate salt and intense heat. Scientists studying fossils say contemporary leather ferns are similar to those that vegetarian dinosaurs fed on millions of years ago.

The rustling you might hear in the dense vegetation could be made by a nine-banded armadillo (*Dasypus novemcinctus*), a species that has migrated from Mexico and Texas across the southeastern United States, as far north as Tennessee and North Carolina. Like a medieval knight, the armadillo is clad in an armored exoskeleton. Bony silvery brown plates sheath its upper body, tail, and the top of its head. It looks as slow and cumbersome as a World War II tank, but when it senses danger it can run away surprisingly fast. It can also roll up into a tight ball to protect its soft, unarmored belly. An armadillo's sharp claws can dig a burrow with lightning speed. It's a strong swimmer, which explains its presence on many Florida and southeastern U.S. barrier islands. It mates in summer, and each litter, born the next spring, has identical quadruplets.

The fringe marsh community is a blend of salt water and fresh water marshes, with open expanses of sawgrass and black rush. High tides generated by storms bring in salt water, and tropical summer rainfall adds fresh water. Sawgrass (*Caldium jamaicense*) a freshwater species, dominates the first half of the marsh. Halophilic, salt-tolerant black rush (*Juncus roemerianus*), dominates the second half of the marsh, closer to the source of the high tides.

The marsh is a teeming city of birds, fish, and insects. Mosquitofish gobble up mosquito larvae, inadvertently fattening themselves into a feast for bigger fish and birds. Turtles and crayfish sate themselves on the numerous marsh grasses. Dragonflies go after insects and worms and become snacks for ospreys, bald eagles, turkey vultures, black vultures, and red-shouldered hawks gliding through the air currents above.

A black vulture (*Coragyps atratus*) can be distinguished from a turkey vulture by its white wing patches and short, stubby tail feathers. The turkey vulture has two-toned, pale, silver and black wings and a longer tail. Both have large wingspans—from 5 to 6 feet—and feed mainly on carcasses of dead animals. They also kill lizards and snakes and pilfer other birds' eggs and nestlings.

Large mammals in the fringe marsh include the raccoon *(Proycon lotor)*, a mostly nocturnal roamer whose wanderings can be traced by its five-toed front and hind footprints. Its black mask is nature's way of characterizing this wily thief, which raids bird, turtle, and reptile nests and comes brazenly into picnic areas and subdivisions to forage. Cute as they are, raccoons frequently carry rabies and contact with them should be avoided.

River otters leave a wide meandering trail in the mud. These playful creatures can often be seen chasing fish and each other through the shallow water. You're far less likely to see a bobcat (*Lynx rufus*). North America's most common species of wildcat hunts by night and by day hides in the shady trees of the fringe marsh and wet hammock.

The brackish pond community of Overlook Pond is a placid, shallow pool almost entirely girded by a fringe of red mangroves. Like the fringe marsh, Overlook Pond is a brackish blend of fresh water and salt water. Summer rains fill it with fresh water, and high tides furnish salt water. Less than 2 feet above sea level, its central open area separates it from the fringe marsh community. Plentiful fish and

**RIVER OTTER**
(Lutra canadensis)
A shy, water-loving mammal seen in coastal rivers and occasionally in marsh areas.

# Collier-Seminole State Park

*It's difficult, but not impossible, to spot bobcats, black bears, and
Florida panthers in this 6,430-acre preserve.*

ROOKERY BAY
HENDERSON CREEK
41 90
JOHNSON BAY
Marco Island Airport
TARPON BAY
951
Marco
BIG MARCO PASS
COLLIER BAY
ADDISON BAY
92
MUD BAY
BLACKWATER ROYAL PALM HAMMOCK CREEK
41 90
Tigertail Beach
92
Marco Beach
GULF OF MEXICO
BARFIELD BAY
BLUE HILL BAY
GOODLAND BAY
892 Goodland
SUGAR BAY
BLACKWATER BAY
Shell Key
BUTTONWOOD BAY
PUMPKIN BAY
CAXAMBAS BAY
Horrs
Island
Tripod Key
FAKIN UNION BAY
SANTINE BAY
Helen Key
Coon Key
Turtle Key
Kice Island
GULLIVAN BAY
Gullivan Key
Morgan Beach
Cape Romano Island
White Horse Key
Panther Key
FAKAHATCHEE PASS
Cape Romano
Round Key
N

● Collier-Seminole State Park

Cape Romano-Ten Thousand
Islands Aquatic Preserve Boundary

Trail

Marsh

Ref: Delorme Florida Atlas and Gazetteer

plants make this an avian smorgasbord. Great egret, little blue heron, green heron, ibis, and other wading birds stalk fish with keen eyes and swift, deadly accurate aim. Pied-billed grebe, mottled duck (*Anas fulvigula*), merganser (*Lophodytes cucullatus*), wood duck (*Aix sponsa*), and green-winged teal (*Anas crecca*) float high on the surface, diving under the water for small fish and aquatic plants.

During summer, The Conservancy of Southwest Florida offers day camps for young people who can learn about the natural environment, canoeing, map and compass reading skills, and other skills that will make them more comfortable in the outdoors.

**Directions:** Drive south on US 41 approximately 7 miles. Turn right on SR 951 and travel 3 miles to Shell Island Road. Turn right again and follow Shell Island Road to the nature center entrance.

**Activities:** Plant and wildlife observation from a 0.5 mile boardwalk through six environmental communities, summer day camps for young people.

**Facilities:** Visitor center, restrooms, gift shop, picnic tables.

**Dates:** Open daily.

**Fees:** Admission fee is charged.

**Closest town:** The preserve is 13 miles southeast of Naples.

**For more information:** The Conservancy of Southwest Florida, 1450 Merrihue Drive, Naples, FL 34102. Phone (941) 262-0304.

# Collier-Seminole State Park

[Fig. 19, Fig. 20] The 6,430-acre preserve, on the Tamiami Trail (US 41), 17 miles southeast of Naples, is a meeting place of cypress and mangrove swamps and tropical forests. The cypress heads, salt marshes, hardwood hammocks and majestic battalions of royal palms have provided at least a resting site for more than 120 species of birds. Bottle-nosed dolphin, alligators, and endangered West Indian manatee are often seen in the park's waterways.

Just after passing through the entrance station, look to your right. This clumsy, Rube Goldbergian-looking piece of machinery is the Bay City Walking Dredge. It was developed in the 1920s to gouge out the Tamiami Trail between Tampa and Miami.

Visitors who hike a 6.5-mile loop trail through slash pines and scrubby pine flatwoods have a good chance of seeing many of the park's resident bird species as well as opossum, armadillo, marsh rabbit, gray squirrel, river otter, raccoon, and white-tailed deer. Much more difficult, if not all but impossible to observe, are bobcats, black bear, and the nearly extinct Florida panther. The western part of the trail normally is wet, and the eastern end is slightly more elevated and drier.

If you bring your own canoe or rent one from the park's concessionaire, you can explore the mangrove-lined tidal waterways and side creeks that wind through the park. Bring a compass and a good sense of direction—it's easy to get confused, even lost, in these crisscrossing creeks, which are subject to strong tidal currents.

The 0.9-mile Royal Palm Hammock Trail goes through white mangrove forest, salt marsh, and tropical hammocks with stands of straight, stately Florida royal palm (*Roystonea regia*). Maturing at 100 feet or more, with thick plumes of dark green, feathery fronds, and clusters of white flowers, the smooth-barked native of Cuba is frequently taken from swamps and marshes to line roadways and driveways.

Collier-Seminole is very popular from November through March, when cooler, drier weather keeps mosquitoes and other pests at their lowest ebb. Hot, humid summer brings out the mosquitoes in vicious black, biting clouds. Even with a heavy dousing of repellent, you can be covered from head to foot in a matter of seconds. You may want to consider a beekeeper's-style hat, with a mesh veil.

Camping is available in over 130 primitive backcountry and full-service sites. Make advance reservations, especially in winter. The park also has a boat ramp and boat basin, offering access to the Gulf of Mexico and Ten Thousand Islands. Saltwater fishing is allowed with the appropriate license. An interpretive museum, designed like a Seminole War blockhouse, has natural history and cultural displays.

**Directions:** US 41, 17 miles southeast of Naples.

**Activities:** Camping, hiking, backpacking, fishing, boating, picnicking.

**Facilities:** Primitive and full-service campgrounds; museum, restrooms, picnic areas; boat ramp; canoe rental.

**Dates:** Open year-round.

**Fees:** There is an admission fee.

**Closest town:** Naples is 17 miles north of the park entrance.

**For more information:** Collier-Seminole State Park, 20200 E. Tamiami Trail, Naples, FL 34114. Phone (941) 394-3397.

# Corkscrew Swamp Sanctuary

[Fig. 18(2)] Nature lovers will find Corkscrew Sanctuary one of the most memorable experiences of their vacation, and bird watchers will delight in the chance to add dozens of new names to their life list in just one afternoon. Nevertheless, were it not for the determined efforts of a consortium of conservation organizations, this primeval chunk of wilderness, which safeguards North America's largest remaining stand of ancient baldcypress trees and hundreds of species of plants, birds, and other animals, would have been lost.

During the 1940s and 1950s, Florida's majestic cypresses were relentlessly cleared for their valuable lumber. Impervious to decay and insects, cypress was the wood of choice for the tens of thousands of new homes mushrooming across post-war America and Europe. What's now Corkscrew Swamp Sanctuary was primed for the saws.

The National Audubon Society was able to rally 14 conservation organizations into the Corkscrew Cypress Rookery Association. They worked out a preservation program with the timber companies that owned the land and purchased the initial acreage in 1954. It is operated today by the National Audubon Society.

Every season is a good season for viewing the sanctuary's wildlife. What you see depends on the time of year, water levels, and the good fortune to be in the right place at the right time. Bring plenty of film, zoom lenses, binoculars, and a bird identification book.

From the visitor center, a 2-mile elevated boardwalk winds through the environmental zones. Before heading out, ask about rare or unusual sightings during the previous days. Early morning and late afternoon are the best times to observe the largest numbers of wildlife. The walk is self-guiding, but Audubon Society volunteers patrol the boardwalk to answer visitors' questions and point out things of special interest.

Plan to take your time, stopping often along the boardwalk. Stay as quiet as possible, and let noisy visitors pass by. With a little patience, and keen observation, you'll be amazed at the birds and other wildlife that will suddenly become visible.

The boardwalk passes over a wetland prairie then plunges right into a mature cypress swamp. Watch where you walk! A pair of southeastern lubber grasshoppers (*Romalea microptera*) might be mating in the middle of the boardwalk. These giant, slow-moving insects—bright yellow, black, and red and up to 2.5 to 3 inches long—have short, stubby wings incapable of flight. The grasshoppers protect themselves by sending out a foul odor that successfully fends off most would-be predators.

A Big Cypress fox squirrel (*Sciurus niger*) often sits on the guard rail, cautiously twitching its nose at the scent of advancing humans. Its reddish brown coat and buff-colored tail markings set it apart from the gray body and white belly of the common Eastern gray squirrel (*Sciurus carolinensis*).

A barred owl (*Strix varia*), patrolling for fish, frogs, and rodents, lands on a low limb and watches stoically as visitors aim cameras and binoculars at his perch. Even when not seen, barred owls are often heard hooting their distinctive "Who-cooks-for-you-who-cooks-for-you."

FOX SQUIRREL
(*Sciurus niger*)

A black and yellow argiope (*Argiope aurania*), a brightly colored member of the orb-weaver family, wait patiently for prey in gigantic, zigzagging webs spun across several tree branches. If you accidentally run into the web, don't be concerned; an argiope is not harmful to humans.

Lettuce Lake, a low, clear area in the

*American alligators are the largest reptiles in North America and the loudest, with males bellowing lustily during the spring mating season. For a reptile, the female is an extraordinary parent.*

middle of the baldcypress swamp, teems with activity. Adult alligators cruise at snout level through big heads of water lettuce (*Pistia stratiotes*). The floating aquatic plant's complex root system is a haven for small fish and crayfish. Don't be tempted to gather it for a salad though: It's toxic to humans.

Under the boardwalk, newly born alligators left on their own soon after birth huddle together for protection on the muddy fringes of the lake. At this stage in life, they have to rely on small fish, frogs, and insects for survival. When they are much older and stronger, they'll be able to pursue large fish, waterfowl, and small mammals.

Brown and green anoles (small lizards, *Anolis sagrei* and *Anolis carolinensis*) scuttle swiftly along the railings. Green tree frogs chirp unseen among the leaves. Large pig frogs (*Rana grylio*) grunt in the water. Their meaty hind legs are a gourmet dish. Mosquitofish feed greedily on mosquito larvae and are in turn a tasty dish for larger fish, birds, and alligators.

Anywhere along the boardwalk you might spot great egrets, little blue heron (*Egretta caerulea*), green heron, wood storks, and black-crowned night heron.

High above, black vultures (*Coragyps atratus*), turkey vultures (*Cathartes aura*), and red-shouldered hawks (*Butteo lineatus*) glide effortlessly through the warm thermals keeping their sharp eyes focused for small prey and carrion on the ground far below.

Fresh from a meal-hunting plunge in the water, anhingas (*Anhinga anhinga*) rest on branches, and spread their silver and black wings to dry. Unlike other water birds, anhingas lack the water repellent coating necessary to keep their feathers waterproof. Anhingas are also nicknamed "snakebirds" because they swim after fish with their long, S-curved necks above the surface of the water.

Double-crested cormorants (*Phalacrocorax aritus*) also lack waterproofing oils and must spread their greenish black wings to dry after a foray in the water. This underwater acrobat is shorter and thicker than an anhinga. It swims with a dolphin's agility, with its hooked beak designed to catch, rather than spear, small and medium size fish. It nests in baldcypress and mangroves, in colonies that include anhinga, herons, and other birds.

Smaller birds often sighted in the sanctuary are great-crested flycatcher (*Myiarchus crinitus*), Eastern phoebe (*Syornis phoebe*), Carolina wren (*Thryothorus ludovicianus*), northern cardinal (*Cardinalis cardinalis*), white-eyed vireo (*Vireo griseus*), pine warbler (*Dendroica pinus*), and northern parula warbler (*Parula americana*).

Visitors frequently hear the rat-tat-tat drumming of pileated woodpeckers, which carve large rectangular nesting cavities in tree trunks. The large black birds with a bright red crown are easy to spot flying through the treetops and landing on the trunk outside their nest cavities. Sometimes they can be seen using their strong beaks to tear away chunks of tree bark in search of insects. After the nesting period, the woodpecker's cozy nest is often taken over by other small birds, squirrels, wood ducks, and rat snakes. The red-bellied woodpecker (*Melanerpes carolinus*), which is smaller and has a small red patch on its head, is often mistaken for the red-headed woodpecker (*Melanerpes erythrocephalus*) which is black and white with a solid red head and neck.

Limpkins (*Aramus guarauna*), a Florida bird species of special concern, can often be seen wading through dense vegetation in shallow water searching for apple snails.

The sanctuary is home to one of North America's largest colonies of wood storks. Also called wood ibis, ironhead, flinthead, and preacher bird, the endangered species is the only member of the stork family that makes its home in the United States. It catches fish and crabs by wading patiently through muddy water with its beak submerged, grabbing its prey and swallowing it instantly. Now you see it now you don't: The closing of a wood stork's beak is one of the swiftest moves in the animal world.

When conditions allow, wood storks nest from November through June. In the sanctuary, large colonies nest together high in baldcypress trees on thin platforms of sticks and vegetation. Males and females bond by clacking their bills and making coordinated body movements. A female typically lays three or four eggs, which incubate from 28 to 32 days. The nesting cycle from mating to fledgling of the young takes about four months, during which adults and chicks consume about 425 to 450 pounds of fish.

To breed successfully, wood storks must constantly consume large amounts of fish. And because storks hunt by feel rather than by sight, fish must be available in abundant, concentrated quantities. During the dry winter season, when water holes normally are reduced, fish are more tightly massed, making it easy for storks to satisfy their chicks' insatiable appetites. When rain and dry cycles don't occur on schedule, or when water flowing to the grasslands is interrupted, the rare birds' nesting activity is sharply curtailed.

Corkscrew's crowning glory is its magnificent stands of baldcypress (*Taxodium disicum*). These giants are the last of the baldcypress forests that once dominated the swamps of the southeastern United States and southern Florida. Most of Corkscrew's cypress trees were saplings when Columbus made his first voyage to the New World at the end of the fifteenth century. Allowed to flourish undisturbed, these 500-year-old titans tower 120 to 130 feet above the floor of the swamp.

Pond cypress (*Taxodium disticum* var. *nutans*) is smaller than baldcypress, growing to a still-impressive 80 to 90 feet. Its bark is lighter gray, and its needles point upward, while those of baldcypress are flatter and straighter.

Red maples are the sanctuary's second largest trees, reaching 90 to 100 feet. Although their counterparts in colder parts of the country lose their leaves in fall and enter a dormant state until spring, the sanctuary's red maples are leafless for only a brief time in midwinter and initiate new growth soon after their leaves fall.

Pond apple (*Annona glabra*) grows to about 50 feet. Its fruit, which looks like a greenish yellow Granny Smith apple, is a favorite food of squirrels, raccoons, birds, and other creatures. The bark is a home for orchids and other air plants.

Strangler fig is one of the predatory plants of the forest. Often reaching 50 to 60 feet or more, the strangler fig's roots are often thought to be vines growing on a host tree. As the roots grow, they wrap around the host tree. The fig's red and yellow fruit is a favorite food of pileated woodpeckers and other birds.

Over two dozen types of ferns provide a lush, tropical groundcover in places. A subspecies of Boston fern (*Nephrolepis biseratta*) is a threatened Florida plant. Strap fern (*Campyloneurum phyllitidis*), a swordlike species that grows in a clump on top of cypress knees and at the base of trees, is listed as a Florida threatened plant.

Resurrection fern, which attaches itself to the trunks and branches of many swamp trees, is a gauge of the sanctuary's rainfall. Leaves that are brown, curled, and seemingly dead indicate a recent lack of precipitation. But after a rainfall, it's possible to watch the "dead" leaves uncurl and turn a brilliant, lively green. Water fern (*Salvinia minima*) is a shade-loving plant that floats on the surface of the water, where it is sometimes misidentified as duckweed, another aquatic plant species.

Spanish moss, which drapes tree branches in wispy grey veils, isn't a moss at all, but an epiphyte, drawing moisture and nutrients only from rainfall and airborne organic matter that it traps. Like other species of air plants, it's not harmful to the host tree. All air plants are part of the Pineapple family.

Swamp lilies bloom virtually year-round, and most profusely in late summer. They're a popular munching food for white-tailed deer. Summer also sees a profusion of swamp hibiscus (*Hibiscus coccineus*), which catches the eye with its enormous, five-petaled, vibrant red flowers up to 8 inches wide on a plant that can grow up to 5 feet tall.

The pine flatwoods community is a high, dry area that lacks some of the exotic flair of the wetland areas and is frequently given only passing scant notice by visitors more anxious to see alligators and flocks of wading birds. The area is only 18 to 20 feet above sea level and briefly floods and quickly drains in summer and fall. It is kept open by periodic natural and controlled man-made fires.

Slash pines are the only member of the Pine family in the sanctuary, and many of them are 100 to 200 years old. They manage to live to such an old age because their thick bark and high canopy protect them from fires. Slash pines killed by lightning remain resistant to rot and may stand in place for decades, continuing to provide roosting areas for ospreys and other birds.

Sabal palms are found in Corkscrew's pine flatwood and sometimes in the swamp. It gets its "cabbage" nickname from its edible heart, a gourmet delicacy which, when removed, is fatal to the tree.

From March through May, the open fields are brilliantly hued with wildflowers. Yellow bachelor's button *(Polygala rugelii)* is easily recognizable by its thimble-shape butter-colored flower that crowns a 1- to 2-foot stalk. Its roots smell like wintergreen. Yelloweyed grass (*Xyris* spp.) is a favorite food of the wild turkey. Its small flowers with three bright yellow petals, bloom in summer and fall. Wax myrtle is abundant in the pine flatwoods and other areas of the swamp. Controlled fires prevent it from shading out sapling pines and other plants that require full sunlight. Wax myrtle berries, similar to bay berries, are sometimes used to make aromatic candles.

In summer and early fall, star-topped sedges (*Dichromena colorata*) form a sea of white along pine flatwood trails. This and other sedges can be identified by their triangular stems.

**Directions:** From Naples, drive US 41/Tamiami Trail north 9 miles, to route 846 (Immokalee Road), then east for 21 miles to the sanctuary entrance.

**Activities:** Bird, animal, and plant viewing.

**Facilities:** Visitor center, gift shop, restrooms, 2-mile boardwalk. A short offshoot boardwalk and 45-seat amphitheater in the wet prairie are reserved for weekly nature education programs for school groups.

**Dates:** Open daily year-round.

**Fees:** An admission fee is charged.

**For more information:** Corkscrew Swamp Sanctuary, 375 Sanctuary Road, Naples, FL 34120. Phone (941) 348-9151. Fax (941) 348-9155.

# Koreshan State Historic Site

[Fig. 18(1)] In the mid-1890s Dr. Cyrus Read Teed, a charismatic former Union Army Medical Corps physician, led his followers into the wilderness, near present-day Corkscrew Swamp Sanctuary, and set about building a commune called New Jerusalem, on the banks of the Estero River. Inspired by a vision he called a "divine illumination," Teed changed his name to Koresh, which means Cyrus in Hebrew.

Hebrews in centuries before Christ often named themselves for Persian King Cyrus the Great, who freed them from bondage in Babylon and allowed them to return to Israel. In recent times, Branch Davidian leader David Koresh also adopted the name. Teed's principal tenets were total celibacy (similar to the Shakers in New England and Kentucky), and a communal sharing of worldly possessions.

The sect practiced equality for women long before the concept of women's suffrage was accepted by American and European society. Koresh envisioned a city of 10 million people, covering 300 square miles. But the commune's population never exceeded 200. Although the Koreshans died out, several of their buildings and artifacts are preserved at the state park.

**Directions:** Located near the small community of Estero. Take US 41 north of Naples to Corkscrew Road then go west. Or take I-75 north to Exit 19 (Corkscrew Road). The site is about 2 miles west of the Interstate.

**Activities:** Camping, picnicking, canoeing in the Estero River, viewing historic sites, narrated tours. A Civil War reenactment is conducted in the fall.

**Facilities:** Campsites, picnic area, restrooms, canoe launching area.

**Dates:** Open year-round.

**Fees:** There is an admission charge.

**Closest town:** Naples is about 20 miles south.

**For more information:** Koreshan State Historic Site, PO Box 7, Estero, FL 33928. Phone (941) 992-0311.

# Lake Trafford

[Fig. 18] Lake Trafford, about 30 miles northeast of Naples, and 3 miles west of the largely Hispanic and Seminole farming community of Immokalee, is the largest lake south of Lake Okeechobee. The 1,500-acre freshwater lake plays a key role in the area's ecosystem, and serves as a destination for anglers wishing to challenge the legendary largemouth bass or fill a cooler with panfish.

The lake is the headwaters of the Corkscrew Swamp Sanctuary to the southwest, the Corkscrew Regional Ecosystem Watershed to the west, and the Fakahatchee Strand System to the south, which includes the Florida Panther National Refuge. These wetlands drain into important estuarine systems such as Estero Bay, Wiggins

Pass at Estero Bay, and Cape Romano. The lake is an integral contributor to the sheet flow that traverses such areas as the Corkscrew Regional Ecosystem Watershed and the Southern Golden Gates Estates area.

The quality of the lake and the associated watershed profoundly affects many wildlife species, and it offers a sanctuary for migrating birds. It's also a vital source of recreation for freshwater fishermen and boaters.

Conservationists compare the lake to a supermarket for migrating birds. During dry seasons, fish accumulate in reduced pockets of water, where they provide easy feeding for wood storks, ibis, herons, egrets, and other wading bird species. When the lake is unhealthy, bird populations in Corkscrew Swamp and other neighboring areas noticeably decline. A large number of alligators make their home in the lake, feeding on the abundant fish and unwary wading birds.

In recent years, Trafford has suffered from excessive organic muck accumulations, loss of submergent plant communities, periodic weed infestations, and several moderate to severe fish kills. In April 1996, a catastrophic fish kill occurred caused by a massive algae bloom. Although the fish populations quickly rebounded, the tragedy rallied support for the lake's restoration.

A deep build-up of organic muck on the bottom of the lake is causing problems with the ecosystem by preventing the growth of native aquatic plants, which freshwater fish depend on during part of their life cycle. The muck was largely generated by hydrilla (*Hydrilla verticillata*), an exotic aquatic plant that found its way into the lake in the early 1980s. The hydrilla took over, choking out native grasses and other vegetation. When dying, or when treated with contact herbicides, the dead hydrilla falls to the lake bottom where it forms the thick layers of sludge. In late 1998, a $16 million federal, state, and local effort was initiated to remove 8 million cubic yards of muck and restore the lake to its natural, healthy state.

Lake Trafford Marina is the lake's commercial hub. Fishing guide "Ski" Olesky and his wife Annie know the troubled lake better than most trained naturalists. Their busy store caters to fishermen from many states and foreign countries, who come here year-round to pursue trophy class largemouth Florida black bass, crappie, bluegill, shellcracker, and other species. Nonanglers take guided boat tours and air boat rides. The Oleskys have been in the forefront of efforts to restore the lake.

**Directions:** Off Collier County Road 82, 40 miles n. of Naples, 3 miles w. of Immokalee.

**Activities:** Fishing, boating, air boat tours.

**Facilities:** Marina store with fishing supplies, books, film, souvenirs, vending machines, restrooms, boat ramps, rental boats, full-service camping sites.

**Dates:** Open year-round.

**Fees:** There is no admission charge.

**Closest town:** Immokalee.

**For more information:** Lake Trafford Marina, 6001 Lake Trafford Road, Imokalee, FL 34142. Phone (941) 657-2401. Fax (941) 658-2401.

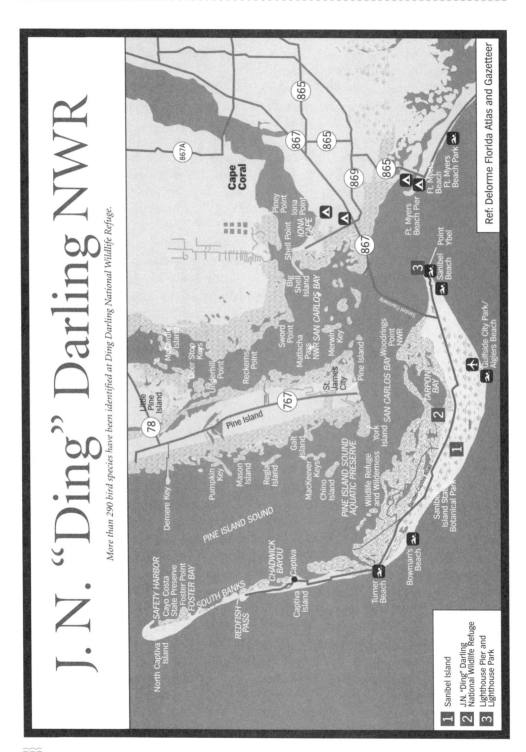

J. N. "Ding" Darling NWR

*More than 290 bird species have been identified at Ding Darling National Wildlife Refuge.*

Ref: Delorme Florida Atlas and Gazetteer

1 Sanibel Island

2 J.N. "Ding" Darling National Wildlife Refuge

3 Lighthouse Pier and Lighthouse Park

# J. N. "Ding" Darling National Wildlife Refuge

[Fig. 21 (2)] Tucked away amid condominiums and the busy beaches of Sanibel Island, the J. N. "Ding" Darling National Wildlife Refuge is a small, but wildlife-laden area that offers some of the best opportunities in Florida to see wading birds. The 5,220-acre refuge, established in 1945, is largely composed of mangrove estuaries and mud flats. Located along the Atlantic Flyway, the refuge serves as a permanent and seasonal residence for more than 290 bird species, some visiting from as far away as the Arctic Circle.

The big attraction is the appropriately named Wildlife Drive, a 5-mile, unpaved but smooth gravel road that winds through the mangroves into the heart of the refuge. Before taking the drive, be sure to pick up a copy of the Wildlife Drive Guide at the visitor center. Plan to take your time and pull over often. You'll discover one scenic view after another of open mud flats and busy wildlife. Sometimes the longer you stay at a spot the more you'll see.

Information signs and a bird viewing tower enhance the drive. Along Alligator Curve, alligators sometimes sun themselves along the banks. At another spot you'll see double-crested cormorants and anhingas swimming and feeding in the clear water. Anhingas spear their prey on their sharp bills and cormorants simply grab their prospective meal.

From the tower you might spot a flock of roseate spoonbills, which are in their brightest plumage between January and March. Mangrove cuckoos, ospreys, red-shouldered hawks, bald eagles, brown pelicans, and common moorhens reside at the refuge year-round and are often seen along the drive.

On any of the shallow flats look for the bluish-colored reddish egret. These dainty wading birds spread their wings to cast a shadow over the water so they can see their prey as they run after it. Other common wading birds in the refuge include great egrets, white ibis, yellow-crowned night herons, and great blue herons.

Scanning the clear waters, you might also see a blue crab walking sideways along the muddy bottom. Although too large to eat, it still gives the birds a wide berth. Raccoons can also be seen snooping carefully along the base of the mangrove trees, searching through the exposed roots for tasty morsels.

Interconnected walking trails lead to other observation points. The Shell Mound Trail winds through tangled vegetation to an ancient Calusa Indian shell mound. Tram tours and guided canoeing and kayak trips are also available during some seasons.

For the best wildlife viewing opportunities plan your trip for low tide when wading birds will be feeding. In the warm months plan your drive for early in the morning or late in the afternoon. In winter, migrating visitors like white pelicans and red-breasted mergansers (*Mergus serrator*) can be spotted.

The refuge was named for J. N. "Ding" Darling, an esteemed political cartoonist and lifelong conservationist. Born in Norwood, Michigan, in 1876, Darling was a two-time Pulitzer Prize-winning cartoonist whose political cartoons appeared in 130 daily newspapers. In Florida he was also known for focusing national attention on the plight of Florida's Key deer with a cartoon that depicted the end of the "toy deer." In 1934, Henry A. Wallace, Franklin Roosevelt's secretary of agriculture, appointed Darling chief of the biological survey (later to become the U.S. Fish and Wildlife Service). As one of his obligations, Darling agreed to do the artwork for the first Duck Stamp.

When Franklin Delano Roosevelt called the first North American Wildlife Conference in 1936, 1,500 conservationists attended. They adopted the constitution for the General Wildlife Federation and elected Darling the first president. This group's name was officially changed to National Wildlife Federation in 1938.

There's a replica of Darling's studio at the visitor center. On the last weekend of January the center celebrates J. N. "Ding" Darling's birthday.

There's also a brief orientation film shown every half hour at the visitor center. Particularly interesting is the refuge time line tracing the area from prehistory to 1978.

Carry insect repellant year-round for mosquitos and no-see-ums. In the summer expect high temperatures and high humidity. Picnicking and camping are not allowed in the refuge. Naturalist presentations and guided tours are mostly available during the winter months. Binoculars and spotting scopes are highly recommended.

**Directions:** From Naples travel north on SR 41, then west on SR 867 onto Sanibel Island. The refuge is 5 miles to the north.

**Activities:** Wildlife observation, hiking, canoeing.

**Facilities:** Visitor center, bookstore, wildlife drive.

**Dates:** Open year-round, sunrise to sunset. Closed on Fridays.

**Fees:** There is a fee to take the Wildlife Drive.

**Closest town:** On Sanibel Island. Fort Myers is 15 miles to the northeast.

**For more information:** J. N. "Ding" Darling NWR, One Wildlife Drive, Sanibel, FL 33957. Phone (941) 472-1100. Web site www.fws.gov/r4eao/wildlife/nwrjnd.html.

# Visiting Naples Area

### ECO-TOURS
### ORCHIDS & EGRETS, INC.

Naturalists lead half-day and full-day trips to the Everglades, Fakahatchee Strand State Preserve, Collier-Seminole State Park, the Ten Thousand Islands, Chokoloskee Bay, Corkscrew Swamp, and other wilderness areas. Pickups are made at all Naples area hotels, and travel is by air-conditioned van and quiet, low-impact boats. Take a camera, a zoom lens, and plenty of film. There are many opportunities to see and photograph manatees, alligators, and many species of birds. Lunch is included on full-day tours.

**For more information:** Orchids & Egrets, 238 Silverado Drive, Naples, FL 34119. Phone (941) 352-8586. Fax (941) 352-8598. Web site www.naturetour.com.

### NAPLES PRINCESS CRUISES

The 90-foot *Naples Princess* and 90-foot *Naples Royal Princess* are easy, comfortable ways to learn about the nature that surrounds the city of Naples. Naturalists from the Conservancy of Southwest Florida describe mangroves, birds, fish, and other animals during two-hour cruises through Naples Bay and into the Gulf of Mexico. A portion of the ticket price is donated to the conservancy.

**Directions:** Tours leave from Old Naples Seaport, 1001 10th Avenue South.

**Activities:** Basic sightseeing cruises, also breakfast, lunch, sunset hors d'oeuvre cruises, and sunset dinner cruises.

**Facilities:** Air-conditioned cabins, outside decks, full service bar, and restrooms.

**Dates:** Boats operate year-round.

**Fees:** There are charges for all tours.

**For more information:** Naples Princess Cruises, 1001 10th Avenue South, Naples, FL 34102. Phone (941) 649-2275.

### TIN CITY

Sightseeing boats and fishing excursions leave from the dock of this former clam shelling plant. Complete with wooden buildings and plank sidewalks, it's also an enjoyable place to browse for souvenirs in 40 shops and enjoy moderately priced seafood restaurants overlooking the waterfront.

**Directions:** Located on Naples Bay, 1200 5th Avenue South, downtown.

**For more information:** Phone (941) 262-4200.

### CARIBBEAN GARDENS

Formerly Jungle Larry's African Safari Park, this 52-acre wildlife and nature attraction includes tram tours through botanical gardens, bird, alligator, and animal shows, a petting zoo, a playground, picnic areas, boat rides, and wildlife lectures.

**Directions:** 1590 Goodlette-Frank Road.

**Activities:** Viewing birds and wild animals, lectures, tram tours, boat rides, animal shows.

**Facilities:** Restrooms, snack bars, petting zoo, walking trails, botanical gardens, playground.

**Dates:** Open daily year-round, except Thanksgiving, Christmas, and Easter.

**Fees:** There is an admission fee and charges for some activities.

**For more information:** Phone (941) 262-5409. Web site www.caribbeangardens.com.

## GOLF COURSES IN THE NAPLES AREA

A number of public and semiprivate courses in the self-proclaimed golf capitol of the world welcome visitors. Call ahead for available tee times and greens fees. Some semiprivate courses may restrict play to members and guests on weekends and other peak times.

### BOYNE USA SOUTH

18100 Royal Tree Parkway. 18-hole, par 72 public course on the edge of Everglades National Park. *Phone (941) 732-5108.*

### GLENN EAGLE

6680 Weston Way, Naples. Semiprivate 18 holes, par 70, designed by Mark Mc-Cumber. *Phone (941) 353-3699.*

### HIBISCUS GOLF CLUB

175 Doral Circle. 18 hole, par 71 public course. *Phone (941) 774-0088.*

### IRONWOOD GOLF CLUB

4710 Lakewood Boulevard. 18 hole, par 54 championship par 3, designed by Arthur Hills and Robert Cupp II. *Phone (941) 775-2584.*

### LELY RESORT-FLAMINGO ISLAND CLUB

8004 Lely Resort Boulevard. 36-hole, par 72 public course. Designed by Robert Trent Jones Sr., the course's hallmarks are hourglass fairways and fingered sand bunkers. The par 3, 159-yard No. 15 is one of Naples' most challenging holes. *Phone (941) 793-2223.*

### MARCO SHORES

1450 Mainsail Drive. 18-hole, par 72, public course, designed by Bruce Devlin and Bob Von Hagge. *Phone (941) 394-2581.*

### PELICAN'S NEST

4450 Bay Creek Drive, Bonita Springs. 36 holes, each 18 par 72, designed by Tom Fazio. *Phone (941) 947-4600.*

### RIVIERA GOLF CLUB

48 Marseilles Drive. 18-hole par 62, public executive course designed by Estelle Gifford. *Phone (941) 774-1081.*

## NAPLES RESTAURANTS

Like other Florida coastal resorts, Naples restaurants highlight fish and shellfish from the Gulf of Mexico and the Atlantic. Adventurous diners can also experience Thai, Japanese, Italian, French, Mexican, Persian, and other ethnic cuisines. A number of trendy cafés, bistros, pubs, wine bars, and coffee houses are tucked among the boutiques in the Fifth Avenue South and Third Street South shopping zones, and the Tin City complex on Naples Bay. Others are on the busy Tamiami Trail (U.S. 41).

### BHA! BHA! PERSIAN BISTRO

847 Vanderbilt Beach Road. The joy at discovering exotic Middle Eastern cuisine in a transient resort town is booted up to pure pleasure with the dining experience. Iranian native Michael Mir's small shopping center restaurant near Vanderbilt Beach and the Ritz-Carlton Naples Hotel is adventure from appetizers to dessert. Beef, lamb, chicken, duck, quail, pheasant, and seafood go Persian with orange saffron sauce, orange zest, almonds, pomegranate and walnut sauces, basmati rice, feta

cheese, mango chutney, sesame, chick peas, yogurt, and saffron. The Sunday brunch buffet is an excellent opportunity to explore the full range of this fascinating cuisine. Casual. Lunch weekdays, dinner daily. Reservations for large groups. *Moderate. Phone (941) 5557.*

### LAFITE RESTAURANT

Registry Resort. 475 Seagate Drive. If all you've ever asked of a rack of lamb is a dollop of mint jelly on the side, and for dessert, a traditional dish of strawberries with whipped cream on top and a slab of shortcake underneath, German-born Chef Wilhelm Gahabka has some imaginative new ideas for your old favorites. At Lafite, a lovely, formal European dining room off the lobby of the Registry Resort, Chef Gahabka's roasted Colorado rack of lamb has a caramelized onion garlic herb crust, spiked with apple mint chutney and Merlot lamb jus. Old faithful strawberries are sweet-and-soured with balsamic vinegar, black peppercorns, and Muscat wine.

Other surprises in his "aggressive American cuisine with continental touches" repertoire include Florida Gulf shrimp in crisp pappadam and arugula red onion slaw; pompano in roasted sesame ginger macadamia crust; and seared filet mignon with porcini pesto sauce. A harpist plays, service is impeccable, the wine list is impressive. It all adds up to a memorable special-occasion dining experience. Very dressy. Reservations are suggested. *Very expensive. Phone (941) 597-3232.*

### MCCABE'S IRISH PUB

The Inn On Fifth, 699 Fifth Avenue South, downtown Naples. While you quaff your Harp and Guinness you can admire the old Irish pub ambience and listen to pipers and singers from Ulster and the Irish Republic playing rollicking traditional tunes. Dig into Irish stew, corned beef and cabbage, potato-leek soup, and nontraditional fusions like Brie dipped in Guinness, fried golden brown and topped with raspberry sauce. Dinner daily. *Inexpensive. Phone (941) 403-7170.*

### SAVANNAH RESTAURANT

5200 Tamiami Trail North. Savannah, the restaurant, was inspired by a 1994 visit to Savannah, the city, by Margaret and Alexander Neumann. They were so impressed by the hospitality they enjoyed in the Georgia port city, they decided to open a restaurant where they could share Georgia and South Carolina Low Country cooking with tourists who had never experienced it. They re-created the languid Old South ambience with ceiling fans, polished hardwood floors, Oriental carpets, interior windows and shutters, and lithographs and pastel watercolors of early nineteenth century Savannah scenes, and plants and flowers native to the Georgia and Carolina coasts. The extensive menu includes Midnight summer salad (a bow to *Midnight in the Garden of Good and Evil*, John Berendt's best-selling tell-all book about a scandalous 1980s Savannah murder), blue cornmeal-fried oysters, Savannah shrimp and crawfish cakes, oyster stew with tasso ham and grits, southern fried chicken, meatloaf, bread pudding, and Jack Daniels chocolate ice cream. Lunch, dinner daily. Dressy. Reservations suggested. *Expensive. Phone (941) 261-2555.*

### TRUFFLES CAFE-BISTRO

8920 North Tamiami Trail (US 41). Truffles is a tried-and-true Naples old-timer. The informal eatery has been on the scene since 1978. Truffles continues to attract its regulars with a combination of deli sandwiches and soups, meal-size salads, and pastas, steak, chicken, pork, seafood, and other hearty entrees, and diet-busting desserts. Casual. Lunch and dinner daily. *Inexpensive to moderate. Phone (941) 597-8119.*

### VESTA'S RESTAURANT AND BAKERY

424 New Market Road, Immokalee. Surrounded by the Immokalee produce fields, this bustling dining room practices southern-style homecooking like you would find in a small town in Alabama or Georgia. Lunchtime plates are filled with meatloaf, fried chicken, hickory-smoked ribs, and barbecued pork with sides of mashed potatoes, green beans, corn, turnip greens, tomatoes, and other freshly picked vegetables. Farm workers and other locals stoke up for the day with biscuits and sausage gravy, country fried steak, grits, eggs, and Mexican-style omelets with fiery jalapenos and onions. Breakfast and lunch weekdays year-round, dinner in winter. *Inexpensive. Phone (941) 657-3311.*

## NAPLES LODGINGS

### COVE INN ON NAPLES BAY

900 Broad Avenue South. Includes 102 efficiencies with refrigerators and microwaves, plus a heated pool. Close to public beach, Naples Bay, downtown shopping and restaurants. *Moderate. Phone (941) 262-7161. Fax (941) 261-6905.*

### THE NAPLES BEACH HOTEL & GOLF CLUB

851 Gulf Shore Boulevard North. In a city as young as Naples, the Naples Beach Hotel is as old as the Pyramids. The forerunner of today's hotel went up in the early 1900s. Its new life began in 1946 when Henry Broadwell Watkins Sr. retired from his Ohio cap gun business, immigrated to Naples, and bought the original Naples Hotel. The original hotel was closed when the new facility was opened at its present location. More than half a century later, Watkins's grandson, Michael Watkins, presides over a family enterprise that enjoys a unique niche in Naples history.

The 315 guest rooms in several low and mid-rise buildings facing the Gulf are cheerfully decorated in bright tropical colors. Guests play tennis and golf on an 18-hole course, enjoy sailing and windsurfing, swim in the Gulf and the freshwater pool. They dine inside or poolside and watch the sun go down at the Sunset Beach Bar. A thoroughly relaxed, unpretentious vacation destination. *Very expensive. Phone (941) 261-2222.*

### OLDE NAPLES INN & SUITES

801 Third Street South. Features 60 efficiency suites, with refrigerators, near downtown and public pier and beach. Amenities include heated pool, bikes, laundry, concierge services. *Moderate. Phone (941) 262-5194.*

### REGISTRY RESORT

475 Seagate Drive. A cushy place to come home to after a long, hot day in the Everglades, the 475-room high-rise, has 50 furnished villas. Facilities include three

heated outdoor pools, seven restaurants, shops, an 18-hole golf course, lighted tennis courts, health club, sailing and other watersports. The hotel is not directly on the beach. However, a three-quarter mile boardwalk and a free tram that operates continuously during the day take guests to Clam Pass Beach County Park. *Very expensive. Phone (941) 597-3147, toll free (800) 247-9810.*

### RITZ-CARLTON NAPLES

280 Vanderbilt Road. Opened in 1985, the Ritz-Carlton Naples has been at or near the top of every national and international "best hotels" list ever since, and collected bushels of Mobile five-star and AAA five-diamond awards. This is definitely not a place to walk through the lobby in your bikini and flip-flops. The imposing Spanish-Mediterranean hotel, with 463 ultradeluxe guest rooms and suites, faces 3 miles of secluded Gulf beaches. Guests have golf privileges at several nearby courses. They can lounge around a freshwater pool designed like a small lagoon, play tennis, go sailing and windsurfing, park the youngsters in kids programs, get a massage and beauty treatments and sit down to the ultimate in gourmet dining and sophisticated enter-tainment. Like other Ritz-Carltons, the Naples hotel displays a collection of eigh-teenth and nineteenth century English paintings and porcelains that would be prized by any major museum. *Very expensive. Phone (941) 598-3300. Fax (941) 598-6690.*

### THE INN ON FIFTH

689 Fifth Avenue South. Opened in 1998 in a restored Spanish-Mediterranean building at the epicenter of the Fifth Avenue shopping and dining zone, the inn's 87 guest rooms and six suites have private balconies and many deluxe features. Ameni-ties include a heated pool, fitness center, full-service spa, valet parking, concierge services and a business center. Guests have golf privileges at several nearby courses. McCabe's Irish Pub, adjacent to the inn and part of the same business, was built in Ireland, disassembled, and shipped lock, stock, and Guinness from the Old Country. *Expensive to very expensive. Phone (941) 403-8777. Fax (941) 403-8778.*

### SEA SHELL MOTEL

82 Ninth Street South. This 30 room motel has efficiencies with refrigerators, microwaves, and cable TV. It has a heated pool, tennis court, coin laundry. *Inexpen-sive. Phone (941)262-5129. Fax (941) 263-0182.*

### TRIANON HOTEL

955 Seventh Avenue South. The first of what is projected to be a chain of small, residential-style hotels opened in downtown Naples in 1998. The owners hope to make their niche in the highly competitive resort hotel industry by emphasizing high-quality, and personalized, superior service. The Naples flagship has 58 large, attractively furnished guest rooms and suites, an outdoor pool, a boardroom-style meeting room, 24-hour security, and free parking.

Rates include complimentary continental breakfast. Afternoon wine and snacks are available. The hotel is a short walk from the Fifth Avenue and Third Street shopping areas, the Tin City waterfront dining and entertainment area, and the Municipal Pier and beach. *Expensive. Phone (941) 435-9600 and toll-free (800) 859-3939.*

### VANDERBILT BEACH RESORT

9225 Gulf Shore Drive North. Renovated in fall 1998, the friendly, kicked-back motel has 65 guest rooms and two-bedroom apartments on popular Vanderbilt Beach. About half the units have kitchens. Guests' amenities include a heated pool, boat ramp, tennis court, and coin laundry. *Moderate to expensive. Phone (941) 597-3144, toll-free (800) 243-9076.*

### VANDERBILT INN ON THE GULF

11000 North Gulfshore Drive North. This inn contains nearly 150 beachfront rooms, including 16 efficiency apartments with kitchens. Amenities include a heated pool, wading pool, rental boats, dining room, and lounge with live entertainment. Adjacent to Delnor-Wiggins State Recreation Area. *Moderate to expensive. Phone (941) 597-3151, toll-free (800) 643-8654. Fax (941) 597-3099.*

### RENTAL COMPANIES

Bluebill Vacation Properties, 26201 Hickory Boulevard, Bonita Springs, FL 34134. *Phone (800) 237-2010. Fax (941) 992-9552.*

Century 21 Olde Naples Realty, 2204 Tamiami Trail North, Naples, FL 34103. *Phone (941) 261-2121, toll-free (800) 421-3112. Fax (941) 262-3439.*

Florida Choice Vacation Home Rentals, 865 Fourth Avenue South, Naples, FL 34102. *Phone (941) 434-8887, toll-free (800) 511-8362. Fax (941) 434-8978.*

Naples Area Vacation Rentals, 3761 Tamiami Trail North, Naples, FL 34103. *Phone (941) 261-7548, toll-free (800) 736-8579. Fax (941) 262-2357.*

### RV PARKS

### CRYSTAL LAKE RV SUBDIVISION RESORT

160 County Road 951, Naples, FL 34119. Includes 489 full-service sites on a lake. Has a heated pool, whirlpool, laundry, game room, clubhouse, shuffleboard. Pets are permitted. *Inexpensive. Phone (941) 353-4212.*

### ENDLESS SUMMER RV PARK

2 Tina Lane, Naples, FL 34104. Features 120 full-service sites with heated pool, laundry, picnic area, shuffleboard. Pets are permitted. *Inexpensive. Phone (941) 643-1511.*

### LAKE TRAFFORD MARINA

6001 Lake Trafford Road, Immokalee, FL 34142. Includes 64, full-service hookups on 1,500-acre recreational lake. Boat ramp, marina, fishing boats, air boat tours. Pets are permitted. (*See* Lake Trafford, page 280). *Inexpensive. Phone (941) 657-2401.*

### NAPLES RV RESORT

3180 County Road 84, Naples. More than 300 full-service sites. Clubhouse, cable TV, heated pool, playground, picnic area. Pets are permitted. *Inexpensive. Phone (941) 352-2101. Fax (941) 455-7271.*

# Appendices

## A. Books and References

*The Alligator: Monarch of the Marsh* by Connie Toops, Florida National Parks and Monuments Association, Homestead, FL 1979.

*Biscayne: The Story Behind the Scenery* by L. Wayne Landrum, KC Publications, Las Vegas, NV 1990.

*Boat and Canoe Camping in the Everglades Backcountry and Ten Thousand Islands Region* by Dennis Kalma, Florida Flair Books, Miami, FL 1988.

*A Canoeing and Kayaking Guide to the Streams of Florida, Volume II, Central and South Peninsula* by Lou Glaros and Doug Sphar, Menasha Ridge Press, Birmingham, AL 1987.

*Coral Reefs of Florida* by Gilbert L. Voss, Pineapple Press, Sarasota, FL 1988.

*A Dredgeman of Cape Sable* by Lawrence E. Will, Glades Historical Society, Belle Glade, FL 1984.

*The Everglades Handbook: Understanding the Ecosystem* by Thomas E. Lodge, St. Lucie Press, Delray Beach, FL 1994.

*The Everglades: River of Grass (50th Anniversary Issue)* by Marjory Stoneman Douglas, Mockingbird Books, St. Simons Island, GA 1997.

*Everglades Wildguide* by Jean Craighead George, Division of Publications, National Park Service, U. S. Department of the Interior, Washington, DC 1997.

*A Field Guide to Snakes of Florida* by Alan Tennant, Gulf Publishing Company, 1997. Houston, TX 1997.

*Fish and Dive Florida and the Keys: A Candid Destination Guide* by M. Timothy O'Keefe and Larry Larsen, Larsen's Outdoor Publishing, Lakeland, FL 1992.

*Fishing Guide to the Upper Keys and Florida Bay* by Martin Smithson, Fishsonian Publications, Melbourne, FL 1997.

*Florida's Birds: A Handbook and Reference* by Herbert W. Kale II, and David S. Maehr, Pineapple Press, Sarasota, FL 1990.

*The Florida Keys: A History of the Pioneers* by John Viele, Pineapple Press, Sarasota, FL 1996.

*The Florida Keys: The Natural Wonders of an Island Paradise* by Jeff Ripple, Voyageur Press, Stillwater, MN 1995.

*Florida Wild Flowers and Roadside Plants* by C. Ritchie Bell and Bryan J. Taylor, Laurel Hill Press, Chapel Hill, NC 1982.

*The Geology of Florida* edited by Anthony F. Randazzo and Douglas S. Jones, University Press of Florida, Gainesville, FL 1997.

*A Guide to the Wilderness Waterway of the Everglades National Park* by William G. Truesdell, University of Miami Press, Coral Gables, FL 1985.

*Indians of North America: The Seminole* by Merwyn S. Garbarino, Chelsea House Publishers, New York, NY 1989.

*Killing Mister Watson* by Peter Matthiessen, Vintage Books, New York, NY 1990.

*Land into Water—Water into Land: A History of Water Management in Florida* by Nelson M. Blake, University Presses of Florida, Tallahassee, FL 1980.

*Legends of the Seminoles* by Betty Mae Jumper and Peter Gallagher, Pineapple Press, Sarasota, FL 1994.

*Man in the Everglades: 2000 Years of Human History in the Everglades National Park* by Charlton W. Tebeau, University of Miami Press, Coral Gables, FL 1968.

*Pine Rockland Plant Guide: A Field Guide to the Plants of South Florida's Pine Rockland Community* by Dr. Daniel F. Austin, Dade County Department of Environmental Resources Management, Miami, FL 1998.

*Sea Stars, Sea Urchins and Allies: Echinoderms of Florida and the Caribbean* by Gordon Hendler, John E. Miller, David L. Pawson, and Porter M. Kier, Smithsonian Institution Press, Washington, DC 1995.

*Snorkeling Guide to Marine Life: Florida Caribbean Bahamas* by Paul Humann and Ned DeLoach, New World Publications, Jacksonville, FL 1995.

*The Southeastern Indians* by Charles Hudson, University of Tennessee Press, Knoxville, TN 1983.

*Sport Fish of Florida* by Vic Dunaway, Wickstrom Publishers, Inc., Miami, FL 1998.

*Totch: A Life in the Everglades* by Peter Matthiessen, University Press of Florida, Gainesville, FL 1993.

*Trees of Everglades National Park and the Florida Keys* by George B. Stevenson, Florida National Parks & Monuments Association, Inc., Homestead, FL 1992.

### WEB SITES

AnglersInfo www.anglersinfo.com/regions/fl/index.html
Big Cypress National Preserve www.nps.gov/bicy
Biscayne National Park www.nps.gov/bisc
Clyde Butcher www.clydebutcher.com
Cyber Island www.cyberisle.com
Dry Tortugas National Park www.nps.gov.drto or www.nps.gov/grto/planning for information on current issues
    regarding uses and plans for future use of Fort Jefferson and the park
Everglades Museum in Everglades City www.colliermuseum.com/everglades.html
Everglades National Park www.nps.gov/ever or www.restudy.org for information on restudy and the plan to save the
    Everglades
Florida Department of Environmental Protection (state parks) www.dep.state.fl.us/parks
Florida Fish and Wildlife Conservation Commission www.state.fl.us/gfc
Florida Keys On-Line Guide www.florida-keys.fl.us/infocc.htm
Florida National Parks and Monuments Association www.nps.gov/ever/fnpma.htm
Florida Outdoors www.florida-outdoors.com
*Florida Sportsman Magazine* www.floridasportsman.com/index.html
Guide to the Everglades and 10,000 Islands www.chamber@florida-everglades.com
VISIT FLORIDA www.flausa.com

### MAP SOURCES

For fishing charts and fishing information statewide contact *Florida Sportsman Magazine*, 5901 SW 74 Street,
    Miami, FL 33143. Phone (305) 661-4222.
*Florida Atlas & Gazetteer* by DeLorme, Freeport, ME 1997. To order contact DeLorme, PO Box 298, Freeport, ME
    04032. Phone (207) 865-4171.
For charts, maps, and information for national parks contact Florida National Parks and Monuments Association,
    Inc., 10 Parachute Key #51, Homestead, FL 33034-6735. Phone (305) 247-1216.

# B. Special Events, Fairs and Festivals

### GENERAL

**Beach "Wet Walks" and Snorkeling Programs**—Bahia Honda State Park. Held regularly July through
November. Other nature walks and history talks throughout the year. Phone (305) 872-2353.

**Living History Weekends**—Fort Zachary Taylor State Historic Site, Key West. Held October through
December. Phone (305) 292-6713.

**Fishing Tournaments**—Literally dozens of fishing tournaments for amateur and professional anglers are held
throughout the Florida Keys. For a *Florida Keys Fishing Tournament Guide* call 1-800-FLA-KEYS and ask for Florida
Keys and Key West pamphlet. Or, write to Florida Keys Fishing Tournaments, PO Box 420358, Summerland Key, FL
33042.

### JANUARY

**Florida Keys Renaissance Faire**—Sombrero Beach, Marathon. Three days of costumed actors and artisans
dressed as King Henry VIII and his cast of knights, minstrels, and wizards. Includes jousting, rat pucking (an early
form of golf), medieval games, arts, crafts, and rides. Phone (305) 658-1540 or 800-2Marathon.

**Key West Race Week**—Key West. Five days of international boat racing that can be viewed anywhere along the
Atlantic side of Key West or from a chartered boat. Phone (617) 639-9545.

### FEBRUARY

**Everglades Seafood Festival**—Everglades City. Annual festival with music, live entertainment, carnival rides,
arts and crafts, and food. Always the first Saturday and Sunday of the month. Phone (941) 695-3941 or 695-4100.

**Pigeon Key Art Festival**—Pigeon Key. At this annual event the key's 5 acres are filled with watercolors, oil
paintings, acrylics, sculptures, and other media of 50 artists showcasing Florida themes. Ranked among the top 200
art shows in the country. Reggae, jazz, Latin, rock, country, and classical musicians perform throughout the two-
day event. Located just south of Marathon off of the old Seven Mile Bridge. First weekend of February. Phone (305)
289-0025.

**Old Island Days**—Key West. A month-long celebration to showcase the community's cultural heritage and the restoration and preservation of the island's unique architectural traditions. Festivities include theatrical productions, musical performances, a children's pageant, and House and Garden Tours. Seventeen houses and gardens are toured on three different weekends. Phone (305) 294-9501.

### MARCH

**Islamorada's Fine Arts and Music Festival**—Islamorada. An annual event at Treasure Village. Fine arts displayed with continuous jazz music each day. Phone (305) 852-0511.

**Original Marathon Seafood Festival**—Marathon. Seafood booths, crafts, and rides. Sponsored by the Chamber of Commerce. Phone (305) 743-5417.

**Seminole Indian Day**—Chokoloskee Island. Celebrate Seminole culture and history in southwestern Florida. Annual event held at Ted Smallwood's Store and Museum. Phone (941) 695-2989.

**Annual Seafood Festival**—Naples Airport. Seafood vendors, arts and crafts, and rides. Phone (941) 436-6462.

**Festival of the Arts**—Downtown Naples. Oldest Fine Art Show with artists from around the country. Entertainment and food. Phone (941) 435-3742.

### APRIL

**Florida Keys Jazz and Blues Festival**—Plantation Yacht Harbor, Plantation Key. Jazz and blues on the main stage or on the water. Big name performers, local talent, and vendors. Phone (305) 853-5905.

**Seven Mile Bridge Run**—Marathon. Every April over 1,500 runners participate in the Seven Mile Bridge Run. A limited number of runners compete, and US 1 is closed during the event. Phone (305) 743-8513.

**Conch Republic Independence Celebration**—Key West. Dates back to a 1982 declaration of independence and surrender by the citizens of the Florida Keys in protest over a U.S. Border Patrol blockade of the islands. Phone (305) 296-0213.

### JUNE

**Super Boat Races**—Key West. High-speed, high-tech boat races in the harbor. Sponsored by Superboat International. Phone (305) 296-8963.

### JULY

**Reef Awareness Week**—A week-long schedule of events throughout all of the Keys including speakers on coral reef ecology, poetry readings, art exhibits, and a sand sculpture contest. Sponsored by American Express. Phone (305) 294-3100.

**Annual Underwater Music Festival**—Looe Key Reef National Marine Sanctuary. Enjoy six hours of specially selected music broadcast via underwater speakers at this National Marine Sanctuary site. Sponsored by the Lower Keys Chamber of Commerce. Phone (800) 872-3722 or (305) 872-2411.

**Hemingway Days Festival**—Key West. This 10-day festival includes writers' workshops, "Papa" Hemingway look-alike contests, a Caribbean street fair, the annual "Running of the Bulls" and even an arm wrestling contest. Phone (305) 294-1136 or 294-4440.

### SEPTEMBER

**Historic Seacraft Race & Festival**—Big Pine Key. This festival's accent is on the maritime history of the Florida Keys. The event includes nonmotorized watercraft races and a kayak paddlers' challenge. Phone (305) 872-3580 or 872-2411.

**Islamorada Heritage Days**—Islamorada. Sponsored by the Chamber of Commerce. Phone (305) 664-4503.

**Clyde Butcher's Annual Labor Day Open House**—Big Cypress Gallery. 52388 Tamiami Trail. Located 0.5 mile east of the Big Cypress National Preserve's Oasis Visitor Center. A three-day event featuring Butcher's newest work, darkroom public tours, a large format camera demonstration, and swamp walks in the backyard. Phone (941) 695-2428.

### OCTOBER

**Indian Key Festival**—Indian Key. Relive history and see historical moments acted out on Indian Key. Vendors and some arts and crafts. Phone (305) 664-4704.

**Octoberfest**—Key Largo at St. Justin Martyr Church. A 3-day event that features a carnival, ethnic food, music, dancing, and professional entertainers. Occurs each year the weekend before Halloween. Phone (305) 852-6939.

**Celebration of the Cigar Festival**—Key West. Based on the history of cigar manufacturing in Key West. A weekend of parties, dinners, historical trolley tours, live jazz, and performers from New York City. Phone (305) 296-2680.

**Florida Keys Jazz and Blues Festival**—Islamorada. Three days of music, arts, crafts, and food vendors. Held each year at the Plantation Yacht Harbor overlooking the bay. Phone (305) 853-5905.

**Goombay Celebration**—Key West. Street fair from Duval Street down to Petronia Street in historic Bahama Village. Live music and ethnic food. Part of Fantasy Fest. Phone (305) 293-8898

**Fantasy Fest**—Duval Street, Key West. A 10-day let-it-all-hang-out Halloween festival complete with costume balls, a fantasy yacht race, a Mardi Gras massacre, and a pet masquerade that concludes with the Twilight Fantasy Parade. Phone (305) 296-1817.

### NOVEMBER

**World Championship Offshore Powerboat Race Week**—Key West. World Championship super boat race. This event attracts more that 50,000 fans for the crowning of the world champions at the conclusion of the year's racing season. View from Mallory Square, Truman Annex, or Fort Zachary Taylor. Sponsored by Superboat International. Phone (305) 296-8963.

**Island Jubilee**—Key Largo. An old country fair at Harry Harris Park and the Upper Keys Arts and Crafts Festival including local performing talent. Phone (305) 451-1414.

**Cayo Carnival Sponsored by Reef Relief**—Key West. A benefit for the protection of Florida's fragile coral reefs. Activities for all ages, food, and music. Phone (305) 294-3100.

**Pirates in Paradise Festival**—Pirate Invasion in Marathon, on Plantation Key, and in Key West. Includes performers from over 40 states! Phone (305) 743-4620 for Marathon festival and (305) 743-4386 for Plantation Key and Key West festivals. Separate weekends.

### DECEMBER

**Miccosukee Tribe of Indians Annual Indian Arts Festival**—Miccosukee Indian Village on Tamiami Trail (US 41). A full week of events featuring colorfully costumed Indians from all over the continental Americas, who join together with song, dance, food, fine Indian arts, jewelry, crafts, and even alligator wrestling.

**Christmas Boat Parade**—Key Largo at Blackwater Sound. Parade of decorated boats and holiday music. Can be seen from land at Upper Keys restaurants near MM 104. Phone (305) 451-4502.

**Annual Historic Seaport Music Festival**—Key West Seaport. Offers a variety of music including blues plus food and beverage vendors. Phone (305) 296-7182.

**Downtown Holiday Festival**—Downtown Naples on 5th Avenue South. Fine arts festival, music, entertainment, and food. Phone (941) 435-3742.

# C. Outdoor Organizations & Agencies

**1000 Friends of Florida.** PO Box 5949, Tallahassee, FL 32314-5948. Web site www.1000fof.usf.edu. Phone (850) 222-6277. A citizen advocacy group that works to help Florida's communities effectively manage growth.

**Center for Marine Conservation.** One Beach Drive SE, Suite 304, St. Petersburg, FL 33701. Web site www.cmc-ocean.org. Phone (813) 895-2188. Florida Keys Field Office: 513 Fleming Street, #14, Key West, FL 33040. Phone (305) 295-3370. A nationwide organization devoted to protecting marine wildlife and habitats.

**Coastal Conservation Association Florida.** 905 East Park Avenue, Tallahassee, FL 32301. Web site www.cca-florida.com. Phone (850) 224-3474. An organization of conservation-oriented anglers and supporters dedicated to protecting marine resources and recreational fishing.

**The Conservancy of Southwest Florida.** 1450 Merrihue Drive, Naples, FL 34102. Web site www.conservancy.org. Phone (941) 262-0304. An organization committed to conserving the biodiversity and natural resources of Southwest Florida's native ecosystems.

**Florida Audubon Society.** 1331 Palmetto Avenue, Suite 110, Winter Park, FL 32789. Web site www.audubon.usf.edu. Phone (407) 539-5700. A statewide organization promoting the protection, preservation, and restoration of birds and all other wildlife, and their habitat through science-based advocacy and education.

**Florida Defenders of the Environment.** 4424 NW 13 Street, Suite C-8, Gainesville, FL 32609. Web site www.stjohnsriver.org/fde. Phone (352) 378-8465. A private, nonprofit organization that works to restore and preserve natural Florida.

**Florida Department of Environmental Protection.** 3900 Commonwealth Boulevard, Tallahassee, FL 32399-3000. Web site www.dep.state.fl.us. Phone (850) 488-1234. State agency charged with conserving and managing Florida's environment and natural resources.

**Florida Fish and Wildlife Conservation Commission.** Everglades Region (includes the Florida Keys), 8535 Northlake Boulevard, West Palm Beach, FL 33412-3303. Web site www.state.fl.us/gfc. Phone (561) 625-5122. State agency that protects Florida's wildlife and freshwater fish. As of July 1, 1999, the GFC will become the Florida Fish and Wildlife Conservation Commission that will regulate both salt and fresh water and wildlife resources.

**Florida Keys Land and Sea Trust.** PO Box 536, Marathon, FL 33050. Phone (305) 743-3900. Works for the preservation of the best remaining natural areas in the Florida Keys.

**Florida Panther Society.** Route 1, Box 1895, White Springs, FL 32096-9611. Web site www.atlantic.net/~oldfla/panther/panther.html. Phone (904) 397-2945. A nonprofit environmental education and support organization for the preservation of the Florida panther.

**Florida Public Interest Research Group.** 704 West Madison Street, Tallahassee, FL 32304. Web site www.pirg.org/floridapirg. Phone (850) 224-3321. A statewide advocacy group that investigates environmental problems, educates the public about solutions, and lobbies for reforms to preserve the environment.

**Florida Wildlife Federation.** PO Box 6870, Tallahassee, FL 32314. Web site www.fwf.usf.edu. Phone (850) 656-7113. A nonprofit, conservation, education organization composed of concerned Floridians with an interest in preserving, managing, and improving Florida's fish, wildlife, soil, water, and plant life.

**Florida Wildlife Federation/National Wildlife Federation Joint Office—Everglades Project.** 5051 Castello Drive, Suite 240, Naples, FL 34103. Web site www.nwf.org/nwf/index.html. Phone (941) 643-4111. An office monitoring and commenting on southwestern Florida development issues that may have negative environmental impacts.

**National Audubon Society—Everglades Ecosystem Restoration Campaign.** 444 Brickell Avenue, Suite 850, Miami, FL 33131-2450. Web site www.audubon.org. Phone (305) 371-6399. A team of scientists, policy experts, educators, and grassroots specialists, working to ensure that the Everglades restoration plan is comprehensive and that there is broad-based public support for restoration.

**National Marine Fisheries Service.** Southeast Regional Office, 9721 Executive Center Drive North, St. Petersburg, FL 33702. Web site caldera.sero.nmfs.gov. Phone (850) 234-6541. A federal agency charged with building sustainable fisheries, recovering protected species, and sustaining healthy coasts.

**National Oceanic & Atmospheric Administration.** U.S. Department of Commerce, 14 Street & Constitution Avenue NW, Room 6013, Washington, DC 20230. Web site www.noaa.gov. Phone (202) 482-6090. Federal agency charged with conserving the nation's coastal and marine resources and with predicting changes in the earth's environment.

**National Park Service.** Southeast Region Office, 100 Alabama Street SW, 1924 Building, Atlanta, GA 30303. Web site www.nps.gov/index.html. Phone (404) 562-3100. The service is charged with conserving the scenery and the natural and historic objects and the wildlife within national parks for now and for the enjoyment of future generations.

**Nature Conservancy, Florida Chapter.** 222 South Westmonte Drive, Suite 300, Altamonte Springs, FL 32714. Web site www.tnc.org/infield/State/Florida/florida.htm. Phone (407) 682-3664. A conservation organization committed to preserving natural diversity by protecting lands and waters and supporting the best examples of all elements of our natural world.

**Nature Conservancy, Florida Keys Initiative.** 201 Front Street, Suite 222, Key West, FL 33040. Web site www.tnc.org. Phone (305) 296-3880. A nonprofit conservation organization whose mission is to preserve the land and marine environments of the Florida Keys.

**Rails to Trails Conservancy of Florida.** 2545 Blairstone Pines Drive, Tallahassee, FL 32314. Web site www.railtrails.org. Phone (850) 942-2379. A nonprofit conservation organization working to create and connect greenways and recreational trails through Florida.

**Reef Relief.** 201 William Street, Key West, FL 33040. Web Site reefrelief.org. Phone (305) 294-3100. Key West-based organization dedicated to preserving and protecting coral reef ecosystems through local, regional, and global efforts.

**Save the Manatee Club.** 500 North Maitland Avenue, Maitland, FL 32751. Web site www.savethemanatee.org. Phone (800) 432-5646 and (407) 539-0990 outside the United States. A nonprofit organization that promotes public education and protection for the endangered West Indies manatee.

**Sierra Club, Florida Chapter.** 475 Central Avenue, Suite M-1, St. Petersburg, FL 33701-3817. Web site www.sierraclub.org/chapters/fl. Phone (813) 824-8813. An organization dedicated to exploring, enjoying, and protecting the wild places of the earth.

**The Trust for Public Land.** 306 North Monroe Street, Tallahassee, FL 32301-7635. Web site www.igc.apc.org/tpl. Phone (850) 222-7911. Creates parks for America's people, from intercity gardens and recreation spots to wilderness, greenways, and bicycling trails.

**U.S. Coast Guard.** District 7 Brickell Plaza Federal Building, 909 SE First Avenue, Miami, FL 33131-3050. Web site www.uscg.mil/contact.html. Phones: Miami (305) 536-5641. Upper Keys (305) 664-4404. Middle Keys (305) 743-6778. Lower Keys (305) 292-8856. Ft. Myers (covers Everglades City and Naples) (941) 463-5755. VHF Channel 16. A federal agency that responds to emergencies on the water.

# D. Outfitters, Marinas, and Boat Rentals

**Banana Bay Resort and Marina.** Dockage, fish and sail charters, watercraft and water sport rentals. Two locations: MM 49.5 Oceanside. 4590 Overseas Highway, Marathon, FL 33050 and 2319 North Roosevelt Boulevard, Key West, FL 33040. Web site www.bananabay.com. Phone (800) BANANA-1.

**Barron River Resort and Marina.** Full-service marina, bait and tackle store, and boat rentals. PO Box 116, Everglades City, FL 34139. Phone (941) 695-3591.

**Big Pine Key Fishing Lodge.** Boat rentals, dive and fishing charters, marina and dockage. MM 33 Oceanside. Box 430513, Big Pine Key, FL 33043. Phone (305) 872-2351.

**Bud Boats.** Boat rental fleet in two locations. Buccaneer Resort and Marina, MM 48.5 Bayside. 2600 Overseas Highway, Marathon, FL 33050. Old Wooden Bridge Fishing Camp and Marina, MM 30 Bayside. Big Pine Key, FL 33043. Phone (305) 743-6316 or (800) 633-2283.

**Bud n' Mary's Marina.** Deep-sea and reef fishing, night trips, and full-service dive center. MM 79.8 Oceanside. 7985 Overseas Highway, Islamorada, FL 33036. Phone (305) 664-2461.

**Chokoloskee Island Park and Marina.** Marina, boat ramp, dockage, boat and motor rentals, and fishing guides. PO Box 430, Chokoloskee, FL 34138. Phone (941) 695-2414.

**Dolphin Marina.** Boat rentals, charters into the Gulf of Mexico and backcountry, bait, tackle, boat ramp, and full-service marina and fuel dock. MM 28.5 Oceanside. 28530 Overseas Highway, Little Torch Key, 33043. Phone (305) 872-2685 or (800) 553-0308.

**Everglades City Chamber of Commerce.** Write or call for a list of area fishing guides and charters. Corner of US 41 and SR 29. PO Box 130, Everglades City, FL 34139. Phone (800) 914-6355 or local (941) 695-3941. Web site www.florida-everglades.com/chamber/members.htm

**Faro Blanco Outfitters.** Flats and offshore guides, fly-fishing and light tackle, boat and kayak rentals, and guided island tours. G-Loomis Pro Shop. MM 48.5 in Marathon's Old Town. 1996 Overseas Highway, Marathon, FL 33050. Phone (800) 759-3276 or (305) 743-0918.

**For Yachts International.** Complete information on boating worldwide. Sailing vessels, motor yachts, and sport-fishing yachts in the Keys and Bahamas. Charters both crewed and bareboat (be your own captain). 99228 Overseas Highway, Key Largo, FL 33050. Phone (305) 453-4000.

**Flamingo Lodge Marina and Outpost.** Provides access to Florida Bay and the backcountry of Everglades National Park. Boat cruises, fishing charters, marina store, boat ramps, boat and canoe rentals. Dock slips, some with electric and water. #1 Flamingo Lodge Highway, Flamingo, FL 33034. Phone (941) 695-3101.

**Florida Fishing Guides.** A list of fishing guides is available on the Coastal Conservation Association Florida's Web site: www.cca-florida.com

**Holiday Inn Marina.** Deep water marina, deep-sea fishing, kayak and boat rentals, scuba diving, snorkeling, and sailing cruises. 99701 Overseas Highway, Key Largo, FL 33037. Phone (305) 451-2121.

**Holiday Isle Marine.** Full service marina offering backcountry and offshore fishing trips, rental boats, dockage, waverunners, sailboarding or parasailing, diving or snorkeling. MM 84 Oceanside. 84001 Overseas Highway, Islamorada, FL 33036. Phone (800) 372-7070 or (305) 664-2321.

**Independent Charter Boat Booking Agency.** Deep sea, reef, backcountry, flats, inshore, trolling, dive trips, daily walk on trips, and private charters. Free. PO Box 522409, Marathon, FL 33052-2409. Phone (305) 743-8636 or (888) 524-8636.

**Marathon Guides Association.** Fishing information guide and list of captains. Marathon Guides Association, PO Box 500065, Marathon, FL 33050.

**Outdoor Resorts—Chokoloskee Island RV Resort and Marina.** Boat, canoe, and kayak rentals; fishing guides; fly-fishing lessons. PO Box 39, Chokoloskee, FL 34138. Phone (941) 695-2881.

**Robbie's.** Three locations: Rental boats at MM 77.5 Bayside. Phone (305) 664-8070. Deep-sea charters and party boats at MM 84.5 Oceanside. Phone (305) 664-9814. Large full-service marina with in/out dry storage for any size boat at Robbie's Boat Yard and Marina at the end of Old Shrimp Road at Stock Island, FL 33040. Phone (305) 294-1124. Mailing address is PO Box 86, Islamorada, FL 33036.

**Sea Boots Outfitters.** Light tackle fishing offshore and backcountry fishing charters. Fly-fishing shop. MM 30 Bayside. PO Box 430652, Big Pine Key, FL 33043. Phone (800) 238-1746 or (305) 745-1530.

**Seelife.** Marine charter company operated by marine scientists who are licensed, insured, and knowledgeable in the biology and natural history of the bay and backcountry from Miami to Marco Island. Offer backcountry fishing, birding, snorkeling, sunset and evening tours, and educational tours. Seats up to four guests. PO Box 45-3035, Miami, FL 33245-3035. Phone (305) 860-5836.

**Whale Harbor Charter Fleet.** Full and half-day offshore and backcountry charters. Phone (305) 664-4511. Fishing party boats with daily trips. Phone (305) 664-4959. MM 84 Oceanside. PO Box 1109, Islamorada, FL 33036.

**World Class Angler.** The mid-Keys store for guided trips, featuring custom rods and rentals, baits, tackle, and a fly department. Open daily. MM 50 Bayside. 5050 Overseas Highway, Marathon, FL 33050. Phone (305) 743-6139.

**World Wide Sportsman.** Booking service for deep-sea fishing trips around the world, a marina, a bait shop, charter fishing guides, fishing gear, and other angling supplies. MM 81.5 Bayside. 81576 Overseas Highway, Islamorada, FL 33036. Web site www.outdoor-world.com. Phone (305) 664-4615.

# E. Florida Fishing Regulations

### SALTWATER

*Fishing Lines—the newsletter* is a quarterly newsletter from the Florida Department of Environmental Protection's Division of Marine Resources. It contains current fishing regulations and is free of charge at most Florida Visitor Centers or by contacting the Florida Department of Environmental Protection, Division of Marine Resources, Mail Station 240, 3900 Commonwealth Boulevard, Tallahassee, Florida 32399-3000. Web site www.dep.state.fl.us. Phone (850) 488-6058.

Saltwater fishing licenses are sold at all county tax collectors' offices and at many bait-and-tackle shops. Licenses may also be obtained over the telephone by dialing toll free (888) 347-4356. The cost differs for residents and nonresidents. Residents can purchase a 10-day or 1-year license. Nonresidents can purchase a 3-day, 7-day, or 1-year license. Special permits are also required for harvesting snook and crawfish (Florida lobster). Charter boats and fishing guides carry commercial licenses that cover their customers.

### SPEARFISHING

Spearing is defined as "the catching or taking of a fish by bow hunting, gigging, spearfishing, or any device used to capture a fish by piercing its body. Spearing does not include the catching or taking of a fish by a hook with hook and line gear or by snagging (snatch hooking).” The use of powerheads, bangsticks, and rebreathers is prohibited.

Species prohibited for harvest by spearing are: billfish (all species), bonefish, Nassau grouper, pompano, spotted eagle ray, tarpon, spotted seatrout, African pompano, sturgeon, Jewfish, red drum, permit, manta ray, snook, weakfish, tripletail, sharks, and all families of ornamental reef fish (surgeonfish, trumpetfish, angelfish, butterflyfish, porcupinefish, cornetfish, squirrelfish, trunkfish, damselfish, parrotfish, pipefish, seahorse, puffers).

Spearfishing is prohibited in the following areas:

— Within 100 yards of a public swimming beach, any commercial or public fishing pier, or any part of a bridge from which public fishing is allowed.

— Within 100 feet of any part of a jetty that is above the surface of the sea--except for the last 500 yards of a jetty that extends more than 1,500 yards from the shoreline.

— In Collier County and in Monroe County from Long Key north to the Dade County line.

— In any body of water under the jurisdiction of the Department of Environmental Protection’s Division of Recreation and Parks. (Possession of spearfishing equipment is prohibited in these areas, unless it is unloaded and properly stored.)

### THE FLORIDA MARINE PATROL

The Florida Marine Patrol provides assistance to boaters and anglers and enforces Florida’s saltwater fishing laws and other state environmental laws and rules. Marine Patrol officers can also provide advice and direction to those who are unfamiliar with Florida’s coastline and waterways. Web site www.dep.state.fl.us/mfc/fabout.htm. Tallahassee Headquarters, phone (800) 342-5367.

### ▓ FRESHWATER

For a *Sport Fishing Regulations Summary* booklet contact the Florida Fish and Wildlife Conservation Commission, Everglades Region (includes the Florida Keys) at 8535 Northlake Boulevard, West Palm Beach, FL 33412-3303. Web site www.state.fl.us/gfc/fising.Phone (561) 625-5122.

Licenses may be purchased from county tax collectors or their subagents, who are generally located at tackle shops, fish camps, hardware stores, and sporting goods stores. Licenses may also be obtained over the telephone by dialing toll free (888) 347-4356. The cost differs for residents and nonresidents. Residents can purchase a 1-year license. Nonresidents can purchase a 3-day, 7-day, or 1-year license.

### EXEMPTIONS:

— Florida residents 65 years of age or older may fish in fresh water if they possess either a Resident Senior Citizen Hunting and Fishing Certificate or proof of age and residency.

— Georgia residents 65 years of age or older who have in their possession a Georgia Honorary Combination Hunting and Fishing License and proof of age.

— Children under 16 years of age.

— Any resident who is a member of the U.S. Armed Forces and is not stationed in Florida but is home on leave for 30 days or less, upon submission of orders.

To Report Wildlife Law Violators, phone (800) 432-2046 or on cellular phones dial *GFC.

# F. Dive Shops

Dive shops in the Florida Keys generally offer a variety of snorkel and dive trips to various locations within the Florida Keys National Marine Sanctuary, John Pennekamp State Park, and Looe Key National Marine Sanctuary. Many also offer custom dive trips, night dives, and snorkel and scuba lessons. For a more complete listing of dive shops in the Florida Keys contact the local chambers of commerce. Or, check the world wide web at www.florida-keys.fl.us/ypdive.htm

**Bud n’ Mary’s Dive Center.** MM 79.8 Oceanside. 7985 Overseas Highway, Islamorada, FL 33036. Phone (305) 664-2211 or (800) 344-7352.

**Captain Slate’s Atlantis Dive Center.** MM 106.5 Oceanside. 51 Garden Cove Drive, Key Largo, FL 33037. Phone (305) 451-1325 or (800) 331-3483.

**Captain Hook’s Marina and Dive Centers.** MM 53 Oceanside. 11833 Overseas Highway, Marathon, FL 33050. Phone (800) 278-4665.

**Hall’s Diving & Snorkeling Center.** MM 48 Bayside. 1994 Overseas Highway. Marathon, FL 33050. Phone (305) 743-5929.

**Holiday Inn Marina.** MM 100 Oceanside. 99701 Overseas Highway, Key Largo, FL 33037. Phone (305) 451-2121 or (800) 935-3483.

**Holiday Isle.** MM 84 Oceanside. 84001 Overseas Highway, Islamorada, FL 33036. Phone (305) 664-2321 ext. 641 or (800) 327-7070.

**Innerspace Dive Shop.** MM 29.5 Oceanside. PO Box 430651, Big Pine Key, FL 33043. Phone (305) 872-2319 or (800) 538-2896.

**John Pennecamp Coral Reef State Park.** MM 102.5. PO Box 1560, Key Largo, FL 33037. Phone (305) 451-1621 or 451-6322.

**Looe Key Reef Resort & Dive Center.** MM 27.5 Oceanside. PO Box 509, Ramrod Key, FL 33042. Phone (800) 942-5397.

**Reef Raiders Dive Shop.** 617 Front Street, Key West, FL 33040. Phone (305) 294-0660.

**Seaclypse Divers.** 6000 Peninsula Avenue, Key West, FL 33040. Phone (800) 626-6396.

**Silent World Dive Center.** MM 103.2 Bayside. PO Box 2363, Key Largo, FL 33037. Phone (305) 451-3252.

**Subtropic Dive Center.** 1605 North Roosevelt Boulevard, Key West, FL 33040. Phone (305) 296-9914.

**Underseas, Inc.** MM 30.5 Oceanside. PO Box 430319, Big Pine Key, FL 33043. Phone (305) 872-2700 or (800) 446-5663.

# G. Glossary

**Algae**—A group of one-celled or many-celled plants, having chlorophyll, without roots, living in water.

**Aquifer**—An underground porous rock formation containing water, especially one that supplies water for wells or springs.

**Bayhead**—A tree island in the freshwater marsh that may be submerged during the wet season; so named because it usually contains redbay or sweet bay trees.

**Bight**—A body of water bounded by a bend or curve in the shore; several are found in Key West.

**Brackish water**—Mixed fresh and salt water.

**Bromeliad**—Nonparasitic air plants from the Pineapple family that are epiphytes.

**Chickee**—An open-sided structure built on a raised platform and covered by a thatched roof; the traditional housing of the Seminole adapted to the southern Florida environment.

**Crustacean**—Animals that wear a segmented shell and have segmented legs are arthropods, such as insects and crustaceans. Crustaceans are arthropods that live in the water and breathe by gills, such as lobsters, barnacles, crabs, and shrimps.

**Detritus**—Decomposed plant and animal matter.

**Ecosystem**—A biological community existing in a specific physical environment.

**Endangered species**—A species that, throughout all or a significant portion of its range, is in danger of extinction.

**Epiphyte**—A nonparasitic plant growing upon or attached to another plant or nonliving structure.

**Estuary**—The portion of a river or coastal wetland affected by the rise and fall of the tide, containing a mixture of fresh and salt water.

**Flats**—Shallow, nearshore waters of the Atlantic and Gulf.

**Habitat**—Where an organism lives; its natural home.

**Hammock**—A dense growth of trees on a slightly elevated area, not wet enough to be a swamp.

**Limestone**—A sedimentary rock derived from the shells and skeletons of animals deposited in seas, and consisting mostly of calcium carbonate.

**Miccosukee Tribe**—One of two federally recognized organizations of Seminole Indians. Incorporated in 1962.

**Nocturnal**—Active at night.

**Periphyton**—An assemblage of small plant organisms (mostly algae) attached to surfaces underwater or floating; may form a spongy mat insulating the ground from total dehydration during the dry season in the Everglades.

**Photosynthesis**—The production of carbohydrates by plants in the presence of chlorophyll and sunlight.

**Plankton**—Aquatic organisms that float at the mercy of the currents or have limited swimming abilities.

**Salt marsh**—An area of soft, wet land periodically flooded by salt water.

**Seminole Tribe**—One of two federally recognized organizations of Seminole Indians. Incorporated in 1957, the Tribe is governed by a constitution and is headed by a council and board of directors.

**Slough**—A channel of slow-moving water in a marsh land.

**Species**—A basic taxonomic group consisting of individuals of common ancestry who strongly resemble each other physiologically and who interbreed, producing fertile offspring.

**Subspecies**—A subdivision of species consisting of individuals different from the rest of the species but still able to interbreed with other members of the species.

**Threatened species**—A species still present in its range but, without significant changes in conditions, may become endangered.

**Zooplankton**—Animal plankton.

# Index